영어 교과 논리 및 논술

영어 교육론 2014~2020학년도 기출 문제

영어 교과 논리 및 논술

: 영어 교육론 2014~2020학년도 기출 문제

ⓒ 오경애, 2020

1판 1쇄 인쇄__2020년 5월 20일
1판 1쇄 발행__2020년 5월 30일

지은이__오경애
펴낸이__홍정표
펴낸곳__글로벌콘텐츠
　　　　등록__제25100-2008-000024호

공급처__(주)글로벌콘텐츠출판그룹
　　　　대표_홍정표　이사_김미미　편집_김수아 이예진 권군오 이상민 홍명지　기획·마케팅__노경민 이종훈
　　　　주소__서울특별시 강동구 풍성로 87-6, 201호
　　　　전화__02) 488-3280　팩스__02) 488-3281
　　　　홈페이지__http://www.gcbook.co.kr
　　　　이메일__edit@gcbook.co.kr

값 18,000원
ISBN 979-11-5852-287-2 13740

영어 교과 논리 및 논술

영어 교육론 2014~2020학년도 기출 문제

들어가며

　　교직과정을 이수하는 학생들이 이수해야 하는 전공 영역에는 교과 교육 영역에 해당하는 교과 교육론, 교과 교재 연구 및 지도법, 그리고 논리 및 논술의 세 과목이 있다. 이 중 논리 및 논술은 "논리적 사고의 근본 법칙을 이해하고 논술에 관한 역량을 배양한다. 또한 체계적인 논술 지도를 위한 글쓰기 지도 능력을 갖추기 위해 필요한 논술법을 학습한다"는 기본 교수 요목을 가지고 있다. 따라서 학술적 목적의 쓰기를 지도하는데, 보통 중등 교사 임용 시험의 문제를 활용해 답안을 작성하는 연습을 같이 수행하고. 이와 더불어 쓰기 교안 작성법과 교수법을 같이 가르친다. 따라서 영어 교과 논리 및 논술은 세 가지 교수 목표를 갖는다고 할 수 있다; 1) 학술적 목적의 논리적인 글쓰기를 할 수 있다, 2) 쓰기 교안을 작성할 수 있다, 3) 쓰기를 지도할 수 있다.

　　영어 교과 논리 및 논술 과목을 강의한 후로 가장 많이 들은 질문은 임용 시험 문제를 어떻게 가르쳐야 하냐는 것이었다. 교과 교육론과 교과 교재 연구 및 지도법을 수강하지 않은 학생들도 있고, 수강했다고 할지라도 난이도가 있는 임용 시험 문제의 답안을 도출하기는 힘들기에 답안을 작성하는 법을 가르치기는 어렵다는 것이 가장 큰 난제였다. 학술적 목적의 글쓰기와 쓰기 지도법은 큰 문제가 아니지만 기출 문제 만큼은 다루기 힘든 것이 사실이었다. 게다가 영어영문학과의 수강생이 적어지면서 몇 년 전부터는 외국어 교과 논리 및 논술이라는 과목명으로 변경되어서 여러 학과의 학생들이 같이 수강함에 따라 영어학, 영문학, 일반영어문제를 같이 풀 수는 없었다. 그렇다고 논리적 글쓰기와 쓰기 지도법만을 가르치며 임용 시험에 대한 준비는 학생들의 전적인 책임으로 맡겨둔다는 것은 너무 무책임한 일이 아닐 수 없다. 학생들이 필요로 하는 부분을 대학이 충족시켜주지 못한 채 학원의 책임과 학생들 개개인의 책임으로 돌릴 수는 없기 때문이다.

이에 따라 2014학년도부터 2020학년도 중등 영어 임용 시험 문제 중 영어 교육론 기출 문제만을 따로 뽑아서 이 책을 기술하게 되었다. 먼저 기출 문제를 영역별로 분리해 관련 이론을 제시해 이론적 배경이 부족한 학생들도 답안을 작성할 수 있게 도왔다. 또한 문제 풀이 과정과 예시 답안을 제시해 학생들에게 이론을 바탕으로 본인의 답안을 작성할 수 있는 가이드라인을 제시했다. 이해를 돕기 위해 한글로 기술했으나 임용 시험이 영어로 출제되기에 중요한 용어는 영어로 따로 제시했다. 또한 기출 문제는 부록으로 첨부했다. 이 책이 임용 시험을 준비하는 학생들과 영어 교과 논리 및 논술과목을 강의하는 교육자들에게 조금이라도 도움이 되기를 바란다.

2020년 5월
오경애

CONTENTS

CONTENTS

영어 교육론 기출 문제 출제 경향표

연도	문제 유형	언어 습득론			영어 교수법			
		언어 습득 이론	학습자 요인	의사소통능력과 중간언어	교수법	4 skills, 문법, 단어, & 발음	교재와 교실 수업	평가
2020 학년도	기입형			전공 Ⓐ 3번 Communicative Competence		전공 Ⓐ 1번 단어	전공 Ⓐ 2번 교실 수업 전공 Ⓑ 2번 교재	
	서술형		전공 Ⓑ 4번 Communication Strategies	전공 Ⓐ 5번 Communicative Competence		전공 Ⓐ 10번 읽기		전공 Ⓑ 6번 평가의 설계 전공 Ⓑ 10번 평가의 설계
	문항 수	0	1	2	0	2	2	2
2019 학년도	기입형		전공 Ⓐ 1번 Learning Styles	전공 Ⓐ 3번 Feedback		전공 Ⓐ 2번 읽기		
	서술형		전공 Ⓑ 4번 Communication Strategies	전공 Ⓐ 11번 Errors		전공 Ⓐ 14번 쓰기		전공 Ⓐ 12번 평가의 설계
	논술형						전공 Ⓑ 8번 교과과정과 교안	
	문항 수	0	2	2	0	2	1	1
2018 학년도	기입형	전공 Ⓐ 1번 Incidental Learning 전공 Ⓐ 7번 Zone of Proximal Development			전공 Ⓐ 3번 Flipped Learning 전공 Ⓐ 10번 TBLT	전공 Ⓐ 8번 단어		
	서술형					전공 Ⓑ 5번 문법		전공 Ⓐ 13번 평가의 종류
	논술형						전공 Ⓑ 8번 교과과정과 교안	
	문항 수	2	0	0	2	2	1	1
2017 학년도 (계속)	기입형					전공 Ⓐ 6번 읽기 전공 Ⓐ 7번 말하기		전공 Ⓐ 1번 평가의 종류

연도	문제 유형	언어 습득론			영어 교수법			
		언어 습득 이론	학습자 요인	의사소통능력과 중간언어	교수법	4 skills, 문법, 단어, & 발음	교재와 교실 수업	평가
2017 학년도	서술형		전공 Ⓑ 4번 Communication Strategies	전공 Ⓐ 8번 Communicative Competence		전공 Ⓑ 서술형 1번 문법	전공 Ⓑ 2번 교재 전공 B 8번 교과과정과 교안	전공 Ⓐ 9번 평가의 원칙
	논술형							
	문항 수	0	1	1	0	3	2	2
2016 학년도	기입형		전공 Ⓐ 7번 World Englishes	전공 Ⓐ 8번 Communicative Competence	전공 Ⓐ 1번 Strategies -based Instruction		전공 Ⓐ 3번 교과과정과 교안	
	서술형			전공 Ⓐ 12번 Feedback		전공 Ⓑ 3번 쓰기 전공 Ⓑ 5번 문법	전공 Ⓑ 1번 과목 설계	전공 Ⓐ 13번 평가의 원칙
	논술형						전공 B 8번 수업참관	
	문항 수	0	1	2	1	2	3	1
2015 학년도	기입형					전공 Ⓐ 5번 읽기	전공 Ⓐ 2번 교재	전공 Ⓐ 3번 평가의 설계
	서술형			전공 Ⓐ 서술형 2번 Feedback	전공 Ⓑ 서술형 1번 Blended Learning		전공 Ⓐ 서술형 1번 교과과정과 교안	
	논술형						전공 Ⓑ 논술형 2번 교실수업	
	문항 수	0	0	1	1	1	3	1
2014 학년도	기입형			전공 Ⓐ 8번 Errors		전공 Ⓐ 10번 읽기	전공 Ⓐ 9번 교과과정과 교안	전공 Ⓐ 7번 평가의 원칙
	서술형					전공 Ⓐ 서술형 6번 문법	전공 Ⓐ 서술형 3번 교재	
	논술형						전공 Ⓑ 논술형 2번 교실수업	
	문항 수	0	0	1	0	2	3	1

제1장

언어 습득론

UNIT 1 학습 이론 및 언어 습득 이론

1 우연적 학습(Incidental Learning)

1. 우연적 학습(Incidental learning)과 의도적 학습(intentional learning)

인지주의 학습 이론에 따르면 정보 처리 방식을 이분법적으로 구분할 수 있다. 즉, 지식은 명시적 지식(explicit knowledge)과 암시적 지식(implicit knowledge)으로 구분할 수 있는데, 이는 서술적 지식(declarative knowledge)과 절차적 지식(procedural knowledge)과 밀접한 연관이 있으며 의도적 학습(intentional learning)과 우연적 학습(incidental learning)의 효율성과도 관련이 있다.

명시적 지식과 암시적 지식을 구별하는 기준은 우리가 그 지식을 명확하게 표현하거나 공유할 수 있는가이다. 즉 명시적 지식은 말이나 글로 쉽게 설명하고 표현할 수 있으나 암시적 지식은 분명 우리가 알고 있음에도 불구하고 설명할 수가 없다. 명시적 지식은 따라서 서술적(declarative)이다. 사실, 개념, 생각처럼 확실하게 서술할 수 있는 것이기에 서술적 지식이라고 할 수 있는 것이다(오경애, 2019). 암시적 지식은 명시적 지식을 활용할 수 있는 방법이라고 할 수 있다. 예를 들어 처음 자전거를 배울 때는 브레이크나 페달, 핸들의 사용법부터 배우고 균형을 잡는 법과 방향을 돌리는 법을 하나하나 배웠을 지라도 일단 자전거를 타는 방법을 습득하게 되면 그러한 것을 생각하지 않고 자연스럽게 타게 된다. 즉, 암시적 지식은 방법에 관한 지식, 기술에 관한 지식이고 절차적 지식과 같은 개념이다.

우연적 학습(incidental learning)이란 기억하고자 하는 의식적인 노력 없이 다른 사람이 하는 말을 듣거나 글을 읽음으로써 단어나 표현 등을 습득하게 되는 것을 의미한다. 반면 의도적 학습(intentional learning)은 시험 준비를 하거나 노래의 가사를 기억하는 것처럼 정보를 기억하고자 의식적으로 노력하는 것을 의미한다. 우연적 학습과 의도적 학습은 암시적 학습(implicit learning), 그리고 명시적 학습(explicit learning)과 중복되는 면이 있다. 그러나 두 개념이 정확하게 일치하는 것은 아니다. 신경 인지학에서는 암시적 학습은 두뇌 전반에 걸쳐 발생한다고 하지만 명시적 학습은 두뇌의 특정 부분에 한정되어 발생한다고 본다.

제 2 언어 습득론(Second Language Acquisition: SLA)에서의 암시적 학습과 명시적 학습은 학습자가 교재에 나온 사실이나 규칙을 학습할 때 무의식적으로 하는지 혹은 의식적으로 하는지에 의해서 구별된다. 이 때 사실이나 규칙은 대부분 문법 현상을 의미한다. 이러한 구분법에 따르면 암시적 학습과 명시적 학습은 우연히(incidentally) 혹은 의도적으로(intentionally) 일어날 수 있다. 그러나 학습이 어떻게 발생했는지에 상관없이 학습된 정보는 사용하지 않게 되면 잊혀 진다. 즉, 우연적 학습이 더 효율적인지 아니면 의도적 학습이 더 효율적인지는 알 수 없다. 우연적 학습과 의도적 학습에 관한 연구는 대부분 단어 습득에 관한 것인데, 읽기를 통한 단어의 우연적 학습이 낮을 때 학습자들에게 단어의 뜻을 찾아보게 하는 의도적 학습이 더 효율적임이 밝혀졌다. 이 때 읽기를 통한 무의식적인 단어의 습득을 "input only"라고 말하고 단어의 뜻까지 찾아보게 하는 것을 "input plus"라고 한다(Hulstijn, 2013).

2. 기술 습득 이론(Skill Acquisition Theory)

Dekeyser(2007b)의 기술 습득 이론(Skill Acquisition Theory)이 기본적으로 주장하는 바는 다음과 같다.

> "...the learning of a wide variety of skills shows a remarkable similarity in development from initial representation of knowledge through initial changes in behavior to eventual fluent, spontaneous, largely effortless, and highly skilled behavior, and that this set of phenomena can be accounted for by a set of basic principles common to acquisition of all skills" (p. 97).

즉, 어떠한 종류의 기술을 배우건 처음에 그에 관한 지식을 배우고, 행동의 변화를 통해서 궁극적으로는 노력 없이도 능숙하게 그것을 해내게 되는 과정이 학습이며 이것은 모든 기술에 다 적용이 된다는 것이다. 이 이론은 명시적 학습(explicit learning)과 암시적 학습(implicit learning)의 이분법적 구도에 명백한 기여를 했다. 이 이론에 따르면 성인은 대부분 명시적 과정을 통해 무엇인가를 배우기 시작하고 그에 따른 충분한 연습을 통해 암시적 과정으로 옮겨가게 된다.

학습의 발전은 서술적 지식(**declarative knowledge**)의 활용을 수반하게 되는 것이며 이 서술적 지식의 습득 후에 절차적 지식(**procedural knowledge**)이 발생한다. 서술적 지식이 절차적 지식으로 바뀌기 위해서는 초기에 습득된 서술적 지식에 질적, 그리고 양적 변화가 필요하다. 그 변화는 자동화(**automatization**)와 재구조화(**restructuring**)에 의해서 발생한다. 이 때 자동화는 학습한 기술을 행하는 속도가 빨라지고 오류의 비율이 현저하게 줄어든 상태를 의미한다. 그리고 재구조화는 지식의 하위 요소들과 그 요소들이 서로 상호작용하는 방법을 바꾸는 과정을 말한다. 이렇게 습득된 절차적 지식의 장점은 필요할 때 마다 이미 만들어진 정보가 즉시 호출된다는 점이다. 이 이론은 또한 스킬을 바탕으로 한 지도의 효과를 증명한다. 즉, 입력(**input**)을 바탕으로 수용적 스킬(**receptive skills**)과 출력(**output**)을 바탕으로 한 생산적 스킬(**productive skill**)에 도움을 준다(Taie, 2014).

1. Read the passage and follow the directions. 【2 points】

Learning a second language (L2) may be viewed as the gradual transformation of performance from controlled to less controlled. This transformation has been called proceduralization or automatization and entails the conversion of declarative knowledge into procedural knowledge. According to this argument, the learning of skills is assumed to start with the explicit provision of relevant declarative knowledge and, through practice, this knowledge can hopefully convert into ability for use. At the same time, it is important to understand that learning an L2 may proceed in a different way. For example, some have wondered if incidental L2 learning is possible as a consequence of doing something else in the L2. Simply put, the question is about the possibility of learning without intention. The answer is still open, but, at present, it appears that people learn faster, more and better when they deliberately apply themselves to learning.

Read Mr. Lee's teaching log below and fill in the blank with the ONE most appropriate word from the passage above.

Through my teaching experience, I've learned that different students learn in different ways. Considering the current trend in teaching and learning, I believe that students should be provided with more opportunities to be exposed to the _____ learning condition. Minsu's case may illustrate that point. At the beginning of the semester, Minsu introduced himself as a book lover. He wanted to read novels in English but was not sure if he could. I suggested that he didn't have to try to comprehend all the details. Indeed,

Minsu has benefitted a lot from reading novels. He said he learned many words and expressions even though he did not make attempts to memorize them. I will continue observing his progress as his way of learning is of great interest.

문제 분석

1) 기술 습득 이론(Skill Acquisition theory)에 대한 암시

● 첫 번째 문단의 전반부에 "declarative knowledge"가 "procedure knowledge"로 변한다는 이론이 언급되어 있다. 이는 기술 습득 이론의 핵심 요소이다.

● "the learning of skills"가 첫 번째 문단의 중간에 언급되어있다. 이는 skill-learning theory, 즉 기술 습득 이론을 풀어쓴 것이다.

● 첫 번째 문단의 후반부에 "incidental learning"이 언급되어 있다.

2) 답안 도출

● 첫 번째 문단은 기술 습득 이론을 바탕으로 해서 제2언어습득을 설명하며 우연적 학습(incidental learning)이 가능하지만 의도적 학습(intentional learning)의 효과가 더 뛰어나다고 마무리 짓고 있다. 이에 반해 두 번째 문단은 현재의 교수법 경향에 따라서 학생들에게 더 많은 우연적 학습의 기회를 주어야 한다고 주장하며 민수라는 학생의 예를 들고 있다.

● 최근 교육 현장에서는 과거에 많이 받아들여졌던 행동주의 및 인지주의 이론이 아닌 구성주의, 혹은 사회문화적 관점의 이론이 활성화되어서 쓰이고 있다. 따라서 이 문제는 인지주의 학습 이론이 주장하는 것처럼 우연적 학습과 의도적 학습이 구분되어 있으며 서술적 지식(declarative knowledge)이 먼저 습득이 되고 절차적 지식(procedural knowledge)으로 변화하는 것이 아니라는 것을 주장하고 있다.

예시 답안

incidental

② 근접 발달 영역(Zone of Proximal Development)

근접 발달 영역(**Zone of Proximal Development: ZPD**)은 Vygotsky의 학습 이론이다. 사회적 구성주의 학습 이론 중 가장 대표적인 이론이며 언어를 포함해서 전 영역에 적용 가능하다. ZPD란 학습자가 혼자서는 할 수 없으나 성인이나 더 잘 하는 사람의 도움에 의해 성취할 수 있는 영역을 의미한다(Brown, 2014). 다음 그림 1은 ZPD를 형상화한 것이다.

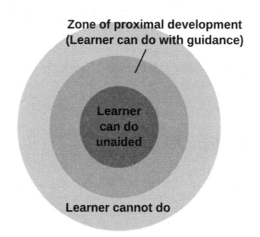

그림 1 : 근접 발달 영역(Zone of Proximal Development)

가장 안쪽에 있는 원이 학습자가 현재 가지고 있는 지식 및 능력을 나타내며 누구의 도움 없이도 혼자 해낼 수 있는 영역이다. 가장 바깥에 있는 원은 학습자가 도움을 받는다고 할지라도 해낼 수 없는 영역이므로 학습이 불가능한 부분이다. 그리고 그 사이에 있는 부분이 ZPD로써 학습자가 도움을 받으면 해낼 수 있는 영역이다. 즉, 이 영역이 교수자나 혹은 학습자보다 더 나은 능력을 가진 사람의 도움이 필요한 부분이다. 가장 바깥에 있는 영역의 학습은 아무리 지도를 한다고 해도 학습자에게는 입력이 안 되는 부분이고 이미 알고 있는 부분을 다시 지도한다는 것은 무의미하기 때문에 ZPD에 속하는 부분을 지도해야지만 학습이 가능하다(Celce-Murcia et al., 2014).

교실 수업에서는 비계 설정(**scaffolding**)이 ZPD에서 학습자의 능력을 고양시키는 대표적 방법으로 알려져 있다. 비계 설정(**scaffolding**)이란 학습자가 특정한 과업을 수행할 수 있도록 그 과업을 작은 단계로 나누어서 시범을 보여주거나 다른 방법을 통해서 성취할 수 있도록 도와주는 교수 방법을 의미하는데 이를 통해 학습자들은 어려운 부분이 있어도 포기하지 않고 단계별로 목표에 도달할 수 있게 된다. 비계 설정은 학습자들이 과업을 성취할 수 있게끔 과업을 단순화시키는 과정이며 학습자들이 적절한 방향으로 갈 수 있도록 도와주는 방법이다. 비계 설정의 여러 방법 중 가장 많이 활용되는 것은 학습자의 주의를 학습활동으로 돌리는 것과 활동을 단순화하는 것이다.

기출 2018 전공 A 기입형 7번

7. Read the dialogue and follow the directions. 【2 points】

(A teacher and a student are talking after seeing a video-clip of a baseball game.)

T: What was happening in the video?

S: A ball, uh, a ball.

T: A ball was thrown.

S: Thrown?

T: Yes, thrown. A ball was thrown.

S: A ball thrown.

T: And who threw the ball?

S: Pitcher. Thrown pitcher.

T: Thrown by the pitcher.

S: By pitcher.

T: Yes, by the pitcher. A ball was thrown by the pitcher.

S: Ball thrown by pitcher.

Note: T= teacher, S= student

Fill in the blank with the FOUR most appropriate words.

> From a socio-cultural perspective, effective learning takes place when what a student attempts to learn is within his or her _____ . This is the distance between what a student can do alone and what he or she can do with scaffolded help from more knowledgeable others like teachers or more capable peers. For learning to be effective, such help should be provided to a student through interaction like the teacher's utterances offered to aid the student in the above dialogue.

문제 분석

1) 근접 발달 영역(Zone of Proximal Development: ZPD)에 대한 암시
● 첫 번째 문단의 교수자와 학습자의 대화를 보면 비계 설정의 예임을 알 수 있다.

● 두 번째 문단의 용어 설명을 보면 사회문화적 관점이라고 언급되어 있으며 학습자가 혼자 할 수 있는 것과 더 잘 알고 있는 다른 사람의 도움을 받아서 할 수 있는 것 사이의 거리라는 근접 발달 영역의 정의가 명확히 나와 있다.

2) 근접 발달 영역에서 비계 설정의 적용
● 첫 번째 문단에서 먼저 교수자는 학습자가 현재 알고 있는 지식을 확인한다. 학습자는 단어("a ball")를 확실히 알고 있는 상태이다. 이 단어에 대한 지식을 발판으로 해서 교수자는 오늘의 학습 목표인 수동태 문장의 사용에 대한 시범을 보여준다("A ball was thrown"). 반복을 통해서 학습자가 "a ball thrown"이라는 한 단계 발전한 구문을 발화하자 교수자는 이를 바탕으로 "by the pitcher"라는 구절을 덧붙인다. 결과적으로 학습자는 단어 중심의 발화에서 "Ball thrown by pitcher"라는 수동태의 의미를 전달할 수 있는 문장의 발화까지 발전해 가는 것을 볼 수 있다.

예시 답안

Zone of Proximal Development

학습자 요인

1 학습 스타일(Learning Styles)

학습 스타일, 혹은 학습자 스타일이란 새로운 정보나 기술을 처리하고 이해하고 습득하는 과정에서 학습자 개개인이 자연발생적이고 습관적으로 선호하는 방법이다(Reid, 1995). 학습자의 학습 스타일은 서로 다르기 때문에 한 교수법이 어떤 학생들에게는 도움이 될 수 있으나 다른 학생들에게는 그렇지 않을 수 있다. 학습자 스타일은 지각적 선호도(**perceptual preference**), 처리 과정 선호도(**processing preference**), 그리고 성격적 선호도(**personality preference**)로 나눌 수 있다. 먼저 지각적 선호도를 살펴보도록 하겠다.

지각적 선호도(**perceptual preference**)는 학습자가 어떤 오감을 바탕으로 정보를 인지하는 것을 선호하는지를 보여준다. 학습자는 자신이 가장 편안하다고 느끼는 육체적이고 지각적인 경로를 통해 주변 정보를 습득하게 된다. 따라서 그 정보가 어떻게 주어지는가에 따라서 학습의 정도가 달라진다. 예를 들어 교수자 중심의 교실에서는 운동 감각을 선호하는 학생들이 불리하다. 심리학을 기본으로 하면 지각적 선호도는 다시 네 가지 기본 유형으로 분류될 수 있다; 시각적(**visual**), 청각적(**auditory**), 운동감각적(**kinesthetic**), 그리고 촉각적(**tactile**) 학습자가 그것이다. 각각의 학습자 유형은 자신이 가장 잘 집중할 수 있는 방법으로 외국어를 학습하고 싶어 하며 그럴 수 있을 때 가장 좋은 결과가 나온다(Rhouma, 2016).

시각적 학습자(**visual learners**)는 정보를 받아들이는 데 있어서 시각에 의존하는 학습자를 의미한다. 이 학습자는 시각 자료, 예를 들어 지도나, 프린트물, 플래쉬 카드, 그림, 도표 등으로 정보가 전달되었을 때 그 정보를 가장 잘 기억한다. 교실 수업에서는 인쇄된 교재나 칠판의 판서를 선호하며 노트 필기를 많이 하며 교수자의 표정이나 몸짓에 주의를 기울인다. 청각적 학습자(**auditory learners**)는 듣기를 선호하는 학습자이다. 청각적 학습자는 강의를 듣거나 토론을 할 때 가장 편안하다고 느낀다. 목소리 톤이나 억양 등을 통해 말 속에 숨어 있는 의미를 찾는데 능숙하기 때문에 녹음이나 녹화된 교재를 선호한다. 운동감각적 학습자(kinesthetic learners)는 몸의 움직임을 통해 정보를 습득하는 학습자이다. 이 학습자는 움직임을 통해 집중을 할 수 있고 학습 활동을 할 때 육체적으로 움직일 필요가 있다. 따라서 가만히 앉아 있어야만 하는 교실 수업은 힘들 수 있으며 야외 수업이라던가, 역할극 등을 선호한다. 마지막으로 촉각적 학습자(tactile learners)는 손을 사용할 때 가장 잘 학습을 할 수 있는 학생들이다. 이들은 손으로 무엇인가를 만들어낼 때 가장 좋은 학습 효과를 보인다. 실험실에서 실험을 하거나, 미술을 하거나, 모형을 만드는 것을 좋아한다. 따라서 학습할 때 무엇인가를 해야 한다고 느낄 때가 많아서 수업 시간에 노트 필기를 하거나 읽을 때 밑줄을 친다(Rhouma, 2016).

두 번째로 처리 과정 선호도(processing preference)를 살펴보면 다음과 같다.

처리 과정 선호도(Processing Preference)	
목표 중심적(goal-oriented)	세부 사항 중심적(detail-oriented)
귀납적(inductive)	연역적(deductive)
종합적(synthetic)	분석적(analytic)
장민감성/장의존성 (field-sensitive/field-dependent)	장둔감성/장독립성 (field-insensitive/field-independent)

표 1: 처리 과정 선호도(Processing Preference)

목표 중심적인 학습자는 전체 그림을 먼저 보는 반면에 세부 사항에 중심적인 학습자는 세부 정보를 먼저 파악한다. 귀납적인 스타일의 학습자는 사례에서 규칙을 찾아내는 것을 선호하는 반면 연역적인 스타일의 학습자는 규칙을 배우고 그 규칙을 사례에 적용하는 것을 선호한다. 또한 종합적인 학습자는 전체를 파악하기 위해 세부 정보를 조합하고 그에 대비해 분석적인 학습자는 그 반대로 먼저 전체를 분해한다. 마지막으로 장에 민감한 혹은 의존적인(field sensitive/field-dependent) 학습자는 전체적인 틀을 파악하는 데 익숙하지만 장에 둔감하거나 독립적인(field-insensitive/field-independent) 학습자는 세부적인 사항을 파악하는 데 더 능숙하다(Celce-Murcia, et al., 2014).

세 번째로 성격적 선호도(personality preference)를 보면 외향적인 학습자와 내향적인 학습자로 나눌 수 있는데, 외향적인 학습자는 다른 학생들과 같이 활동을 하며 배우는 것을 선호하는 반면 내향적인 학습자는 혼자서 공부하는 것을 선호한다(Celce-Murcia, et al., 2014).

1. Read the questionnaire in \<A> and the teacher's note in \<B>, and follow the directions. 【2 points】

───────────── \<A> ─────────────

This questionnaire is designed to identify students' learning styles. Each category (A, B, C, D) has 10 items. Students are asked to read each item and check their preferences.

	Learning Style Questionnaire	4	3	2	1
A	1. I understand better when I hear instructions.				
	2. I remember information better when I listen to lectures than when I read books.				
	3. I like to listen to radio shows and discussions more than reading the newspaper.				
	⋮				
B	1. I like to look at graphs, images, and pictures when I study.				
	2. I follow directions better when the teacher writes them on the board.				
	3. I can easily understand information on a map.				
	⋮				
C	1. I enjoy working with my hands or making things.				
	2. I remember things better when I build models or do projects.				
	3. I like to 'finger spell' when I learn words.				
	⋮				

	:			
D	1. I like activities that involve moving around.			
	2. I prefer to learn by doing something active.			
	3. I learn the best when I go on field trips.			
	:			

Note : 4=strongly agree, 3=agree, 2=disagree, 1=strongly disagree

---

\<B\>

Based on the findings of the questionnaire conducted in my class, I have noticed that four students each have a major learning style.

Scores of the four students			
Youngmi	Minsu	Taeho	Suji
A = 38	A = 18	A = 15	A = 13
B = 11	B = 36	B = 12	B = 14
C = 10	C = 10	C = 40	C = 12
D = 12	D = 12	D = 11	D = 36

This week, I am going to teach names of wild animals, like 'ostrich' and 'rhinoceros', by trying different activities to address these students' different learning styles. Youngmi scored the highest in category A, showing that she is an auditory learner. So I will let her listen to a recording and say the names of animals out loud. Minsu's high score in category B shows that he is a visual learner. I will let him look at images of animals and read the corresponding names. The person who had the highest score in C was Taeho, who is a tactile learner. I am going to use origami so he can use his hands to fold papers into animal shapes. This will help him learn their names better. Lastly, Suji's score in category D shows that she is a(n) _____ learner. For her, I am planning to do an animal charade activity where she acts like different animals and others guess the names of them. I think she will enjoy moving around the classroom. In these ways, I want to maximize students' learning outcomes in my class.

Based on the information in <A> and <B>, fill in the blank in <B> with the ONE most appropriate word.

1) 학습 스타일(learning styles)에 관한 제시

● 문단 <A>의 앞에 학습자의 "learning styles"에 관한 설문조사라고 나와 있다.

● 문단<B>에서 "auditory learner", "visual learner", "tactile learner"라는 용어가 제시 되어 있다.

2) 답안 도출

● 문단 <A>의 설문 문항을 보면 네 가지의 각각 다른 학습 스타일이 제시 되어 있고 문단 <B>에서 학생들의 점수는 각각 한 가지의 학습 스타일을 선호함을 보여주고 있다. 수지는 설문 문항의 D section에서 높은 점수를 받았으며 교수자가 디자인한 학습 활동은 수지가 선호하는 몸의 움직임을 활용한 것이다.

kinesthetic

2 세계 영어(World Englishes)

영어는 현재 69개국에서 주요한 언어나 공식 언어로 쓰이고 있다. 오늘날 80%의 대화가 영어로 행해지지만 그 중 단지 10~12%만이 영어를 모국어나 공식 언어로 하고 있는 화자 간에 행해진다. 이는 결국 영어 사용자들이나 그들이 사용하는 영어가 매우 다양해졌다는 것을 의미한다. 영어는 이제 영어의 소유권이 더 이상 영어를 모국어로 하는 화자에게 국한되어 있지 않다는 의미에서 국제어로서의 영어(**English as an International Language: EIL**)라고 불리기도 하고, 영어가 가진 경제, 기술, 그리고 문화적 권력 때문에 많은 사람들이 영어를 사용한다는 의미에서 세계어로서의 영어(**English as a Global Language**), 그리고 영어의 종류(**variety**)가 하나가 아닌 여러 개라는 의미에서 세계 영어(**World Englishes: WE**)라고 불린다(Eslami et al., 2019).

세계 영어(**World Englishes**)는 영어가 더 이상 영어를 모국어로 하는 화자만의 소유물이 아니라 국제어, 세계어, 혹은 링구아 프랑카(**lingua franca**)로 자리 매김했다는 의식에서 출발한다. **Kachru**는 영어 사용 국가들을 세 가지로 분류했다. 첫째는 inner circle로서 영어가 처음 확산되었던 시기를 기준으로 해서 영어를 사용하는 국가들이다. inner circle에는 영국, 미국, 호주, 캐나다, 뉴질랜드 등이 포함된다. 두 번째로 outer circle은 영국과 미국이 식민지를 확장하면서 지배 언어로 영어를 사용하게 됨에 따라 현재도 그 국가의 공식 언어로 영어를 사용하고 있는 국가들이다. 인도, 필리핀, 방글라데시, 말레이시아, 나이지리아, 케냐 등이 이에 속한다. 마지막으로 expanding circle에는 영어가 공식 언어는 아니지만 중요한 외국어로써 역할을 하고 있는 국가들로써 한국, 중국, 일본, 러시아와 같은 나라들이 속해 있다(Nam, 2019).

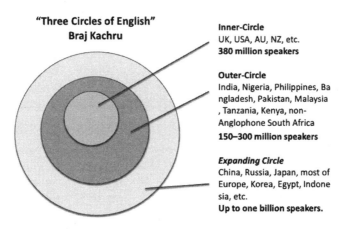

그림 2: Kachru의 Three Circle Model

따라서 교사 교육 프로그램에는 다음과 같은 내용이 포함되어야 한다. 교사는 1) 언어학적 차이로 인해 발생하는 의사소통의 오류에 대한 교육을 받아야 하며, 2) 다양한 소재를 활용해서 다른 영어를 사용하는 화자에 대한 내용이 들어있는 문화적 교재를 활용할 수 있어야 하며, 3) 다양한 영어에서 나오는 어려움에 대비할 수 있도록 세계 영어(**World Englishes**)를 초기부터 접해야 한다 (Matsuda, 2017).

기출   2016 전공 A 7번

7. Read the online discussion about Hyun's opinion and fill in the blank with TWO words from the passage. 【2 points】

Hyun

As an international language, English has many varieties used and taught around the world. Have you ever thought about English varieties?

$\text{like it } 28 \mid \text{recommend it } 15$

Sarah

Yes! There are many varieties of English. Americans, Australians, Brits and Canadians have many variations in how they use English. Naturally, this exists between non-native speakers, too. I think we should be aware of this reality. Many English teachers in the world today are non-native speakers of English. We need to consider this issue for teacher training and language instruction.

Bill

I agree. Although I am a native English teacher, like many of you, we need to recognize the validity of a variety of

Englishes, or better known as, _____.
These include established outer-circle varieties such as Indian English, Singaporean English, and Nigerian English.

Min

Perhaps, but what about standardization? Shouldn't we focus on one clearly understood form of the language for consistency and intelligibility?

Jun

I don't think that is applicable in all cases, Min. The needs and attitudes of students, teachers, and administrators have an influence on the norm or standard adopted for instruction; it is thus best that local norms be respected whenever possible.

문제 분석

- Hyun의 글에서 국제어로써 영어는 많은 "varieties"를 가지고 있다고 제시되어 있다.

- Sarah는 이에 대해 영어 교사 중 비원어민이 많으니 교사 교육과 언어 지도에 이를 고려할 필요가 있다고 한다.

- Bill은 "a variety of Englishes"의 타당성에 대해 언급하며 "outer circle"이라는 용어를 사용한다. 이 때 Bill이 처음으로 영어를 복수형, 즉 "Englishes"라고 사용한 것에 주목한다.

예시 답안

World Englishes

3 의사소통 전략(Communication Strategies)

의사소통 전략(Communication Strategies: CS)은 광범위한 개념으로 많은 내용들이 연관되어 있다. 이론적으로는 상호작용 가설(interaction hypothesis)을 기반으로 해서 두 화자가 의사소통을 하기 위한 방법으로서의 의미 협상(meaning negotiation)과 의사소통 능력의 부족함을 만회하기 위한 보상 전략(compensatory 혹은 compensation strategies)이 그것이다.

먼저 Long은 상호작용 가설(interaction hypothesis)을 통해 화자들이 언어적 형태, 대화 구조, 그리고 전달하고자 하는 정보의 내용을 조절하며 대화할 때 나타나는 문제를 피하거나 고친다고 주장한다. Long은 그의 가설에서 수정된 입력(modified input)과 수정된 상호작용(modified interaction)을 구분했다. 수정된 입력(modified input)은 언어 능력이 부족한 화자에게 의사를 전달하기 위해 언어적 형태를 변경하는 것을 의미하는 반면, 수정된 상호작용(modified interaction)은 담화 중 상호작용의 구조를 변경하는 것이다. 이러한 구조의 변경은 주로 분명하게 말하기 요청(clarification requests), 확인 점검(confirmation checks), 반복(repetition), 이해 점검(comprehension checks) 등으로 나타나는데, 이를 의미 협상(meaning negotiation, 혹은 negotiation of meaning)이라고 부른다(Wei, 2012).

의미 협상(meaning negotiation)을 보다 자세하게 살펴보자. 분명하게 말하기 요청(clarification requests)은 화자가 전달하고자 한 내용이 제대로 전달이 되었는지 확인하는데 사용하는 중요한 전략이다. 보통 화자가 전달한 말을 이해하지 못했을 때 청자가 요청한다. 다음의 예를 보자.

(1)
NS : Did you go shopping with your mom or with your friends?

NNS : No no I ‑ what? What you say? [asking for clarification]

NS : Did you go to the mall with your mom or with your friends?

NNS : Go to mall?

NS interlocutor : Yes.

NNS : Oh! With my friends.

(* NS: Native Speaker, NNS: Non-Native Speaker)

위의 예를 보면 NNS가 "No no I ‑ what? What you say?"라고 분명하게 말하기 요청

(**clarification request**)을 하자 NS가 "Did you go to the mall with your mom or with your friends?"라고 반복해서 말해준다.

다음의 예는 확인 점검(**confirmation checks**)을 보여준다. 확인 점검은 청자가 한 말을 제대로 이해했는지 화자가 확인하는 것이다.

(2)

NS : Did Andy get high marks? I mean good scores?

NNS : High marks? [confirmation check]

NS : Good grades, like 80 and 90. Did he get those scores?

NNS : Oh, maybe. I am not sure.

예 (2)를 보면 NNS가 "High marks?"라고 말한다. 이는 NS가 처음에 말한 "good scores"를 제대로 이해하지 못했기에 본인이 이해한 "high marks"가 맞는지 확인한 것이다.

이해 점검(**comprehension checks**)은 화자가 전달하고자 하는 메시지가 제대로 전달이 되었는지 확인하는 것을 의미한다. 다음의 예는 이해 점검을 나타낸다.

(3)

NS : What are you talking about?

NNS : Sta……

NS : Sta……?

NNS : Yes. Something made with concrete like real man, animal. But fake. You know what I mean? [comprehension check]

NS interlocutor : Hhhmmm.

NNS : Like Liberty in New York, understand? [comprehension check]

NS : Oh yes. STATUE!

NNS : Yes, statue.

예 (3)을 보면 NNS의 제한적 단어 능력으로 인해 의사소통 문제가 야기된다. 그러자 NNS는 단어를 "Yes. Something made with concrete like real man, animal. But fake"라고 설명한다. 그리고 NS가 이해했는지 "You know what I mean?"이라고 물어본다. 그럼에도 불구하고 NS가 이해하지 못한 것 같자 예를 들어서 "like Liberty in New York"이라고 다시 한 번 설명한 후 "understand?"
라고 이해 점검(comprehension check)을 한다(Masrizal, 2014).

두 번째로 Gass는 의미 협상(meaning negotiation)이 일어나는 반복적인 패턴을 모델화했다.
방아쇠(trigger) → 표시기(indicator) → 응답(response) → 응답에 대한 반응(reaction to
response)이 그것이다. 방아쇠(trigger)는 청자가 이해하는데 문제를 일으킨 화자의 발화를 의미한
다. 표시기(indicator)는 청자가 이해하는데 문제가 있음을 표현한 것으로써 분명하게 말하기 요청
(clarification requests), 확인 점검(confirmation checks), 이해 점검(comprehension checks)
등의 상호작용적 움직임(interactional moves)이 이에 속한다. 응답(response)은 청자의 요청에 대
한 화자의 답변이고, 응답에 대한 반응(reaction to response)은 화자의 답변에 대한 청자의 반응을
의미한다(Yeh & Lai, 2017). 다음의 예를 보자.

(4)

T: Tell me the most popular dishes in Taiwan. (trigger)

S: Um ⋯⋯ You say "xiao-chi"? Most popular ⋯⋯ (indicator)

T: Yeah. The two most popular dishes in Taiwan. (response)

S: I think one of them is stinky tofu, and the other is fried chicken. (reaction to
   response)

(* T=Teacher, S=Student)

(Yeh & Lai, 2017)

예 (4)를 보면 S는 T가 한 말을 이해하지 못한다. 이 때 T가 한 말은 방아쇠(**trigger**)가 되고, 이해하
지 못했다는 S의 발화 "Um ⋯⋯ You say "xiao-chi"? Most popular ⋯⋯"는 표시기(**indicator**)
가 된다. T가 다시 "Yeah. The two most popular dishes in Taiwan."이라고 말하자 S는 그에 따
른 적절한 답변을 한다. 이 때 T가 다시 되풀이 한 발화는 반응(**response**)이 되고 S가 한 적절한 답
변은 응답에 대한 반응(**reaction to response**)이 되는 것이다.

마지막으로 언어적 능력의 부족함으로 인해 발생하는 의사소통 문제를 다양한 방법으로 만회하
고자 하는 전략을 보상 전략(**compensatory/compensation strategies**)이라고 한다. 이 때 보상
전략은 의미 협상(**meaning negotiation**)과 관련이 있으나 대화의 상호작용이나 의미 협상의 유형

을 의미하는 것이 아니라 화자가 사용하는 전략만을 의미한다. 보상 전략에는 여러 가지 종류가 있다. 조립식 문형(prefabricated patterns), 회피(avoidance), 바꾸어 말하기(paraphrase), 우회적 화법(circumlocution), 근접 대체어(approximation), 단어 만들기(word coinage), 도움 요청(appeal to authority), 언어 전환(code-switching), 마임(mime), 직역(literal translation) 등이 그것이다. 이 이외에도 여러 가지가 있으나 언급된 것만을 우선적으로 살펴보겠다.

먼저 조립식 문형(prefabricated patterns)은 화자가 본인이 말하는 것의 문법적 구조나 단어는 모르지만 어떤 특정한 상황에서 규칙적으로 특정 패턴을 쓴다는 것을 인지하고 사용하는 구문이다. 예를 들어 "do you~"라는 구문을 인지한 화자가 상대방에게 무엇을 물어볼 때 지속적으로 "do you~"를 사용하지만 you가 주어이고 의문문을 만들기 위해 do 조동사를 사용한다는 것을 모른다면 이는 조립식 문형(prefabricated patterns)에 해당된다.

회피(avoidance)는 가장 많이 사용되는 전략으로 주제 회피(topic avoidance), 문구 회피(message avoidance), 그리고 의미 회피(semantic avoidance)로 나눌 수 있다. 주제 회피는 주제 자체를 피하는 것이고 문구 회피는 문구 포기(message abandonment)로 불리기도 하는데 주제에 대해서 말을 시작하긴 했으나 중간에 의미 전달을 할 수 없게 되어서 말을 안 하게 되는 것이고, 의미 회피는 단어나 문법 규칙을 몰라서 사용을 피하게 되는 것을 의미한다. Brown(2014)은 의미 회피를 다시 하류 범주로 구분하여 구문적 회피(syntactic avoidance)와 어휘적 회피(lexical avoidance)로 나눴고 또한 발음을 피하는 음운론적 회피(phonological avoidance)도 덧붙였다.

바꾸어 말하기(paraphrase)는 전달하고자 하는 바를 다른 형태나 단어로 대체하는 것을 의미하는데 이는 더 어려운 언어를 피하기 위함이다. 따라서 바꾸어 말하기는 의미 회피(semantic avoidance)와 밀접한 관련이 있다고 할 수 있다. 혹자는 바꾸어 말하기의 종류로 우회적 화법(circumlocution), 근접 대체어(approximation), 단어 만들기(word coinage)를 들기도 하지만 보통은 우회적 화법, 근접 대체어, 단어 만들기는 독립된 개념으로 본다. 그럼에도 불구하고 이 개념들은 모두 서로 관련이 있다. 예를 들어 바꾸어 말하기를 보다 확장한 형태가 우회적 화법이다. 우회적 화법은 단어를 설명하거나 묘사하는 것을 의미한다. 만일 "a revolving door"라는 단어를 몰랐을 때, "You know, the door that goes round..."라고 말한다면 이는 우회적 화법에 해당한다. 근접 대체어는 화자가 하나의 단어나 문장 구조를 알고 있는 상태에서 그것이 맞지는 않지만 의미가 통하기에 그냥 사용하는 전략을 의미한다. 예를 들어 "waterpipe"가 정확한 용어지만 그냥 "pipe"라고 말한다면 이는 근접 대체어에 해당한다. 단어 만들기도 바꾸어 말하기의 한 형태로 보는 경우가 있다. 단어 만들기는 모르는 단어를 표현하기 위해 영어로 단어를 만들어 내는 것을 의미한다. 예를 들어 "balloon"을 몰랐을 때 "airball"이라고 표현한다면 이는 단어 만들기에 해당한다.

도움 요청하기(**appeal to authority**)는 간혹 "appeal for assistance" 혹은 "appeal for help" 라고 불리기도 하는데 이는 화자가 사전을 찾아보거나 다른 사람에게 도움을 요청해서 맞는지 물어보는 것을 의미한다. 언어 전환(**code-switching**)은 모르는 부분을 모국어로 전환해서 말하는 것을 지칭한다. 마임(**mime**)은 신체 등을 사용해서 의미를 전달하고자 하는 것인데 비언어적 신호 (**nonverbal signals**)라고 불리기도 한다. 직역(**literal translation**)은 모국어를 그대로 직역해서 영어로 옮기는 것을 의미한다(Uhm, 2000).

기출 **2020** **전공 B** **4번**

4. Read the passage in <A> and the interaction in <B>, and follow the directions. 【4 points】

──────────── <A> ────────────

When problems in conveying meaning occur in conversational interactions, interlocutors need to interrupt the flow and negotiate meaning in order to overcome communication breakdowns and to understand what the conversation is about. A negotiation routine may have a sequence of four components:

• A trigger is an utterance that causes communication difficulty.

• An indicator alerts the speaker of the trigger that a problem exists.

• A response is the component through which the speaker of the trigger attempts to resolve the communication difficulty.

• A reaction to response can tell the speaker of the trigger whether or not the problem has been resolved.

(The following is a student-student talk occurring in the morning.)

S1: You didn't come to the baseball practice yesterday. What happened?

S2: Nothing serious. I had to study for an exam.

S1: I am sorry you missed the practice. Have you taken the exam yet?

S2: Yes. I took it a little while ago.

S1: How did you do?

S2: Hopefully I did OK. I didn't get any sleep last night.

S1: I guess you must be drained.

S2: Drained? What do you mean?

S1: It's similar to 'tired.'

S2: Oh, I see. Yeah, I am very tired.

S1: You need to take a break.

S2: I sure do, but I think I am going to eat something first.

Note: S = student

Identify an utterance from <B> that is a response mentioned in <A>, and explain how the speaker attempts to resolve the communication difficulty with the identified utterance. Then, identify an utterance from <B> that is a reaction to response mentioned in <A>, and explain whether the communication difficulty is resolved with the identified utterance.

문제 분석 📊🔍

● 문단 <A>에서 "negotiation of meaning"에 관한 문제라는 주제가 제시되어 있다. 즉, 협상의 패턴이 "routine"이라는 단어로 제시되어 있으며 "a trigger", "an indicator", "a response", "a reaction to the response"라는 단계가 제시된다.

● 문단 <B>에서 S1의 "I guess you must be drained"에서 의사소통의 문제가 야기되므로 그 발화는 "a trigger"에 해당하고, 이에 대한 "an indicator"가 S2의 "Drained? What do you mean?"

으로 표현되고 있다.

● 문제에서는 그 다음 과정인 "a response"를 제시한 후 어떻게 의사소통의 문제를 해결하는지 묻고, 그에 대한 reaction to response를 제시하기를 요구하고 있다. 따라서 이 문제는 의미 협상 (**negotiation of meaning**)이 일어나는 과정을 이해하고 있는지, 이를 수행할 수 있는지 확인하는 문제이다.

예시 답안

The response is S1's utterance, "It is similar to 'tired'". When S2 did not understand the word, "drained", S1 tries to negotiate meaning by offering a different word with a similar meaning. With S1's response, S1 shows a reaction to response by stating "Oh, I see. Yeah, I am very tired". S1's utterance indicates that the communication difficulty is resolved.

4. Read the passages and follow the directions. 【4 points】

─────────────────── <A> ───────────────────

(Below is a student's writing and a conversation with his teacher about the writing.)

Students writing

> Someone first showed the bicycle to the public in the late 18th century. People first thought it was not safe or comfortable. But many creative people improved it. So, many people use the bicycle widely as a form of transportation or for exercise today. Bicycle makers manufacture lighter, faster and stronger bicycles now than before. Because of that, more people ride the bicycle around the world these days than any time in the past. But they used some unique types of cycles in the old days like the four-cycle.

Teacher-student one-on-one conference

T: What is this writing about?

S: It's about the bicycle. Do you ride a bicycle?

T: Yes, I sometime do. So your writing is not about people who produce or use the bicycle.

S: That's right.

T: OK, the main theme is the bicycle. But none of the sentences has the bicycle as its subject.

S: I know. But if the bicycle becomes the subject, then I have to use many passives. They are complicated and difficult. So I tried not to use them.

T: But it would be better to use the bicycle as the subject in most sentences. That way, it will become clear that the main focus of your writing is the bicycle.

S: Well, okay. I'll try.

T: You used the word "manufacture." Did you know this word?

S: No, I didn't. At first, I wanted to use "make" but then the sentence looked a bit awkward because the subject is "makers." It would go like "Bicycle makers make."

T: I see.

S: So I looked up a different word in a dictionary that has the same meaning as "make."

T: That works. What about this word "four-cycle?" What do you mean? Are you trying to describe a bicycle but with four wheels?

S: Yes, I am. I added "four" to "cycle" just like "bi" is put before "cycle" in bicycle.

T: Oh, it is called "quadricycle." "Quadri" means four just as "bi" means two.

Note: T=teacher, S=student

─────────────────── <B> ───────────────────

When writing as well as speaking in a second language, learners who have limited command of the second language may have to use a variety of strategies that can compensate for their lack of knowledge of the target language grammar and vocabulary in order to effectively get their intended meaning or message across to a reader or listener. Strategies employed for this purpose include avoidance, code switching, word coinage, appeal to authority, and using prefabricated patterns. As these strategies constitute a significant part of strategic competence, advances in the learners' ability to effectively use them play a considerable role in promoting their communicative competence.

Based upon the student's writing and his dialogue with the teacher in <A>, identify THREE strategies the student used from those mentioned in <B>. Then, provide corresponding evidence for each identified strategy from <A>.

문제 분석 〖▥Q〗

● 문단 <B>에서 "strategies" "compensate"라는 단어가 나오고 부족한 언어 실력을 만회하기 위한 전략이라는 정의가 제시되어 있으므로 보상 전략에 관련된 문제임을 알 수 있다.

● 보상 전략으로써 "avoidance, code switching, word coinage, appeal to authority, using prefabricated patterns"가 문단 <B>에서 제시된다.

● 그 전략에 해당하는 예를 <A>에서 찾아서 예와 함께 기술하면 된다.

예시 답안 〖✎〗

The three strategies the student used are 1) avoidance, 2) appeal to authority, and 3) word coinage. The student states that s/he tried not to use the bicycle as the subject to avoid using a passive voice. Thus, the student used the avoidance strategy. The student also looked up the word, "manufacture", which is appeal to authority. Last, the student made up the word, "four-cycle" because s/he did not know the word "quadricyle". The strategy is word coinage.

4. Read the passages and follow the directions. 【4 points】

─────────── <A> ───────────

Meaning-negotiation strategies such as comprehension checks, clarification requests, and confirmation checks may aid comprehension during conversational interaction. First, comprehension checks are defined as the moves by which one interlocutor seeks, to make sure that the other has understood correctly. Second, clarification requests are the moves by which one interlocutor requests assistance in understanding the other's preceding utterance. finally, confirmation checks refer to the moves used by one interlocutor to confirm whether he or she correctly has understood what the other has said.

─────────── <B> ───────────

Miss Jeong has been instructing her students to actively utilize meaning-negotiation strategies stated in <A> during speaking activities. One day, she interviewed two of her students, Mijin and Haerim, about the strategies that they had used during previous speaking activities. The following are excerpts from the interview:

Mijin : When I didn't understand what my friends said during speaking activities, I usually said, "Could you repeat what you said?" or "I am sorry?" Sometimes I tried to check whether my friends clearly understood what I said by saying, "You know what I mean?"

Haerim: Well, during speaking activities, when I had difficulties comprehending what my friends said, I didn't say anything and pretended to understand what they said. I felt it embarrassing to show my lack of understanding to my friends. However, when I talked about something during speaking activities, I often said, "Do you understand?" in order to see if my utterances were understood well by my friends.

Based on the passage in <A>, write down all the meaning-negotiation strategies that Mijin and Haerim used respectively, along with their corresponding utterances from each student in <B>.

문제 분석 ‖Q

● 문단 <A>에서 "meaning-negotiation strategies"에 대한 문제임이 제시되어 있고 그에 해당하는 전략들이 "comprehension checks, clarification requests, and confirmation checks"로 제시되어 있다.

● 문제에서 문단 <B>에서 사용된 전략과 예를 함께 기술하라고 나와 있으므로 각 화자가 사용한 전략을 찾아서 기술하면 된다.

예시 답안 ✍

Mijin uses two strategies. The first one is a clarification request, such as "Could you repeat what you said?" or "I am sorry", and the second one is a comprehension check, such as "You know what I mean?". Haerim employes only a comprehension check, such as "Do you understand?"

UNIT 3 의사소통 능력

1 의사소통 능력(Communicative Competence)

의사소통 능력(communicative competence)은 Chomsky의 언어적 능력(linguistic competence)에 대항하는 개념으로 등장했다. 언어적 능력이 문법적으로 맞는 문장을 화자가 말하는 능력을 의미한다면, 의사소통 능력은 화자가 상황에 적절한 사회적 규칙을 반영하는 언어의 형태를 선택할 수 있는 능력을 의미한다. 따라서 의사소통 능력은 특정한 상황에서 누가 말하고 말하지 않을지, 언제 말하고, 언제 침묵할지, 누구에게 말하고 상대방의 지위나 역할에 따라 어떻게 말하고, 어떤 비언어적 행동을 취할 것인가 등에 관한 지식을 의미한다. 이러한 의사소통 능력은 사회 언어학과 밀접한 관련이 있는 개념이다.

Canale과 Swain(1980)은 의사소통 능력을 네 가지로 구분해서 설명했다. 첫째는 문법적 능력(grammatical competence)으로 문법적으로 맞는 발화를 할 수 있는 능력이다. 여기에는 문법적 형태뿐만 아니라 어휘나 음운 등 모든 언어적 코드가 들어갈 수 있다. 두 번째는 담화 능력(discourse competence)으로써 일관적인 발화를 할 수 있는 능력이다. 즉, 작은 단위의 발화를 이어서 전체 담화를 가능하게 하는 능력이다. 세 번째로 사회 언어적 능력(sociolinguistic competence)은 사회 언어적으로 적절한 발화를 할 수 있는 능력을 의미하는데. 사회 문화적 규칙을 따른다는 것은 그 언어가 사용되는 사회적 상황을 이해할 수 있다는 것을 말한다. 마지막으로 전략적 능력(strategic competence)은 의사소통 시 문제가 생겼을 때 이를 해결할 수 있는 능력이다. 전략적 능력은 의사소통 전략(communication strategies)을 사용해서 문제를 수정할 수 있는 능력뿐만 아니라 의사소통의 효율성을 향상시키기 위한 전략을 모두 포함한다.

Bachman(1990)은 Canale과 Swain의 의사소통 능력을 보다 자세하게 나눴다. 그 첫 번째는 조직적 능력(organizational competence)인데 문법적 능력(grammatical competence)과 문맥적 능력(contextual competence)으로 다시 나뉜다. 문법적 능력이 언어의 사용법과 관련이 있다면, 문맥적 능력은 개별적인 발화를 합하여 하나의 일관된 담화로 만드는 능력이다. 두 번째는 화용적 능력(pragmatic competence)으로써 상대방이 잘 이해할 수 있는 언어의 기능을 사용할 수 있는 능력과 주어진 상황에 적절한 언어의 능력을 사용할 수 있는 지식을 합한 것이라고 할 수 있다. 마지막으로 전략적 능력(strategic competence)은 평가, 계획, 수행이라는 요소를 모두 포함한 능력으로써 다른 능력의 부족함을 만회할 수 있는 능력이다. 즉 제한적인 언어 능력을 가장 효율적으로 사용할 수 있게 하는 능력이라고 할 수 있다.

　　Celce-Murcia, Brinton과 Ann Snow(1995)는 여기에 덧붙여 행동적 능력(actional competence)을 제안했다. 행동적 능력은 유의미한 모든 화행(speech acts)을 이해하고 사용할 수 있는 능력을 의미한다. 여기서 화행(speech acts)이란 사회 언어학에서 의사소통 능력과 관련이 있는 또 하나의 개념으로써 말을 하나의 행위로 정의한 것이다. 즉, 우리가 하는 모든 발화를 하나의 행위로 정의한다면 발화는 실질적으로 사용된 단어나 문법과는 다른 기능적인 가치를 갖게 된다. 따라서 발화를 형태가 아닌 기능에 따라 구별할 수 있게 되는 것이다. 예를 들어 "창문 닫아"라고 말하는 것과 "여기 춥다"라고 말하는 것은 문법적으로 전혀 다른 형태지만 둘 다 창문 닫기를 요구하는 같은 기능을 가지고 있다. 이 때 우리가 사용하는 두 가지 발화를 다 "locutions"라고 한다. 발화 행위(locutionary act)는 말을 하는 행위 자체를 말하며, 이 때 발화는 의미를 전달할 수 있는 기본 요소를 다 갖추고 있어야 한다. 이 발화 행위에 어떤 의도가 있다면 이를 발화 수반 행위(illocutionary act)라고 표현한다. 위에 든 두 가지 예는 모두 추우니 창문을 닫았으면 좋겠다는 의도된 목적을 가지고 있으므로 발화 수반 행위(illocutionary act)에 해당한다. 만약 발화 수반 행위가 청자로 하여금 어떤 행동을 하도록 야기한다면 이는 발화 효과(perlocutionary force)를 갖게 된 것이다. 창문을 닫았으면 한다는 발화 수반 행위(illocutionary act)가 행해졌을 때 누군가, "그래" 하고 창문을 닫았다면 "창문 닫아" 혹은 "여기 춥다"라는 발화 효과(perlocutionary force)가 행동을 취하게 만들었고 화자의 목적은 성취된 것이다(Wardhaugh & Fuller, 2015). 이렇듯 발화 수반 행위에 따른 결과나 효과가 발생하기를 기대한다면 이를 발화 효과 행위(perlocutionary act)리고 한다(Wardhaugh & Fuller, 2015).

　　사회 언어학의 도구로 많이 쓰이는 연구 방법은 담화 분석(discourse analysis)이나 대화 분석(conversation analysis)이다. 담화 분석은 자연적으로 발생하는 연속적인 문장, 즉 담화를 연구하는 것으로써 언어를 전달하고자 하는 사람이 무엇을 전달하고자 했고, 듣는 사람이 그것을 어떻게 해석하는가가 담화 분석의 주요 주제이다. 대화 분석은 대화에서 사람들 사이의 상호 작용을 연구하는 것으로써 순서 바꾸기(turn-taking)를 주로 살펴보는데, 순서 바꾸기란 한 화자가 말을 하고 또 다른 화자가 그에 이어 말을 하는 것을 의미한다. 두 연구 방법 모두 실생활에서 언어가 어떻게 사용되고 있는지에 집중하기 때문에 실생활에서 사용되는 모든 언어적 요소, 예를 들어 단어나 문법 구조, 장르뿐만 아니라 비언어적 의사소통(nonverbal communication)과 순서 바꾸기(turn-taking), 방해(interruptions), 청자 반응(listener response) 등과 같은 대화적 코드(conversational codes)도 분석 대상이다. 다만 대화 분석은 사회학에서 기원했기에 사회적 상호 작용에 보다 중점을 두며 한 주제가 시작되어 끝날 때까지의 전체 대화를 중심으로 순서 바꾸기를 살펴본다는 것과 분석의 결과물이 메시지의 전달에서 끝나는 것이 아니라 그 대화가 갖는 사회적 의미와 행동에 중점을 둔다는 사실이 담화 분석과 다르다고 할 수 있다. 두 연구 방법 모두 사회언어학에서 많이 쓰이고 있는데, 연구의 도구로 많이 쓰이는 언어 양식(speech styles)과 담화 표지(discourse markers)를 살펴보고, 용어가 까다로운 비언어적 의사소통(nonverbal communication)도 자세하게 살펴보도록 하겠다.

먼저 언어 양식(speech styles)이란 화자가 사용하는 언어의 형태를 의미하는데, 이것은 형식(formality)에 따라 달라진다. 보통 얼마나 형식을 갖추는가에 따라 달라진다. 보통 얼마나 형식을 갖추는가에 따라 다음과 같이 분류된다; 1) 동결 문체(frozen style), 2) 공식 문체(formal style), 3) 자문 문체(consultative style), 4) 약식 문체(casual style), 5) 친밀 문체(intimate style). 동결 문체(frozen style)는 대중에게 연설할 때 사용하는 가장 형식적인 언어의 형태이고, 공식 문체(formal style)는 중요하거나 심각한 상황에서 사용되는 스타일이며, 자문 문체(consultative style)는 소모임에서 많이 사용하는 형태로 잠깐 만난 사이라던가 처음 만난 사람들 사이에 많이 사용된다. 반면 약식 문체(casual style)는 편안한 상대와 대화할 때 사용되는 형태이며 친밀 문체(intimate style)는 가족이라던가, 아주 친한 사이에서 사용되는 형태이다. 특히 공식 문체는 화자가 발음, 단어나 문장 구조의 선택에 신경을 쓸 때 사용되는 것으로써 환경, 지역, 사회적 계층, 나이, 성별 등에 따라 영향을 받는다(Joos, 1967).

담화 표지(discourse markers)는 화자나 작가가 전달하는 의미를 청자나 독자가 잘 이해하게끔 하는 역할을 한다. 예를 들어 "yeah", "so", "OK", "right?" 등은 모두 담화 표지에 해당한다. 담화 표지는 차례가 바뀜을 보여주거나, 생각을 잘 연결하거나, 화자의 태도 등을 단어나 구를 사용해서 알려준다. 담화 표지에는 여러 종류가 있지만 맞장구(backchannel), 울타리(hedges), 그리고 전방조응적(대용적) 단어(anaphoric words), 후방조응적 단어(cataphoric words), 외조응적 단어(exophoric words)를 살펴보도록 하겠다. 이 중 맞장구(backchannel 혹은 backchannel cues)

는 청자가 주의를 기울이고 있거나, 이해거나, 동의하고 있다는 것을 화자에게 알려주기 위한 담화 표지로써 특별한 정보를 전달하지 않는다. 주로 "yeah", "uh-huh", "hmm", and "right" 등이 사용된다. 울타리(**hedges**)는 화자가 애매모호하거나 불분명함을 나타내기 위해서 쓰는 도구로써 형용사나, 부사 혹은 부가의문문이 쓰일 수도 있다. 다음의 예를 보자.

1) There might just be a few **insignificant** problems we need to address. (adjective)
2) The party was **somewhat** spoiled by the return of the parents. (adverb)
3) **I'm not an expert but** you might want to try restarting your computer. (clause)
4) That's false, **isn't it?** (tag question clause)

위의 문장에서 굵게 표시되어 있는 부분을 보면 전체 문맥에서 반드시 필요하지는 않지만 사용됨으로써 화자가 어떤 주장을 하는데 있어서 확실성이 감소된다. 마지막으로 전방조응적(대용적) 단어(**anaphoric words**), 후방조응적 단어(**cataphoric words**), 외조응적 단어(**exophoric words**)는 문맥의 일관성을 강화시키기 위한 방법으로 사용된다. 전방조응적(대용적) 단어는 이미 언급된 단어를 다시 가리키기 위한 것이고, 후방조응적 단어는 후에 언급될 것을 미리 가리키는 말이며, 외조응적 단어는 대화에서는 언급되지 않는 것을 가리킬 때 쓰는 말이다.

1) 전방조응적(대용적) 단어(anaphoric words)

Michael went to the bank. **He** was annoyed because **it** was closed

→ **He**는 Michael을 의미하고 **it**은 bank를 의미한다. 이 때 이 두 단어는 모두 전방조응적(대용적) 단어이다.

2) 후방조응적(cataphoric words)

Although I phone **her** every week, my mother still complains that I don't keep in touch often enough.

→ **her**는 my mother를 의미하는 후방조응적 단어이다.

3) 외조응적 단어(exophoric words)

"**They**'re late again, can you believe it?" "I know! Well, **they**'d better get here soon or it'll get cold."

→ **they**는 두 사람의 대화에서 언급된 적이 없는 외조응적 단어이다.

(출처 : 위키피디아)

마지막으로 비언어적 의사소통(**nonverbal communication**)은 과거에는 단어나 언어를 제외한 의사소통이라고 받아들여졌으나 최근에는 구어로 하는 대화와 같은 성격을 지닌다고 여겨진다. 구어로 하는 대화가 의미를 지속적으로 전달한다면 비언어적 의사소통은 의미가 전달되는 방법을 나타낸다는 것이다. 비언어적 의사소통에는 신체 언어학(**kinesics**), 눈맞춤(**oculesics**), 옷과 소지품(**artifacts** 혹은 **artifactics**), 감각학(**kinesthetics** 혹은 **haptics**), 소리(**vocalics**), 후각(**olfactics**), 근접 공간학(**proxemics**), 그리고 시간학(**chronemics**) 등이 있다.

먼저 신체 언어학(**kinesics**)은 제스처나 포즈, 표정 등을 포함한 몸의 움직임을 의미한다. 눈맞춤(**oculesics**)은 눈맞춤이나 얼마나 오랫동안 쳐다보는가에 관한 것이다. 특히 눈맞춤은 문화에 따라 차이가 많다고 알려져 있다. 옷과 소지품(**artifacts** 혹은 **artifactics**)은 옷이나 소지품을 의미한다. 감각학(**kinesthetics** 혹은 **haptics**)은 신체 접촉을 말한다. 소리(**vocalics**)는 말로 전달하는 의미를 제외한, 억양, 음색, 발음, 소리의 크기 등을 포함한다. 후각(**olfactics**)은 냄새나 향을 이용한 대화이지만 잘 연구된 분야는 아니다. 근접 공간학(**proxemics**)은 대화할 때 필요한 개인적 공간을 의미한다. 이 공간도 화자간의 관계나 문화에 따라 차이가 있다고 알려져 있다. 시간학(**chronemics**)은 시간에 대한 개념, 걷는 간격, 얼마나 신속하게 일을 처리하는가에 관한 연구이다(Mishra, 2018).

기출 **2020** **전공 A** **3번**

3. Read the passage in <A> and the conversation between two teachers in <B>, and follow the directions. 【2 points】

─────────── <A> ───────────

The way you speak is affected in many ways. For example, how much attention you are paying to your speech may be one factor. When you are not paying much attention to the way you are speaking, your speech may be more casual. By contrast, if you are conscious about the way you are speaking, your output will be less casual. The social position of the person with whom you are engaging in conversation may also affect your language output. It is natural to use more formal language when you speak to someone whose social position is above yours. The sociolinguistic concept of solidarity should also be considered. If your interlocutor comes from the same speech community or shares a similar social or cultural identity with you, you will feel connected to him or her, and this will affect the way you deliver your message. In addition, where you are affects the formality of your output. When you are in a formal situation, such as a business meeting, you naturally use more formal language, and the opposite is true as well. Lastly, the channel or medium of language, that is, whether you deliver your message through speech or writing, can be another critical factor that affects your speech. All of these things need to be considered carefully, because they constitute what is called pragmatic competence which relies very heavily on conventional, culturally appropriate, and socially acceptable ways of interacting.

――――――――――――――――――― <B> ―――――――――――――――――――

T1: What are you writing?

T2: Oh, this is a recommendation letter for Miri.

T1: I see. She is very active in school activities, so you must have a lot to write about her.

T2: Yes, she is a good student, but she doesn't know how to adapt her conversational style when making a request.

T1: Hmm... what do you mean by that?

T2: When Miri approached me, she said, "Hi, teacher, can you write me a recommendation letter?"

T1: Haha... I understand what you mean. Some of my students also seem to have trouble making their speech style appropriate to the situation.

Miri is just one example.

T2: Exactly! Still, I feel it's my responsibility to show them how speech styles differ across various situations. Hey, why don't we offer a special lecture on this topic?

T1: Definitely! We can invite a guest speaker who can show the importance of selecting the appropriate conversational style to match the _____ of the situation.

Note: T = teacher

Fill in the blank in <B> with the ONE most appropriate word from <A>.

문제 분석

● 문단 <A>의 마지막 부분에 이것이 "pragmatic competence"에 관련이 있다고 되어 있으므로 의사소통 능력(**communicative competence**) 중 화용적 능력(**pragmatic competence**)에 해당하는 문제임을 알 수 있다. 문단 <A>에서 "the way you speak"이 "paying attention to your speech", "social position of the person", "solidarity", "where you are", "channel of the language"의 다섯 가지 요소에 따라고 달라진다고 나와 있다.

● 문단 <B>의 사례는 언어 양식(**speech styles**)이 상황에 따라 달라지는 것을 아직 습득하지 못한 학생의 부적절한 요청 구문이 문제가 된 것임을 보여준다. 문단 <A>에 언급되어 있는 하나의 단어를 사용해야 하므로 상황의 어떤 점에 따라 언어 양식이 달라지는 지에 중점을 두어 단어를 찾으면 된다.

예시 답안

formality

5. Read the passage in <A> and the interaction in <B>, and follow the directions.
【4 points】

———————————— <A> ————————————

　　Different words and phrases can be used to organize the structure and manage the flow of ongoing conversations. Language elements of this function include different types such as conjunctions, cataphoric words, hedges, and back channel cues. Conjunctions join words, phrases, or clauses together. Cataphoric words refer forward to other words which will be used later in the conversation. Hedges are words or phrases employed not to express the truth of a statement categorically, and back channel cues indicate that one is paying attention to his or her interlocutor's speech. As using these types of language is associated with discourse and strategic competence, the ability to use them in an effective way constitutes part of communicative competence.

———————————— <B> ————————————

(Two students are doing a task on finding differences between each other's pictures without showing them to each other.)

S1: Do you see any people in your picture?

S2: I have a man. He is tall.

S1: Is he the only person?

S2: I also have a woman in my picture.

S1: There are two in mine, too. What are they doing?

S2: They are sitting together.

S1: That's one difference. They are standing in mine.

S2: What is the woman wearing?

S1: She is wearing a jacket.

S2: What color is it?

S1: It's black.

S2: That is the same in my picture.

S1: Oh, wait, on her jacket, I found this. There is a letter P on it.

S2: I also see a P on her jacket in my picture.

S1: What about the man? What is he wearing?

S2: He is in a blue coat. It is sort of neat.

S1: The man's coat is brown in mine. That's another difference.

Note: S = student

Identify TWO types among those mentioned in <A> that are used in <B>. Then, provide evidence for each identified type from <B>.

문제 분석 🔍

● 문단 <A>에서 담화 표지(**discourse markers**)들의 예가 "conjunctions, cataphoric words, hedges, and back channel cues"로 제시되어 있고 각각의 정의도 함께 제시되어 있다. 문제에서 <B>에서 사용된 것들을 찾아보라고 했는데 <B>의 대화에는 "back channel cues"와 단어, 구, 문장 등을 연결하는 "conjunction"은 나와 있지 않다. 따라서 사용된 담화 표지는 "cataphoric words"와 "hedges"임을 알 수 있다.

예시 답안 ✏️

The two types used in <B> are 1) cataphoric words and 2) hedges. In S1's utterance, "Oh, wait, on her jacket, I found this. There is a letter P on it", "this" indicates a letter P. Thus, "this" is a cataphoric word. Also, S2 says "It is sort of neat". "sort of" is used as a hedge in the statement.

8. Read the passages and follow the directions. 【2 points】

<A>

Non-verbal communication is an important aspect of intercultural communication. It includes the following categories, which also apply to cultural norms in public space. First, there is kinesics, which is the use of gestures or body language. A second category is oculesics, which refers to eye contact and eye movement. Eyes can provide signals as to one's mood, such as being interested, bored, empathetic, or annoyed. Third, there is proxemics, which relates to physical distance between interlocutors (and other people in public spaces). A fourth category is kinesthetics (also called haptics), meaning touching or making physical contact with someone. Across cultures, norms relating to these categories can vary significantly, which can lead to misunderstandings or inappropriate behavior in cross-cultural situations.

<B>

A group of students in Ms. Lee's school won a regional English contest and they received an all-expense-paid trip to Seattle as a reward. In preparation, Ms. Lee tutored them on how to be polite, which included lessons comparing cultural norms and non-verbal communication in Korea and America. However, the following event occurred.

After arriving in Seattle, they were hungry, so they asked their shuttle bus driver to stop at the nearest fast food restaurant, but it was busy and the line was long. A student, Gyumin, led the group through the line. As the line moved, so did Gyumin, inching ever so closer to the front. He was excited—this was his first time in a restaurant abroad—and he was eager to order his meal. However, Ms. Lee noticed something recurring. Gyumin was closely following a middle-aged American man in line, and as the line moved forward, Ms. Lee saw that the man frequently turned his head to the side and, with a scrunched forehead, gazed down at Gyumin for a moment as if to tell him something. Ms. Lee quietly pulled Gyumin aside and the following exchange occurred:

T: Gyumin, do you remember what I taught you about lining up?

S: You mean not to bump into anyone? I didn't!

T: No, no, not that. Rather, do you remember the arm's length rule?

S: Oh, that!

T: It's okay. Just remember it for next time. We want to be polite while we are here.

S: Okay. I got it.

Note: T = teacher, S = student

Given the information in <A>, write the ONE most appropriate category that Gyumin violated in <B> in regards to cultural norms in America.

문제 분석

● 문단 <A>에 "nonverbal communication"이라는 주제가 제시되어 있고 "kinesics", "oculesics", "proxemics", "kinesthetics"라는 네 가지 소분류가 제시되어 있다. 문단 <B>의 예에 "arm's length's rule"이라고 설명되어 있으므로 개인이 필요한 공간에 관한 문제라는 것을 알 수 있다.

예시 답안

Proxemics

8. Read the conversation between a teacher and a student and follow the directions.
【2 points】

> (*Sujin, who is in an exchange programme in England, is having a conversation with her teacher, Ms. Connor.*)
>
> Sujin: Hi, how're you doing?
>
> Ms. Connor: I'm doing well. Are you alright?
>
> Sujin: Yes. Um . . . I have fun . . . but still intimidated by talking to people in English.
>
> Ms. Connor: What's the problem?
>
> Sujin: I have my British friend Kate in my class. Yesterday, she told me, "I like your jacket! Really unusual. Great on you." So I said, "Really? I don't think so." I felt she was rather embarrassed and something was wrong.
>
> Ms. Connor: Oh, you should just say, "Thank you" in that situation. Remember, cultural norms involving language use differ from country to country. Don't worry, you're on the right track. It's a normal process of learning in a new culture.
>
> Sujin: Oh, I see. I should have understood her and said, "Thanks." OK, thank you very much.

Complete the comments by filling in ① with TWO words and by filling in ② with ONE word. Write your answers in the correct order.

> Sujin experienced misunderstanding as she performed a ____①____ of compliment response in an interaction with her British friend. Since cultures differ from one another and language is inextricably interwoven

with culture, cultural knowledge of language use in context plays a crucial role in cross-cultural communication. This entails the concept of ____②____ competence, one of the core components of communicative competence, which enables learners to use the L2 in socioculturally appropriate ways.

문제 분석

- 첫 번째 문단의 사례를 보면 학생이 문화적 차이에서 기인하는 의사소통의 문제점을 겪었다는 것을 알 수 있다. 두 번째 문단의 ②에 해당하는 용어의 설명을 보면 의사소통 능력(**communicative competence**) 중 사회문화적으로 적절한 방법으로 L2를 사용하게 하는 능력이라고 제시되어 있으므로 Canale과 Swain의 분류법을 따랐다는 것을 유추할 수 있다.

- 두 번째 문단의 빈칸 ①은 compliment response를 "perform"했다는 것이 유일한 힌트이다. 이 것은 발화를 행위로 간주했다는 것을 의미하므로 화행(**speech acts**)과 관련되어 있다는 것을 알 수 있다. 화행의 세 가지 종류인 발화 행위(**locutionary act**), 발화 수반 행위(**illocutionary act**), 그 리고 발화 효과 행위(**perlocutionary act**) 중 학생의 발화는 의미를 전달할 수 있는 기본 요소가 갖춰진 것이므로 발화 행위라고 할 수 있다. 그러나 발화의 의도가 제대로 전달이 안 되었기에 발화 수반 행위가 수행되었다고 할 수는 없다.

예시 답안

① locutionary act
② sociolinguistic

4 중간 언어

중간 언어(**interlanguage**)란 모국어와 목표 언어 사이의 중간 단계에 있는 학습자의 언어 체계를 의미한다. 중간 언어는 오류 분석(**error analysis**)이 적용되는 분야이다. 오류 분석은 외국어 혹은 L2 학습자의 언어를 분석하는 방법으로써 오류를 알아내고, 설명하고, 분석하고, 평가하는데 중요한 역할을 한다(Lan, 2019).

① 오류(Errors)

학습자 언어의 오류(**errors**)는 체계적이고 지속적으로 발생하는 속성을 지닌다. 이는 지속적으로 발생하지 않는 실수(**mistakes**)와 구별된다. 학습자 언어의 오류는 그 오류의 기원에 따라 분류된다. 먼저 모국어와 목표 언어와의 차이에 의해 발생하는 언어 간 오류(**interlingual errors**)와 목표 언어를 학습하는 과정에서 발생하는 언어 내 오류(**intralingual errors**)로 구분할 수 있다.

언어 간 오류는 간섭(**interference**), 언어 전이(**language transfer**) 혹은 교차 언어적 오류(**cross-linguistic errors**)라고도 불리는데, 학습자의 모국어가 목표어의 습득에 해로운 영향을 끼칠 때 발생한다(Kaweera, 2013). 따라서 이는 부정적 전이(**negative transfer**)라고 할 수 있다. 즉, 언어 간 오류는 전이 오류(**transfer errors**)에 의해 야기된다고 할 수 있다. 언어 내 오류는 발달상 오류(**developmental errors**)로써 학습자가 가지고 있는 목표 언어에 관한 지식의 한계에 의해 발생한다. 학습자가 목표 언어에 관한 부분적인 지식을 광범위하게 적용하면서 나타나는 오류이기에 과잉일반화(**overgeneralization**)가 상당 부분을 차지한다(Sari, 2016). 따라서 언어 간 오류는 간섭(**interference**), 언어 내 오류는 과잉일반화(**overgeneralization**)이라고 부른다(Lan, 2019).

11. Read the passage in <A> and the teacher's log in <B>, and follow the directions.
【4 points】

─────────────── <A> ───────────────

    Language transfer refers to the effects of the learner's previous language knowledge or performance on subsequent language learning. Transfer can be categorized into positive and negative transfer. Negative transfer can be further divided into two types – overgeneralization and interference.

─────────────── <B> ───────────────

(Following is a teacher's reflection on a task for her Korean students.)

Teacher's log

    I conducted a task that required students in pairs to ask and answer questions in class yesterday. At the beginning of the task, I heard a student asking, "Don't you like bananas?" His partner answered, "No, I eat them everyday. They are good for my health." And another student said, "Yes, I never eat them. But I like mangos," when responding to "Don't you like oranges?" I noticed many other students make such errors later in the course of the task. So I decided to tap into the errors and explained them to students after the task. I gave them further question-and-answer exercises to provide opportunities to practice what I explained before the class was over.

Identify the type of negative transfer in <B> based on <A>. Then, provide TWO examples of the identified type from <B> and explain why they exemplify the identified type in terms of whether transfer occurs intralingually or interlingually.

문제 분석 📊🔍

● 문단 <A>의 첫 부분에 "language transfer"라는 주제가 나와 있고 그 중 부정적인 전이를 "overgeneralizaiton"과 "interference"라고 한다고 용어가 정의되어 있다.

● 문단 <B>의 예를 보면 학생들이 부정어가 들어가 있는 질문에 대한 답을 할 때 영어를 사용하는 화자가 하듯이 긍정과 부정의 의미로 답하는 것이 아니라 한국어 화자들이 하듯이 동의와 반대의 개념으로 yes와 no를 사용 하는 것을 알 수 있다. 따라서 이는 모국어에서부터 야기된 언어 간 오류 (**interlingual errors**)임을 알 수 있다.

● 문제에서 전이가 "interlingual" 혹은 "intralingual" 일어났는지 찾고 예를 제시하라고 했으므로 해당하는 예와 함께 "interlingual transfer"임을 밝히면 된다.

예시 답안 ✍️

The type of negative transfer is interference. The examples of the interference are 1) "No, I eat them everyday" and 2) "Yes, I never eat them". The examples show that the direct influence of students' 1st language, Korean. Korean speakers answer "yes" or "no" based on agreement or disagreement, but English speakers use "yes" or "no" in terms of positiveness or negativeness. Thus, the examples show the negative transfer of students' 1st language which has occurred interlingually.

8. Read the interaction between a teacher and a student, and follow the directions. 【2 points】

> *(The teacher asks her student, Dongho, what he did over the weekend.)*
>
> T: Hi, Dongho, how was your weekend?
> S: Hello, uh, have, had fun.
> T: You had fun, oh, good. Did you go anywhere?
> S: Yeah, uh, I go, go, went to uncle, uncle's home.
> T: What did you do there? Did you do something interesting?
> S: I play, played with childs. Uncle have childs, three childs.
> T: Your uncle has three children?
> S: Yeah, uh, one boy and two girls. So three childs.
> T: Do you like them?
> S: Yeah. They're fun. They'e good to me.
>
> * T = teacher, S = student

Complete the comments on the interaction by filling in the blank with ONE word.

> Language errors may occur as a result of discrepancies between the learner's interlanguage and the target language. One main source of such errors is called _____ , one example of which is seen in the student's use of *childs* in the given interaction.

문제 분석

1) 과잉일반화(Overgeneralization)에 대한 암시

● 교수자와 학습자의 대화에서 학습자가 지속적으로 "childs"라는 단어를 사용한다.

● "Language errors"라는 말이 두 번째 문단에 제시되어 있으며 "language errors"는 학습자의 "interlanguage"와 "target language" 사이의 "discrepancy"에서 나올 수 있다고 정의 내린다.

● 그러한 오류의 요인 중 하나의 예가 "childs"라고 설명하고 있다.

2) 과잉일반화(Overgeneralization)란?

● 1970년대에 대두되기 시작한 오류 분석(**error analysis**)은 제 2언어 학습자의 오류를 분석해서 학습자가 정말 알고 있는 것이 무엇인지를 파악하는데 그 목표를 두고 있다. 이 오류 분석은 학습자의 L2도 모국어와 같이 예견 가능하고 규칙이 있는 언어라는 이론에 바탕을 두고 있다. 이에 따라 Selinker(1972)는 학습자의 언어를 "interlanguage"라고 이름 짓는다.

● 오류 분석에서 학습자의 언어는 크게 두 가지로 나누는데 그 첫째는 발달상 오류(**developmental errors**)로써 학습자가 이해하고 있는 제 2언어 시스템 자체를 반영한다. 이 오류가 발달상 오류라고 불리는 까닭은 모국어 학습과 비슷한 양상을 보이기 때문이다. 이 발달상 오류는 다시 과잉일반화(**overgeneralization**)와 단순화(**simplication**)로 나뉜다. 이때 과잉일반화는 학습자가 이해한 제 2언어의 규칙을 적용하면 안 되는 곳에도 적용하는 것을 의미하며 단순화는 문장의 일부 요소가 결핍된 것을 의미한다. 두 번째는 간섭(**interference**)이나 간섭 오류(**interference errors**)라고 불리며 모국어가 제 2언어에 부정적으로 영향을 미치는 것을 의미한다.

예시 답안

overgeneralization

2 | 피드백(Feedback)

교수자와 학생간의 상호 작용을 중시하는 현 영어 교육의 현장에서 교정적 피드백(**corrective feedback**)은 중요한 역할을 수행하고 있다. 학습자의 오류에 대한 교수자의 교정적 피드백은 학습자가 자신의 영어 실력과 목표 언어 사이의 차이를 인지하고 그들의 출력(**output**)을 수정하도록 돕는다. 오류를 수정하는 과정에서 학습자는 본인의 L2를 재구성하며 이것이 결국 영어 습득을 촉진시키는 것이다.

교수자의 교정적 피드백의 종류는 여러 방법으로 나뉠 수 있으나 크게 다음의 여섯 가지로 분류된다.

1) 고쳐 말하기(recast): 교수자가 학습자의 오류를 수정해서 말하는 것으로써 대표적인 암시적 피드백(**implicit feedback**)이다. 즉, 학습자가 대화를 유지하게 하는 것이 주된 목표이지만 그 와 동시에 오류도 인지할 수 있기를 바랄 때 쓰는 방법이다.

(예) S: He go to the store yesterday.

　　 T: He went to the store. (recast)

　　 *S=Student, T=Teacher

2) 명시적 교정(explicit correction): 학습자가 오류를 범했음을 명백하게 알려주는 방법으로써 암시적 피드백(**implicit feedback**)과는 반대되는 명시적 피드백(**explicit feedback**)의 한 종류이다.

(예) S: He go to the store yesterday.

　　 T: Not "go". You should use "went". (explicit correction)

3) 설명 요청(clarification request): 학습자의 발화 중 무엇인가가 틀리다는 것을 알려주는 방법이다. 보통 "Sorry?", "Pardon me", "I don't understand what you said", "Excuse me?" 등을 사용한다.

(예) S: He go to the store yesterday.

　　 T: Sorry? (clarification request)

4) 반복(Repetition): 교수자가 학습자의 오류를 반복하는 방법이다. 반복(**repetition**)을 하는 이 유는 학습자가 스스로 오류를 수정하게 하기 위함이고 보통 오류가 생긴 부분을 강조해서 발화한다.

(예)　S: He go to the store yesterday.

　　　T: He GO (강조) to the store yesterday? (repetition)

5) 유도해내기(elicitation): 학습자가 스스로 오류를 수정하도록 하기 위해 유도해 내는 방법이 다. 학생이 오류를 인지하도록 질문을 하거나 오류가 있었던 부분으로 유도해 낸다.

(예1)　S: He go to the store yesterday.

　　　　T: What did he do? (elicitation)

(예2)　S: He has a long hair.

　　　　T: He has...(elicitation)

6) 상위언어적 피드백(Metalinguistic feedback): 상위언어적 피드백(**metalinguistic feedback**)은 학습자의 오류를 수정한 형태에 관한 언급을 하거나 정보를 제공, 또는 질문 등을 함으로써 수정하게끔 하는 것이다. 대표적인 명시적 피드백의 방법이지만 맞는 형태 를 제시하지는 않는다.

(예)　S : He go to the store yesterday.

　　　T: Use past tense for the verb. (metalinguistic feedback)

(Wu, 2006)

　학습자가 오류를 범했을 때 교수자의 교정적 피드백에 반응을 보이는 것을 흡수(**uptake**)라고 한 다. 교수자가 학습자 발화의 오류 부분을 환기 시켜주었을 때 즉각적으로 반응을 보인다면 흡수가 발 생했다고 할 수 있다(Lyster & Ranta, 1997). 흡수는 학습자가 오류에 주의를 기울였다는 증거가 될 수 있는데 성공적인 것과 그렇지 않은 것으로 나눌 수 있다. 성공적인 흡수는 수정이 된 것이고 (**repair**) 성공적이지 않은 흡수는 수정이 필요한(**needs repair**) 상태로 남아있게 된다(Zhao, 2009).

3. Read the dialogue and follow the directions. 【2 points】

> T: What are you going to do this weekend?
>
> S: I will go to a market with my mom.
>
> T: Is there anything you want to buy?
>
> S: Eggs. Many eggs.
>
> T: Is that all you want?
>
> S: No. I will buy many bread and cheese, too.
>
> T: (1) <u>Well, you said you will buy... buy...</u>
>
> S: Buy bread and cheese. Ah, buy a lot of bread. I will buy a lot of bread and cheese.
>
> T: Why will you buy them?
>
> S: I like to make sandwiches. I will make many sandwiches.
>
> T: Do you have any other plans?
>
> S: I have many homework so I will study for many hours.
>
> T: (2) <u>Well, what word do we use with homework?</u>
>
> S: Many homeworks? No, a lot of? Yes, a lot of homework.
>
> *Note*: T=teacher, S= student

Fill in the blank with the ONE most appropriate word.

> _____ refers to a type of the teacher's corrective feedback that directly induces the correct form of an error from the learner. One technique of this is to induce the correct form of an error by prompting the learner to reformulate the error and complete his or her own utterances, which is seen in the teacher's first corrective feedback, (1), in the dialogue.

Another technique is to use questions to lead the learner to produce correct forms as shown in the teacher's second corrective feedback, (2), in the dialogue.

문제 분석

- 두 번째 문단에 "the teacher's corrective feedback"이라고 주제가 제시되어 있다. 또한 학습자 오류의 올바른 형태를 유도해 내는 것이라고 정의하며 학습자가 오류를 재구성하도록 유도하는 것과(1) 질문을 던져서 학습자가 올바른 형태를 말하도록 이끄는 것이라고 (2) 설명한다.
- 첫 번째 문단의 (1)을 보면 오류가 있는 바로 앞부분까지 말해서 학습자가 오류가 있는 부분을 인지하고 수정해서 다시 발화하도록 유도하고 있으며 (2)에서는 질문을 해서 학습자가 올바른 형태를 말하도록 하고 있다.

예시 답안

elicitation

12. Read the passage in <A> and the conversation in <B>, and follow the directions.
【4 points】

──────────── <A> ────────────

Mr. Jeon's Thoughts

There are various types of teacher corrective feedback on learners' grammatical errors, including clarification request, elicitation, metalinguistic feedback and recast. I believe that corrective feedback may not have an immediate impact but it should meet certain requirements in order to facilitate language learning. I think corrective feedback should not explicitly indicate that an error has occurred so that it does not embarrass the learner inadvertently and disrupt the flow of ongoing communication. I also find it important that corrective feedback should contain a targetlike alternative to the learner's ill-formed output. Such an alternative form enables the learner to make a comparison of his or her problematic form and its correct form, which constitutes a cognitive process facilitative of language learning.

──────────── <B> ────────────

S: I am very worried.

T: Really? What are you worried about, Minjae?

S: Math exam for tomorrow. I don't studied yesterday.

T: You didn't study yesterday?

S: No, I didn't studied.

T: Please tell me why. What happened?

S: I did volunteering all day long. So I don't had time to study.

T: Well, Minjae, "don't had" is not the right past tense form.

S: Uh, I didn't had time, time to study.

Note: T = teacher, S = student

Identify the teacher's TWO corrective feedback utterances in <B> and select their respective type from those mentioned in <A>. Then explain how only ONE of the utterances meets what Mr. Jeon believes is required for effective corrective feedback in <A>.

문제 분석 🔍

● 문단 <A>에 "types of teacher corrective feedback"이 "clarification requestion, elicitation, metalinguistic feedback, and recast"로 제시되어 있다.

● 문단 <B>에서 교수자의 2번째와 4번째 발화에 feedback이 들어있다. (ex) "You didn't study yesterday?" "'don't had' is not the right past tense form."

● 문단 <A>에 제시된 피드백 유형 중 두 번째 문단의 예와 맞는 것을 제시하고 둘 중 Mr. Jeon의 주장과 일치하는 것을 고른다.

예시 답안 ✏️

The teacher gave feedback to the students, first using recast ("You didn't study yesterday") and second a metalinguistic feedback ("'don't had' is not the right past tense form"). Out of those, only recast meets Mr. Jeon's opinion on effective feedback. Mr. Jeon believes that explicit feedback interrupts conversation and the effective feedback should include a corrective form of the learner's ill-formed output. Since the teacher's metalinguistic feedback interrupts the conversation and recast contains the corrective form of the student's error, recast successfully meets Mr. Jeon's opinion.

2. Read the passage in <A> and the conversation in <B>, and follow the directions. 【5 points】

────────────── <A> ──────────────

In negotiation of meaning, "uptake" refers to an interlocutor's immediate response to his or her partner's signal of noncomprehension. In uptake, the interlocutor often uses a variety of communication strategies such as message abandonment, topic change, circumlocution, word coinage, foreignizing, and code switching.

────────────── <B> ──────────────

The following is part of a teacher-student interaction that contains negotiation of meaning.

T: Hi, Sangjee. How was your weekend?

S: Hello. Well, I had a busy weekend.

T: Did you go anywhere?

S: No, I stayed home all weekend.

T: Why were you busy, then?

S: I had to fly ten chickens.

T: Uh, what? What did you do?

S: Uh, you know, put chickens in oil, very hot oil, kind of bake them.

T: Oh, you FRIED them!

S: Yeah, I fried them with my mother.

T: Why did you have to fry that many chickens?

S: We had a big party on Sunday. My grandfather's birthday. Many people came.

> T: Oh, so that's why you fried so many. The party must have been a lot of fun.
>
> *Note*: T = teacher, S = student

Identify where the uptake takes place by writing the specific utterance from <B>, and select the strategy used in the uptake from those in <A>. Then explain how the utterance in the uptake shows the selected strategy.

문제 분석 📊🔍

1) 답안 도출 방법

● 문단 <A>에 흡수(**uptake**)에 관한 정의가 흡수를 할 수 있는 다양한 의사소통 전략과 함께 소개되고 있다.

● 두 번째 문단을 보면 의사소통에 문제가 생긴 부분은 교사의 4번째 발화라는 것을 알 수 있고 학생이 즉시 "uptake"를 하는 것을 볼 수 있다.

● 학생의 "uptake"가 문단 <A>에 제시된 "message abandonment, topic change, circumlocution, word coinage, foreignizing, code switching" 중 어떤 것에 해당하는지 된다.

● 다른 단어를 사용해서 의도했던 "fry"의 의미를 전달하고자 했으므로 "circumlocution"이 학생이 선택한 방법이다.

2) 의사소통 전략(communication strategies)이란?

● 1972년에 Selinker가 처음 소개한 용어로 학습자가 의도한 의미를 언어적 지식의 부족으로 인해 전달하지 못할 때 쓰는 전략이다. 1) **circumlocution**: 학습자가 다른 단어나 구를 이용해 의미를 전달한다. 2) **avoidance**: 다른 문장, 단어를 사용하거나 주제를 회피하는 전략이다. 3) **word coinage**: 모르는 단어를 대체하기 위해 새로운 단어를 만들어내는 전략이다. 4) **code-switching**: 모국어로 대체해서 말을 한다. 5) **asking for clarification**: 맞는 단어를 물어보거나 도움을 구한다. 6) **non-verbal strategies**: 제스처를 사용한다.

When the intended meaning of "fry" was not successfully understood, the student tried to repair it by saying "Uh, you know, put chickens in oil very hot oil, kind of bake them." The communication strategy that the student used is circumlocution. Circumlocution refers to a learner's strategy of using different words or phrases to express the intended meaning. In the given conversation, the student compensated the message by explaining what the student did using different words and phrases, so circumlocution is used.

제2장

영어 교수법

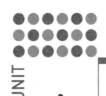

UNIT **1** 교수법

① 과업 중심 교수법(Task-Based Language Teaching)

과업 중심 교수법(Task-based language teaching: TBLT)은 외국어 교과목이나 개별적인 수업을 "과업"중심으로 계획하는 교수법이다. 이 때 과업은 목표 과업(**target tasks**)과 교육적 과업(**pedagogical tasks**)으로 구별되는데 목표 과업은 실생활에서 사용되는 언어를 의미하고 교육적 과업은 교실 수업에서 발생하는 언어 사용을 의미한다(Nunan, 2004).

목표 과업을 예로 들자면 옷을 사거나, 비행기 예약을 하거나, 운전면허 시험을 보거나 길을 찾는 등 사람들이 일상생활이나 직장 등에서 하는 모든 일을 말한다(Long, 1985). 이러한 목표 과업을 효율적으로 수행하도록 교실 수업에서 수행하는 교육적 과업은 듣기 활동을 통해 지도를 그리거나, 양식을 기입하는 등의 다양한 활동을 모두 포함한다(Richards et al., 1986). 즉 교육적 과업은 목표 과업을 향후에 성공적으로 수행하게 하기 위한 작업이라고 할 수 있다.

과업 중심 교수법이 형태 중심의 언어 수업과 구별되는 점은 의미 전달에 중점을 두고 있다는 것이다. Nunan(2004)은 교육적 과업의 정의를 학습자가 목표 언어로 이해하고, 조작하고, 생산해내거나 상호 작용을 하는 수업 활동이라고 정의하며 주된 활동은 형태를 조작하는 것이 아닌 의미를 전달하기 위해 문법 지식을 사용하는 것이라고 했다. 과업의 특성은 다음과 같다.

1) 주된 목표는 의미에 있어야 한다.
2) 다른 사람이 한 말을 그대로 되풀이하지 않는다.
3) 실생활의 활동과 비교할만한 관계가 있다.
4) 과업의 완수에 우선순위가 있다.
5) 과업의 평가는 결과물에 달려있다.

(Skehan, 1998)

즉 실생활과 관련이 있는 과업을 완성하는 것이 수업의 주된 목표이며 교실 활동은 학습자가 가진 언어 지식을 활용해 의사소통을 활성화하는 것을 중심으로 하고 있다.

다음은 과업 중심 교수법을 활용한 교안을 만들기 위한 예이다.

Steps and Process	Example
[needs analysis]	Airline flight attendance
target tasks ↓ (classify at more abstract level)	1. serve breakfast, lunch, dinner, drinks. snacks... 2. check life vests, oxygen cylinders, seat belts... 3. Check overhead bins, luggage stowed under seats, passengers in assigned seats....
target task types ↓ (derive)	1. Serve food and beverages 2. Check safety equipment 3. Prepare for takeoff
pedagogic tasks ↓ (classify and sequences)	1a. Identify choices between two food items (taped cues +picture choices) 1b. Identify choices among multiple items (taped cues +picture choices) 1c. Responds to take choices when some items are unavailable (taped cues + picture choices) ⋮ 1n. Full simulation with verbal presentation of choices and identification of passenger selection (the exit task)
task syllabus	

표 2: 과업 중심 교안 작성을 위한 단계(Long, 2015)

위의 표를 보면 요구 분석(**needs analysis**)을 통해 항공 승무원이 되고자 하는 학습자들에게 필요한 목표 과업을 선정한다. 목표 과업이 식사를 준비하고, 구명조끼 등을 확인하고, 선반이나 짐 등을 확인하는 것으로 결정이 되자 이러한 목표 과업을 수행하기 위한 교실 활동을 고안한다. 그 후 과업 강의 계획표가 만들어지는 것이다.

10. Read the passages and follow the directions. 【4 points】

─────────────── <A> ───────────────

   Task-based language teaching (TBLT) holds a central place in current second language acquisition research and also in language pedagogy. Some suggest there are six main steps in designing, implementing, and evaluating a TBLT program.

〈 1 〉	〈 2 〉	〈 3 〉
Target tasks are identified through a needs analysis.	The target tasks are grouped into target task-types.	Pedagogic tasks are derived.

〈 4 〉	〈 5 〉	〈 6 〉
A task syllabus is developed with its primary focus on communication not on linguistic forms.	The task syllabus is implemented in classrooms via various techniques of focus on form.	Student achievement is assessed using task-based tests.

─────────────── <B> ───────────────

Mr. Kim designed and implemented a TBLT program based on the six steps described in <A>.

• Step 1. He did some questionnaire surveys with his students and interviewed fellow teachers to identify what his students would really want to do in everyday life.

• Step 2. He grouped the identified real-world tasks (e.g., purchasing a train ticket, booking a room, renting a car) into more general categories (e.g., planning a trip).

- Step 3. He developed tasks that his students would perform in the classroom. Those tasks were expected to elicit communicative language use in the classroom.
- Step 4. He designed a syllabus with a central aim of presenting different grammatical items one at a time and teaching them separately.
- Step 5. He drew student attention to linguistic forms when needed, while the primary focus of the lessons was still on communication during task performance.
- Step 6. He assessed the student outcomes, focusing on whether and how much they accomplished each given task.

Identify the step in <B> that does not match with its corresponding suggestion in <A>. Then, explain how that identified step deviates from its suggestion in <A>. Do NOT copy more than FOUR consecutive words from the passage.

문제 분석 📊🔍

- 문단 <A>에 "Task-based language teaching (TBLT)"라는 주제가 제시되어 있고 TBLT 교과 목을 디자인하고, 수행하고, 평가하기 위한 여섯 가지의 단계가 함께 제시되어 있다. TBLT 수업 모델은 하나로 통일되어 있지 않고 학자 마다 다른 수업 모델이 있으므로 시험 문제에 제시된 바를 따르는 것이 좋다.

- 문단 <B>에 문단 <A>에서 제시된 여섯 가지의 단계를 바탕으로 해서 Mr. Kim이 만들어낸 Step 이 나와 있다.

- 문단 <A>의 제안에 따르지 않은 단계를 <B>에서 찾아서 어떤 부분이 맞지 않는지를 설명하면 된다.

예시 답안 ✏️

Step 4 in <B> does not match with the suggestion in <A>. While the fourth step in <A> suggests focusing on communication, Step 4 in <B> focuses on grammatical items. Thus, it deviates from the suggestion provided in <A>.

2 전략 중심 교수법(Strategies-based Instruction)

전략 중심 교수법(Strategies-based Instruction: SBI)을 보다 효율적으로 이해하기 위해서 먼저 전략이 무엇인지에 대해서 알 필요가 있다. 전략은 여러 가지로 분류될 수 있는데, 크게 언어 학습 전략을 중심으로 살펴보겠다. 언어 학습 전략이란 학습자가 목표 언어에 대한 지식과 이해를 향상시키고자 하는 목표를 가지고 사용하는 전략이다. 보통 인지(cognitive), 상위 인지(metacognitive), 사회적(social), 그리고 정의적(affective) 전략으로 나뉜다.

먼저 인지 전략(cognitive strategies)은 목표 언어를 식별하고, 기억하고, 저장하고, 다시 상기하는 전략을 의미한다. 예를 들어 새로운 언어를 이해하기 위해 기존 지식을 사용하거나, 새로운 문단을 이해하는 데 문법 지식을 활용하거나, 주제에 따라 단어를 분류하는 것 등이 이에 해당한다. 두 번째로 상위인지 전략(metacognitive strategies)은 미리 계획을 세우거나, 스스로 평가를 하거나, 모니터 하는 전략이다. 예를 들어 그 날의 수업을 위해 교재를 미리 예습하거나, 말하기 전에 생각을 정리하는 등의 전략이 이에 속한다. 사회적 전략(social strategies)은 다른 화자와 상호 작용을 하기 위해 학습자가 선택하는 행동이다. 질문을 하거나, 다른 학생이 과업을 완수하도록 돕는다거나, 다른 사람과 같이 협력하는 것이 이에 해당한다. 정의적 전략(affective strategies)은 학습자의 동기, 감정, 그리고 자세를 조절하는 전략이다. 예를 들어 불안을 감소시키거나, 자기 자신에게 용기를 북돋아주거나, 스스로에게 보상을 하는 전략 등이 이에 속한다(Cohan et al., 1996).

이러한 전략을 활용하는 방법을 가르쳐 주는 전략 중심 교수법은 1960년대부터 꾸준히 발달을 해서 지금은 스타일과 전략 중심 교수법(styles-and strategies-based instruction: SSBI)이라고 불린다. 즉 모든 학습자가 같은 전략을 사용하는 것이 아니라 학습자가 선호하는 스타일에 따라 전략의 사용이 달라짐을 인지하고 개개인의 학습자에 맞는 접근법을 채택하게 된 것이다. 학습자가 전략을 사용하게 하는 SSBI에는 다음과 같은 단계가 있다.

1) **전략 준비(Strategy Preparation):** 학습자가 전혀 전략을 모르고 있을 수는 없으므로 어떤 전략을 알고 있고 사용하고 있는 지 파악한다.

2) **전략 인식 상승(Strategy Awareness-Raising):** 학습 과정이 어떻게 구성되어 있는지, 학습자가 선호하는 학습 스타일은 무엇인지, 이미 사용하고 있는 전략은 무엇인지, 학습자가 얼

마나 학습을 책임 있게 주도하고 있는지, 학습자의 전략 사용을 평가하기 위해서 어떤 접근법을 사용하는지에 관해서 학습자가 깨닫게 만드는 과정이다.

3) **전략 지도(Strategy Instruction)**: 어떻게, 언제, 왜 특정한 전략을 사용할 수 있는지 가르쳐준다. 이 때 교수자는 전략을 설명하고, 예를 들어서 사용 방법을 보여준다.

4) **전략 연습(Strategy Practice)**: 학습자가 배운 전략을 시험해 볼 수 있는 기회를 제공한다. 이 연습 과정은 ① 활동을 위해 사용할 전략을 계획하거나, ② 특정한 전략을 사용하고 있음을 상기시켜주거나, ③ 활동이 끝난 후 전략의 사용과 효과를 정리해 주는 방법을 포함한다.

5) **전략의 개인화(Personalization of Strategies)**: 학습자는 어떻게 전략을 사용했는지를 스스로 평가하고 다른 학습 과정에서도 응용할 수 있는 방법을 찾아본다.

(Cohen & Weaver, 2005)

1. Read the lesson procedure and follow the directions. 【2 points】

> **Lesson Procedure**
>
> 1. Ss listen to a recorded conversation about the topic of the lesson.
> 2. T asks Ss to make associations among key words and to guess the meaning of the words from context. Then T teaches new vocabulary.
> 3. Ss read passages and find semantic clues to get the main idea.
> 4. Ss reread the passages and scan for specific information.
> 5. Ss, in groups, do categorizing activities.
> 6. Ss discuss the topic and write a short comment on it.
> 7. T hands out the checklist and has Ss keep a daily log after school for one week.
>
> A Daily Learning Log
>
> Name: Jihae Park
> ※ Respond to each of the following statements with a checkmark (✔).
>
> | | Day 1 | | | Day 2 | | | Day 3 | | | Day 4 | | | Day 5 | | |
> |---|---|---|---|---|---|---|---|---|---|---|---|---|---|---|---|
> | | 1 | 2 | 3 | 1 | 2 | 3 | 1 | 2 | 3 | 1 | 2 | 3 | 1 | 2 | 3 |
> | 1. I make guesses to understand unfamiliar words. | | | | | | | | | | | | | | | |
> | 2. I first read over passages quickly, and then go back and reread them. | | | | | | | | | | | | | | | |
> | 3. I make summaries of the text that I read in English. | | | | | | | | | | | | | | | |
> | 19. I ask a friend questions about schoolwork. | | | | | | | | | | | | | | | |
> | 20. I write down my feelings in a language learning diary. | | | | | | | | | | | | | | | |
>
> *Note*: 1 = Never, 2 = Sometimes, 3 = Always
>
> *Note*: T = teacher, S = student

Complete the comments by filling in the blanks with the SAME word.

> The lesson procedure shows that the students are instructed to practice various kinds of _____ during the class. Also, they are encouraged to be aware of their use of _____ by keeping a daily learning log.

문제 분석

● 첫 번째 문단의 수업 과정을 보면 단어의 뜻, 글의 주제, 특정한 정보를 찾기 위한 전략이 포함되어 있다.

● 수업 과정은 전략 설명, 전략 연습, 그리고 전략의 개인적 활용 방법을 포함하고 있다.

● 교사가 학생에게 나눠준 "A Daily Learning Log"의 문항을 분석해 보면 인지 전략, 사회적 전략, 정의적 전략이 포함되어 있음을 알 수 있다.

예시 답안

strategies

3 테크놀로지와 교실 수업(Technology and Classroom Teaching)

정보와 기술이 발달함에 따라 학습자가 유의미한 학습을 할 수 있도록 교실 수업에 기술을 접합시키는 방법이 빠른 속도로 발달하고 있다. 특히 컴퓨터 매개 통신(**Computer Mediated Communication: CMC**)과 인터넷의 발달로 학습자와의 상호 작용과 의사소통의 기회가 확장되었다. 그 중 보편화된 혼합형 학습(**blended learning**)과 거꾸로 학습법(**flipped learning**)을 살펴보겠다.

혼합형 학습(**blended learning**)은 면대면 교실 수업과 온라인 학습을 합한 개념이다. 테크놀로지가 학습의 과정에 포함될 때 혼합형 학습이라고 부르며 이는 전통적 교실 수업에 몇 가지 혜택을 가져다주었다. 먼저 학생들의 시간 관리 능력을 향상시키는데 도움을 준다. 학생들이 교실 밖에서 학업을 완수해야 하기 때문에 언제 학습을 해야 할 지 선택할 수 있는 자율성과 유연성이 보장된다. 두 번째로 학생들이 학습을 향상시키기 위해 테크놀로지를 사용할 수 있는 기회를 제공하고 이로 인해 수업에 더 능동적으로 참여할 수 있게 한다. 마지막으로 교사가 테크놀로지를 보다 효율적으로 활용할 수 있게 해준다. 트위터나 페이스북과 같은 SNS도 혼합형 학습에 사용되고 있으며 이는 학생이 교실 수업과 같은 딱딱한 학습 환경이 아니라 자유로운 상황에서도 학습이 가능하다는 것을 인지하게 해준다. 최근에는 구글 클래스룸이나 **Edmodo** 등과 같은 교육적 플랫폼이 전 세계적으로 많이 개발되고 있으며 교실 학습과 모바일 학습이 균형을 이룰 때 보다 실용적이고 효율적인 교육적 효과가 있음이 입증되고 있다(Hosseinpour et al., 2019).

거꾸로 학습법(**flipped learning**)은 2006년에 처음으로 등장한 용어로써 영상을 통해 개별 학생에게 지도가 이뤄지는 지도법을 의미한다. 전통적인 교실 수업 시간은 최소화되고 교실 수업은 학생들이 모둠 활동으로 문제를 기반으로 한 학습, 토론, 질의, 프로젝트 등을 하기 위한 시간과 장소로 활용된다. 교사는 학생들에게 필요한 것이 무엇인지 끊임없이 탐구해 그것을 제공하는 역할을 수행한다. 초기에는 영상을 통해서 수업 내용을 전달하고 교사가 지도의 중심에 서는 모델이었지만 그 후 학생 개개인의 학습 속도에 맞춰서 영상 수업의 내용이 달라지는 것으로 발달했다. 현재는 교사가 지도자의 역할을 하는 것이 아니라 학생들이 교실 수업의 중심이 되고, 지도 전략의 목표는 깊이 있고 지속적인 지식의 전달이 되었다. 따라서 교사는 풍부한 학습 경험을 제공하는 역할을 수행하게 된다(Bergmann & Sams, 2014).

한국에서는 "거꾸로 학습법"이라는 이름으로 큰 반향을 일으켰으며 교육부도 2015년부터 학생들의 학습 능력을 강화할 수 있는 교수법으로 권장하고 있다. 현재 대학교를 비롯하여 중등학교에서 많이 활용되고 있고 긍정적인 학습 결과를 보여주는 연구도 많이 나오고 있으나 아직 논란의 여지도 많고 적용 원칙에 대해서는 더 많은 연구가 필요하다.

기출 2015 전공 B 서술형 1번

1. Read the passage in <A> and the table in <B>, and follow the directions. 【5 points】

<A>

As part of an effort to maximize opportunities for her students to interact with others in English, Ms. Park, a high school English teacher, plans to design her lessons from a blended learning perspective. She is considering having the students interact with each other and her both online and offline. She designs lessons as follows: Online activities are based on a synchronous computer-mediated communication (CMC) interaction, and the transcripts of the online interaction are used a couple of days later for offline discussion.

Realizing that many of her students seem shy, frustrated, and uncomfortable with face-to-face discussion, she would like to use a CMC tool to help students get ready for an offline discussion. By examining their online production with peers and the teacher, she believes that CMC activities will guarantee more equalized opportunities for participation and make students' errors more salient and thus open to feedback and correction.

─ <B> ─

Evaluation of Three CMC Tools

Criteria ＼ Tools	Tool A	Tool B	Tool C
Easy to Use	Y	Y	Y
Saving and Archiving	Y	N	N
Real-Time Interaction	N	Y	Y
Video Chatting	N	Y	N
Online Dictionary	Y	N	N

Note: Y = Yes, N =No

Based on the information in <A> and <B>, identify the tool you would recommend for Ms. Park, and provide TWO reasons for your recommendation.

문제 분석 📊🔍

- 문단 <A>에 "blended learning"이라는 힌트가 먼저 제시되며 혼합형 학습(blended learning)에 대한 설명이 네 번째 줄에 "students interact with each other and her both online and offline"이라고 나와 있다.

- 이 때 "online activities"의 핵심이 다시 "synchronous computer-mediated communication (CMC) interaction" 그리고 "the transcripts of the offline discussion"이라는 조건으로 주어진다.

- 위의 조건에 따른 CMC tool을 문단 <B>에서 골라본다면 먼저 saving과 archiving이 안 되는 Tool B를 제외할 수 있다. Offline discussion을 위한 transcripts를 얻을 수 없기 때문이다. 또한 real-time interaction이 안 되는 Tool A도 제외할 수 있는데 이는 synchronous CMC가 불가능하다는 것을 의미하기 때문이다. 따라서 조건에 가장 적절한 도구는 Tool C이다.

The most appropriate tool for Ms. Park's lesson is Tool C. In the paragraph <A>, Ms. Park indicates two important conditions for the CMC tool for her lesson plans with a blended learning perspective. Those are 1) "synchronous computer-mediated communication (CMC) interaction" and 2) "the transcripts of the offline discussion". Since Tool A does not allow real-time interaction, it is not suitable for synchronous CMC interaction. Also, Tool B does not have functions to save and archive, so the transcripts cannot be used for later offline discussion. Thus, Tool C is the best option out of the three.

3. Read the dialogue and follow the directions. 【2 points】

> T1: There's no doubt that young children beginning school need the basics of reading, writing, and math.
>
> T2: I agree, but the big problem is determining the best way for them to get it. I think the classic mode of a teacher at the chalkboard, and books and homework is outdated.
>
> T1: True. That's why I have been looking at some teaching literature based on the ideas Jonathan Bergman and Aaron Sams came up with.
>
> T2: What do they suggest?
>
> T1: Well, they have reconsidered the role of the traditional classroom and home. So home becomes a classroom, and vice versa in this way of learning. Students view lecture materials, usually in the form of videos, as homework before class.
>
> T2: That's interesting. What's the focus in class?
>
> T1: That's the best part. Class time is reserved for activities such as interactive discussions or collaborative work supervised by the teacher.
>
> T2: I like it. But how does it benefit the students?
>
> T1: They can study the lectures at home at their own pace, or re-watch the videos, if needed, or even skip parts they already understand.
>
> T2: Right. And then, in class the teacher is present when they apply new knowledge. What about traditional homework?
>
> T1: That can be done in class, too. So, the teacher can gain insights into whatever concepts, if any, their students are struggling with and adjust the class accordingly.
>
> T2: What does the literature say about its effectiveness?

T1: Amazingly, according to one study, 71% of teachers who have tried this approach in their classes noticed improved grades, and 80% reported improved student attitudes, as well.

T2: That's fantastic. Let me read that when you're done. I want to look further into this.

Note: T= teacher

Fill in the blank with the ONE most appropriate word.

The teaching approach discussed by the two teachers is known technically as _____ learning in educational settings.

문제 분석 🔍

● 첫 번째 문단에 학교에 처음 입학하는 학생들이 읽기, 쓰기, 수학의 기초가 필요하다고 나와 있다. 이는 문제에서 요구하는 교수법이 영어 교수법에만 국한된 것이 아님을 암시한다.

● 거꾸로 학습법(flipped learning)의 주창자로 유명한 "Jonathan Bergman"과 "Aaron Sams"가 대화 중 언급된다.

● 교실과 가정의 역할이 뒤바뀐 학습법이라고 나오고 학생은 교실에서 비디오로 수업을 듣고 학교에서는 활동을 한다고 나와 있다.

예시 답안 ✍️

flipped

UNIT 2 지도법

1 읽기(Reading)

　　읽기 교수에는 정독(**intensive reading**)과 다독(**extensive reading**) 두 가지가 있다. 정독은 단어, 구, 문장 하나하나를 체계적으로 분석해서 가능한 많은 의미를 해석해 내는 방법이다. 학습자는 집중해서 독해를 해야 하기 때문에 쉽게 지칠 수 있어서 장시간 정독을 하기는 어렵다. 정독은 상향식(**bottom-up**) 접근법을 사용해서, 단어와 읽기 전략뿐만 아니라 상위인지 전략의 중요성 등을 지도하는 것이다(Celce-Murcia et al., 2014). 정독이 새로운 읽기 전략이나 새 단어를 직접적으로 가르치기 위해 작은 단위의 읽기에 중점을 두는 반면 다독은 보다 많은 양의 읽기에 중점을 둔다. 다독은 긴 글을 특별한 전략 없이 읽는 것이다. 특히 학문적 목적의 독해에서는 다독을 통해서 읽기 능력, 언어 능력, 단어, 철자, 쓰기 등을 향상할 수 있다. 다독은 또한 'reading for pleasure'라고 알려져 있는데 모르는 단어를 찾아볼 필요 없이 언어 실력을 늘릴 수 있기 때문이다(Brown, 2015).

　　독해 능력을 향상시키기 위해서는 정독과 다독이 모두 행해져야 한다. 예를 들어 단어 학습의 새 전략을 가르쳤다면 그 전략은 다독을 하는 동안에 자연스럽게 활용될 수 있다. 즉, 다독은 단순히 많이 읽으라고 독려하는 것 이상의 목적을 갖게 된다. 특히 중간 정도의 영어 실력을 가지고 있는 학습자에게 두 가지 종류의 읽기 지도가 이뤄진다면 훨씬 더 나은 효과를 가질 수 있다(Celce-Murcia et al., 2014).

　　읽기 지도를 할 때 사용하는 원칙 중 하나는 SQ3R을 따르는 것이다. SQ3R은 Survey, Question, Read, Recite, Review의 줄임말로써 읽기를 하기 위한 5가지 절차이다. 먼저 훑어보기(**survey**) 단계에서는 주제를 찾기 위해 빠른 속도로 내용을 훑어본다. 두 번째 질문(**question**) 단계에서 글에서 알고 싶은 내용이 무엇인가에 대해서 질문을 한다. 세 번째 읽기(**read**) 단계에서는 두 번째 단계의 질문에 대한 답을 찾으면서 글을 읽는다. 네 번째 낭독(**recite**)단계에서 말을 하거나 글을 쓰면서 중요한 포인트를 정리한다. 마지막 검토(review)단계에서 읽은 내용 중 중요한 부분을 판단하고 장기적으로 관련된 정보에 결합해서 넣는다.

학습자의 독해 능력을 향상시키기 위해서 보다 능동적인 읽기 전략이 활용되고 있다. 읽기 교수는 보통 'before(pre)-reading', 'during(while) reading', 그리고 'after(post)-reading'으로 나눠진다. 'Before(pre)-reading' 단계의 목표는 다음과 같다.

1) 읽기의 목적을 파악한다.
2) 학습자가 가지고 있는 이전 지식을 확인한다.
3) 단어나 중요한 개념과 같이 독해에 필요한 정보는 제공한다.
4) 기대감을 수립한다.
5) 호기심을 자극한다.
6) 자신감과 동기를 부여한다.
7) 글의 구조를 파악한다.
8) 읽기 목표를 파악하거나, 글을 검토하거나, 주제를 추측하는 등의 pre-reading 전략을 보여주고 연습시킨다.

Before-reading 단계에서 저자가 글을 쓴 목적을 파악하고 학습자가 주제에 관해서 알고 있는 것을 파악하는 과정을 이전 지식 활성화(activating prior knowledge)라고 하는데 이와 밀접한 관련이 있는 것이 스키마(schemata) 이론이다. 학습자는 본인이 이미 가지고 있는 개념에 근거하여, 특히 언어적 지식과 세상에 대한 지식을 바탕으로 해서 자신의 정보, 지식, 감정, 경험, 문화를 글에 투영한다. 스키마는 두 가지로 분류될 수 있다. 1) 내용 스키마(content schemata)와 2) 형식 스키마(formal schemata)가 그것이다. 내용 스키마는 우리가 사람, 세계, 문화, 그리고 우주에 관해서 알고 있는 지식을 의미하며 형식 스키마는 언어와 담화 구조에 관한 지식을 의미한다(Brown, 2015). 스키마를 활성화하기 위해서 교수자는 학습자의 경험과 관련이 있는 질문을 할 수도 있고, 주제에 관한 토론을 하게 할 수도 있다. 또한 전체 글을 미리 훑어봄으로써 구조를 파악하고, 제목이나, 표, 그림, 용어 등을 살펴본 후 무엇에 관한 내용인지 예견하게 할 수 있다. 이를 예견(prediction, predicting, 혹은 prediction techniques)이라고 한다.

During(while)-reading 단계의 목표는 다음과 같다;

1) 이해를 촉진시키기 위해 읽기를 유도한다. 예를 들어 그래프 분류도(**graphic organizer**)를 작성하게 할 수 있다. 그래프 분류도는 표, 차트, 그래프, 연도표 등 읽기에서 나온 정보를 시각적으로 보여주는 것이다. 이 그래프 분류도는 내용상 관계를 보여준다.

2) 학습자가 의미를 구성하고 이해를 모니터하도록 돕는다.

3) 학습자가 읽는 것과 자신의 알고 있는 것을 연결해서 읽고 있는 글을 평가하도록 돕는다.

4) 내용을 계속 요약하도록 돕는다.

5) 이 단계에서 많이 쓰는 전략을 보여주고 연습하도록 돕는다. 이해도를 모니터링 하는 것, 어려운 점을 파악하는 것, 잘못 이해한 것을 고치는 것이 그것이다.

6) 이해를 돕고, 전략을 개발하는 것에 관한 토론을 도모하도록 한다.

(Celce-Murcia et al., 2014)

During(while)-reading에서 가장 많이 쓰이는 전략은 skimming과 scanning이고, 그 외 윤곽그리기(**outlining**), 추론하기(**inferencing**), 요약하기(**summarizing**), 소리 내어 생각하기(**think-aloud**) 등이 쓰인다. 먼저 skimming은 보통 읽기보다 세 배나 네 배 정도 빠른 속도로 읽는 것을 의미하는데 정해진 시간에 많은 양의 글을 읽어야 할 때 쓰인다. Skimming을 할 때는 모든 단어를 다 읽는 것이 아니라 가장 중요한 정보나 주제만을 파악한다. Skimming의 단계는 다음과 같다. 1) 각 문단의 첫 번째 줄을 읽는다, 2) 각 문단의 마지막 줄을 읽는다, 그리고 3) 그 사이의 주요 단어를 읽는다. Skimming은 전체적인 문맥이나 주제를 파악할 때 주로 쓰이기 때문에 보통 하향식 처리(**top-down processing**)를 많이 사용한다. 하향식 처리는 학습자가 가지고 있는 지식과 경험을 바탕으로 전체적인 맥락을 먼저 파악하는 것이다. 모든 세부 정보를 다 번역할 필요가 없고 문단의 주제는 보통 첫 번째와 마지막 줄에 위치하기 때문이다. 반면 scanning은 학습자가 주제가 아닌 세부적인 내용에 집중할 때 사용된다. 예를 들어 날짜, 이름, 장소 등 특별한 정보를 찾을 때 이 전략을 사용한다. Scanning은 글에서 특정한 정보를 빠른 속도로 찾아내는 과정으로써 전체 글을 다 읽지 않고도 특정 정보를 도출하기 위해 사용된다. 빠른 속도로 페이지를 넘기며 특정 단어나 구를 찾아내는 것이다. Scanning을 잘 사용하기 위해서는 다음과 같은 방법을 사용한다. 1) 찾아야 할 특정한 정보만을 기억한다, 2) 필요한 정보를 찾아내는데 도움이 되는 힌트를 알아낸다, 그리고 3) 그 힌트를 찾기 위해 페이지를 빠른 속도로 훑어나간다. 만약 힌트를 찾으면 필요한 정보가 있는 부분을 찬찬히 읽는다. 이러한 과정을 수행하면서 학습자는 높은 집중력을 갖게 된다(Yusuf et al., 2017).

During (while)-reading에서 사용되는 활동 중 쓰기와 관련된 활동은 개요나 요점을 정리하는 윤곽 그리기(**outlining**), 그래프 분류도(**graphic organizer**), 그리고 요약하기(**summarizing**) 등이 있다. 이 중 그래프 분류도는 윤곽 그리기의 도구로 활용되기도 한다. 윤곽 그리기는 주요 개념들 간의 관계를 파악하고 그 개념들을 순서에 맞게 정리하는 높은 수준의 활동으로써 주제와 주제를 보완 설명하는 하부 개념들을 전체 그림으로 보여준다. 윤곽 그리기는 상위인지 전략을 활용하는데 글의 내용을 직접적으로 보여주는 지도와 같은 역할을 하기 때문이다. 윤곽 그리기는 독해에서 매우 중요한 역할을 하며 이를 활용함으로써 독해 능력이 향상된다. 따라서 그래프 분류도를 포함한 윤곽 그리기는 독해의 기본이 되는 정보를 알아낼 수 있는 기본적인 활동이라고 할 수 있다. 게다가 윤곽 그리기는 글이 포함하고 있는 개념과 정보를 순서에 맞게 시각화해서 보여주기 때문에 더욱 효과적이다. 윤곽 그리기의 다섯 가지 기능은 다음과 같다. 1) 학습자가 중요한 개념에 집중할 수 있도록 한다, 2) 글의 구조에 익숙해지게 한다, 3) 오래 기억하게 한다, 4) 보조 교재로 활용될 수 있다, 그리고 5) 학습자가 적극적으로 참여할 수 있게 한다(Tan, 2015).

During (while)-reading에서 활용되는 또 하나의 전략은 추론하기(**inferencing**)이다. 독해에서 추론하기는 문맥의 뜻을 추론해 내는 것과 문맥에서 단어의 뜻을 유추해 내는 두 가지의 영역으로 나눌 수 있다. 먼저 문맥에 숨겨진 의미를 찾아내는 추론하기는 보통 "행간 읽기(**read between the lines**)"라고 말한다. 직접적으로 서술되어 있지 않다고 문맥의 전체적인 의미를 파악하기 위해 숨겨진 의미를 감지해 내거나 글을 내용을 바탕으로 해서 스스로 결론을 도출해 내는 기술이기 때문이다. 이때 학습자는 문맥에 나와 있지 않은 외부의 정보를 활용하기도 하고 본인이 가지고 있는 배경 지식을 활용하기도 한다(Cain & Oakhill, 1999).

'단어의 뜻 추측하기(**guessing word meaning**)'라고 표현되는 단어의 추론은 그 단어가 포함되어 있는 문장이나 바로 앞 뒤 문장의 해석을 통해 단어의 뜻을 추측하는 것이다. 단어의 뜻을 추측하는 것은 두 가지의 요소에 의해 결정되는데, 하나는 학습자에 관련된 역량으로 단어 용량, 문법 지식, 언어의 숙련도, 세부 사항에 주목하는 능력, 인지적이고 정신적인 노력, 그리고 성격에 의해 결정된다. 두 번째는 문맥에 관련된 변인으로 단어와 문맥의 특징, 그리고 내용에서의 실마리와 주제의 익숙함이다. 학습자가 가장 많이 쓰는 전략은 문맥에서 실마리를 찾아 단어의 뜻을 추측하는 것이다(Cetinasci, 2014).

During (while)-reading 단계에서 쓸 수 있는 여러 가지 활동 중 마지막으로 제시할 것은 '소리 내어 생각하기(**think-aloud**)'이다. 교수자는 학생들에게 문제 풀이 과정이나 읽기 과정에서 소리 내서 말하라고 지시한다. 이 지시는 학생들이 무엇을 생각하는지 말하도록 반복적으로 행해질 수도 있다. 학생들은 생각이 떠오르는 대로 계속 말하면서 글을 읽는다. 소리 내서 말하는 것은 사고의 과정을 방해하지 않는다. 형식에 구애받지 않고 거의 자동 반사적으로 말을 하기 때문이다. 심리학에 기초를 둔 이 활동은 심리학적 이론을 문제 해결 방법에 적용한 것이다. 말을 하면서 주어진 활동, 즉 읽기를 하거나 문제를 풀라고 교수자가 지시를 하고 학생들이 말을 하면서 본인의 생각을 모니터 할 수 있고 따라서 이해가 향상된다. 자신의 생각을 모니터링 하면서 보다 잘 이해하기 위해서 문장을 다시 읽거나 필요한 정보를 찾을 수 있게 되기 때문이다. 소리 내어 생각하기는 수동적인 읽기가 아닌 대표적인 적극적 읽기 활동이다.

After(post)-reading 단계의 목표는 다음과 같다.

1) 이해를 확인한다.
2) 글의 구조가 어떻게 이해를 돕는지 찾아본다.
3) 다시 읽기 활동 등을 통해 읽기의 유창성 발달을 돕는다.
4) 학생들이 글에서 얻은 정보를 요약하고, 조합하고, 평가하고, 통합하고, 확장하고, 응용하도록 한다.
5) 학생들이 저자나 글의 부분을 비판할 수 있게 한다.
6) 요약된 내용을 완성하게 하거나, 소주제를 순서대로 정리하거나, 주제와 세부사항을 분류하거나 하는 활동을 통해서 성공적으로 독해를 해냈음을 인지하게 한다.
7) 읽은 내용을 생각해보거나 다른 글과 접목시켜보는 등의 전형적인 post-reading 전략을 보여주고 연습할 수 있게 한다.

(Celce-Murcia et al., 2014)

After(post)-reading 활동은 매우 다양하다. 학습자가 내용을 요약하고, 반영하고, 질문을 할 수 있도록 다양한 활동을 이용할 수 있다. During (while)-reading 단계에서 사용되었던 윤곽 그리기(**outlining**), 요약하기(**summarizing**), 추론하기(**inferencing**)도 활용할 수 있고 글의 내용에 관한 질문에 대한 답을 하거나, 작가의 의도를 파악하거나 비판하기 위한 토론 등 위에 서술된 목표를 성취하기 위한 많은 활동이 가능하다.

그 외 교실 수업에서 읽기 활동으로 많이 쓰이는 방법 중 하나는 빈 칸 메우기(**cloze**)활동이다. 보통 일곱 번째 단어를 빈칸으로 두고 학생들이 빈칸을 채우게끔 한다. 정해진 비율로 단어를 지우기 때문에 이러한 방법을 정해진 비율로 지우기(**fixed-ratio deletion**)라고 하고 의미나 문법 등 특정한 교육 목표에 따라 지우면 합리적 지우기(**rational deletion**)라고 부른다. Cloze에서 변화된 활동이 C-test와

cloze-elide procedure이다. C-test는 한 단어 건너 하나씩 단어의 반을 지우는 것이며, cloze-elide procedure는 내용에 상관이 없는 단어를 삽입하고 학생들이 그 단어를 지우게 하는 것이다.

Cloze 활동의 채점을 할 때는 두 가지 방법이 쓰이는데 하나는 정확한 단어 채점(exact word scoring)이고 또 하나는 적절한 단어 채점(appropriate word scoring)이다. 정확한 단어 채점은 정확한 단어만을 맞는 것으로 간주하는 것이고 적절한 단어 채점은 똑같지는 않아도 의미가 비슷한 단어는 맞는 것이라고 간주하는 것이다. 읽기 활동으로서 cloze는 이해가 중요하기 때문에 정확한 단어 채점과 적절한 단어 채점 두 가지 방법을 다 사용할 수 있다. 그러나 듣기 활동에 cloze를 활용할 때는 학생들의 듣기 실력을 향상시키는데 그 목적을 두고 있기 때문에 정확한 단어나 구를 써야하는 정확한 단어 채점 방식을 주로 사용한다(Brown & Abywickrama, 2010).

기출 2020 전공 A 10번

10. Read the passage in <A> and the lesson plan in <B>, and follow the directions. 【4 points】

───────────── <A> ─────────────

Teachers can employ a variety of techniques when teaching reading that will help enhance students' reading comprehension. For instance, at the preparation stage, the prediction technique can be used: Pictures or photos and titles can be viewed quickly to give the students an idea of the overall content of the text. While reading, if students find some words difficult, the teacher may help them to guess their meanings by looking at the surrounding words. Also, as for the reading content, the teacher can employ the outlining technique, which can help the students see the overall organization of the text by reconstructing the ideas or events. After reading, diverse techniques can be used in order to check the students' level of comprehension: scrambled stories, finding the author's purpose, and examining grammatical structures.

(Below is part of Mr. Kim's lesson plan. He is preparing a handout for his students.)

Objectives	• Students will read the text about modern tourists and find the main idea. • Students will identify the topic and the details of the text based on the handout. • Students will write a summary about the text based on information given in the handout.

Teaching-Learning Activities		
Introduction	Greeting & Roll-call	• T and Ss exchange greetings. • T checks if all the Ss are present.
Development	Activity 1	• T hands out a reading text, "Tourists Today." • T asks Ss to skim through the text. • T asks if Ss understand the gist of the text. • T asks Ss to read the text again. • T distributes the handout about the reading text.

Note: T = teacher, S = student

Tourists Today

Many contemporary tourists avoid encountering reality directly but thrive on psuedo-events in their tourism experiences thus affecting tourism entrepreneurs and indigenous populations. For one, many tourists prefer to stay in comfortable accomodations, thereby separating themselves from the local people and environment. For instance, sleeping in a hotel filled with the comforts of home may insulate them from the fact that they are in a foreign land. In addition, much of the tourism industry is bolstered by the use of tourist-focused institutions such as museums and shopping centers. The needs of the contemporary tourists have induced entrepreneurs to build tourist attractions for the sole purpose of entertaining visitors. This detracts from the colorful local culture and presents a false view of the indigenous cultures. The other group affected by modern tourism is the local population. These people find themselves learning languages in a contrived way based on the changing tides of tourist groups solely for marketing purposes. Furthermore, when curious visitors do venture outside their cultural bubbles, they enjoy, albeit intrusively, watching locals doing their daily tasks, thereby making them the subject of the tourist gaze. In sum, while tourism is on the rise, the trend is to maintain a distance from the real environment rather than to see the locations for their own values, and this negatively affects tourism entrepreneurs and local people.

Handout

Topic sentence: Modern tourists' demands _____

_____

A. Effects on tourism entrepreneurs
   • Provide comfortable accommodations
   • Create tourist-focused entertainment attractions

B. Effects on local populations
   • Learn tourists' languages
   • Become the objects of the tourist gaze

Based on <A>, identify the technique that the teacher employed in the handout in <B>. Then, complete the topic sentence in the handout. Do NOT copy more than FOUR consecutive words from <B>.

문제 분석 📊🔍

- 문단 <A>에 읽기 지도에 필요한 전략들이 제시되어 있다. 예) preparation stage: the prediction technique, while reading: guessing words' meaning, the outline technique, after reading: scrambled stories, finding the author's purpose, and examining grammatical structures.

- 문단 <B>에 수업 목표와 함께 "while-reading"의 앞부분이 나와 있다. 또한 문단 <B>에 수업에 사용되는 글과 교수자가 나눠주는 핸드아웃도 함께 제시되어 있다.

- 핸드아웃을 보면 글의 개요가 정리되어 있음을 알 수 있다. 따라서 문단 <A>에 제시되어 있는 "while-reading"의 전략 중 윤곽 그리기(**outline technique**)가 쓰였음을 알 수 있다.

- 핸드아웃의 주제문을 보면 "Modern tourists' demands"가 주어이고 서술부가 비어 있다. 문단 <B>에 제시된 글을 보면 여행객들이 요구하는 것들과 그것이 지역 주민에게 어떠한 영향을 미치는가에 대한 두 가지 부분으로 나눠져 있음을 알 수 있다. 따라서 핸드아웃에 요약된 내용을 참고해서 그 부분을 서술하면 된다.

예시 답안 ✍️

Mr. Kim uses the outlining technique. The topic sentence is "Modern tourists' demands to experience local life indirectly influence negatively on the tourism industry and local people."

2. Read the conversation between two teachers and follow the directions. 【2 points】

> T1: My students are having trouble with plural nouns. I'm thinking of trying a new task.
>
> T2: What's your idea?
>
> T1: I'm planning to give a short text where every seventh word is blanked out. Students have to guess the correct word for each blank to make a complete sentence.
>
> T2: Well, that might be a bit difficult for beginning level students. I did a similar activity last semester. I gave a text where I blanked out only plural nouns so that students could focus on them.
>
> T1: Oh, I see.
>
> T2: You can also give students only parts of words in the blanks and ask them to restore each word in the text.
>
> T1: Hmm, that seems interesting. Well, then, for my students, I'll try to use only plural nouns in the written text and ask my students to fill in the blanks. Thanks for the suggestion.
>
> *Note*: T1=teacher 1, T2=teacher 2

Complete the comments by filling in the blank with the ONE most appropriate word.

> In the above dialogue, the two teachers are talking about teaching plural nouns through three types of gap-filling tasks which require students to read the texts and fill in the blanks. The gap-filling described by the teachers here is _____ , which can be readily adapted for pedagogical tasks in classrooms.

● 두 교사의 대화를 분석해 보면 빈 칸 메우기(cloze) 활동에 대해서 말하고 있음을 알 수 있다. 교사 1은 일곱 번째 단어를 지우는 정해진 비율로 지우기(**fixed-ratio deletion**)에 관해서 설명하고 있고, 교사 2는 명사의 복수형만을 지우는 합리적 지우기(**rational deletion**)에 관해서 설명하고 있다. 또한 교사 2는 단어의 일부분만을 지우는 C-test의 변형된 형태를 설명하고 있다.

● 제시된 구문에서 교사들이 빈칸을 채우는 세 가지 방법에 대해서 이야기 하고 있는데 그것을 한 단어로 표현하라고 했으므로 정답은 "cloze"가 된다.

예시 답안

cloze

기출 2017 전공 A 6번

6. Read the passage and follow the directions. 【2 points】

> The following is part of a lesson procedure that aims to facilitate students' comprehension of a text concerning global warming.
>
> **Steps:**
> 1. Before reading the text, T activates Ss' background knowledge concerning global warming and provides other relevant information to help Ss to have a better comprehension of the text.
> 2. T instructs Ss to read the text quickly in order to grasp the main ideas. In doing so, T tells them not to read every word.
> 3. T asks Ss to reread it quickly for specific information, such as the type of

disasters caused by global warming.

4. T instructs Ss to read the text again at their own pace.

5. T checks Ss' overall comprehension by having them write a brief summary of the text.

6. T then checks Ss' understanding of the details by using a cloze activity.

Note: T = teacher, S = student

Identify the two kinds of expeditious reading that the teacher instructs students to use in steps 2 and 3 with ONE word, respectively. Write them in the order that they appear.

문제 분석

- Step 2에서 학생들은 주제를 파악하기 위해 글을 빠른 속도로 읽고 교수자는 모든 단어를 읽을 필요가 없다고 하고 있다.

- Step 3에서 학생들은 글을 빠른 속도로 읽으며 특정 정보를 찾는다.

- 따라서 while-reading에서 많이 쓰이는 skimming과 scanning 전략임을 알 수 있다. 각각 한 단어로 써야 하며 순서대로 써야 한다는 점에 유의해야 한다.

예시 답안

skimming, scanning

5. Read the conversation between two high school English teachers, and identify the type of reading that Ms. Kim recommends to Mr. Hong. Use TWO words. 【2 points】

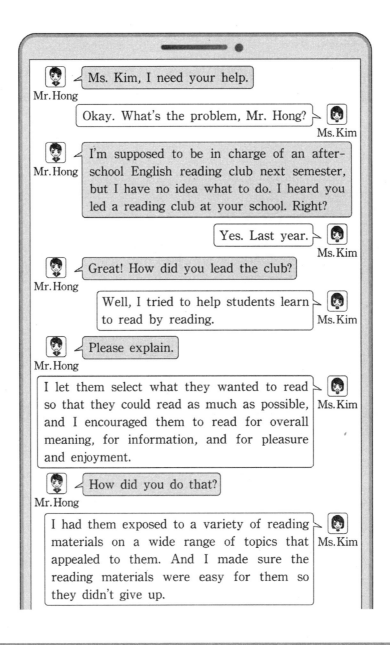

Mr. Hong: Ms. Kim, I need your help.

Ms. Kim: Okay. What's the problem, Mr. Hong?

Mr. Hong: I'm supposed to be in charge of an after-school English reading club next semester, but I have no idea what to do. I heard you led a reading club at your school. Right?

Ms. Kim: Yes. Last year.

Mr. Hong: Great! How did you lead the club?

Ms. Kim: Well, I tried to help students learn to read by reading.

Mr. Hong: Please explain.

Ms. Kim: I let them select what they wanted to read so that they could read as much as possible, and I encouraged them to read for overall meaning, for information, and for pleasure and enjoyment.

Mr. Hong: How did you do that?

Ms. Kim: I had them exposed to a variety of reading materials on a wide range of topics that appealed to them. And I made sure the reading materials were easy for them so they didn't give up.

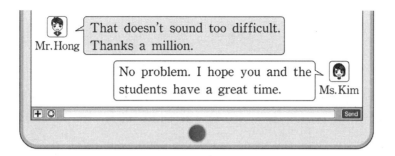

문제 분석

● Mr. Hong은 방과 후 프로그램으로 영어 읽기 클럽을 운영해야 한다. 이에 대한 조언으로 Mr. Kim이 제시하는 읽기 방법에 대한 힌트는 먼저 그의 세 번째 발화에서 "read by reading", 네 번째 발화에서 "read as much as possible" 과 "for pleasure and enjoyment" 등이다. 또한 다양한 주제로 구성되어 있는 다양한 읽기 자료를 준비해서 학생들이 흥미를 갖게 하고 읽기 쉬운 자료를 준비한다는 보완 설명이 나와 있다. 이러한 힌트들은 다독의 특징이다.

예시 답안

extensive reading

10. Below are an excerpt from a reading text and part of a student's think-aloud data generated while reading it. Based on the think-aloud data, identify the reading strategy that the student is using. Use ONE word. 【2 points】

Computers have the potential to accomplish great things. With the right software, they could help make science tangible or teach neglected topics like art and music. They could help students form a concrete idea of society by displaying on screen a version of the city in which they live.

In practice, computers make our worst educational nightmares come true. While we bemoan the decline of literacy, computers discount words in favor of pictures or video. While we fret about the decreasing cogency of public debate, computers dismiss linear argument and promote fast, shallow romps across the information landscape. While we worry about basic skills, we allow into the classroom software that will do a student's arithmetic or correct his spelling.

> Well, nightmares? The author thinks computers do harm to education.

> Hmm . . . the author is blaming computer software for a decline in basic skills.

● 학생이 "think-aloud" 활동을 하면서 사용하고 있는 읽기 전략을 찾는 문제이다.

● 학생이 "think-aloud" 활동을 하면서 녹음한 첫 번째 데이터를 보면 사용한 "nightmares"라는 단어가 사용되었다는 점에서 글을 쓴 저자가 컴퓨터가 교육에 부정적인 영향을 미친다고 생각한다고 유추한다. 또한 '기본 기술에 대해 걱정하고 있는 반면 소프트웨어가 수학이나 철자 교정 등 교실수업에 사용되도록 허락 한다'라는 구절을 읽고 말한 두 번째 데이터는 저자가 컴퓨터 소프트웨어 탓을 하고 있다는 것을 추론해내었음을 보여준다.

예시 답안 ✏️

inferencing

2 문법(Grammar)

영어 교수법에서 가장 큰 변화를 겪은 것이 아마도 문법 교육일 것이다. 교수법을 바탕으로 설명하자면 문법 번역식 교수법(**Grammar Translation Method: GTM**)이 유행하던 시기에는 문법 수업을 바탕으로 강의 계획이 수립되고 수업도 문법 중심으로 이뤄졌다. 문법 규칙에 관한 직접적 설명과 연습문제 풀이로 수업이 진행이 되었으며 영어가 아닌 모국어로 수업이 진행이 되었다. 그러나 직접 교수법(**Direct Method**)은 영어로 수업이 진행이 되었으며 문법 진도에 맞춰서 강의 계획이 설계되었다고 해도 문법 규칙을 직접적으로 설명하지는 않았다. 그 후에 나온 청화식 교수법(**Audiolingual Method**)은 문법 규칙의 직접적 설명이 직접 교수법보다 더 배제되었다. 행동주의 심리학에 근거를 두고 있었던 청화식 교수법에서는 문장의 패턴을 반복적으로 연습하는 것이 주된 교실 활동이었다. 문장의 패턴이 문법에 바탕을 두고 쉬운 것부터 어려운 것까지 단계별로 구성이 되어있었지만 반복 학습을 통해 행동의 변화를 추구하는 청화식 교수법에는 문법 지도가 포함되지 않았다(Thornbury, 1999).

이후 Chomsky의 이론에 영향을 받은 자연적 접근법(**Natural Approach**)이 1950년대 말에서 60년대 초에 도입이 되면서 반복 연습은 사라지게 되었다. 모든 인간은 언어를 학습할 수 있는 장치(**Language Acquisition Device: LAD**)를 가지고 태어난다는 그의 이론은 Krashen의 입력 가설(**Input Hypothesis**)과 함께 영어 교수법에 많은 영향을 미쳐서 인지주의 학습 이론이 유행하던 시기에는 문법을 포함해서 어떤 종류건 간에 형식적이고 의도적인 언어 수업은 교실 수업에 포함되지 않았다. 교수자의 역할은 학습자가 이해할 수 있는 입력(**comprehensible input**)을 제공해 주는 것이었고 학습자가 모국어를 습득하는 것과 같은 환경에서 자연스럽게 외국어를 습득하게 하는 자연적 접근법을 활용하는 교실 수업에서 문법은 설 자리가 없었다(Thornbury, 1999).

1970년대에 와서 사회언어학의 영향으로 의사소통 중심 교수법(**Communicative Language Teaching: CLT**)이 발달하면서 의사소통 능력은 단순한 문법 지식 이상이 필요하다는 것이 확실시되었다. 초기의 깊은 의사소통 중심 교수법(**Deep-end CLT**)은 문법을 바탕으로 한 강의 계획이나 문법 수업을 배제했지만 후기의 얕은 의사소통 중심 교수법(**Shallow-end CLT**)은 기능 중심의 문법을 수업의 중요한 일부분으로 취급하게 되었다. 현재 의사소통 중심 교수법이나 과업 중심 교수법(**Task-based Language Teaching: TBLT**)도 문법 지도를 일정 부분 포함하는 방식으로 변화했다(Thonbury, 1999).

문법 수업이 언어 습득을 도와준다는 것은 이제 반론의 여지가 없는 확실한 주장처럼 보인다. 그러나 문법 지도를 어떻게 얼마나 하는지에 관해서는 아직도 이견이 많다. 먼저 문법 지도라는 용어보다는 형태 기반 수업(**form-focused instruction: FFI**)이라는 용어가 광범위하게 사용되고 있다. 형태 기반 수업은 "학습자가 언어의 형태가 주의를 기울일 수 있도록 유도하는 계획적이거나 우연한 학습 지도 활동(any planned or incidental instructional activity that is intended to induce language learners to pay attention to linguistic form)"(Ellis, 2012, p. 271)이라고 정의내릴 수 있다. 이 정의를 자세히 살펴보면 교수자가 미리 문법을 지도할 계획을 가지고 준비해서 교실에 들어가는 경우나, 수업 도중 필요에 의해서 계획에 없던 문법 활동을 하게 되는 경우를 모두 포함한다는 것을 알 수 있다. 또한 문법 번역식 교수법이 문법의 규칙을 학습자에게 직접적으로 지도했던 것과는 다르게 학습자가 문법의 형태에 주의를 기울일 수 있도록 유도하는 것이 목표라는 것을 알 수 있다. 이는 기존의 문법 지도와는 현저한 차이가 있다.

현재 문법 지도법은 직접적인(**explicit** 혹은 **overt**) 방법과 간접적인(**implicit** 혹은 **covert**) 방법 두 가지로 나눠진다. 직접 교수법(**explicit presentation of forms**)은 말 그대로 문법 규칙을 직접적으로 보여주는 것이고 문법 용어를 사용하기도 한다. 그러나 간접 교수법은 문법 용어를 사용하지 않고 의사소통 중심의 활동을 하면서 문제가 되는 문법 요소를 다루는 것이다. 학생들이 문장을 분석하거나 교수자가 용어를 사용해 문법 규칙을 설명하는 단계 없이 다른 학생들과 교실 활동을 하거나 교사와 대화를 하면서 자연스럽게 규칙을 습득하게 된다(Brown, 2015).

교실 수업에서 문법 지도가 이뤄지는 대부분의 경우는 직접적인 방법이고 직접 교수법에는 연역적 접근법(**deductive approach**)과 귀납적 접근법(**inductive approach**)이 있다. Brown(2015)은 귀추적 접근법(**abductive approach**)도 함께 제시한다. 먼저 연역적 접근법은 문법 규칙을 제시하고 그 문법 규칙이 적용되는 예를 보여준다. 따라서 연역적 접근법은 규칙에 기초한(**rule-driven**) 학습이라고 할 수 있다. 귀납적 접근법은 예를 먼저 제시하고 학습자가 제시된 예를 통해서 문법 규칙을 발견할 수 있게 한다. 따라서 규칙을 발견하는(**rule-discovery**) 학습이라고 할 수 있다 (Thonbury, 1999). 귀추적 접근법은 이와는 달리 먼저 제시된 문제나 문장을 바탕으로 가설을 세우는 것으로 시작한다. 따라서 학습자는 가설을 하나씩 적용해 나가면서 맞는 규칙을 찾아낼 수 있다 (Brown, 2015).

과거에 연역적 방법으로만 문법을 지도하던 것과 달리 문법 지도 방법이 귀납적이나 귀추적으로 변화하게 된 이유는 두 가지 이론의 영향이라고 할 수 있다. 그것은 "형태 중심(**focus on form**)"과 "인식 상승(**consciousness-raising**)"이다. 먼저 형태 중심(**focus on form**)에 관해 설명하겠다. 현재의 문법 교육은 1) 형태(**form**), 2) 의미(**meaning**), 3)기능(**function**)으로 나눠진다. 즉, 1) 어떻게 만들어지고, 2) 어떤 의미를 가지며, 3) 언제 그리고 왜 사용이 되는지 지도가 되어야 한다 (Celce-Murcia et al., 2014). 과거의 문법 교육은 형태에 집중되어 있었는데, 왜 현재는 세 가지 부분으로 나눠지게 된 것일까? 입력 처리(Input Processing) 이론은 이러한 문법 지도의 정당성을 증명한다.

입력 처리(Input Processing)는 학습자가 형태와 의미와의 관계를 찾아내고자 하는 상황에서 발생한다. 즉, 학습자의 정보 처리 능력은 한계를 가지고 있기 때문에 동시에 형태와 의미를 인지할 수 없다는 것이다. 따라서 학습자는 형태를 인지하기 전에 의미를 먼저 파악하게 된다. 이러한 학습자의 특성을 바탕으로 만들어낸 문법 교수법이 처리 교수(Processing Instruction: PI)이다. 입력 처리에는 다음과 같은 원칙들이 있다.

1) **의미 우선성의 원칙(Primacy of Meaning Principle):** 학습자는 형태를 파악하기 전에 의미를 먼저 파악한다.

2) **내용어 우선성의 원칙(The primacy of content words principle):** 학습자는 무엇보다도 내용을 먼저 처리한다.

3) **단어 선호도의 원칙(The lexical preference principle):** 학습자는 의미를 파악하기 위해서 문법적 형태보다는 단어에 의존한다.

4) **비반복 선호도의 원칙(The preference for nonredundancy principle):** 학습자는 반복적인 문법적 형태보다는 반복적이지 않은 문법적 형태를 먼저 파악한다.

5) **무의미 이전에 의미 원칙(The meaning before nonmeaning principle):** 학습자는 의미가 없는 형태보다는 의미가 있는 형태를 먼저 파악한다.

6) **문장의 위치 원칙(The sentence location principle):** 학습자는 문장의 맨 앞에 있는 단어를 먼저 파악한다.

7) **사건의 확률 원칙(The event probabilities principle):** 학습자는 단어의 순서보다는 사건이 일어날 수 있는 확률에 더 의존한다.

8) **수단의 유용성 원칙(The availability of recourses principle):** 학습자는 집중할 수 있는 여력을 다 소비하면 안 된다.

이러한 원칙들을 바탕으로 한 문법 수업을 처리 교수(Processing Instruction: PI)라고 하는데 PI는 형태 중심 문법 수업(focus on form)의 한 가지 형태로써 다음과 같은 특징을 가지고 있다.

1) 목표 구조에 관한 직접적 정보
2) 정보 처리 전략에 관한 직접적 정보
3) 구조화된 입력 활동(structured input activities)

구조화된 입력 활동(structured input activities)은 다음과 같은 가이드라인에 따라서 개발할 수 있다.

1) 한 번에 하나의 규칙만 제시한다.
2) 의미에 중점을 두도록 한다.
3) 문장을 담화로 연결한다.
4) 듣기와 읽기를 다 사용해서 입력을 제공하도록 한다.
5) 학습자가 듣거나 읽을 때 무엇을 하도록 한다.
6) 학습자의 정보 처리 전략을 염두에 둔다.

(VanPattern, 2004)

다시 현재의 문법 지도 방법에 영향을 미친 "형태 중심(focus on form)"으로 돌아가자면 형태 중심은 형태, 의미, 그리고 기능을 의사소통 상황에서 지도할 수 있는 문법 교수 방법이다. 기존의 문법 교수법을 흔히 focus on formS 라고 하는데, 이 교수법은 형태에만 집중하기에 문법 교육의 효과가 떨어진다. 또한 의미를 알려주기 위해서는 "의미 중심(focus on meaning)"과 병행되어야 한다. 형태 중심(focus on form)은 focus on formS와의 구별을 위해서 FonF라고 주로 표기한다. FonF는 의미를 알고 있는 학습자가 형태의 오류를 반복할 때 형태에 집중할 수 있게 함으로써 화석화를 방지하는 역할을 한다.

FonF과 관련이 있는 또 하나의 개념은 의식 상승(consciousness raising)이다. 과거 인지주의 학습이론의 영향과 Krashen의 입력 가설(input hypothesis)을 바탕으로 한 교실 수업이 학습자를 수동적인 존재로 보았다면 현재는 구성주의 학습 이론의 영향으로 학습자가 주의를 기울이고 의식적인 노력을 함으로써 학습이 발생한다고 본다. 즉, 학습자가 목표가 되는 문법을 "알아챔(noticing)"으로써 문법의 형태가 학습된다는 것이다. 이때 교수자의 역할은 학습자가 문법 규칙을 인지하고 습득하도록 돕는 것이다. 문법 교육은 기본적으로 문법 규칙에 대한 학습자의 의식을 상승시키는 것이라고 할 수 있고, 학습자가 문법 규칙을 습득하지 못한다고 해도 추후에 적당한 때가 오면 습득할 수 있게 하는 정보 처리 과정을 유발하게 하는 것이다(Thonbury, 1999).

　　구조화된 입력 활동(**structured input activities**)처럼 직접적인 문법 지도를 위해서는 의식 상승 기법도 하나의 활동으로 활용될 수 있다. 예를 들어 귀납적 접근법을 사용해서 학습자에게 예를 주고 규칙을 찾아보라고 한 후 문법 설명을 함으로써 그 문법 규칙에 대한 학습자의 인식을 고양시킬 수 있다. 그와 비슷하게 학습자의 인식을 높이는 전략으로써 **the garden path** 활동을 활용할 수 있다. The garden path는 학습자에게 문법 규칙의 전체를 알려주는 것이 아니라 일부분만을 알려주고 학습자가 부분적인 규칙을 사용해서 과잉일반화(**overgeneralization**)의 오류를 범하면 틀린 부분을 알려줌으로써 틀리기 쉬운 문법 규칙에 대한 인식을 높여주는 방법이다(Celce-Murcia et al., 2014).

5. Read Ms. Lee's opinions about the grammar lesson in <A> and the sample lesson plan in <B>, and follow the directions. 【4 points】

───────────────── <A> ─────────────────

I think teachers should keep in mind that the ultimate goal of any grammar lesson is to build up communicative ability. In order to achieve this goal, I believe that classroom activities should not focus on practicing structures and patterns in a meaningless way. Instead, they should be designed to involve students in real communication. By doing so, grammar lessons will be able to encourage the students' interest in learning and elicit more active and meaningful interaction with others in the classroom.

───────────────── <B> ─────────────────

Subject	High School English	Students	1st-year students
Title	Lesson 9 My Dream	Date	Nov. 24th
Objectives	• Students will familiarize themselves with the expression "If I were … ." • Students will be able to communicate using the expression "If I were …."		

Teaching-Learning Activities		
Introduction	Greeting & Roll-call	• T and Ss exchange greetings. • T checks if all the Ss are present.
	Review	• T reviews materials from the previous lesson.
	Stating the Objectives	• T introduces the objective of the lesson.

Develop-ment	Activity 1	• T hands out a text that contains several instances of "If I were … ." • Ss scan the text and highlight all the sentences including "If I were … ." • Ss check the ones they highlighted with T. • T tells Ss to pay attention to the verb form "were."
	Activity 2	• T tells Ss that she is going to read a passage on "My Dream." • T explains difficult words in the passage. • T reads the passage at a normal pace. • Ss jot down the key words in the passage as T reads. • Ss reconstruct the passage individually. • T hands out the original text to Ss.
	Activity 3	• T has Ss form groups of three. • T asks Ss to think of a job they would like to have in the future. • Ss use "If I were …" to share their opinions about their future dream jobs. • Assuming that their dreams come true, two Ss take a reporter's role and interview the other S asking how he or she feels about his or her job. • Ss take turns and continue the activity.
	Activity 4	• T hands out a worksheet. • Ss put together sentence fragments to form complete sentences. • T reads out complete sentences and each S checks their own answers. • T writes three more sentences using "If I were … " on the board. • T asks Ss to read the sentences.
Consoli-dation	Review	• T reviews what Ss learned.
	Closure	• T hands out homework and announces the next lesson. • T says goodbye to Ss.

Note: T= teacher, S= student

Based on <A>, choose the ONE most appropriate activity in the development stage that reflects Ms. Lee' opinions. Then, support your choice with evidence from <B>. Do NOT copy more than FOUR consecutive words from the passage.

문제 분석 📊🔍

1) Focus on form에 관한 암시

● 문단 <A>에서 Miss Lee는 문법 교수의 궁극적 목표는 의사소통능력을 향상시키는 것이라는 견해를 보여준다. 따라서 교실 활동의 의미를 바탕으로 하지 않은 문법 연습을 지양해야 한다고 주장하고 있다.

● 또한 문법 교수는 의미 있는 상호 작용을 추구해야 하며 학생들의 실질적인 의사소통 능력을 증진시키기 위해서 설계되어야한다고 문단 <A>에 나와 있다.

2) 형태 중심 교수법(form-focused instruction)을 바탕으로 활동 찾기

● Activity 1: 목표 문법 규칙인 "If I were…"를 찾도록 함으로써 학습자가 form을 습득할 수 있도록 한다. 그러나 학습된 형태의 의미를 습득할 수 없다.

● Activity 2: Dictogloss를 통해서 학습자들이 text 안의 가정법 구문을 인지할 수 있도록 하고 있다. 그러나 의사소통능력의 향상에 기여할 수 있는 여지가 없다.

● Activity 3: 그룹 활동을 통해서 학습자들이 "If I were…" 구문을 사용할 수 있도록 함으로써 형태의 의미 두 가지 부분을 의사소통을 함으로써 실질적인 대화 내용을 통해 학습하도록 하고 있다.

● Activity 4: 학습자들이 문장완성을 통해서 "If I were…"의 형태에 익숙해 질 수 있도록 한다. 그러나 언제 어떻게 쓰이는지에 관한 학습에는 기여하지 않는다.

예시 답안 📝

The most appropriate activity is Activity 3. Miss Lee states that a grammar lesson should develop communicative skills. While Activity, 1,2, and 4 engage students in only the structures of the target grammar, "If I were…", Activity 3 is designed for students to practice "If I were…" in a meaningful way. Since students talk about their dream jobs using the target grammar feature, Activity 3 increases students' communicative ability in meaningful interaction.

1. Read the passages and the teaching journals, and follow the directions. 【4 points】

─────────────── \<A\> ───────────────

Form-focused instruction (FFI) can be split into two types: focus on form*S* and focus on form. According to R. Ellis (2001), FFI "includes both traditional approaches to teaching forms based on structural syllabi and more communicative approaches, where attention to form arises out of activities that are primarily meaning-focused"(p. 2).

─────────────── \<B\> ───────────────

[Mr. Song]

My students often tell me that they feel overwhelmed by the number of grammatical structures they have to learn. While thinking about ways to help students develop grammatical competence, I decided to teach grammar explicitly in class. Today I spent most of the class time on explaining grammatical rules using meta-linguistic terms. Although some of the students initially showed some interest in learning about the rules, many of them got bored, with some dozing off after ten minutes or so.

[Miss Oh]

Most of my students find grammatical rules difficult and boring. So I decided to implement a new approach. For this approach, I typed up the reading passage in the textbook and deliberately italicized the target structures, hoping that this would help my students notice how the target structures function. After I passed out the reconstructed reading passage, I had my students read it by themselves and then work together in groups, cross-checking their understanding.

Referring to the terms in <A>, identify the type of form-focused instruction exemplified in each of the teachers' teaching journals, and explain with supporting evidence from <B>. Do NOT copy more than FOUR consecutive words from the passage.

문제 분석

1) 형태 중심 교수법(form-focused instruction)의 종류

- 문단 <A>에서 "form-focused instruction(FFI)"이 "focus on form*S*"와 "focus on form" 두 가지 종류로 나눠질 수 있다고 나와 있다.

- 문단 <A>에서 두 종류의 문법 수업이 1) 강의 계획서에 따라 전통적으로 문법을 가르치는 교수법과 2) 의미 중심의 활동에서 문법에 중점을 두고 있는 의사소통 중심적인 교수법이라고 설명되어 있다.

- 따라서 "focus on form*S*"와 "focus on form" 중 어느 것이 전통적인 교수법에 해당하고 어느 것이 의사소통 중심의 교수법에 적합한지 구별할 수 있는 능력을 요한다.

- 문단 <B>에서 Mr. Song의 교수법은 더 전통적인 문법 교수법에 가깝고, Miss Oh의 교수법은 의미 중심에 가깝다.

2) Focus on form*S*와 Focus on form의 차이점

- Focus on form*S*는 오직 언어 형태에만 집중을 두어 가르치는 것으로써 문장 형태에 중점을 두어 가르친 기존의 문법 교수법과 흡사하다. Focus on form*S*는 focus on meaning과 비교되기도 하는데, focus on meaning은 문장의 형식에는 전혀 중점을 두지 않고 의미에 치중하는 교수법을 말한다. Focus on form*S*는 학습자가 학습된 문법을 실생활에 사용하지 못하는 비효율성 때문에 비판을 받았고 이에 대한 대안으로 대두된 것이 Michael Long이 1988년에 제안한 Focus on form(FonF)이다. FonF는 학습자가 이미 사용하고 있는 문장의 문법 규칙을 깨닫게 만드는 교수법으로써 문법의 의미와 사용법을 학습자가 알고 있다는 전제 조건하에 수행되는 문법 활동이다. 또한 FonF은 의사소통 중심 교수법에서 결핍되어 있다고 비판을 받은 문법 학습을 효과적으로 할 수 있다는 것이 장점이다.

Mr. Song's approach is focus on form*S*; he taught grammar explicitly in class and strictly focused on forms without meaning. Yet, Miss Oh's approach is focus on form. By typing the target structure in italic, she had her students aware of the target structure and the way it worked in the passage.

기출 **2016** 전공 B 5번

5. Read the passage in <A> and examine the teaching procedures in <B>, and follow the directions. 【4 points】

───── <A> ─────

Language learning can be classified into different types in various ways in terms of how learners process linguistic form to acquire rules that govern its use. One way is to distinguish inductive learning from deductive learning. This distinction is made by taking into account how a rule is learned in relation with its specific instances.

───── <B> ─────

(Below are parts of two teachers' instruction procedures for teaching past tense verb forms in hypothetical conditionals.)

Teacher A's Class
- T explains to Ss that past tense verb forms should be used in sentences with if clauses to describe hypothetical situations.
- T asks Ss to complete sentences with appropriate verb forms to show hypothetical situations.

1. I _____(can) fly to you, if I _____(be) a superhero.
2. If he _____(have) a time machine, he _____(will) go
   back in time.

• T asks Ss to read a short text with sentences describing hypothetical situations.

> If I had a spaceship, I would fly to Mars. I would also build my own house there and live forever, if there were both oxygen and water. Unfortunately, I don't have lots of money to buy a spaceship. . . .

• T asks Ss to write a paragraph starting with the given expression.

If I lived on Mars, . . .

Teacher B's Class

• T gives back the written texts about hypothetical situations Ss produced in the previous class and provides their reformulated texts T has produced at the same time. Only incorrect verb forms in Ss' writings are changed in T's reformulation as in the examples below.

<A student's original writing>

If I have last year to live over again, I will exercise more and eat less junk food because I can be healthier. I will spend more time with my friends and have better grades, if I am more active and watch less TV. . . .

<The teacher's reformulated text>

If I had last year to live over again, I would exercise more and eat less junk food because I could be healthier. I would spend more time with my friends and have better grades, if I were more active and watched less TV. . . .

- T asks Ss to compare T's reformulated sample with their writings and to underline all the words in the sample that are different from those in their writings.

- T asks Ss to find what the underlined words have in common and in what way they differ from the ones used in their original writings in terms of language form.

- T asks Ss to work out the rule that applies to all their underlined words based on their findings in the previous step.

Note: T = teacher, S = student

Identify the type of learning applied to each class in <B> based on <A>. Then explain how each class orients students toward its identified type of learning with supporting evidence.

문제 분석 ⅢQ

1) 답안 도출 단계

- 문단 <A>에서 문법 학습을 "inductive learning"과 "deductive learning"으로 나누고 있다.

- 문단 <B>에서 두 교사의 가정법 수업이 각각 "inductive learning"과 "deductive learning"을 바탕으로 구성되어 제시되고 있다.

- 따라서 문단 <B>에서 제시된 수업을 실례로 들어 어떤 것이 inductive이고 어떤 것이 deductive 인지 설명하면 된다.

2) 귀납적 학습(inductive learning)과 연역적 학습(deductive learning)이란?

● 귀납적인 학습법은 학습자 중심 학습법으로써 학생들이 주어진 개념을 스스로 깨달을 수 있게 하는 학습법이다. 따라서 먼저 적절한 예를 주어서 어떻게 그 개념이 사용되는지 규칙을 스스로 찾게 유도한다.

● 연역적인 학습법은 교수자 중심의 학습법으로써 교수자가 새로운 개념을 설명하고 학습자로 하여금 그 개념을 이용해 연습을 하게 함으로써 주어진 개념을 숙지시키는 학습법이다. 이러한 연역적 학습법은 교수자가 짧은 시간 안에 많은 문법 규칙을 가르칠 수 있기에 선호되어 왔으나 다음과 같은 점에서 비판을 받는다. 1) 문법을 내용과 분리해서 가르친다. 2) 따라서 문법의 의미와 기능에는 거의 중점을 두지 않는다. 3) 기계적인 연습이 반복된다. 4) 따라서 높은 문법 지식에도 불구하고 그 문법 지식을 사용할 수 없을 때가 많다.

예시 답안

Teacher A's class makes use of deductive learning while Teacher B's class uses inductive learning. Teacher A first explains the rule and has students practice the rule using different activities. However, Teacher B gives examples first and helps students notice the target feature and finally formulate the rule.

6. Read the passage in <A> and examine the teaching procedure in <B>. Then follow the directions. 【3 points】

--- <A> ---

Processing instruction, a type of focus-on-form instruction, is based on the assumption that when processing input, L2 learners have difficulty in attending to form and meaning at the same time due to working memory limitations. Not surprisingly, they tend to give priority to meaning and tend not to notice details of form. Processing instruction uses several principles to explain what learners attend to in the input and why. Below are some of these principles.

The Lexical Preference Principle: In (1), both -*es* and *boy* convey the same information, 'he third person singular' Yet, learners prefer to focus on the lexical item, *boy,* to arrive at meaning, and often ignore the grammatical item, -*es*, while processing the sentence.

  (1) The *boy* studi*es* in the library, not at home.

The First Noun Principle: Learners tend to process the first noun or pronoun they encounter in a sentence as the agent of action. For example, they may misinterpret (2) as "Jack collected the data for the project."

  (2) *Jack* let *Joe* collect the data for the project.

The Event Possibilities Principle: Event possibilities refer to the likelihood of one noun being the agent of action as opposed to another. Since it is more likely in the real world that a dog would bite a man than the other way around, learners would likely misinterpret (3) as "The dog bit the farmer."

(3) The dog was bitten by the farmer.

In processing instruction, teachers provide students with structured input activities, taking into consideration the principles above. In a structured input activity, students are forced to attend to form in order to comprehend a sentence.

--- <B> ---

Teaching Procedure

1. Explicit Explanation

Explain how a past tense sentence is constructed in English. Then inform students of why they tend not to notice the past tense marker -*ed* and thus misinterpret past tense sentences.

2. Structured Input Activity

Have students read six sentences and decide whether they describe an activity that was done in the past or usually happens in the present. Then, check the answers together.

Sentences	Present	Past
(1) They watched television at night.	☐	☐
(2) They watch television at night.	☐	☐
(3) I walk to school on Mondays.	☐	☐
(4) I walked to school on Mondays.	☐	☐
(5) We played soccer on weekends.	☐	☐
(6) We play soccer on weekends.	☐	☐

Identify the principle in <A> that the teaching procedure in <B> focuses on. Then explain how the structured input activity in <B> helps students correctly process the target form for meaning.

![문제 분석 아이콘] 문제 분석 ⅢQ

1) 답안 도출 방법

- 문단 <A>에 "processing instruction"에 관한 설명이 나오고 3개의 원칙이 소개되어 있다.

- 문단 <B>에 "processing instruction"을 그대로 응용한 교수법이 소개되어 있다.

- 문단 <B>의 활동을 보면 먼저 과거시제의 형태를 설명하고 두 번째로 과거시제의 형태의 중요성을 설명하고 마지막으로 학습자가 "structured input activity"를 하게 하는 전형적인 processing instruction의 요소를 따르고 있다.

- 이 "structured input activity"의 핵심은 제시된 문장들의 차이를 의미로 유추할 수 있는 여지가 전혀 없기 때문에 학습자가 과거시제 marker인 -ed 에 집중할 수밖에 없다는 것이다.

2) 처리 교수(Processing Instruction)란?

- VanPattern(2004)이 효과를 입증한 input을 바탕으로 한 문법 교수법을 지칭한다. 처리 교수 (**Processing Instruction**)의 가장 중요한 특징은 학습자가 어떠한 실마리, 기존의 지식, 혹은 내용에 의지해도 이해할 수 없는 문장이 예로 주어져야 한다는 것이다. 이는 학습자가 의미가 아닌 형태에만 집중하게 하는 효과가 있다.

![예시 답안 아이콘] 예시 답안 ✍

The teaching procedure in <B> focuses on the lexical preference principle exhibited in <A> since the teacher tries to help students notice the past tense marker, -ed. The students cannot use any meaningful sources from the exemplified sentences because the sentences in a pair are identical except the past tense marker, -ed. Thus, the students have to focus on the target form without depending on meaning.

3 쓰기(Writing)

쓰기 교수법을 이해하는 데 있어서 가장 중요한 것은 과정 중심의 교수법(**the process approach**)과 결과 중심의 교수법(**the product approach**)을 구분하는 것이다. 과거의 쓰기 교수법은 결과물을 중심으로 만들어졌고 평가도 최종 결과물을 바탕으로 이뤄졌다. 최종 결과물이 정해져 있는 기준을 충족하면 성공적인 것으로 평가되었고(**summative assessment**), 교수자는 그 기준을 충족하고 있는 모델을 제시하고 학습자는 최대한 그 모델과 비슷하게 쓰기 과제를 수행하는 방식으로 수업이 진행되었다. 그러나 최근 경향은 학습자를 작가로 보고 내용의 발전에 보다 중점을 두고 쓰기 수업이 진행되고 있다. 이러한 경향을 과정 중심 교수법(**the process approach**)이라고 한다. 과정 중심 교수법의 가장 큰 특징은 학습자가 결과물 하나를 제출하는 것이 아니라 과제물을 여러 번 제출하면서 내용과 표현에 관한 피드백을 지속적으로 받는 데 있다. 이러한 피드백을 형성적 피드백(**formative feedback**)이라고 한다(Brown, 2015).

구성주의 학습 이론을 생각해 보면 과정 중심의 교수법이 쓰기 수업에 더 적합하다는 것을 알 수 있다. 학습자는 본인이 가지고 있는 언어 능력에서 근접 발달 영역(**zone of proximal development**)으로 발전을 할 수 있지만 그 영역을 초월한 단계에는 교수자의 도움이 있어도 도달할 수가 없다. 따라서 결과물 중심의 교수법을 활용해서 아무리 모델을 제시해도 학습자의 쓰기 능력이 부족하다면 그 모델 수준 정도의 쓰기를 해낼 수 없다. 그렇다면 학습자는 좌절을 겪을 것이고 이는 학습에 부정적인 영향을 미치게 된다. 그러나 과정 중심의 교수법에서 교수자가 피드백을 주게 되면 학습자는 본인이 가지고 있는 쓰기 능력을 바탕으로 해서 수정을 하게 됨으로 근접 발달 영역으로 쉽게 발전할 수 있게 된다. 따라서 과정 중심 교수법이 쓰기 지도에 있어서 훨씬 효과적이라고 할 수 있다.

과정 중심의 교수법은 다음과 같은 단계를 거치게 된다.

1) **전 쓰기(Pre-writing)**: 구조화된 활동을 통해서 내용이나 동기를 제공함 Ex) 주제에 관한 토론, 읽기, 브레인스토밍, 개요잡기(**outlining**) 등
2) **쓰기(Writing)**: 형식 보다는 내용을 중점을 둔 초안 작성
3) **반응(Response)**: 글에 관한 반응 Ex) Peer review, 그룹 토론, 교수자의 피드백이나 상담(**conference**)
4) **수정(Revising)**: 초안에 관한 피드백을 바탕으로 해서 내용을 다시 구성함
5) **편집(Editing)**: 문법이나 단어 등 형식을 다듬어서 교정을 봄

6) 후 쓰기(Post-writing): 결과물을 공유하거나 보여줌

7) 평가(Evaluating): 교수자나 학생들이 평가를 함

(Celce-Murcia et al., 2014)

위의 단계로 대표되는 과정 중심의 교수법에서는 학생들이 초안을 제출하면 피드백을 받게 된다(3단계). 그 후 학생들은 글을 수정하고 편집하게 된다(4, 5단계). 이 때 피드백은 내용을 중심으로 하는 것이 원칙이며 내용이 수정된 이후 마지막 단계에서 문장의 정확성에 대한 피드백이 이뤄지게 된다. 위에 제시된 2, 3, 4의 단계는 내용이 완성될 때까지 여러 번에 거쳐 되풀이 될 수 있다. 내용이 완성되면 문장 단위의 피드백이 이뤄지는데 문장의 정확성을 위한 문법이나 단어에 대한 피드백도 틀린 부분을 맞게 고쳐서 주는 것이 아니라 다양한 기호를 통해 힌트를 제시함으로써 학습자가 스스로 생각해서 고칠 수 있게 한다. 이에 따라 교수자가 지도하고 이끄는 수업이 아니라 학생들의 쓰기 능력을 바탕으로 구성되는 학습자 중심의 교실 수업이 가능해진다.

교수자의 역할은 써야 될 글의 장르(genres)를 정하고 그 장르에 맞는 언어(register)를 제시해 주며 학습자가 가지고 있는 지식을 불러오는 것으로 시작된다고 할 수 있다. 이때 학습자가 가지고 있는 기존의 지식을 스키마(schematic knowledge)라고 하는데, 이는 네 가지로 세분될 수 있다. 1) 장르에 관한 지식, 2) 세상에 관한 일반적인 지식, 3) 사회문화적 지식, 그리고 4) 주제에 관한 지식이다. 전 쓰기 단계에서 이 스키마를 잘 활성화시키면 글의 내용이 보다 잘 발전할 수 있다(Harmer, 2004).

글의 내용이 충분히 발전하면, 글의 구성에 대한 지도가 실시된다. 글의 구성에 대한 지도는 주로 결합성(cohesion)과 일관성(coherence)에 대한 것이다. Harmer(2014)에 따르면 결합성은 단어적 결합(lexical cohesion)과 문법적 결합(grammatical cohesion)으로 나눠진다. 단어적 결합은 나왔던 단어를 반복해서 쓰거나 개념적으로 연결되어 있는 단어를 씀으로써 글의 결합도를 높여서 독자가 글의 구성을 따라가기 쉽게 만드는 방법이다. 문법적 결합은 1) 대명사나 소유격 사용, 2) 관사 사용, 3) 시제 일치, 4) 접속사 사용 등이 있다. 이 때 이미 나왔던 단어를 지칭하고자 한다면 전방조응적(대용적) 지시(anaphoric reference)가 사용되었다고 하고 이후에 나올 단어를 지칭한다면 후방조응적 지시(cataphoric reference)라고 하며, 글에 언급은 되지 않았지만 독자가 이미 알고 있는 것을 지칭한다면 외조응적 지시(exophoric reference)라고 한다. 일관성(coherence)은 저자가 글을 쓴 목적과 생각의 과정을 독자가 마치 사용설명서를 읽듯이 따라갈 수 있게 하는 것을 의미한다. 보통 결합적 장치(cohesive devices), 즉 다양한 종류의 접속사를 사용하면 일관성이 높아진

다고 하지만 잘 써진 글은 결합적 장치가 사용되건 사용되지 않건 높은 일관성을 가지고 있다. 예를 들어 글의 주제와 전혀 상관이 없는 문장이 들어가 있다면 일관성이 떨어진다고 할 수 있다.

14. Read the passage in <A> and part of a lesson procedure in <B>, and follow the directions. 【4 points】

─────────────── <A> ───────────────

(Below are suggestions from a conference for teaching L2 writing.)

To help students to write effectively...

(a) Start with pre-writing activities with little emphasis on ungrammaticalities and incorrect spelling.

(b) Have drafting and revising stages in a recursive way.

(c) Provide meaning-focused feedback.

(d) Offer students opportunities to think about their own writing.

─────────────── <B> ───────────────

(The following is part of Ms. Song's lesson procedure for teaching how to write an argumentative essay.)

Steps:

1. T provides background information about artificial intelligence and Ss watch videos related to the topic.

2. Ss discuss the topic in groups and brainstorm.

3. Ss sketch their ideas and write the first drafts, focusing on content.

4. T reviews Ss' drafts and provides corrective feedback that reformulates ill-formed expressions.

5. Ss revise their drafts once, based on the feedback, and then hand in their final drafts to T.

6. T asks Ss to write reflective journals about their writing.

Note: T= teacher, Ss=students

Identify TWO suggestions from <A> that Ms. Song does NOT implement in <B>. Then, support your answers with evidence from <B>.

![문제 분석 아이콘]

- 문단 <A>에 과정 중심의 교수법(**the process approach**)이 제시되어 있다. 쓰기 과정의 초반에는 문법 등의 형식에 크게 구애받지 않고 몇 번의 draft를 통해 내용의 완성도를 높인다. 이때 피드백도 의미 중심으로 이뤄진다.

- 문단 <B>에서 Ms. Song은 결과 중심의 교수법(**the product approach**)에 해당하는 교수법을 일부 보이고 있다. 즉 4번에서 내용이 아닌 문법에 관한 피드백이 이뤄졌으며 5번에서 원고 수정이 문법에 관한 피드백을 바탕으로 한번만 이뤄졌음을 알 수 있다. 이는 학습자를 작가로 보고 내용에 대해 반복적인 피드백을 주는 과정 중심의 교수법과는 대조되는 내용이다.

- 문제에서 Ms. Song이 수행하지 않은 제안을 두 개 찾고 그에 따른 증거를 제시하라고 했으므로 문단<A>에서 두 개의 제안을, 문단 <B>에서 증거를 제시하면 된다.

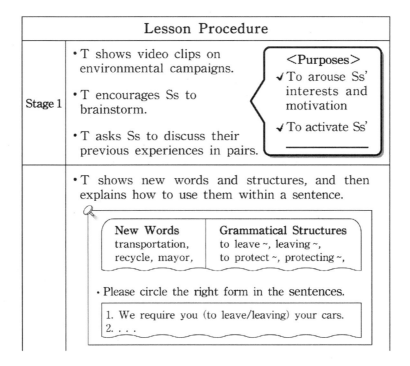
The two suggestions that Ms. Song does not implement are (b) Have drafting and revising stages in a recursive way and (c) Provide meaning-focused feedback. According to Ms. Song's lesson procedure in <B>, she provides corrective feedback for ill-formed expressions. It indicates that she provides form-focused feedback, instead of meaning-focused feedback, suggested in <A>. Also, students revise drafts only once and submit the final draft in <B>. Yet, multiple drafts and revision in a recursive way is suggested in <A>.

기출 **2016** 전공 B **3번**

3. Read part of a lesson plan and follow the directions. 【4 points】

Lesson Procedure		
Stage 1	• T shows video clips on environmental campaigns. • T encourages Ss to brainstorm. • T asks Ss to discuss their previous experiences in pairs.	<Purposes> ✓ To arouse Ss' interests and motivation ✓ To activate Ss' _____
	• T shows new words and structures, and then explains how to use them within a sentence. New Words: transportation, recycle, mayor, Grammatical Structures: to leave ~, leaving ~, to protect ~, protecting ~, • Please circle the right form in the sentences. 1. We require you (to leave/leaving) your cars. 2. . . .	

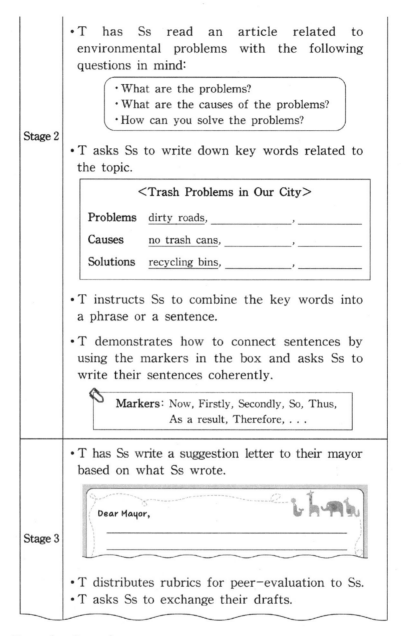

| Stage 2 | • T has Ss read an article related to environmental problems with the following questions in mind:

・What are the problems?
・What are the causes of the problems?
・How can you solve the problems?

• T asks Ss to write down key words related to the topic.

<Trash Problems in Our City>

Problems　dirty roads, _____, _____

Causes　　no trash cans, _____, _____

Solutions　recycling bins, _____, _____

• T instructs Ss to combine the key words into a phrase or a sentence.

• T demonstrates how to connect sentences by using the markers in the box and asks Ss to write their sentences coherently.

Markers: Now, Firstly, Secondly, So, Thus, As a result, Therefore, . . . |
| Stage 3 | • T has Ss write a suggestion letter to their mayor based on what Ss wrote.

Dear Mayor,
_____
_____

• T distributes rubrics for peer-evaluation to Ss.
• T asks Ss to exchange their drafts. |

Note: T = teacher, S = student

Fill in the blank in the <Purposes> box in Stage 1 with ONE word. Then identify ONE way the teacher directly prepares students to write a well-organized suggestion letter in Stage 2, and explain it with evidence. Do NOT copy more than FIVE consecutive words from the passage.

- Stage 1에서 영상을 보거나 토론을 하는 활동을 한다. 이는 학생들의 관심과 schemata를 불러오는 활동이다.

- 문제에서 학생들이 "well-organized suggestion letter"를 쓰도록 교수자가 준비시키는 방법을 Stage 2에서 찾으라고 했다. Stage 2에서는 단어와 문법, 글의 주제를 이해하기 위한 질문과 쓰기, 그리고 transitional markers의 사용이 들어가 있다. 이 중 글의 구성에 관한 것은 transitional markers이므로 이에 대한 증거를 제시하면 된다.

예시 답안

Schemata. One way that the teacher helps students write a well-organized letter is to teach transitional markers. The transitional markers shown in Stage 2 increases the coherence of a writing. By practicing how to utilize the transitional markers, such as "now", "firstly", "so", "thus" etc., the organization of students' writing will be better constructed.

4 말하기(Speaking)

발음 지도에 있어서 가장 많이 쓰이고 효과적인 활동은 최소 대립쌍(minimal pairs)을 활용하는 것이다. 최소 대립쌍은 하나의 음소만 다르고 나머지는 다 같은 단어의 쌍을 의미한다. 교수자는 학생들이 어려움을 느끼는 소리에 집중해서 연습시키는 방법으로 최소 대립쌍을 많이 활용하고 있다. 예를 들어 "cat"과 "cut"을 반복해서 듣고 연습을 하게 해서 두 개의 모음 발음을 구별하기 힘들어하는 학생을 도울 수 있는 것이다(Kelly, 2000).

최근에 의사소통 중심 교수법과 과업 중심 교수법의 영향으로 단순 반복을 하는 최소 대립쌍보다는 내용을 중심으로 연습을 하게 하는 의미 있는 최소 대립쌍(meaningful minimal pairs)이 활용되고 있다. 다음의 예를 보자.

> T: This pen leaks.
>
> S: Then don't write with it.
>
> T: This pan leaks.
>
> S: Then don't cook with it.

(Brown, 2015)

위의 예에서 학생들이 어려움을 겪고 있는 것은 단모임 'a'와 'e'의 구분이다. 단순히 문제가 되는 음소가 들어있는 단어를 들려주고 따라하게 하는 것이 아니라 문장 내에서 그 단어의 쓰임새를 알 수 있게 예문을 구성했기에 학생들의 의미를 생각하면서 발음을 구별하게 된다. 이는 학생들이 더 오랫동안 발음의 차이를 기억하게 만드는 효과를 가지고 있다.

기출 2017 전공 A 7번

7. Read the passage and fill in each blank with TWO words. (Use the SAME answer for both blanks.) 【2 points】

> S: Could you give me some advice on how I can improve my pronunciation?
>
> T: Yes, of course. Are you having trouble pronouncing a particular word?
>
> S: I can't think of any right now, but there are a lot of sounds in English that I can't pronounce.
>
> T: Can you give me an example?
>
> S: The word *right*. R is very difficult for me.
>
> T: Oh, that's because the consonant *r* doesn't exist in the Korean sound system. Then, you should practice pronunciation with a lot of

_____ . For example, the words *river* and *liver* have only one sound difference in the same position, but it makes a big difference in meaning.

S: Oh, I see. So, I guess *fine* and *pine* would be another example of _____ , right?

T: Yes, you're right. If you want to be able to pronounce *right*, you first need to be able to hear the difference between *right* and *light*. There are so many other examples, like *rice* and *lice*, *rode* and *load*, etc.

S: I can't hear the difference between those words, either.

T: I know they are difficult, but with enough practice, you will be able to hear the difference and pronounce them correctly.

Note: T = teacher, S = student

문제 분석

1) 최소 대립쌍(minimal pairs)에 관한 암시
- 첫 줄에 발음을 향상시키기 위한 방법이라고 제시되어 있다.
- 특정한 발음에 대한 어려움이 제시되어 있다.
- 같은 위치에 한 소리만 다른 단어들이 예로 제시되어 있다.

2) 최소 대립쌍(minimal pairs)이란?
- 단어나 구 중 한 음소만 다른 단어들의 쌍이다. 최소 대립쌍은 발음지도에 가장 도움이 된다고 알려져 있다. 최소 대립쌍은 먼저 학습자가 익숙하지 않은 발음에 대한 인지도를 높여주고 그에 따라 그 특정한 발음을 학습할 수 있는 기회를 제공해 준다. 최근에는 최소 대립쌍을 이용한 발음 학습에 내용을 덧붙여 의미와 함께 학습할 수 있는 방법이 더 인기를 끌고 있다.

예시 답안

minimal pairs

5 단어(Vocabulary)

  그간 단어 능력에 관해서 다양한 논의가 이뤄졌지만 가장 전통적인 관점은 단어 수업에는 형태(**form**), 의미(**meaning**), 그리고 기능(**function/use**)이 모두 포함되어야 한다는 것이다. 학습자들은 단어 지식을 중요하게 생각한다. 왜냐하면 부족한 단어 실력은 의사소통에 큰 문제를 야기하기 때문이다. 게다가 문법 규칙을 알고 있다고 해도 알고 있는 단어의 개수가 적다면 여전히 목표어를 이해할 수 없다. 따라서 단어 지식의 다양한 면들에 관한 연구는 단어를 완전히 안다는 것은 발음, 철자, 형태, 의미 등을 모두 포함하는 광범위한 언어학적 지식을 가지고 있다는 의미임을 밝혀냈다. 이에 따라 단어 지식은 단어의 범위(**breadth**)와 깊이(**depth**)로 나눠진다. 단어의 범위는 학습자가 그 단어에 대해서 얼마나 알고 있는 가와는 상관없이 알고 있는 단어의 개수를 의미한다. 즉, 알고 있는 단어의 질과는 관련 없이 알고 있는 단어의 수를 말한다. 반면 단어 지식의 깊이는 특정한 단어를 얼마나 알고 있는가를 의미한다. 발음, 철자, 형태소적 특성, 통사론적 특성, 의미, 레지스터, 담화적 특징, 그리고 빈도가 이에 속한다. 단어 지식의 깊이는 표면적인 의미의 이해가 아닌 자주 사용되는 단어의 유용성에 대한 것이다. 이러한 단어 지식의 깊이는 독해 능력을 향상시키는데 결정적인 역할을 한다(Caro & Mendinueta, 2017).

  단어 지식의 깊이는 학습자가 다양한 상황에서 적절한 단어를 쓸 수 있도록 해준다. 그 중의 하나는 완곡어법(**euphemism**)이다. 완곡어법은 정중하거나 덜 직접적인 표현을 활용해서 말하기 어렵거나 부끄러운 주제를 말해야 할 때 사용하는 어법이다. 특히 몸의 상태나 죽음과 같은 주제를 말해야 할 때 직접적인 표현은 삼가게 된다. "Ugly" 대신에 "plain"이라는 단어를 사용한다던가, "toilet" 대신에 "bathroom", "die" 대신에 "pass away", "kill" 대신에 "put down"이나 "put to sleep"을 사용하는 것이 실질적인 예가 될 수 있다.

1. Read the passage in <A> and the teacher's journal in <B>, and follow the directions. 【2 points】

───────────── <A> ─────────────

Vocabulary is a core component of language knowledge and provides much of the basis for how well learners listen, speak, read, and write. Without extensive knowledge of vocabulary or diverse strategies for acquiring new words, learners are often unable to produce as much language as they would like.

Knowing a word does not simply mean knowing its surface meaning. Rather, it involves knowing diverse aspects of lexical knowledge in depth including phonological and morphological forms and syntactic and semantic structures. Therefore, activities that integrate lexical knowledge of form, meaning, and use should be included in class.

───────────── <B> ─────────────

Teacher's Journal

Ms. Kang and I read an article on teaching vocabulary and discussed how we can improve the way we teach vocabulary. We realized that we have been heavily focused on expanding the size of our students' vocabulary. As a result, they seem to know a lot of words but do not understand or use them properly in context. So, we came up with the following activities that we believe help our students develop _____ of vocabulary knowledge across form, meaning, and use.

Vocabulary activities to be implemented:

- Trying to pronounce the target words by listening to a recorded text
- Analyzing parts of the target words (e.g., prefixes and suffixes)
- Guessing the meanings of the target words using contextual cues
- Studying concordance examples to see various contexts and collocation patterns
- Writing a short story using the target words

Fill in the blank in <B> with the ONE most appropriate word from <A>.

문제 분석

● 문단 <A>에서 단어를 안다는 것은 표면적인 의미를 아는 것이 아니라 음운론적 그리고 형태소적인 형태와, 통사론적이고 의미론적인 구조를 포함하는 다양한 면의 단어 지식을 깊이 있게 아는 것이라고 나와 있다. 따라서 형태, 의미, 그리고 사용법을 함께 가르쳐야 한다고 주장한다.

● 문단 <B>에서 교사들의 저널을 보면 그간 단어의 범위를 확장하는데 집중해 왔으므로 단어 지식의 무엇을 발달시키기 위한 활동을 고안해 냈다고 한다. 그 무엇이 빈 칸으로 되어 있고, 제시된 단어 활동을 분석해 보면 발음, 형태소, 의미, 사용법을 모두 포함하고 있음을 알 수 있다.

● 학습자가 단어의 형태, 의미, 기능을 모두 습득하도록 하는 활동이 문단 <B>에서 예로 제시되어 있고 문단 <A>의 내용은 단어의 범위보다는 단어의 깊이에 중점을 두고 있다. 따라서 단어 지식의 깊이를 발달시키기 위한 활동임을 유추해 낼 수 있다.

예시 답안

depth

8. Read the dialogue and fill in both blanks with the ONE most appropriate word. (Use the SAME word in both blanks.)【2 points】

> S: Ms. Lee, can I ask you a question?
>
> T: Sure, go ahead.
>
> S: I went over your feedback on my essay, and I really appreciate it. You pointed out the expression "die" could be revised to "pass away."
>
> T: Yes, I did.
>
> S: I don't understand the difference between the two expressions. As far as I understand, they have the same meaning.
>
> T: Oh, I see. That's actually an example of a(n) _____ .
>
> S: Hmm ... .
>
> T: Let me make it clearer with another example. How do you think someone would feel if they were called "poor"?
>
> S: Well, they may feel bad.
>
> T: Okay, what about "less privileged"?
>
> S: Oh, I understand your point. Two words or expressions may mean the same thing, but we may have different feelings and attitudes about them.
>
> T: That's the point. A(n) _____ is a polite word or expression that you use instead of a more direct one, to avoid shocking or upsetting someone.
>
> S: Interesting!
>
> T: Good.
>
> S: Thank you, Ms. Lee. Your feedback is always helpful.

Note: T= teacher, S= student

문제 분석

● 단어에 관한 문제라는 단서가 학생의 두 번째 발화에서 나와 있다.

● "die"와 "pass away"의 차이점을 모른다고 나와 있다.

● 교사가 예를 들 때 "poor"가 "less privileged"로 바꿔 쓰인다고 했고 직접적인 표현보다는 예의 있는 표현이라고 설명하며 그 이유가 다른 사람의 마음을 상하게 하지 않기 위해서라고 설명했다.

예시 답안

euphemism

UNIT 3

교재(Textbooks)

교재는 다양한 언어 학습과 교육 과정에 있어서 가장 중심적인 부분이고 학습자와 교수자 모두에게 도움을 준다. 교재 선정(textbook selection)과 교재 평가(textbook evaluation) 과정에 대한 연구는 다양하지만 보통 일반적인 기준을 바탕으로 한 점검표를 만들 수 있다. 이 점검표는 일반적으로 교재의 외형, 내용, 교육 프로그램의 목표와 방법, 교수자가 필요로 하는 점이 포함되어 있고 또한 교재를 얼마나 쉽게 구입할 수 있는가도 포함될 수 있다(Amerian & Khaivar, 2014).

교재 선정을 하는데 있어서 다양한 접근법이 있지만 가장 실용적인 방법 중 하나는 교육 과정의 목표와 교육 과정을 먼저 고려하고, 연습 문제나 활동과 같은 세부 사항을 나중에 고려하는 것이다. 혹자는 학생들의 배경, 교과목 강의 계획과 학교에 관한 정보를 바탕으로 해 교재를 다섯 권이나 열 권 정도 선정한 후 세 단계의 과정을 거치는 것을 제안한다. 첫 번째 단계에서는 교재의 차례나 내용을 훑어보면서 목적, 구성, 방법 등을 살펴보고, 두 번째 단계에서 교재의 내용을 신중하게 검토해서 두 세권으로 축소한다. 그리고 마지막 단계에서 양적 질적 검토를 통해 교재를 선정한다는 것이다(Celce-Murcia & McIntosh, 1979). 이를 보다 자세하게 나누면 다음과 같은 선정 과정을 제시할 수 있다.

1) **과목과 교육 과정에 맞는 교재 선정**: 교재를 선정하기 전에 교수자들은 먼저 교육 과정을 잘 검토해서 교육 과정의 목표에 맞는 교재들을 선정한다. 즉, 교재가 교과목 목표의 상당 부분을 반영하고 있어야 한다. 그 후 교재의 내용이 학습자들에게 적절한지 판단한다. 예를 들어 대학 입학을 준비하는 학생들이 학문 목적의 영어(English for Academic Purpose)를 필요로 한다면 다른 학생들은 영어에 대한 문해 능력만을 원할 수도 있다.

2) **교재에 나와 있는 언어 스킬 검토**: 교육 과정에서 예를 들어 읽기 능력에 보다 집중을 하고자 한다면 교재가 정말 읽기 능력을 중심으로 구성이 되어 있는지 검토해야 한다. 또한 정말 읽기 능력을 효율적으로 가르치고 있는지 아니면 단순하게 연습 문제만이 나와 있는지도 검토해야 한다.

3) 연습 문제와 활동 검토: 교재의 연습 문제나 활동을 검토할 때 다음과 같은 질문이 유용하다.

① **연습 문제와 활동이 학습자의 언어 습득에 도움이 되는가?**: 교재에 포함되어 있는 많은 연습 문제가 교수자에게는 편리하지만 학습자의 언어 발달에는 기여하지 않는 경우가 많다. 교재에는 학습자가 본인이 가지고 있는 언어 능력을 확장하고 연습할 수 있는 활동들이 포함되어야 한다. 예를 들어 정보 격차 활동(information gaps), 직쏘 활동(jigsaw), 역할극 등이 그것이다.

② **연습 문제가 제어된 활동(controlled activities)과 자유 활동(free activities)을 골고루 갖추고 있는가?**: 제어된 활동(controlled activities)이란 빈 칸 채우기와 같이 정답이 하나만 있는 활동이고, 자유 활동(free activities)은 토론 등과 같이 학습자의 창의력과 지식에 따라 다양한 답이 나올 수 있는 활동이다. 학습자들의 언어 실력을 효과적으로 향상시키기 위해서 두 가지 종류의 활동이 모두 필요하다.

③ **연습 문제가 진도에 따라 난이도가 높아지는가?**: 학생들의 언어 실력이 향상됨에 따라 연습 문제는 언어적인 그리고 인지적인 면에서 쉬운 것에서부터 보다 복잡하고 어려운 것으로 발전해 가야 한다. 이러한 방법으로 학생들에게 지속적으로 지적 자극을 줄 수 있다.

④ **연습 문제가 다양하고 학생들의 노력을 요구하는가?**: 학생들이 같은 연습 문제만을 본다면 익숙해지기는 하겠지만 학생들에게 지속적으로 동기를 부여하기 위해서는 각 과마다 새로운 활동이 제시되면 좋다.

4) 실용적인 문제 검토: 가격이나 접근성과 같은 실질적인 문제를 검토한다. 모든 교재가 필요한 때에 바로 구입할 수 있는 것이 아니므로 교재 선정은 충분한 시간을 두고 미리 행해지는 것이 좋다.

(Garinger, 2002)

교재 평가(textbook evaluation)는 교수자가 교재에 대해서 정확하고 체계적인 이해를 할 수 있다는 면에서 중요하다. 교재 평가는 시기에 따라 세 가지로 나뉘는데, 미래에 사용될 교재에 대한 평가인 '사용 전 평가'와, 현재 사용하고 있는 교재에 대한 평가인 '사용 중 평가', 그리고 사용한 후에 평가하는 '사용 후 평가'가 그것이다. 교재 평가를 통해서 특정 교재에 대한 장점과 단점을 알 수 있고 이는 이후 교재를 각색(text adaptation)하는데도 도움이 된다. 어떤 상황에서는 괜찮았던 교재가 다른 교육 상황에서는 문제가 될 수도 있기에 교재 평가에 앞서 교재의 역할, 교수자와 학습자에 관한 정보 수집이 선행되어야 한다. 교재 평가는 필요조건에 관한 해결책을 찾는 과정으로써 네 개의 단계로 나눠지는데, 그 단계는 1) 기준 세우기, 2) 주관적 분석, 3) 객관적 분석, 그리고 4) 필요조건 충족이다(Amerian & Khaivar, 2014).

교재 선정의 기준 중 하나로 최근에 제시되기 시작한 것이 진위성(authenticity)이다. 진위성이란 교재의 내용과 언어가 교실 밖 세계를 얼마나 반영하는가에 관한 것이다. 영어 교육계에서 교재에 사용된 대화와 실제 원어민이 사용하는 대화와의 차이점이 문제로 대두된 후에, 학습자가 자연스러운 언어에 노출되어야 한다는 주장이 나왔다. 이후 영어 교재의 대화는 실제 사용되는 언어로 많이 바뀌고 있다. 그러나 한편에서는 원어민 화자를 위한 언어는 영어를 모국어로 하지 않는 화자가 학습자인 교실 상황에서는 어울리지 않기 때문에 교실 수업에서 노출되는 언어의 진위성은 환상에 불과하다는 비판이 있다. 또한 교재에서 사용되는 언어가 실질적으로 원어민들이 사용하는 언어라고 할지라도 주제는 여전히 인위적이라는 비판도 있다(Siegel, 2014).

이에 따라 교재의 언어를 진위성이 담보되어 있는 것으로 바꾸는 방법 이외에 진위성이 있는 교재(authentic materials)를 사용하는 방법도 늘고 있다. 진위성이 있는 교재는 언어 교수라는 목적을 위해 특별히 고안된 예만을 사용하는 교재의 반대되는 개념으로써 실질적인 언어의 사용을 담고 있는 교재를 의미한다. 따라서 진위성이 있는 교재는 원어민에 의해서 만들어진 원어민을 위한 글이되는 것이고 언어 교수를 목표로 해서 만들어진 교재가 아닌 것이다. 혹자는 이러한 정의에 반대해서 진위성이 있는 글(authentic text)은 가르치기 위해서가 아니라 의사소통을 위해 만들어진 것이며 진위성이 있는 활동(authentic task)은 언어를 연습하기 위해서가 아니라 의사소통을 하기 위한 활동을 의미한다고 주장한다. 이 주장에 따르면 일상생활을 수행하기 위해 고안된 수업 활동은 모두 진위성이 있는 활동에 속하게 된다. 그러나 진위성이 있는 교재는 보통 다음의 세 가지로 분류될 수 있다. 1) 일상생활에서 사용되는 글(영수증, 보고서, 사용 설명서, 편지, 이메일, 지원서 등), 2) 방송에서 사용되는 글(신문, 잡지, 텔레비전, 라디오, 영화, 책 등), 3) 웹사이트 (Sierocka, 2012).

교재의 진위성은 교재의 각색(textbook adaptation)과 대비되는 개념이다. 교재의 진위성이 현실에서 사용되는 언어를 교재에 반영하거나 현실에서 사용되는 글을 그대로 사용하는 것이라면 교재 각색은 교재를 더 효율적이고 유연하게 만드는 전략을 적용하는 것을 의미한다. 이러한 각색은 다음과 같은 이유로 이뤄진다.

1) 불필요한 내용을 제거하기 위해
2) 개인의 다양성을 고려하기 위해
3) 학습자의 학습 전략과 인지 스타일에 바탕을 둔 내용을 제공하기 위해
4) 학습자의 문화와 가치를 바탕으로 한 내용에 맞추기 위해
5) 능력 있는 학습자에게 도전 의식을 부여하기 위해

6) 교육 과정에 학습자의 참여를 확대하기 위해

7) 학습자의 관심과 목표를 성취하기 위해

8) 학습자의 스트레스와 불안을 감소시키기 위해

(Halim & Halim, 2016)

교재의 채택(**textbook adoption**)은 각색과 반대되는 개념으로써 제공된 교재를 권위 있는 것으로 받아들이고 거의 각색을 하지 않거나 아예 안하는 것을 의미한다. 교재를 그대로 채택하는 것을 비판하는 것은 교재의 각색이 때로 필수적일 수 있기 때문이다. 효율성과 적절함을 성취하기 위해서 교재 각색은 개인화(**personalizing**), 지역화(**localizing**), 현대화(**modernizing**)라는 목표를 지닌다(Sierocka, 2012).

교재를 각색하기 위한 다양한 기술은 다음과 같다. 1) 첨가(**adding**), 2) 제거(**deleting**), 3) 수정(**modifying**), 4) 단순화(**simplifying**), 5) 재배치(**reordering**), 그리고 6) 교재 교체(**replacing materials**)가 있다. 첨가는 교재에 내용을 더함으로써 보완하는 방법으로써 반드시 마지막에 덧붙여질 필요 없이 초반부터 덧붙이기도 한다. 제거는 첨가의 반대 개념으로써 교재의 일부분이 빠지는 것인데 보통 첨가와 함께 쓰인다. 수정은 교재 내용을 향상시키기 위해서 행하는 모든 변화를 말한다. 일반적으로 교재를 보다 의사소통 중심적으로 바꾸고 보다 현실적인 언어를 사용하며 학생들이 관심 있는 주제로 바꾸는데 사용된다. 단순화는 수정의 한 방법으로써 문장의 구조를 단순하게 만들거나 내용을 단순화하는 것을 의미한다. 재배치는 교재 내용의 일부분을 다른 순서로 재구성하는 것이다. 한 과에서 순서를 바꾸기도 하도 과의 순서를 바꾸기도 한다. 마지막으로 교재를 교체하는 것은 교재의 일부분을 다른 교재로 대체하는 것을 의미한다(Halim & Halim, 2016).

위에서 언급한 교재의 수정(**textbook modification**)은 학습자의 영어 실력에 맞춰서 수정한다는 개념은 아니다. 최근에 중시되는 교재의 진위성을 유지하는데 있어서 가장 큰 문제는 학습자의 언어 실력에 맞지 않을 수 있다는 것이다. 학습자의 언어 실력에 맞는 사실적인 교재를 선정하는 것이 좋으나 대부분의 경우에 사실적인 내용에 학습자의 언어 실력까지 고려한 교재를 찾기란 쉽지 않다. 따라서 혹자는 진위성이 담보된 교재가 반드시 학습자에게 좋은 것만은 아니라고 주장한다. 특히 낮은 언어 실력을 가진 학습자에게 맞는 진위성 있는 교재를 찾는 것은 더욱 어렵다. 결과적으로 교실 현장에서는 진위성이 있는 글을 학습자의 실력에 맞춰서 바꾸는 언어적 수정(**linguistic modification**)이 많이 사용된다. 말을 할 때 핵심어를 강조하거나, 쉬운 단어를 사용하거나 반복함으로써 학습자의 이해를 돕는 것은 흔히 볼 수 있는 언어적 수정이다. 또한 읽기 수업을 위한 교재의 텍스트를 학습자가 보다 잘 이해할 수 있게끔 수정한다. 이를 텍스트 수정(**text modification**)이라고 부른다. 읽기를 용이하게 하기 위해서 문장 단위의 수정이 이뤄질 때 단어와 문장 구조의 두 가지 면을 수정하게 된다. 이를 어휘 수정(**lexical modification**)과 구문 수정(**syntactic modification**)이라고 한다(Brewer, 2008).

특히 언어 실력이 낮은 학습자를 돕는 방법에는 단순화(**simplification**)와 상술(**elaboration**)이 있다. 단순화에는 단어를 단순화하는 단어 단순화(**lexical simplification**)와 문장의 구조를 쉽게 만드는 문장 단순화(**syntactic simplification**)가 있는데 많이 사용되는 쉬운 단어를 사용하고 주어, 동사, 목적어의 가장 쉬운 기본 구조의 문장을 활용함으로써 학습자가 문장을 명확하게 이해하도록 돕는다. 또한 글의 내용을 반복하고 길게 설명함으로써 학습자의 이해를 돕는 상술(**elaboration**)은 학습자의 독해를 향상시키는 것으로 알려져 있다(Brewer, 2008).

2. Read the conversation between two teachers and follow the directions. 【2 points】

> (*Two teachers are evaluating two textbooks, Textbook A and Textbook B, in order to select the one that their students are going to use next year. This is part of their conversation.*)

T1: So, why don't we start with the first criterion? I went with Textbook A.

T2: May I ask you why?

T1: I think that the illustrations and graphics in Textbook A portray people in the target culture more realistically.

T2: Yeah! Textbook A contains very realistic visuals that can provide our students with cultural information more accurately.

T1: Good! Then, what about the second criterion?

T2: Well, I think Textbook B is the better of the two. I couldn't give Textbook A a good score, because it appears to aim at explicit learning with many contrived examples of the language.

T1: Hmm... could you clarify your point a bit more?

T2: Well, I mean the texts and dialogues in Textbook A are oversimplified.

T1: I had the same impression, but don't you think that they may help our students by focusing their attention on the target features?

T2: You may be right, but I think that such texts might deprive them of the opportunities for acquisition provided by rich texts.

T1: Oh, I see. That's a pretty good point.

T2: So, in my opinion, Textbook B can provide more exposure to language as it is actually used in the real world outside the classroom.

T1: Yeah! From that point of view, Textbook B will be intrinsically more interesting and motivating to our students.

T2: I agree. Okay, then, I think we are ready to move on to the next evaluation criterion.

Note: T = teacher

Fill in the blank with the ONE most appropriate word.

> There are many criteria that can be used in textbook evaluation. The teachers, T1 and T2, are mainly focusing on, first, the criterion of reality of visuals and then, the other criterion of _____ . In the dialogue, the latter is specifically related to language use shown in the textbooks.

문제 분석

● 첫 번째 문단에서 두 교사가 교재를 평가하고 있는데 이는 교재를 선정하기 위한 것이라고 제시되어 있다. 따라서 이 문제는 교재 선정을 위한 사전 평가에 관한 문제임을 알 수 있다.

● 두 교사의 대화 내용을 보면 이미 교재를 선정하기 위한 기준이 준비되어 있다는 것을 알 수 있고 첫 번째 기준에 대한 대화 내용이 1) 사실적인 삽화와 같은 시각 자료와 2) 사실적인 언어를 접할 기회를 중심으로 구성되어 있다.

● 특히 A 교재의 단점으로 "oversimplification"이 언급되어 있고 B 교재의 장점으로 "more exposure to language as it is actually used in the real world"로 교재의 진위성에 대한 문제임을 암시하고 있다.

예시 답안

authenticity

2. Read the passages and follow the directions. 【4 points】

──────────── <A> ────────────

Materials can be adapted for many reasons, for example, to localize, to modernize, or to personalize. We can localize materials to make them more applicable to our local context. We can modernize materials when they are outdated in terms of English usage or content. We can also personalize materials by making them more relevant to learner needs and interests. Materials adaptation can be carried out by using a number of different techniques, as shown in the figure.

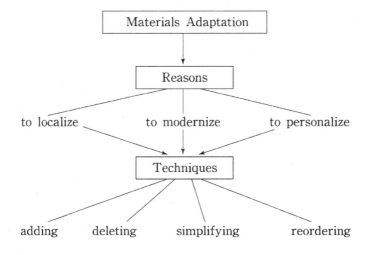

──────────── <B> ────────────

Mr. Lee is teaching first-year middle school students whose proficiency levels are very low. After conducting a needs analysis, he has learned that the students find the writing sections of the textbook difficult and that they are interested in sports. While he is planning a writing lesson for next week, he realizes that there is only one pre-writing activity in Unit 1 of the textbook. He thinks that one activity is not enough for his students to develop ideas for writing. Thus, he is going to increase the number of the pre-writing activities from one to three. In addition, thinking that the reading passage on sports in Unit 3 will better suit learner interests than the reading text in Unit 1, he decides to switch the two reading texts. He believes that this change will help his students become better prepared for writing and more engaged in English language learning.

Referring to the terms in <A>, explain the reason why Mr. Lee wants to adapt the materials, and identify which techniques he is going to use for materials adaptation. Do NOT copy more than FOUR consecutive words from the passage

문제 분석 III○

● 문단 <A>에서 주제가 교재의 각색(**textbook adaptation**)으로 나와 있으며 그 세 가지 이유가 지역화(**localization**), 현대화(**modernization**), 그리고 개인화(**personalization**)로 제시되어 있다. 또한 이 세 가지 이유를 위한 기술로써 첨가(**adding**). 제거(**deleting**), 단순화(**simplifying**), 그리고 재배치(**reordering**)가 언급되어 있다.

● 문단 <B>에서 교사가 영어 실력이 낮은 학생들을 가르치며 요구 분석(**needs analysis**)을 한 결과 쓰기 활동을 어려워하고 스포츠에 관심이 있음을 알게 되었다고 나와 있다. 교사는 쓰기 활동을 늘리기로 했고, 스포츠에 관한 내용이 들어 있는 과를 앞으로 옮기기로 했다고 한다.

● 문제에서 문단 <A>에 제시되어 있는 용어를 사용해서 왜 교사가 교재를 각색하고자 하는 이유와 사용하고자 하는 기술을 설명하라고 요구하고 있다.

예시 답안

Mr. Lee wants to personalize the materials to meet students' needs and interests. Since his students have low English proficiency, he is going to add more writing activities. Also, he will reorder reading passages to satisfy students' interests. Thus, the techniques that will be used are "adding" and "reordering".

2. Read Mr. Han's materials for his level-differentiated classes, and follow the directions. 【2 points】

The original text is for 2nd year high school students.

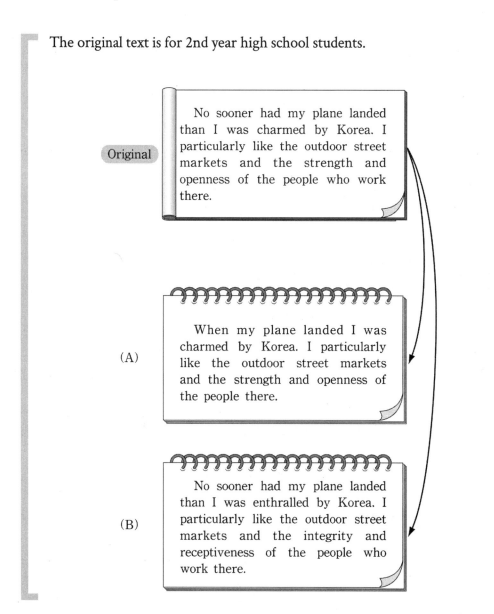

Original

No sooner had my plane landed than I was charmed by Korea. I particularly like the outdoor street markets and the strength and openness of the people who work there.

(A)

When my plane landed I was charmed by Korea. I particularly like the outdoor street markets and the strength and openness of the people there.

(B)

No sooner had my plane landed than I was enthralled by Korea. I particularly like the outdoor street markets and the integrity and receptiveness of the people who work there.

Complete the comments by filling in each blank with ONE word. Write your answers in the correct order.

> The original text has been adapted to suit the students' English proficiency levels. (A) shows how input is simplified through _____①_____ modification to make the original text easier for the lower level students. (B) shows how input is adapted through _____②_____ modification to make the original text more challenging for the upper level students.

문제 분석 📊🔍

- 첫 번째 문단에서 수준별 수업을 위해 교재 내용이 수정된 것을 볼 수 있다.

- 두 번째 문단에서 교재 내용의 난이도를 쉽게 하기 위해서 수정한 방법 ① 과 난이도를 높게 하기 위해서는 수정한 방법 ②에 관해서 설명하고 있다.

- 첫 번째 문단의 (A)와 (B)를 분석해 보면 (A)는 문법의 수정이, 그리고 (B)는 단어의 수정이 일어났음을 알 수 있다.

예시 답안 ✏️

① syntactic
② lexical

3. Read Mr. Park's comments in <A> and examine the results of a textbook evaluation by a review committee in <B>. Then follow the directions. 【3 points】

<A>

Mr. Park: The goal of my class is to help students use the language to communicate and perform authentic tasks. So I want to spend most of my class time letting students rehearse tasks they need to perform outside the classroom. I also want my students to have a lot of opportunities to work together so that they can use their linguistic knowledge to convey meaning rather than just practice form.

<B>

Evaluation Criteria	Textbook A			Textbook B			Textbook C		
	1	2	3	1	2	3	1	2	3
pattern drill activities		✓		✓					✓
role-play based on real-life situations		✓				✓		✓	
pronunciation tips			✓	✓					✓
regular grammar review			✓	✓			✓		
group projects	✓					✓		✓	

* 1=poor, 2=average, 3=good

Considering the information in <A> and <B>, identify the textbook you would recommend for Mr. Park and provide TWO reasons for recommending it based on its characteristics.

● 문단 <A>에 교재 선정을 위한 수업의 목표가 의사소통을 위한 언어의 사용과 사실적인 활동을 하는 것으로 제시되어 있다. 교사가 원하는 활동은 교실 밖에서 언어를 사용할 수 있게 수업 시간에 실생활과 비슷한 활동을 연습하는 것이고 특히 그룹 활동을 선호하고 있다.

● 문단 <B>의 평가 기준표를 보면 "role-play based on real-life situations"와 "group projects"가 교사가 원하는 수업 활동과 목표에 근접하다는 것을 알 수 있다. 따라서 그 두 부분에서 높은 점수를 받은 교재를 추천하면 된다.

예시 답안 ✍️

Textbook B would be most suitable for Mr. Park's class. According to the results of a textbook evaluation, Textbook B received the highest mark for "role-play based on real-life situations" and "group projects". Since Mr. Park prefers his students to perform authentic tasks and group work, Textbook B meets the goal of Mr. Park's class.

교과 과정과 교안
(Curriculum and Lesson Plan)

4

Brown(2015)은 교과 과정(**curriculum**)과 프로그램(**program**)을 구별해서 정의한다. 그에 따르면 교과 과정이 하나의 프로그램이나 과목에 대한 목표, 교과 내용, 과정, 평가를 모두 포함한 교육 과정을 의미하고 프로그램은 학교나 학원에서 제공하는 수업이나 과목의 집합체를 의미하는데 보통 학위나 자격증을 따기 위한 과정에서 들어야 하는 수업이나 과목들 전체를 지칭한다. 예를 들어 고등학교에 재학 중이라면 고등학교 "프로그램"에 있는 것이고, 졸업하기 위해서 순서대로 정해진 여러 과목들을 들어야 하는데, 이것을 교과 과정이라고 하는 것이다. 만일 한 대학의 영어영문학과에 재학 중이라면 학부 과정(**undergraduate program**)에 있는 것이고, 영어영문학을 전공하고 있는 것이며, 영어영문학사를 취득하기 위해서는 정해진 교과 과정(**curriculum**)을 이수해야하는 것이다. 이 때 수강해야 하는 하나의 과목을 course 또는 class이라고 부르며 각 과목당 강의계획서(**syllabus**)가 존재한다. 이 강의 계획서를 바탕으로 매 수업 시간마다 정해진 교수 목표를 수행하기 위해 만들어진 것인 교안(**lesson plan**)인 것이다.

교과 과정(**curriculum**)과 강의 계획서(**syllabus**)는 다음과 같은 차이가 있다. 먼저 교과 과정에서 기획하는 데 중심이 되는 세 개의 과정은 계획, 수행, 그리고 평가이다. 이 세 개의 과정은 전체 교과 과정과 각 과목에 적용되며, 그 결과물로 강의 계획서, 수업 계획, 그리고 평가 도구가 나온다. 다만 교과 과정은 전체 프로그램에 다 적용이 되고 강의 계획서는 하나의 과목에만 적용이 된다는 차이점이 있다. 또한 강의 계획서는 계획에서 그치지만 교과 과정은 수행과 평가라는 과정을 다 포함한다는 특징이 있다(Celce-Murcia, et al., 2014).

교과목을 만들기 위해서 가장 먼저 해야 할 일은 상황 분석(**situation analysis**)으로써 교육 환경과 학생들의 요구 사항 등을 분석하는 것이다. 교육 환경, 학급의 특성, 교수자 특성, 수업 내용의 관할, 그리고 평가 요구 사항 등을 분석해 교과목 설계의 기본 틀을 마련한다. 일단 교과목의 기본 틀을 만들었으면 요구 분석(**needs analysis**)을 수행한다. 요구 분석을 통해 교과목의 목표를 설계하고 교과목 설계자와 학생들의 의견을 수렴한다. 이 때 요구는 객관적 요구(**objective needs**)와 주관적 요구(subjective needs)로 나눌 수 있는데, 객관적 요구는 시험 결과, 설문 조사 결과, 교사 보고서 등을 통해서 나온 데이터를 바탕으로 교육 행정가들에 의해 비교적 쉽게 측정되는 요구이다. 반면 주관적 요구는 학생들의 관점에서 본 요구 사항들로 실제 학생들이 필요로 하는 것과는 다를 수 있다 (Brown, 2015).

최근에 학습자가 중심이 되는 교수법이 주로 활용됨에 따라 Nunan의(1988) 학습자 중심 모델 (learner-centered model)이 많이 쓰이고 있다. 그의 모델은 결과물 중심 모델과 과정 중심 모델이 합쳐진 것으로써 여섯 개의 과정을 거치면서 지속적인 피드백과 평가가 시행된다. 먼저 요구 분석 (needs analysis)이 행해지고, 교수 목표가 설정되며(goal identification), 그 후 학습 목표가 정해진다(objective setting). 이렇게 정해진 교수 목표와 학습 목표에 따라 교재가 개발되며 (materials development), 학습 활동이 정해지고(learning activities), 학습의 형태와 환경이 결정된다(learning mode & environment). 마지막으로 학기 말에 과목에 대한 평가(assessment & evaluation)를 실시한다. 이러한 절차 속에서 교과목에 관련이 있는 다른 교육자와 학생들에게 피드백을 받고 평가를 하는 과정이 지속된다.

이러한 과정을 통해 결정된 교과목에는 교수 목표(goals)와 학습 목표(objectives)가 있다. 교수 목표는 전체 교육 과정에 조화를 이뤄야 하며 달성 가능하고 바람직한 것이어야 한다. 학습 목표는 교수 목표의 하위 개념으로써 교수 목표보다 구체적이다. 즉 학습 목표는 학생들이 성취해야 하는 특정 지식, 행동, 또는 기술을 구체적으로 설명한다. 이렇게 교과목의 교수 목표와 학습 목표에 따라 강의 계획서가 만들어지고 교재와 평가 체계가 구축되면 하나의 과목이 만들어지는 것이다(Brown, 2015).

한 과목의 강의 계획서(syllabus)는 그 과목에 대한 많은 정보를 제공한다. 강의 계획서는 과목의 교수 목표와 학습 목표, 학습 주제 그리고 평가 기준 등을 포함하기 때문이다. 특히 언어 과목의 강의 계획서는 수학이나 역사와 같은 다른 과목과는 다르게 여러 가지 종류가 있다. 먼저 문법 중심의 강의 계획서(grammatical, formal, 혹은 structural syllabus)는 문법 구조를 중심으로 구성되어 있다. 예를 들어, 동사, 의문문, 절 등이 주요 학습 주제가 된다. 그러나 문법 중심의 강의 계획서는 주로 문장 단위의 문법 지식을 쌓는데 중점을 두었기 때문에 많은 비판을 받았다. 학습자가 언어에 관한 지식을 습득할 뿐이지 그 언어를 사용하는 법을 배우지 못한다는 것이다. 두 번째로 개념과 기능 중심의 강의 계획서(notional-functional syllabus)가 있다. 의사소통을 목적으로 하는 언어의 기능과 의사소통의 주제가 되는 개념을 중심으로 구성되어 있으므로 최근의 의사소통 중심 교수법에 부합하는 강의 계획서이다. 특이 이 강의 계획서는 학습자의 요구를 파악하는 것이 중요하다. 세 번째로 과업 중심의 강의 계획서(task-based syllabus)는 과업이 중심이 된다. 과업을 완수하기 위해서 학습자는 본인의 언어 실력을 최대한으로 활용하게 된다. 네 번째로 기술을 바탕으로 한 접근법(**skills-based approaches**)은 말하기, 쓰기, 듣기, 읽기의 네 가지 기술을 바탕으로 강의를 계획한다. 강의 계획서는 상황을 중심으로 구성되어 있어서 학습자가 상황에 따라 적절한 기술과 전략을 사용할 수 있다. 이 이외에도 단어 중심의 강의 계획서(**lexical syllabus**), 장르 중심의 강의 계획서(**genre or text-based syllabus**), 프로젝트 중심의 강의 계획서(**project-based language learning**), 내용 중심의 강의 계획서(**content-based instruction** 또는 **content and language integrated learning**), 과정 중심의 강의 계획서(**negotiated syllabus**) 등이 있다.

강의 계획서에 따라 각 주의 차시에 맞는 교안(**lesson plan**)을 짜게 되는데, 이 교안에도 역시 교과목의 목표에 따라 각 차시에 맞는 교수 목표(**goals**)와 학습 목표(**objectives**)가 있다. 특히 학습 목표는 학생들이 성취해야 하는 구체적인 목표를 명백하게 기술해야한다. 학습 목표는 최종 목표(**terminal objectives**)와 세부 목표(**enabling objectives**)로 나눌 수 있는데, 최종 목표는 교수자가 평가할 수 있는 최종적인 학습 결과물을 의미하고 세부 목표는 그 최종 목표에 도달하기 위한 중간 과정이라고 할 수 있다(Brown, 2015). 또한 대부분의 학습 목표는 학생들의 수업 활동을 통해서 성취할 수 있는 결과물을 중심으로 설계되어야 한다. 즉 각 활동마다 하나의 학습 목표가 있어야 하는 것이다. 목표가 설정이 되었으면 그 다음 단계로 수업 교재나 교구(**materials and equipment**)를 기술하고 수업의 과정(**procedures**)을 기술하게 되는데, 수업 과정은 단계별로 세부적으로 기술한다. 수업 과정에는 수업의 시작을 어떻게 할지, 어떤 활동들을 할 것이며, 마무리는 어떻게 할지가 포함된다. 이후 평가(**assessment**)가 들어가고 과제(**extra-class work**)를 주는 것으로 교안은 마무리가 된다(Brown, 2015; Celce-Murcia et al., 2014).

2. Read the passage in <A> and a teacher's note in <B>, and follow the directions. 【2 points】

───────── <A> ─────────

Curriculum design is a series of systematic efforts to develop a curriculum that satisfies the target learners as well as teachers. Researchers suggest that there are five main stages in the process of designing a curriculum.

```
┌──────────────────────────────┐
│          _____            │
└──────────────────────────────┘
                ⇓
┌──────────────────────────────┐
│      Goal Specifications      │
└──────────────────────────────┘
                ⇓
┌──────────────────────────────┐
│     Materials Development     │
└──────────────────────────────┘
                ⇓
┌──────────────────────────────┐
│  Language Teaching & Learning │
└──────────────────────────────┘
                ⇓
┌──────────────────────────────┐
│      Curriculum Evaluation    │
└──────────────────────────────┘
```

───────── <B> ─────────

Teacher's Note

I am planning to develop a new English course for winter session, so I wanted to establish the basis for developing the curriculum. The first step of this process requires me to systematically collect and analyze areas of necessity for my students in order to satisfy their language learning requirements. So, I created a survey which asked students questions about their English deficiencies and the difficulties they face in performing certain language tasks in their current classes. It also asked them about the methods they enjoy learning through as well as the types of English skills that they want to improve. For the second step of this process, I wanted to get more information about the students' preferred learning styles and interests, so I referred to my classroom observation notes to learn about them. I then asked my school's principal to show me the results of their placement tests to gain an understanding of their levels of linguistic proficiency and background experience. Furthermore, I interviewed students both in groups and individually to get more detailed information. In short, I conducted _____ by collecting all these data.

문제 분석

- 교육 과정 개발에 관한 문제이다. 교육 과정에 대한 개발 단계가 다섯 개로 문단 <A>에 제시되어 있다.

- 문단 <B>에 교육 과정 개발의 첫 번째 단계에 대한 설명이 나와 있고 마지막 줄에 이러한 데이터를 수집함으로써 무엇을 한 것인지 빈 칸을 채우게끔 되어 있다. 이 빈 칸은 문단 <A>의 첫 번째에 제시되어 있는 빈 칸과 같은 것이다.

- 교사가 수집한 데이터는 학습자가 필요로 하는 영역을 체계적으로 수집하고 분석하는 과정에서 실시한 설문조사 결과와 학습자의 학습 스타일을 알기 위해 관찰한 바와 배치 고사 결과, 학생들과의 면담을 포함한다. 이는 모두 학습자가 필요한 바를 파악하기 위한 것이다.

예시 답안

needs analysis

1. Examine the survey results in <A> and part of the interview with the teacher who taught Practical English II in <B>, and follow the directions. 【4 points】

<A>

A school administrator conducted a survey with 60 students from two classes of Ms. Lee's Practical English II in order to improve the course in the future.

Evaluation of Practical English II

Content	Number of respondents per category			
	1	2	3	4
(1) I feel I achieved my learning objectives as a result of taking this course.	4	9	25	22
(2) I feel more confident in my self-expression in English as a result of taking this course.	5	9	24	22
(3) I feel the supplementary material used in this course was helpful.	5	6	25	24
(4) I feel my speaking performance was assessed effectively based on the tests and assignments given.	29	22	8	1

Note: 1=strongly disagree, 2=disagree, 3=agree, 4=strongly agree

---

<B>

A: Your Practical English II was very satisfying for students. What do you think made it so successful?

T: Well, I thought it was necessary to make decisions about what would be taught and how it would be taught before designing a course, so I did a survey and interviews.

A: You mean you chose the teaching materials, contents, and activities based on what your students wanted to learn?

T: That's right. The results also provided me with a lot of information about what my students needed to learn or change, their learning styles, interests, proficiency levels, etc. Based on that information, I decided on the course objectives, contents, and activities.

A: You must have been very busy working on designing the course before it started. What about assessment?

T: Students just took one major test at the end of the semester. I regret that I evaluated only their learning product.

A: You mean just once over the semester?

T: Yes, I thought it was impossible to assess their speaking performance regularly by myself and I gave one major test to the students. So I was actually unable to gather information on the developmental process of their speaking abilities.

. . .

A: Okay. Thank you for your time.

Note: A = administrator, T = teacher

Describe ONE strong point with evidence of what the teacher did for the success of the Practical English II course. Then describe ONE weak point of what the teacher did in the course, and suggest ONE possible solution from the teacher's standpoint.

문제 분석 [ıllQ]

● 교과목의 평가에 관한 문제이다. 학기가 마무리된 후 과목에 대한 평가를 통해 더 발전적인 수업을 차후에 제공할 수 있다.

● 문단 <A>에서 교육 행정가가 한 설문조사 결과에 따르면 학습 목표 달성, 영어 말하기 실력 향상,

교재에 대한 만족도는 모두 높은 점수를 받았으나 말하기 평가와 과제는 낮은 점수를 받았다.

● 문단 <B>의 교사와 교육 행정가의 대화를 분석해 보면 학습자에 대한 요구 분석을 통해 교과목을 설계한 것이 높은 점수의 원인이었고, 말하기를 정기적으로 평가하는 것이 힘들어서 결과 중심의 평가를 했다는 것을 알 수 있다.

● 문제에서 장점과 단점을 증거를 들어 설명하고 교수자의 입장에서 단점을 극복할 수 있는 해결 방법을 제시하라고 했으므로 요구 분석을 장점의 증거로 제시하고 단점으로써 말하기 평가를 들고 정기적으로 평가를 실시할 수 있는 방법을 제시하면 된다.

예시 답안

The strong point is that the teacher designed the course based on the needs of students through surveys and interviews. The weak point of the course is that the teacher gave only one summative speaking test. To be able to assess students' ongoing process, portfolios, which includes audio/video-recording of oral performance, will be a possible solution.

1. Read the lesson procedure and write the TWO lesson objectives. Do NOT copy more than FIVE consecutive words from the passage. 【5 points】

The following is a sample lesson plan of culture-integrated language learning for 2nd year middle school students.

Lesson Procedure

(1) Students watch a video clip that shows an experiment, which is summarized below.

> The experiment shows that American mothers used twice as many object labels as Japanese mothers ("piggie," "doggie") and Japanese mothers engaged in twice as many social routines of teaching politeness norms (empathy and greetings). An American mother's pattern might go like this: "That's a car. See the car? You like it? It's got nice wheels." A Japanese mother might say: "Here! It's a vroom vroom. I give it to you. Now give this to me. Yes! Thank you." American children are learning that the world is mostly a place with objects, Japanese children that the world is mostly about relationships. Relationships usually involve a verb. Verbs are more important in Asian languages than in English. Asians tend to use an expression like "Drink more?" rather than "More tea?" when they perceive there is a need. Americans are noun-oriented, pointing objects out to their children, naming them, and telling them about their attributes. Nouns denote categories.

(2) Students share their own experiences about noun-oriented expressions as opposed to verb-oriented ones, and discuss different ways of thinking

for those expressions.

(3) Students do Activity 1 in order to learn a variety of noun-oriented English expressions.

<Activity 1> Fill in the blanks with appropriate words.

Verb-Oriented Expressions	Noun-Oriented Expressions
He works hard.	He is a hard worker.
My head aches.	I _____ .
He is very humorous.	He has a good _____ .
. . .	. . .

---

(4) Students discuss why noun-oriented expressions are more frequently used in English than verb-oriented ones.

(5) Students engage in the following activity to reinforce their awareness of the cultural difference between the West and the East.

Q: If you have a bad cold, which of the following wouldn't you say?

A: ① I've got a stuffy nose.

② I have a runny nose.

③ My nose is sick.

문제 분석

- 수업에 대한 설명이 문화 통합 언어 학습(culture-integrated language learning)이라고 나와 있으므로 언어와 문화 두 가지를 배우는 수업임을 알 수 있다.

- 두 개의 학습 목표를 찾는 문제인데. 학습 목표는 대부분 활동의 결과물을 반영하고 있으므로 두 개의 활동을 찾으면 <Activity 1>과 (5)번의 활동이 이에 해당함을 알 수 있다.

● <Activity 1>은 동사를 중심으로 한 표현을 명사를 중심으로 한 표현으로 바꾸는 것으로써 언어적인 면을 연습하는 활동이다. (5)번의 활동은 서양과 동양의 문화적 차이에 대한 인식을 강화하기 위한 활동이라는 설명이 나와 있다. 비디오의 내용이 정리된 (1)번의 지문을 읽어보면 일본의 엄마들은 동사를 중심으로 한 표현을 주로 하는데 반해 미국의 엄마들은 명사를 중심으로 한 표현을 주로 한다고 명시되어 있다. 따라서 문화적 차이에 따라 명사를 중심으로 한 표현과 동사를 중심으로 한 표현을 사용함을 인지하고 사용하지 않아야 할 표현으로 동사를 중심으로 한 표현을 선택할 수 있게 하는 활동이다.

❏ 내용 중심 교수법(content-based instruction)

내용 중심 교수법(Content-based instruction: CBI)의 강의 계획서는 교과목과 언어 학습 두 가지를 중심으로 만들어진다. 중심을 어디에 두느냐에 따라 접근법이 다양해 질 수 있는데, 교과목 즉 내용에 중심을 두게 되면 목표 언어는 내용을 배우는 수단이 되고, 언어에 둔다면 내용은 언어를 학습할 수 있는 수단이 된다(Celce-Murcia et al., 2014). 위의 문제에 나와 있는 교안은 언어에 중심을 두고 있는 내용 중심 교수법의 교안이며 내용 중심 교수법의 교안은 언어적 목표와 내용적 목표 두 가지를 모두 포함해야 한다.

❏ 명사 중심, 혹은 동사 중심의 표현

영어와 일본어를 비교해 보면 영어는 명사 중심이고 일본어는 동사 중심임을 알 수 있다. 특히 어린아이가 영어를 모국어로 배울 때 명사의 수가 압도적으로 많으며 한국어나 중국어를 모국어로 하는 아이들은 그렇지 않다. 영어나 유럽의 언어들은 주어로 사용되는 명사가 목적어와 동사를 통제하는 반면 일본어는 동사의 성격에 따라 전체 문장이 통제된다. 따라서 영어는 사람을 더 중심으로 보는 반면 일본어는 상황을 더 중심으로 본다. 영어 교육에 있어서도 일본어와 영어 사이의 구조적 차이를 학습자가 인지하게 하고 영어를 사용하고자 할 때 일본어에서는 숨겨진 목적어를 찾게 함으로써 좋은 성과를 거둘 수 있다(Ishikawa, 2015).

예시 답안

First, students will be able to change the verb-oriented expressions to the noun-oriented ones. Second, students will be able to notice the cultural difference from various expressions and identify the verb-oriented expression.

9. Read the lesson procedure and complete the objectives by filling in each blank with TWO words. Write your answers in the correct order. 【2 points】

Students: 2nd year middle school students

Approximate time: 45 minutes

Lesson objectives:

Students will be able:

• to describe a daily routine using correct verb forms and ___①___ from a sample paragraph

• to revise writing through___②___ on first drafts

Lesson Procedure

1. The teacher asks students what they do when they get home every day.

2. Students take turns asking and answering questions about their daily routine in pairs. Students take notes on each other's answers.

3. The teacher provides a sample paragraph, and students choose the correct expressions.

> (As soon as/Since) Taebin finishes school, he goes to taekwondo. When he arrives, he puts on his workout clothes, and (first/then) he practices. (After/Before) he finishes, he rides his bike home. (As soon as/After that), he takes a shower. (After/Next), he eats his dinner. (Before/When) he finishes dinner, he does his homework. (Before/While) he goes to bed, he brushes his teeth.

4. Students use their notes to write a short paragraph about their partner's daily routine.

5. Students exchange writings and underline their partner's mistakes using the checklist.
   - Are the present forms of verbs used correctly?
   - Are the events described in time order?
   - Is time order indicated using the expressions focused upon in the sample paragraph?
   - Is punctuation used correctly?

6. Students rewrite their paragraph based on Step 5.

문제 분석

- 학습 목표를 기술하는 문제이다. 두 개의 학습 목표가 일상생활 묘사하기(**to describe a daily routine**)와 글을 교정하는 것(**to revise writing**)으로 나와 있으므로 그에 해당하는 활동을 먼저 찾는다.

- 3번의 활동이 일상생활을 묘사하는 것이고 5번의 활동이 교정을 하는 것이므로 각 활동을 자세하게 분석하면 3번은 시간과 순서를 나타내는 적절한 접속사와 접속 부사를 찾는 것이고, 5번은 점검표를 사용해 상대방의 실수에 밑줄을 쳐주는 것임을 알 수 있다.

- 따라서 빈 칸에 들어갈 말은 "time-order transitions"와 "peer editing"이 된다.

예시 답안

① time-order transitions
② peer editing

교실 수업
(Classroom Teaching)

교실 수업에 관련된 문제는 다양하고 광범위한 범위에서 출제가 된다. 교실 수업에서 활용하는 활동, 교수자와 학생들과의 상호 작용 혹은 학생들 간의 상호 작용, 교수자의 역할을 포함한 교실 수업 관리 등 실질적인 교실 수업에서 마주할 수 있는 모든 분야가 다 포함된다고 할 수 있다. 사실 수업 설계부터 평가까지 영어 교수법의 모든 분야가 포함되기에, 교실 수업에서 이론이 어떻게 구현되어야 하는지를 물어보는 문제라고 할 수 있다. 이에 따라 기출 문제 영역을 중심으로 교실 수업에서 쓰일 수 있는 활동과 교실 수업 관리를 포함한 전반적인 부분을 설명하도록 하겠다.

먼저 교실 수업에서 많이 쓰이는 용어를 정의하겠다. 접근법(approach)은 언어와 언어 학습의 이론을 의미하는데 이 이론이 어떠한 원칙을 바탕으로 언어 수업을 진행할지를 결정한다. 설계(design)라고 함은 언어 교수법의 목적, 강의 계획서와 같은 언어 수업 내용의 선택과 구성, 과업(tasks)과 활동(activities), 교수자와 학생의 역할, 교재 등을 선정하고 결정하는 과정을 의미한다. 그리고 수업 과정(procedure)은 언어 교수와 학습에 활용하는 활동과 연습 모두를 포함하는 것이다(Celce-Murcia et al., 2014).

과업(task)은 의사소통의 목적을 위해 만들어진 특정한 형태의 연속적인 기법(techniques)을 의미한다. 그리고 활동(activities)은 교수자의 지시를 받고 정해진 시간에 행해지는 학생들의 행동을 지칭한다. 활동에는 특정한 학습 목표가 있고 역할극이나, 게임 등이 그 예가 될 수 있다. 기법(techniques)은 교수자나 학생들이 수행하는 다양한 활동을 모두 포함하는 폭 넓은 개념이다. 연습이나 전략도 모두 기법(techniques)에 속하며 수업 시간에 특정한 목적의식을 가지고 교수자의 계획 하에 행해지는 모든 활동을 기법이라고 한다(Brown, 2015).

Brown(2015)은 기법(techniques)을 여러 가지로 분류했다. 먼저 제어된 기법(controlled technique)과 개방형(open-ended technique)으로 분류하자면 제어된 기법은 교수자가 기대하고 있는 반응을 유도해 내기 위해 제한된 대화 내에서 대부분 언어의 형태에 중점을 두어 행해진다. 반면 개방형 기법은 학생들이 의미에 중점을 두고 자연 발생적인 대화를 하는 것이다. 이를 교실 활동에 응용해 본다면, 교수자가 오늘 학습할 내용을 제시하고 설명한 후에 학생들은 제어된 활동(**controlled practice**)을 통해서 그 부분을 연습을 하게 된다. 이때 오늘 새로 학습한 부분을 제외한 나머지 부분, 예를 들어 문법이나 단어는 이미 학습자가 알고 있는 부분으로써 주의를 기울일 필요가 없는 부분이어야 한다. 이는 학습자가 오늘 새로 학습한 형태에 집중할 수 있게 하기 위함이다. 이렇게 제어된 활동을 통해서 충분히 연습을 한 후에 의사소통 활동(**communicative practice**)으로 넘어가게 되는데, 이 의사소통 활동은 실제 일상생활에서 마주할 수 있는 상황과 최대한 비슷하게 만들어져야 한다.

또한 그는 기계적인 기법(**mechanical technique**), 의미적인 기법(**meaningful technique**), 그리고 의사소통적인 기법(**communicative technique**)으로 구분하기도 했다. 기계적 기법에 속하는 활동인 훈련(**drill**)은 보통 기계적인 훈련(**mechanical drill**)을 의미한다. 단순 반복적으로 들은 것을 그대로 따라 하기도 하고 빈 칸을 채우기도 한다. 의미적인 기법은 단순하게 반복한다는 점은 같지만 의미가 있는 상황이나 내용을 생각하며 훈련하는 것이다. 다음은 의미적 훈련(**meaningful drill**)의 예이다.

> T: The woman is outside, [pointing out the window at a woman] Where is she, Hiro?
>
> SI: The woman is outside.
>
> T: Right, she's outside. Keiko, where is she?
>
> S2: She's outside.
>
> T: Good, Keiko, she's outside. Now, class, we are inside. Hiroko, where are we?
>
> S3: We are inside.
>
> (Brown, 2015, p. 223)

위의 예를 보면 "outside"와 "inside"를 반복적으로 연습하고 있지만 내용을 담고 있는 문장 안에서 사용함으로써 학습자의 이해를 돕고 실생활에서 사용되는 상황과 비슷하게 만들고 있다.

의사소통적 기법은 하나의 목표를 가지고 정해진 대화의 형식 없이 반복하는 것이다. 다음은 과거 시제를 연습하기 위한 의사소통적 기법의 예이다.

> T: Good morning, class. Last weekend I went to a restaurant and I ate salmon. Juan, what did you do last weekend?
>
> Juan: I went to park and I play soccer.
>
> T: Juan, you play soccer or you played soccer?

Juan: Oh . . . eh . . . I played soccer.

T: Good! Ying, did you go to the park last weekend?

Ying: No.

T: What did you do?

Ying: I went to a movie.

T: Great, and what did you do, Fay?

(Brown, 2015, p. 224)

위의 예를 보면 의미 있는 기법과는 다르게 정해진 문장 구조를 따르는 것이 아니라 대화를 하면서 다만 과거 시제의 습득과 연습에 집중하고 있다.

이렇듯 단순한 훈련(drill)도 의미 있는 상황에서 의사소통을 중심으로 연습하게 된 것은 상호작용이 중시되는 교실 수업과도 밀접한 관련이 있다. 교수자의 역할도 교실 수업의 분위기에 따라서 달라지는데 통제관(controller), 감독관(director), 관리자(manager), 촉진자(facilitator), 그리고 자원(resource)이 있다(Brown, 2015). 통제관으로서의 교수자는 교실 수업 전반을 미리 계획하고 통제한다. 따라서 상호작용이 중심이 되는 수업이 불가능한 것은 아니지만 힘들 수 있다. 감독관으로서의 교수자는 수업 과정이 제대로 진행되도록 감독하며 학생들이 언어활동을 하도록 돕는다. 관리자로서의 교수자는 수업 계획을 세우지만 학생들이 정해진 교실 수업의 목표 안에서 자유롭게 의사소통을 하도록 허용한다. 그리고 촉진자로서의 교수자는 학습자가 스스로 학습을 할 수 있게 돕는 역할을 한다. 마지막으로서 자원으로서의 교수자는 거꾸로 학습법(flipped learning)에서 쉽게 볼 수 있는 역할로 학생들이 도움을 요청할 때를 제외하고는 학습자가 스스로 학습하는데 개입하지 않는다. 즉, 교수자로서의 역할이 가장 작다고 할 수 있다.

교실 수업에서 상호작용이 중요하다는 것은 대부분의 교실 활동이 교수자와 학생 혹은 학생과 학생 사이의 의사소통 활동 중심으로 이루어진다는 의미이다. 따라서 짝 활동(pair work)과 모둠 활동(group work)이 교실 활동의 주가 된다. 교수자와 학생 사이의 상호작용은 IRE와 IRF로 구별할 수 있다(Celce-Murcia et al., 2014). IRE는 "Initiation → Response → Evaluation"의 줄임말로써 교수자가 질문을 던지고(initiation), 학생이 그에 대한 답을 하면(response) 학생이 학습 내용을 잘 이해했는지는 평가하는 것이다(evaluation). 이때 교수자가 사용하는 질문은 대부분의 경우 전시 질문(display questions)으로써 이미 답이 정해져 있는 것이다. 학습자가 개념을 이해했는지를 물어 보는 질문이므로 개념 질문(concept questions)라고도 한다. IRF는 "Initiation ➔ Response ➔ Feedback"의 줄임말로써 교수자가 질문을 하고(initiation) 학생이 이에 대한 답을 했을 때(response) 그에 관한 피드백을 주는 것이다(feedback). 교수자의 질문에는 정답이 있는 것이 아니고 학습자가 가급적 발화를 많이 하도록 유도하는 목적이 있기 때문에 관련 질문(referential question)을 주로 사용한다. 관련 질문이란 정답이 없는 질문을 의미한다. 또한 교수자의 피드백은 주로 학습자 발화의 오류를 수정하기 위해서 사용된다.

학생들 간의 상호작용은 짝 활동과 모둠 활동으로 이뤄진다. 짝 활동은 그 자체로도 많이 활용되고 때로는 모둠 활동을 위한 단계로써 활용되기도 한다. 짝 활동은 모둠 활동 보다 편리한데, 이는 주로 짧은 시간 내에 이뤄지고 교수자 입장에서 준비할 필요가 적고 학생들 입장에서도 움직일 필요가 없기 때문이다. 그러나 짝 활동의 가장 커다란 장점은 누구나 예외 없이 의사소통 활동에 참여하게 된다는 데 있다. 반면 모둠 활동은 짝 활동 보다는 많은 시간과 준비 과정이 필요하다. 모둠 활동은 학생들이 모두 참여할 수 있지만 몇몇 학생들에 의해 주도될 수 있다는 단점이 존재한다(Celce-Murcia, et al., 2014). 따라서 성공적인 모둠 활동을 위해서 교수자의 준비가 많이 필요한데 다음과 같은 기술들이 조직적인 모둠 활동에 큰 도움을 줄 수 있다 (Brown, 2015).

1) 게임
2) 역할극(role-play)
3) 모의실험(simulations): 역할극과 기본적인 개념은 같지만 다른 점은 보통 더 많은 학생들이 더 복잡한 구조에 참여한다는 데 있다. 예) 무인도에 갇힌 상황 등
4) 드라마: 역할극보다 더 정형화된 형태이다.
5) 프로젝트
6) 면담
7) 브레인스톰(brainstorming)
8) 정보 격차(information gap): 정보 격차(information gap)는 매우 다양하고 광범위한 활동을 포함하고 있다. 부족한 정보를 채우는 활동은 모두 정보 격차 활동이라고 할 수 있다.
9) 직쏘(jigsaw): 정보 격차 활동의 한 형태로써 그룹의 멤버가 각자 일정 부분의 정보를 가지고 있으면 그것을 모아서 전체 정보를 완성하는 것이다. 퍼즐 맞추기와 같다.
10) 문제 해결(problem solving): 하나의 문제를 각 그룹이 해결하는 것이다.
11) 의사 결정(decision making): 문제 해결 활동의 일부분 혹은 그와 연결할 수 있는 활동으로써 여러 해결 방법 중 하나를 결정하는 것이다.

12) 의견 교환(opinion exchange): 논란의 여지가 있는 주제를 가지고 중급 이상의 학생들이 자신의 의견을 교환하며 토론하는 것이다.

이러한 짝 활동과 모둠 활동은 많은 수의 학생들을 가르칠 때도 유용하게 사용될 수 있다. 대부분의 중등 영어 교실은 수십 명의 학생들로 구성되어 있다. 이렇게 많은 수의 학생들을 가르칠 때는 학생들의 영어 실력도 다르고 개개인의 학생들에게 피드백을 주기가 힘들기 때문에 학습자 중심의 수업이 아닌 교수자 중심의 수업, 즉 강의 중심의 수업으로 진행되기 쉽다. 그러나 조금만 주의를 기울이면 의사소통 중심의 교실 활동을 이어나갈 수 있다. 다음은 의사소통 중심의 교실활동에 유용한 조언이다.

1) 학생들의 이름을 외우고 사용함으로써 각각의 학생들이 모두 소중하다는 것을 느끼게 한다.
2) 가능한 많이 상호작용이 가능한 활동을 한다.
3) 짝 활동과 모둠 활동을 활용해서 학생들이 영어를 가급적 많이 사용할 수 있도록 한다.
4) 오디오 자료나 비디오 자료 등을 활용해서 많은 듣기 활동을 할 수 있도록 한다.
5) 학우들의 교정(peer-editing), 피드백, 평가를 이용해서 가능할 때 마다 쓰기 활동을 한다.
6) 학생들에게 다양한 과제를 내준다.
7) 모든 학생들의 쓰기 과제를 한 번에 걷지 않는다.
8) 작은 "학습 센터"를 교실에 만들어서 학생들이 개별적인 학습을 할 수 있도록 한다.
9) 비공식적인 대화 모임이나 스터디 모임을 만든다.

(Brown, 2015, p. 297)

이렇듯 많은 수의 학생들을 가르칠 때도 최대한 개별화해서 영어 수업의 효과를 증진시킬 수 있다. 그 외에도 학생들의 영어 수준 편차가 심한 경우도 가르치는데 어려움을 겪을 수 있다. 영어 수준이 다른 학생들을 가르칠 때는 다음과 같은 방법을 따르면 도움이 된다.

1) 학생들의 영어 수준을 과하게 일반화하는 오류를 범하지 않는다. 학생들이 보여주는 영어 실력이 실제 영어 수준을 반영하는지, 아니면 다른 이유가 있는지 살펴본다.
2) 수업 활동을 학생들 개개인에게 최대한 맞춘다. 학생들 개개인이 필요로 하는 부분이 무엇인지 파악해서 같은 수업 활동이라도 변형을 준다.
3) 학생들이 선택할 수 있게 한다. 수업 활동을 학생들이 선택하게 하면 더 좋은 효과를 볼 수 있다.

4) 기술적 도움을 활용한다. 인터넷이나 다른 기술적 도움을 활용해 다양한 자극을 줄 수 있도록 한다.

5) 중간 단계의 학생들에게 맞춰서 수업을 진행한다.

6) 모둠 활동을 다양하게 준비한다.

(Brown, 2015, p. 299)

교실 수업 관리와 더불어 한 가지 짚고 넘어가야 할 부분은 수업 참관(class observation)이다. 수업 참관은 선임 교사가 할 수도 있고, 다른 동료 교사가 할 수도 있지만 참관 기준표만 잘 만든다면 스스로 할 수도 있다. 교실 현장을 바탕으로 한 연구가 많이 실시됨에 따라 타인의 수업 참관에 부담을 갖는 교사들의 수도 줄어들고 있다(Brown, 2015). 사실 수업 참관은 새로운 아이디어나 기술을 습득하는데 있어 도움이 되는 수단이 될 수 있다. 보통 수업의 준비 단계, 교육의 방법과 내용, 교사와 학생간의 상호작용 등으로 분류해서 참관 기준표를 만들고 이를 바탕으로 교실 수업을 객관화해서 볼 수 있기 때문이다.

8. Read the passage in <A> and the two teachers' reflections in <B>, and follow the directions. 【10 points】

─────────── <A> ───────────

Mr. Kim and Ms. Jo, English teachers, attended a workshop for language teachers where they both gained a lot of useful information to promote student learning. Below is part of the information from the workshop.

Teachers need to...
(1) keep in mind that their course goals and/or procedures can be modified.
(2) offer students a variety of learning strategies to develop learner autonomy.
(3) involve students in self-/peer-evaluation instead of evaluating them alone.
(4) assess students frequently throughout the semester.

─────────── <B> ───────────

(Below are the two teachers' reflections after the workshop.)

Mr. Kim's reflection

To develop English writing abilities, my students engaged in writing activities. I simply assumed that paragraph writing would be enough for my students. However, I realized that I should change the initial course goal after assessing my students' first classroom writings. Their writing abilities were well above my expectations so I changed the goal set earlier and included essays. Since I believe that one-shot assessment at the end of the course is not effective for enhancing student learning, I carried out assessment periodically over the whole course period. I also believe assessment should be objective and that students' self-assessments are rather subjective in some ways. So, I did all the periodic assessments by myself, not asking students to evaluate their own work.

Ms. Jo's reflection

In my class, students were expected to develop debating skills in English. I organized my lesson in this way: brief mini-lectures, short video presentations to provide content for debating practice, followed by small group debating practice. I taught a range of learning strategies so that my students could become independent language learners utilizing those strategies whenever needed. For improving students' oral skills, I thought that arranging assessments multiple times, not just once, would be better. So I carried out assessments every two weeks during my instructional period. Based on the results of the assessments, I noticed that strictly following the lesson procedure was rather challenging to my students. However, I kept the same procedure over the course period since I believe maintaining consistency is crucial in order not to confuse students.

Write TWO paragraphs based on <A> and <B>. In the first paragraph, identify TWO elements from <A> that Mr. Kim employed in his course and ONE element that he did not employ, and provide evidence from <B> for each identified one. In the second paragraph, identify TWO elements from <A> that Ms. Jo employed in her course and ONE element that she did not employ, and provide evidence from <B> for each identified one.

● 사회 문화적 관점과 구성주의 학습 이론의 영향을 받아서 영어 교수법도 미리 정해 놓은 바에 따라, 혹은 교수자의 특성에 맞춰서 진행되는 것이 아니라 학습자 개개인에 맞춰서, 그리고 상황에 따라 융통성 있게 적용되고 있다. 문단 <A>에서 제시된 정보는 이러한 경향을 잘 반영하고 있다. (1) 과목의 목표나 과정은 수정될 수 있다. (2) 학습자 자율성을 발달시키기 위해서 학습 전략을 제시해야 한다. (3) 교사가 모든 평가를 혼자 하는 것이 아니라 학습자 스스로가 또는 학우들이 평가할 수 있도록 한다. 이는 교사가 교실에서 가진 권위와 권력을 학생들과 나누는 좋은 방법이 될 뿐만 아니라 학습자가 자기 주도성을 갖게 함으로써 학습 동기를 높이고 능동적인 학습자로써 성취감을 높일 수 있게 한다. (4) 평가는 자주, 다양한 방법으로 실시된다. 여러 번에 걸친 평가가 객관적인 결과를 도출할 수 있기 때문이다.

● 문단 <B>에서 김 선생님은 쓰기 과목을 가르칠 때 첫 평가 후 학습 목표를 수정한다. 또한 한 번의 평가는 효율적이지 않다고 생각했기 때문에 학기 중에 주기적으로 평가를 실시한다. 그러나 학생들이 스스로 평가하는 것은 주관적 요소가 강하다고 믿었기에 평가는 스스로 한다. 이 때 채점 기준표(rubric)를 사용한다면 객관적인 판단이 가능하다. 그러나 이는 문단 <A>에서 제시된 (3)의 방법과 일치하지 않는다. 조 선생님은 말하기 수업에서 학생들에게 학습 전략을 가르쳐 준다. 또한 평가를 2주에 한 번씩 실시한다. 그러나 평가의 결과가 학생들이 어려움을 겪고 있다는 것을 반영하고 있음에도 불구하고 수업 방식을 변경하지는 않는다. 이는 문단 <A>의 (1)의 조언을 반영하지 않은 것이다.

● 문제에서 각 선생님이 문단 <A>에서 제시된 정보 중 따른 것과 그렇지 않은 것을 제시하고 문단 <B>에서 증거를 제시하라고 나와 있으므로 각각의 문단에 선생님들이 따른 두 개의 정보와 따르지 않은 하나의 정보를 쓰면 된다.

Mr. Kim followed the first and the fourth information from the workshop, which are "modifying the course goal" and "assessing students frequently". However, he did not follow the third information, "involving students in self-/peer-evaluation". First, Mr. Kim modified the initial goal based on the students' writing proficiency. Second, Mr. Kim carried out assessment throughout the semester. It shows that he followed the first and the fourth information in <A>. However, he believed that students' self-assessments are subjective, so he did all the assessments. It indicates that he did not employ the third element in <A>.

Ms. Jo followed the second and fourth information from the workshop, which are "offering students a variety of learning strategies" and "assessing students frequently" However, she did not follow the first information, "modifying the course goals and/or procedures". First, Ms. Jo taught various learning strategies to develop students' independence. Second, she performed the assessments multiple times. They correspond to the second and the fourth element in <A>. However, she did not employ the first element. She stated that maintaining consistency was essential, so she kept the same procedure throughout the semester in spite that students found it challenging.

8. Read the passage in <A> and the teacher talk in <B>, and follow the directions.
【10 points】

──────────── <A> ────────────

(Below are notes that Ms. Shin, a new teacher, took of her senior teacher's advice on how to make her class communicatively oriented.)

Senior teacher's suggestions

- Objective: Get class centered on language functions rather than grammatical structures.
- Error targeted: Focus only on global errors impeding communication of meaning.
- Strategy: Encourage the use of communication strategies.
- Feedback: Provide correction implicitly.

──────────── <B> ────────────

(Below is Ms. Shin's talk at the beginning and closure of her single-activity class.)

Today, you are going to practice how to make requests using the question forms you learned from the last class. To do this, you will be doing an activity in pairs where you need to fill in a book order form by asking your partner for the necessary information. While doing this, you will get a chance to use the question forms to make requests. If you can't come up with the exact words to express the meaning you intend during the activity, you can try using similar words you know or even gestures, instead. Now, I will hand out the copies of the order form. Then, you can begin the activity with the student next to you. You'll work in pairs. OK, here are your copies.

$$\vdots$$

All right, now it's time to wrap up. I think you all did a great job on the form-filling activity exactly as I told you when the class started. But there is one and only one language element I want to briefly point out today. I noticed some of you missed 's' in some verbs like "He come" while talking. It should be "comes" not "come" though meaning is still clear without 's.' Apart from this, you seem to be fairly familiar with making requests now. Next time, we will focus on how to ask for permission.

Write TWO paragraphs based on <A> and <B>. In the first paragraph, identify TWO suggestions from <A> that Ms. Shin's class conforms to and provide evidence for each identified suggestion from <B>. In the second paragraph, identify TWO suggestions from <A> that Ms. Shin's class does not conform to and explain how with evidence from <B>.

문제 분석 ᴸᴸQ

- 문단 <A>에 제시된 조언은 다음과 같다. 1) 수업 목표를 문법 구조가 아닌 언어의 기능에 맞춘다, 2) 의사소통에 저해되는 전반적인 오류(global errors)에 집중한다, 3) 의사소통 전략의 사용을 장려한다, 그리고 4) 암시적인 수정을 제공한다.

- 문단 <B>에서 신 선생님은 수업 목표를 "요청하기" 그리고 "허락 구하기"로 정했음을 알 수 있다. 따라서 기능을 중심으로 한 수업 목표가 설정되었음을 알 수 있다. 또한 단어가 생각나지 않는다면 비슷한 단어나 몸짓을 사용하라고 조언했으므로 의사소통 전략의 사용을 장려한 것이다. 그러나 오류의 수정에 있어서는 지엽적 오류를 명시적으로 수정했음을 알 수 있다.

❑ 전반적 오류(global errors) 대 지엽적 오류(local errors)

학습자 오류를 구분하는 여러 가지 구별 방법 중 의사소통을 기준으로 구분하면 전반적 오류와 지엽적 오류로 나눌 수 있다. 전반적 오류는 의사소통에 문제를 야기해서 이해가 안 되는 경우를 의미하고 지엽적 오류는 의사소통은 가능하지만 부분적으로 오류가 있는 경우를 의미한다. 오류 수정에 있어서 전반적 오류는 수정을 하는 것을 원칙으로 하고 지엽적 오류는 수정을 하지 않거나 학습 목표와 관련이 있는 경우에 한해서 수정하는 것을 원칙으로 한다.

예시 답안

Ms. Shin conforms to two suggestions from her senior teacher's advice. First, the objectives of her class are based on language functions. In <B>, she states that students will practice how to make requests and the focus of next class is asking for permission. Thus, her class has concentrated on language functions. Second, she encourages her students to use communication strategies. She tells her students to use similar words or gestures when they can't come up with the exact words.

However, she fails to follow the other two suggestions, "focusing on global errors" and "providing implicit feedback". First, she focuses on a local error, which does not interfere with communication. She states not to miss "-s" at the end of a verb after the third person singular subject. Also she provides explicit feedback rather than implicit feedback by pointing out what was incorrect and how to correct it.

8. Read the two lesson procedures for teaching comparatives in <A> and <B>, and follow the directions. 【10 points】

──────────────── <A> ────────────────

Class A

Lesson objectives: Ss will be able to discuss and present their travel experiences using comparatives.

1. T tells a story about travel experiences.

> *Let me tell you about two trips I took, one to Singapore and the other to Bangkok. I really enjoyed my trip to Bangkok. It was more interesting than my trip to Singapore. Singapore was a little more boring than Bangkok. Although Singapore was cleaner and nicer, I thought Bangkok was a more fun city to travel in.*

2. T articulates the lesson objectives and asks Ss to form groups of six.

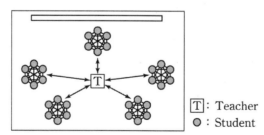

⬚: Teacher
●: Student

3. Ss begin a consensus building activity. During this activity, Ss compare locations according to a list of given adjectives (e.g., safe, beautiful, historic) on a worksheet. (T helps Ss as needed.)

	Your chosen place	Your group's agreed-upon place
safe	*Busan*	*Daegu*
beautiful	*Jeju*	*Jeju*
historic		
...		
_____ (*your idea*)		

Ss compare and discuss their ideas using comparatives.

(T gives feedback. Ss correct ill-formed utterances.)

     S: Busan is beautifuler.

     T: Beautifuler?

     S: Beautiful, more beautiful.

     T: More beautiful?

     S: Busan is more beautiful.

     T: More beautiful. OK.

4. In groups, Ss discuss where the better and worse places to visit are.

   (T walks around the classroom to see if all the Ss are participating in the discussion. If Ss are reluctant to join in group work, T encourages them to participate.)

5. Ss work on a summary together within their group. T allows Ss to choose a role within their group (e.g., leader, timekeeper, note-taker, reporter). (T monitors their work and helps out as needed.)

6. Each group presents their summary to the class.

   ....

Note: T = teacher, S = student

Class B

Lesson objectives:

(1) Ss will learn comparative forms;

(2) Ss will be able to make sentences using comparatives.

1. T explains the grammatical form of comparatives and writes the following chart on the board:

safe	safer
beautiful	more beautiful
cheap	cheaper
expensive	more expensive
...	...

(T stays at the front of the class the entire time, and Ss sit in orderly rows in silence.)

2. T instructs Ss to pay attention to the lesson.

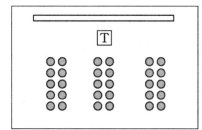

T : Teacher
○ : Student

3. T plays a recording line-by-line, and Ss listen and repeat.

(T instructs them to repeat in unison.)

Recording	Students
A: What is cheaper, taking trains or taking buses?	What is cheaper, taking trains or taking buses?
B: Taking buses is cheaper than taking trains.	Taking buses is cheaper than taking trains

| A: Which one is safer?
B: Taking trains is safer than taking buses. | Which one is safer?
Taking trains is safer than taking buses. |

4. T checks if Ss understand the comparative forms.

   (T asks questions, Ss answer individually, and T gives feedback.)

       T: What is the comparative form of 'safe'?

       S: Safer.

       T: Good. What about 'beautiful'?

       S: More beautiful.

       T: Very good. Then what about 'cheap'?

       S: More cheaper.

       T: No, not 'more cheaper'. It's 'cheaper'.

5. Ss do more choral repetition.

   (T plays the recording again, pausing it after key phrases, and Ss repeat them immediately.)

6. T asks Ss to repeat key phrases individually.

   (T corrects Ss' errors explicitly.)

   ....

Note: T = teacher, S = student

Write TWO paragraphs. In the first paragraph, identify and compare the roles of the teacher in each class, and explain them with evidence from the text. In the second paragraph, explain and compare how the teacher in each class manages the classroom with evidence from the text.

- Class A와 Class B가 정반대의 수업 양식을 보여주고 있다. 또한 문제에서 요구하는 바는 두 교사의 역할을 비교하고 교실 관리의 차이점을 비교하는 것이다.

- Class A에서는 학생 중심의 활동이 이뤄져서 학생들이 풍부한 상호작용을 하며 학습 목표를 성취해 감을 알 수 있고 Class B에서는 교사 중심의 수업이 이뤄지고 교실 활동은 단순 반복과 따라 하기가 주가 됨을 알 수 있다. 따라서 이에 해당하는 교사의 역할을 쓰고 예를 들면 된다.

- 교실 수업 관리는 먼저 수업 목표를 공유하는데 있어서 차이점을 보이고 있고, 좌석 배치가 두 번째 차이점, 마지막으로 상호작용이 다르다는 것을 알 수 있다. Class A의 교사는 학생들의 주의를 집중하고 스키마를 불러오는 활동 후 수업 목표를 제시한 반면 Class B의 교사는 바로 문법 설명을 한다. 좌석 배치는 Class A의 학생들이 여섯 명이 같이 모둠 활동을 할 수 있는 구조인 반면에 Class B에서는 교사를 바라보며 앉을 수 있게 되어 있다. 상호작용을 보면 Class A의 학생들이 협동과 토론을 주로 한 반면, Class B의 학생들은 교사와의 상호작용이 전부임을 알 수 있다.

While the teacher in Class A plays a role of a facilitator, the teacher in Class B plays a role of a controller. A teacher as a facilitator guides students to find their own ways to learn and helps them whenever they have difficulties. Thus, students are in charge of their own learning. However, a teacher as a controller is in charge of every procedure of a lesson. The teacher in Class A conforms to the role of facilitator in that s/he guides students perform the activity and gives feedback when needed. Thus, students in groups are in charge of learning how to use comparatives with the teacher's encouragement for active participation. The teacher in Class B fits into the role of a controller because s/he is the center of classroom activities. The teacher controls all procedures during the lesson, and there is not much room for students to have creative language use.

Also two teachers manage classes quite differently. In terms of lesson objectives, the teacher in Class A gathers students' attention by sharing his or her experience first and then states the objectives for the day. Yet, the teacher in Class B does not state the lesson objectives but jumps into the grammar lesson. Second, the seating arrangements are different. The configurations of Class A is for students to have interactive conversation, but the desks in Class B are lined up in columns facing the teacher. Third, the types of interaction is different. Students in Class A are interactive participants doing collaborative work and discussion. Yet, the students in Class B interact only with the teacher by doing choral repetition and drilling.

3. Read the activity procedure and identify the type of learning activity with ONE word. 【2 points】

	Activity Procedure
Step 1	• T places various information on a different job in each of the four corners in the classroom. (Each corner is labelled with a different letter, A, B, C, or D.) • T assigns individual Ss a letter (A, B, C, or D) in order to create four groups of four Ss, each of which is a base group composed of A to D.
Step 2	• T provides Ss in each base group with handouts. (Each handout has a set of questions about four different jobs.) • T helps Ss understand that they should be interdependent upon one another not only for their own learning but also for the learning of others throughout the activity. • T informs Ss which corner to go to based on their letter in order to form four different expert groups.
Step 3	• Ss move to their expert groups and find out information about different jobs through discussions and answer the questions on the handouts. • T circulates within the groups and makes sure each of the Ss has all the answers.

| | • Ss return to their initial base groups and exchange the information through discussing what they learned in the expert groups.
Step 4 | • All the base groups present their findings to the whole class and decide which job they would like most.

Note: T = teacher, S = student

문제 분석 🔍

● 네 개의 단계를 가지고 있는 수업 활동의 명칭을 제시하는 문제이다. 첫 번째 단계에 "다양한 정보 (**various information**)"라는 단어가 나와 있으므로 정보와 관계되어 있고 여러 가지 정보를 활용하는 활동임을 알 수 있다.

● 교사는 A, B, C, D의 각 코너에 네 개의 직업에 대한 정보를 비치해 놓고, 학생들에게 A, B, C, D라는 글자를 준다. 따라서 A, B, C, D로 구성된 학생들이 네 개의 기본 그룹을 형성한다. 교사는 네 개의 직업에 대한 질문이 담겨 있는 인쇄물을 나눠준 상태이고 학생들은 그 질문에 답을 찾아야 한다. 이 때 A를 가진 학생들은 모두 A의 코너, B를 가진 학생들은 모두 B의 코너, C를 가진 학생들은 C의 코너, D를 가진 학생들은 D의 코너에 모여서 비치되어 있는 정보를 활용해 그 직업에 대한 전문가 그룹이 되어 각 직업에 대해 토론하고 인쇄물에 답을 쓴다. 그 후 학생들은 다시 기본 그룹으로 돌아가 자신들이 배워온 정보를 바탕으로 해서 나머지 정보를 채우는 것이다.

● 기본적으로 정보 격차(**information gap**) 활동이지만 문제에서 하나의 단어로 된 활동이라고 되어 있으므로 정보 격차 활동 중 각각의 구성원이 특정한 정보를 가지고 있고 전체 정보를 모으는 것을 목표로 하는 활동은 직쏘(**jigsaw**)이다.

예시 답안 ✏️

jigsaw

8. Examine the consulting report about Ms. Song's English class and follow the directions. 【10 points】

Teacher: Ms. Song	Consultant: Mr. Cho	Date: Dec. 2nd
Before consultation	In my class, I taught grammatical structures as follows: T: She will go swimming. (showing a picture of 'John riding a bike') "Ride a bike." S1: John will ride a bike. T: Good. (showing a picture of 'Mary playing the piano') "Play the piano." S2: Mary will play the piano. T: Very good. (showing a picture of 'Tom visiting a museum') "Visit a museum." S3: Tom visit a museum. T: No, you should say, "Tom will visit a museum." . . . T: (showing a picture of 'people going to a movie') What will they do? S4: They will go to a movie. T: Very good. (turning to S5, showing a picture of 'students singing a song') What will they do? . . . I expected my students to learn practiced structures, but they still had difficulty in using them in real context.	

Mr. Cho's advice	The following are pieces of Mr. Cho's advice: • Utilize an e-portfolio. • Use other types of questions. • Employ various authentic materials. • Provide other types of feedback. • Assign specific roles to students in group work.
After consultation	After the consultation, I made changes in teaching grammar as follows: T: Good morning, class. Winter vacation is coming soon. I will go to Jeju Island and travel around. Minji, what will you do this vacation? S1: I go to Grandma's house in Busan. T: Minji, I go to Grandma's house? S1: Oh. . . eh. . . I will go to Grandma's house. T: Perfect! What about Bora? Do you have any plans? S2: Um. . . I. . . I take guitar lessons. T: I take guitar lessons? S2: Uh. . . I will take guitar lessons. T: Good! What a great plan! Why do you want to do that? . . .

Note: T = teacher, S = student

Write TWO paragraphs. In the first paragraph, identify the type of teaching technique which Ms. Song used before the consultation and explain the technique with evidence. In the second paragraph, identify TWO changes that Ms. Song made based on Mr. Cho's advice, and then explain those two changes by comparing the classes before and after consultation with evidence.

● 교사 중심의 단순 반복, 형태 중심의 수업을 학습자 중심, 의미 중심의 수업으로 바꾸는 문제이다.

● 먼저 Mr. Cho의 조언은 "e-포트폴리오 사용", "다른 종류의 질문 형태를 사용", "다양하고 진위성이 있는 교재의 사용", "다른 종류의 피드백 제공", 그리고 "모둠 활동에서 학생들에게 특정한 역할을 주기"로 구성되어 있다. 이는 모두 학습자 중심, 의사소통 중심의 학습법에서 많이 사용되는 특징들이다. Ms. Song의 이전 교실 수업 내용을 보면 문법 구조를 가르치는데 있어서 단순 반복 학습을 했다는 것을 알 수 있고 이에 대한 문제로 실제 상황에서는 사용할 수 없다는 것이 나와 있다.

● 조언 이후의 수업 내용을 보면, 학습자가 창의적으로 언어를 사용할 수 있는 질문을 많이 하고, 틀린 표현에 대한 피드백에서 올바른 형태가 직접적으로 제공되지 않는다는 것을 알 수 있다. 따라서 이 두 가지 부분을 중심으로 서술하면 된다.

Ms. Song used mechanical drills before the consultation. Mechanical drills focus on a minimal number of language forms through repetition and typically have only one answer. Drills range from simple repetition to substitution format. Before consultation, Ms. Song provided a model sentence and the phrase that students should use when they repeated. Students substituted the part using the given phrase. Thus, students were able to focus on the form of a future tense from the base form of a verb. Yet, the activity shows no connection with reality.

After the consultation, Ms. Song has made two changes. First, she uses other types of questions. She used only a display question before the consultation, but after the consultation, she uses mostly referential questions. When she asked "What will they do?" before the consultation, she already knew the answer, and there was only one correct answer, Yet, when she asks "what will you do this vacation?" or "why do you want to do that?" after the consultation, there is no right or wrong answers. Second, she provides a different type of feedback. While she used the explicit correction before, she uses repetition after the consultation. For example, when S3 made an error, she said "no" and provided a correct form before the consultation. However, after the consultation, she simply repeats students' errors with changing intonation, such as "I go to Grandma's house?" and "I take guitar lessons?"

2. Read two middle school students' opinions about an English lesson posted on the online bulletin board and their teacher's teaching log, and follow the directions. 【10 points】

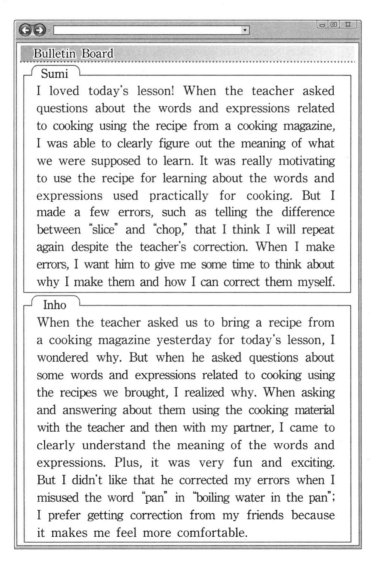

My Teaching Log

What I put emphasis on in today's class

I always want my students to have a clear understanding of what I teach, so today I tried to teach the points using materials used in real life rather than the ones in the textbook. To my surprise, they really loved the way I taught today. They participated in the lesson with a lot of enthusiasm.

The things I have to improve in the next class

While leading the activity, for convenience' sake, I corrected the errors that students made. Considering their opinions, however, I have to use alternate ways to give them a chance to correct their errors individually or in pairs.

In one paragraph, identify ONE feature of the teacher's lesson that the students liked, and explain TWO reasons why they liked it. In another paragraph, address ONE problem with the lesson, and suggest TWO solutions from the teacher's standpoint by supporting them with rationale. Both paragraphs must be based only on the bulletin board and the teaching log above.

문제 분석

● 진위성이 있는 교재 사용의 중요성과 암시적 피드백에 관한 문제이다. 두 중학교 학생이 게시판에 올린 내용을 보면 모두 요리법에 나온 단어와 표현이 이해하기 쉽고 재밌었다고 하고 있다. 그러나 두 학생은 선생님의 직접적인 오류 수정에는 문제를 제기하고 있다.

● 교사의 수업 기록도 이에 일치한다. 학생들이 명확하게 이해하기를 원했기 때문에 실생활에 사용되는 교재를 사용했고, 편리함 때문에 오류를 수정해주었지만 학생들이 스스로 오류를 수정할 수 있는 기회를 줘야겠다고 적혀 있다.

● 문제에서 학생들이 좋아했던 점 하나와 이유, 하나의 문제와 교사의 입장에서 두 가지 해결 방법을 제시하라고 했기 때문에 이에 해당하는 내용을 기술하면 된다.

Two students posted their preference on the lesson on the online bulletin board. They both indicated that the use of authentic material was what they liked. First reason was that it was motivating to learn the practical words and expressions. Second, it was easier for them to understand the meaning of words and expressions much clearly.

However, they did not appreciate the teacher's direct correction. They either wanted to correct errors by themselves or by peers. The alternate ways could be implicit feedback and peer correction. Instead of explicitly correct students' errors, the teacher could take advantage of recast, elicitation, or repetition to give students time to reflect on the feedback and correct the errors by themselves. Also peer correction will help students feel more comfortable since they can correct each other.

2. Examine the class observation checklist and notes completed by a middle school English teacher after observing a colleague's class, and follow the directions.【10 points】

Observation Checklist

Instructor: *Sumi Kim*　　Unit: *4. Personal Health*
Topic: *How to treat acne*　Function: *Giving advice*
Period: *2/8*　　　　　　Date: *Nov. 11*

Areas	Criteria	Scale*
Lesson Preparation	• have a clearly developed lesson plan	1 –②– 3
	• prepare interesting multimedia materials	1 --- 2 –③
Instructional Strategies	• give clear directions	1 –②– 3
	• use an appropriate grouping strategy for group activities	①– 2 --- 3
	• provide level-appropriate activities	1 –②– 3
Affective Aspects	• create a warm and accepting atmosphere	1 --- 2 –③

* 1 = poor, 2 = average, 3 = good

Notes

- A fun video clip on acne. SS loved it.
- T was kind and patient.
- Group activity (Same-ability grouping)
  ▸ Higher-level students did well. Had no problems.
  ▸ Lower-level students had a hard time completing the task. Seemed like they needed some help.

In one paragraph, identify one strong point and one weak point of the lesson based on the data above. Support each of your choices with details from both the checklist and the notes. In another paragraph, address the problems the lower-level students are experiencing by suggesting two possible solutions and supporting them with your rationales.

문제 분석

- 학생들의 배경 지식을 상기시키기 위한 멀티미디어의 사용과 다양한 영어 실력을 가진 학생들을 가르치기 위한 전략을 묻는 문제이다.

- 참관표와 기록을 보면 재미있는 멀티미디어 사용에 높은 점수를 받았으나 적절한 그룹을 구성하는 데는 낮은 점수를 받았음을 알 수 있다. 참관 기록에는 높은 영어 실력을 가진 학생들은 활동을 잘한 반면 낮은 영어 실력을 가진 학생들은 어려움을 겪었다고 되어 있고 같은 영어 실력을 가진 학생들로 그룹을 구성했다고 나와 있다.

- 문제에서 장점 하나와 단점 하나를 기술하고 낮은 영어 실력을 가진 학생들이 겪는 문제를 해결하기 위한 방안을 두 개 제시하라고 되어 있으므로 낮은 수준을 가진 학생들을 가르치는 방법 중 해당하는 방법을 제시하면 된다. 이 때 같은 수준의 그룹 활동이 문제로 제시되어 있음을 상기하고 방안을 제시한다.

예시 답안

The class observation checklist reveals that the lesson has one strong point and one weak point. The strong point is the use of interesting multimedia materials, and the weak point is an inappropriate grouping strategy. According to the observation notes, students loved fun video clips. Yet, the homogeneous group strategy to make a same-ability group was proven to be ineffective; While higher-level students had no problem completing the tasks, lower-level students had a hard time completing the tasks.

To solve the problems that the lower-level students are experiencing, first varying ranges in the same group and second extra support with clear direction would help. First, if the teacher places students of different levels in the same group, the students would interact with each other to complete the tasks. By doing so, lower-level students would benefit from higher-level students. Second, the teacher can provide extra support to lower-level students by providing clear direction using simple language and the use of L1 at times. The clear description of how to do activities will help students go beyond their abilities.

6 평가(Assessment)

평가에 관해 논하기 전에 먼저 관련 용어를 정의하도록 하겠다. 평가(**assessment**)는 한 사람의 어떤 특성의 수준이나 정도를 측정하고 감정하는 것이다. 교육 현장에서 평가는 지속적으로 이뤄지며 다양한 방법으로 실시된다. 교사의 질문에 대한 학생의 답이나 쓰기 결과물도 모두 평가에 속한다. 반면 시험(**tests**)은 평가의 한 종류로써 모든 학습자가 본인이 가진 능력을 최대한 활용해서 가장 좋은 성과를 도출해내는 것이며 교과 과정의 일부분으로써 모두 같은 시간에 보는 것이다. 시험은 한 사람의 능력을 측정하는 하나의 도구로써 어떤 방법으로 측정할지가 명확해야 한다. 즉, 객관식 시험인지, 채점 기준표가 있는 쓰기 시험인지, 혹은 질문지가 있는 면담인지 직접적으로 나타나 있어야 한다는 것이다. 또한 시험은 시험을 보는 사람의 능력을 반드시 직접적인 과정이나 규칙을 통해 정량화해서 측정해야 한다(Brown & Abywickrama, 2010).

또한 측정(**measurement**)과 심사(**evaluation**)도 평가나 시험과 혼돈할 수 있는 개념이다. 측정(**measurement**)은 학습자의 수행 능력을 정량화하는 것이다. 즉, 학습자의 수행 능력에 순위와 등급을 매기는 것이다. 측정은 양적(**quantitative**) 혹은 질적(**qualitative**)으로 행해질 수 있는데, 양적 측정이 학습자의 수행 능력을 정확하게 묘사하고 다른 학습자와의 비교를 용이하게 하는 장점이 있는 반면 질적 측정은 채점 기준표(**rubrics**)를 바탕으로 하기 때문에 교사가 학습자에게 구체적이고 개별화된 피드백을 주는 효과가 있다. 심사(**evaluation**)는 시험 또는 평가의 결과가 어떠한 결정을 내리는 데 도움을 주는 것을 의미한다. 즉, 심사는 시험의 결과를 해석하고 그 결과가 어떠한 의미가 있는지 판단하는 과정이다. 예를 들어 시험 성적은 측정된 것이다. 그리고 그 시험 성적이 좋은지 나쁜지를 가리는 것이 심사인 것이다. 다음의 그림은 평가, 시험, 측정, 심사의 관계를 보여준다.

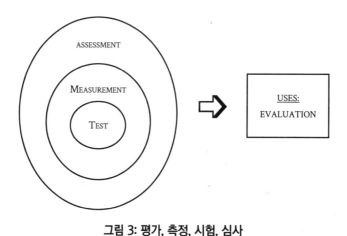

그림 3: 평가, 측정, 시험, 심사

평가의 종류(Types of Assessment)

평가는 먼저 비공식적인 평가(informal assessment)와 공식적인 평가(formal assessment)로 구분할 수 있다. 비공식적인 평가는 다양한 형태로 구현된다. 계획하지 않은 질문과 답변, 학습자에게 주는 즉각적인 피드백, 쓰기 과제에 남기는 의견 등 학생의 언어 능력에 대해서 정해진 결론을 내리고자 하는 의도 없이 실시되는 평가가 비공식적인 평가에 해당한다. 반면 공식적인 평가는 체계적으로 계획한 평가로써 교사가 학생의 성취도를 평가하기 위해 만들어진 것이다. 예를 들어 모든 시험은 다 공식적인 평가에 해당한다. 그러나 모든 공식적인 평가가 다 시험은 아니다. 시험 성적만이 학생의 성취도를 나타낸다고 할 수는 없기 때문이다.

Brown과 Abywickrama(2010)는 평가를 다시 형성 평가(formative assessment)와 총괄 평가(summative assessment)로 분류하고 있다. 형성 평가는 학습자가 언어 능력을 습득해 가는 과정을 평가하는 것이고 총괄 평가는 통상적으로 학기 말에 학습자가 학습한 것 혹은 성취한 것을 평가하는 것이다. 비공식적인 평가는 모두 형성 평가라고 할 수 있다. 학습자가 지속적으로 발전할 수 있도록 돕는 목표를 가지고 있기 때문이다. 반면 기말 고사는 총괄 평가의 대표적인 예다. 기말 고사는 학습자가 한 학기 동안 얼마나 수업 목표를 성취했는지를 평가하기 때문이다. 과거에는 총괄 평가가 평가의 대부분을 차지하고 있었지만 현재는 형성 평가를 더 중시하고 있다. 이는 교사가 형성 평가를 통해 학습자의 언어 발달에 관한 중요한 정보를 알 수 있기 때문이다. 또한 과거에 총괄 평가로 해석

되었던 퀴즈, 중간고사 등도 형성 평가의 성격을 가질 수 있음을 알게 되었다.

시험의 종류를 채점 기준으로 살펴본다면 상대 평가(**norm-referenced tests**)와 절대 평가(**criterion-referenced tests**)로 구별할 수 있다. 상대 평가는 수험생의 점수를 평균, 중간값, 표준편차, 그리고 백분위로 해석하는 것을 의미한다. 이 방식은 수험생을 등수로 구별하는 목적으로 사용된다. 예를 들어 TOEFL, TOEIC 등 표준화된 영어 시험은 상대 평가방식을 취하고 있다. 반면 절대 평가는 보통 등급의 형태로 수험생에게 피드백을 주기 위한 것이다. 따라서 학생들의 점수 분포는 문제가 되지 않으며 얼마나 평가의 기준으로 제시된 목표를 성취했는지가 중요하다. 예를 들어 OPIc 시험은 절대 평가이다. ACTFL 가이드라인에 나와 있는 등급별 능력을 가지고 있는지를 보기 때문이다.

평가의 목적에 따라서 시험을 분류한다면 성취도 시험(**achievement tests**), 진단 시험(**diagnostic tests**), 배치 시험(**placement tests**), 언어 능력 시험(**proficiency tests**), 적성 시험(**aptitude tests**) 등으로 나눌 수 있다. 첫째, 성취도 시험(**achievement tests**)은 학습자의 성취도를 학기 단위, 교재의 한 과, 또는 수업의 한 차시 등의 단위로 측정하기 위한 시험이다. 학습자가 정해진 수업 목표를 얼마나 성취했는지를 측정하기 때문에 반드시 범위가 정해져야 하고 수업 목표와 관련된 내용을 측정해야 한다. 보통 학기의 끝이나 수업의 끝에 행해지기 때문에 총괄 평가적인 특징이 있으나 다음 수업의 자료로 쓰인다면 형성 평가로 활용될 수도 있다. 둘째, 진단 시험(**diagnostic tests**)은 학습자가 배워야 할 언어의 측면을 진단하기 위한 것이다. 진단 시험은 교사가 학습자가 어려움을 겪고 있는 부분을 미리 알아내서 추후에 도움을 주고자 만들어진다. 따라서 성취도 시험이 이미 학습한 부분을 측정하기 위해서 학기 말에 행해진다면 진단 시험은 학기 초에 행해진다. 셋째 배치 시험(**placement tests**)은 학생들을 실력에 맞는 반에 배치하기 위해서 행해진다. 일반적으로 앞으로 가르칠 교재에서 항목을 선택해서 시험을 보지만 기존에 있는 영어 능력 시험을 이용하기도 한다. 넷째, 언어 능력 시험(**proficiency tests**)은 전반적인 언어 실력을 측정하기 위한 시험으로써 통상적으로 객관식 문항으로 이뤄져 있으며, 대부분 총괄 평가이며, 또한 상대 평가이다. TOEIC이나 TOEFL 등이 이에 속한다. 마지막으로 적성 시험(**aptitude tests**)은 외국어 과목을 학습하기 전에 그 외국어를 배울 능력이 측정하기 위한 것이다. 그러나 적성 시험은 기존의 시험이 언어의 적성보다는 학문적 능력을 평가한다는 비판을 받은 후로 영어 교육 현장에서는 거의 사용되지 않는다(Brown & Abywickrama, 2010).

최근에는 의사소통 중심 교수법의 영향으로 학습자들의 언어 사용 능력이 중시됨에 따라 객관식 문항 위주의 시험에서 벗어난 수행 평가(**performance-based assessment**)가 각광을 받고 있다. 수행 평가는 말하기와 쓰기 결과물을 포함하며 통합 기술(**integrated skills**)을 활용하여 시험을 보기도 하고 상호 작용을 일으키는 활동을 활용해 평가하기도 한다(Brown & Abywickrama, 2010). 우리나라도 중등 영어 과목에서 수행 평가가 일정 부분을 차지하고 있다. 수행 평가는 시험을 보는 학생이 어떤 과업(tasks)을 완수해야 하기 때문에 과업 중심 평가(task-based assessment)로 불리기도 한다. 다음은 수행 평가의 특징이다.

1) 학생들은 정해진 선택지 안에서 고르는 것이 아니라 스스로 만들어 낸 답변을 해야 한다.
2) 높은 수준의 사고를 활용해 개방형 답변을 한다.
3) 과업은 의미 중심적이고 진위성이 담보되어야 한다.
4) 과업은 말하기, 쓰기, 읽기, 듣기가 복합적으로 포함되어야 한다.
5) 과정과 결과물이 모두 평가된다.
6) 얼마나 많이 알고 있는지가 아닌 얼마나 깊이 알고 있는지가 평가된다.

(O'malley & Valdez, 1996, p. 5)

수행 평가이외에도 기존의 객관식 시험을 대체할 수 있는 다양한 평가 방법이 사용되고 있다. 먼저 채점 기준표(rubrics)의 사용이다. 채점 기준표는 수행 평가를 공정하게 하기 위한 도구로써 보통 말하기와 쓰기 평가에서 개방형 답변을 공정하게 채점하기 위해서 사용된다(Brown & Abywickrama, 2010). 평가를 하는 기준이 영역별로 나눠져 있으며 그 기준이 자세하게 설명되어 있다. 기준은 유창성(fluency)과 정확성(accuracy)이 모두 포함되어야 한다.

두 번째는 포트폴리오(portfolios)를 들 수 있다. 포트폴리오는 결과물뿐만 아니라 과정이 모두 담긴다는 점이 가장 큰 특색이라고 할 수 있다. 포트폴리오는 정해진 영역에서 학생들의 노력, 발전, 그리고 성과물을 보여줄 수 있는 모든 것들을 합한 것이다(Genesee & Upshur, 1996). 보통 작문의 초안부터 마지막 원고까지, 보고서, 프로젝트, 발표 개요, 시나 산문과 같은 창작물, 사진, 신문이나 잡지 스크랩, 오디오나 비디오 녹화물, 일기 같은 개인적 기록물, 시험 성적과 과제물, 강의 노트, 평가 등이 포함된다(Brown & Abywickrama, 2010).

세 번째로 저널(journals)을 들 수 있다. 개인의 생각이나 감정, 목표를 향한 발전 과정 등을 자유롭게 쓰는 것인데 교육 현장에서는 언어를 배우는 과정을 기록하거나, 문법 학습의 기록, 읽기 숙제에 대한 반응, 전략 중심 학습법에 대한 기록, 자기 평가 기록 등 다양한 목표를 가진 저널을 활용할 수 있다. 또한 교사와 학생간의 교류를 촉진하는 방법으로써 대화 저널(dialogue journals)이 사용되기도 한다. 대화 저널은 초등학교에서 과제로 낸 일기장에 선생님이 의견을 적어서 돌려주던 방식을 생각하면 이해하기 쉽다.

네 번째로 회의(**conferences**)와 면담(**interviews**)이 있다. 쓰기 수업에서 학생들의 발전 과정에 관해서 이야기를 나누는 형태로 많이 활용되고 있으며 포트폴리오나 저널과 함께 활용되기도 한다. 면담은 회의의 한 형태로써 평가의 목적을 가지고 학생과 이야기를 나눌 때 면담(**interviews**)이라고 하는데, 이는 우리가 생각하는 전형적인 면담이 아니라 학생의 말하기나 학습 스타일을 평가하기 위한 목적이 있을 때 사용되는 용어이다(Brown & Abywickrama, 2010). OPIc 시험을 생각하면 이해하기 쉬울 것이다. 소프트웨어를 활용하기는 하지만 수준별로 구성된 질문에 수험자가 대답을 하는 형태를 취하고 있는데 말하기 능력을 측정하기 위하여 면담의 형태로 질문 문항이 구성되어 있기 때문이다.

다섯 번째로 관찰(**observations**)이 있다. 교실에서 일어나는 일상적인 관찰이 아니라 체계적으로 계획이 세워진 과정을 의미 한다. 보통 점검표(**checklist**)를 활용해서 관찰하고 싶은 영역을 체계적으로 점검한다. 마지막으로 자가 평가(**self-assessment**)와 동료 평가(**peer assessment**)가 있는데 자가 평가는 학습자의 자기 주도적 학습을 장려하고 내적 동기를 부여한다는 장점을 가지고 있고 동료 평가는 협동 수업이라는 원칙 하에서 서로가 서로의 학습에 도움이 된다는 점을 인지하게 한다. 또한 자가 평가와 동료 평가는 둘 다 학습자 중심의 언어 교실을 만드는데 기여한다고 할 수 있다(Brown & Abywickrama, 2010).

13. Read the dialogue and follow the directions. 【4 points】

> T: Come here, Sumin. How was your vacation?
>
> S: Pretty good. Thank you, Ms. Kim. Actually, I'm so happy to be taking English classes from you this year.
>
> T: Good! You're really welcome in my class. Okay, then, let's talk about the test you had.
>
> S: You mean the reading test you gave us in the first class? Actually, I was wondering why you gave us a test instead of going directly into the textbook.
>
> T: Right, your class hasn't had a lesson yet. It was mainly to see how much you are ready for this semester and give you individual attention for any strong and weak points you have.
>
> S: I see. So, how were the results?
>
> T: Hmm … . Overall, you did quite well. Especially, you did well on the grammar questions. But it appears you had a bit of trouble with some words in the reading texts.
>
> S: You're right. Some words are really hard to memorize although I keep trying.
>
> T: I understand. Well, why don't you try to learn them through a context particularly relevant to you? That will be helpful, I believe.
>
> S: Thank you for your advice, Ms. Kim.
>
> *Note*: T= teacher, S= student

Fill in the blank with the ONE most appropriate word. Then, support your answer with evidence from the dialogue.

Tests can be categorized according to the purposes for which they are carried out. In this respect, the test that Ms. Kim and Sumin are talking about is an example of a(n) _____ test.

문제 분석 📊🔍

● 교사와 학생의 대화를 보면 진단 시험(**diagnostic test**)에 대한 암시가 나와 있다. 먼저 시험이 첫 번째 수업에서 행해졌다. 또한 주로 학습자가 얼마나 준비가 되어있는지, 학습자 개개인별로 강점과 약점을 파악하기 위한 시험이라고 제시되어있다. 마지막으로 시험 결과에 대한 피드백이 학습자가 어려워하는 특정한 부분에 집중되어 있다.

● 진단 시험(**diagnostic test**)은 언어의 특정한 측면을 진단하기 위해 설계된 시험으로써, 학습자가 이미 성취한 것이 무엇인지, 그렇지 못한 것은 무엇인지를 파악하여 교육 과정의 계획 및 실천에 반영하는데 필요한 의사 결정을 하기 위해 실시한다. 이러한 진단 시험은 해당 교육 과정이 종료된 후 실시되는 일반 성취도 평가를 그대로 이용하는 것이 아니라 학생들에게 즉시 필요한 교육 내용에 대한 정보를 파악하기 위해 별도로 진단 평가를 개발하여 실시하는 것이 일반적이다.

예시 답안 ✍️

Diagnostic Test. The answer is a diagnostic test for two reasons. First, the test was administered in the first class. Second, the teacher clearly stated that the test was to determine weather the student was ready for the semester and to find out the student's strong and weak points. Since a diagnostic test is designed to find out the difficulties for learners usually in the beginning of a semester, the test is a diagnostic test.

1. Read the dialogue and follow the directions. 【2 points】

> **Student—teacher Meeting**
>
> T: Well, looking back over the last twelve weeks, I can see that you have written many drafts for the three essay writing assignments.
>
> S: Yes, I have. I have a lot of things here.
>
> T: Of all your essays, which one do you think is the best?
>
> S: I think the persuasive essay I wrote is the best.
>
> T: What makes you think so? Maybe you can tell me how you wrote it.
>
> S: Well ... I think the topic I chose was quite engaging. I enjoyed the writing process throughout. And it feels good being able to see the progress I've made.
>
> T: Yes, that's the benefit of this kind of project. I can see some improvement in your use of transitions. Your ideas are nicely connected and organized now.
>
> S: Thanks. What else should I include?
>
> T: Well, did you work on the self-assessment form and the editing checklist?
>
> S: Yes, I did. I completed them and included them with all of my drafts right here.
>
> T: Perfect! I'll be able to finish grading all of your work by the end of next week.
>
> *Note*: T = teacher, S = student

Complete the following by filling in both blanks with ONE word. (Use the SAME word.)

_____ can include essays, reports, journals, video or audio-recorded learner language data, students' self-assessment, teachers' written feedback, homework, conference forms, etc. As collections of these items, _____ can be useful for assessing student performance in that they can lead students to have ownership over their process of learning and allow teachers to pay attention to students' progress as well as achievement.

문제 분석

● 첫 번째 문단에 "writing assignments"라고 토픽이 소개되고 학습자가 여러 가지 것들을 많이 가지고 있다고 말하고 있다.

● 빈 칸이 들어 있는 두 번째 문단에서 에세이, 보고서, 저널 등 다양한 형태가 모두 포함될 수 있다고 나와 있다. 마지막으로 학습자가 학습의 과정을 스스로 주도하는데 도움이 되며 교수자가 학습자의 성취뿐만 아니라 성취 과정에도 집중할 수 있도록 돕기에 유용하다고 나와 있다.

❏ Portfolios란?

대체 평가의 여러 형태 중 하나인 포트폴리오는 그 구성에 있어서 의사소통을 기본 틀로 하고 있어서 인기가 높다. 포트폴리오는 학습자와 그 외의 사람들에게 학습자의 노력, 과정, 그리고 성취를 보여주는 다양한 결과물의 모음이다. 문제에서 제시된 대로 에세이, 보고서, 작문, 시, 감상문, 일기, 오디오나 비디오로 녹음된 학습자의 언어 등 어떠한 것이라도 포함될 수 있다.

예시 답안

portfolios

2 평가의 원칙(Principles of Assessment)

평가에는 다섯 가지의 원칙이 있다. 실용도(**practicality**), 신뢰도(**reliability**), 타당도(**validity**), 진위도(**authenticity**), 그리고 역류 효과(**washback**)가 그것이다. 먼저 실용도는 평가를 만들고, 시행하고, 채점하는데 있어서 얼마나 행정적으로 편리한가를 나타내는 원칙이다. 시험 문제를 만들고 실시하는데 있어서 드는 비용이나 시간, 채점의 용이함, 결과 보고의 용이함이 실용도에 속한다(Brown & Abywickrama, 2010). 실용적인 시험이란 예산 안에 들고, 적절한 시간 안에 시험을 치를 수 있으며, 시험을 실시하는 방법에 대한 지시가 명백하며, 만들고 채점하는 시간과 노력을 감안한 시험이다.

신뢰도(**reliability**)는 시험을 믿을 수 있는지에 관한 원칙이다. 예를 들어 같은 시험을 두 번 시행했을 때 같은 결과가 나온다면 신뢰할 수 있는 시험이라고 할 수 있다. 신뢰할 수 있는 시험이란 두 번 이상 실시했을 때 시험 조건이 같아야 하고, 채점에 관한 뚜렷한 지시가 있어야 하며, 채점 기준표(**rubrics**)가 동일해야 하고, 채점자가 그 채점 기준표를 일관되게 적용해야 하며, 애매모호한 문제가 없는 시험이다(Brown & Abywickrama, 2010). 신뢰도는 영향을 미치는 요인을 기준으로 몇 가지로 나눌 수 있다. 먼저 학생과 관련된 신뢰도(**student-related reliability**)이다. 만일 학생이 시험을 보는 날 아팠다거나 시험 문제의 답을 실력으로 맞힌 것이 아니라 찍어서 좋은 점수가 나왔다면 학생과 관련된 신뢰도는 낮아지게 된다.

그러나 교사 입장에서 그보다 더 중요한 신뢰도는 채점자 신뢰도(**rater reliability**)이다. 즉 채점자의 주관적 생각이나 오류가 채점 과정에 삽입될 여지가 있는 것이다. 채점자 신뢰도는 다시 채점자 간 신뢰도(**inter-rater reliability**)와 채점자 내 신뢰도(**intra-rater reliability**)로 나눠지는데, 채점자 간 신뢰도는 두 명 이상의 채점자가 같은 시험을 채점했을 때 결과가 얼마나 일치하느냐에 따라 달라지고 채점자 내 신뢰도는 한 사람의 채점자가 채점을 했을 때 시험 결과가 얼마나 일관적인가에 따라 달라진다(Brown & Abywickrama, 2010). 예를 들어 학생에 대해 편견을 가지고 있다거나 혹은 채점을 하다가 집중도가 떨어진다면 채점자 내 신뢰도가 낮아지게 된다. 채점자 신뢰도를 높이기 위해서는 여러 명의 채점자가 평가를 하는 방법을 쓸 수 있고, 채점자가 한 명이라면 반복 채점을 함으로써 신뢰도를 높일 수 있다. 세 번째로 시험 행정 신뢰도(**test administration reliability**)가 있다. 시험을 보는 환경이 신뢰도에 영향을 주는 것으로써 시험장의 온도, 소음, 시험지 인쇄의 품질 등이 이에 해당한다. 마지막으로 시험 신뢰도(**test reliability**)가 있는데 이는 시험 자체의 신뢰도를 의미한다. 예를 들어 객관식 시험에서는 문항의 난이도가 얼마나 고르게 분포되어 있으며 선택지가 얼마나 잘 만들어져 있는지가 관건이고 주관식 시험에서는 얼마나 객관적으로 답안이 맞고 틀린지를 결정하는가가 관건이다.

세 번째 원칙은 타당도(validity)이다. 타당도란 평가하고자 하는 영역이 제대로 평가되는가에 관한 것이다. 타당한 시험이란 측정하고자 의도한 영역이 정확하게 측정되는 시험이고, 관련이 없는 사항들은 측정하지 않으며, 학생들의 수행 능력을 가급적 많이 활용하며, 시험의 기준에 맞는 문항들을 이용하고, 시험을 보는 사람의 능력에 관한 유용하고 유의미한 정보를 제공하며, 이론적 배경이 탄탄한 시험이다(Brown & Abywickrama, 2010). 타당도는 다시 다섯 개의 하위 범주로 나눠진다. 먼저 내용과 관련된 증거(content-related evidence)를 보면 시험의 영역에 해당하는 능력을 수험자가 활용해 시험 문제를 풀고, 시험의 결과가 그 능력을 나타내고 있음을 의미한다. 예를 들어 학습자의 말하기 능력을 측정하고자 하는 시험인데 객관식 문항의 지필 고사라면 내용과 관련된 증거가 약해서 타당도가 낮아지게 된다. 즉 평가하고자 하는 영역을 직접적으로 측정한다면 내용과 관련된 타당도가 높아지는 것이다. 두 번째로 기준과 관련된 증거(criterion-related evidence)가 있다. 대부분의 절대 평가에서 학생들이 성취해야만 하는 기준이 정해져 있다. 그렇다면 평가는 그 기준에 맞춰서 만들어져야 하고 그 결과는 다른 기준과 견줄 수 있어야 한다. 예를 들어 학생의 표준 영어 능력 시험 점수가 높다면 학교의 영어 점수도 높을 것이라고 가정할 수 있으며, 실제 영어 실력도 좋아야 한다.

기준과 관련된 증거는 다시 두 가지로 분류할 수 있는데 공인 타당도(concurrent validity)와 예측 타당도(predictive validity)이다(Brown & Abywickrama, 2010). 공인 타당도는 시험의 결과가 그에 해당하는 수행 결과와 일치할 때 높아진다. 예를 들자면 읽기와 듣기로 구성된 영어 기말고사에서 높은 점수를 받았는데 그 점수가 학생의 실제 읽기와 듣기 능력을 반영하지 않는다면 공인 타당도가 낮은 것이다. 예측 타당도는 시험의 결과가 미래에 학생의 성공 여부를 나타내는 정도이다. 영어 시험의 결과가 이후 반 배치의 기준이 되거나 다음 단계로 넘어갈 수 있는지를 판단할 수 있는 기준이 된다면 예측 타당도가 높다고 할 수 있다. 세 번째로 구인과 관련된 증거(construct-related evidence)가 있다. 여기서 구인(construct)이란 이론이나 가설을 의미하는데, 우리가 보통 언어 능력, 의사소통 능력, 유창성이라고 말하는 것은 언어적 이론이고 자존감, 동기는 심리학적 이론이다 (Brown & Abywickrama, 2010). 따라서 이론과 관련된 증거 혹은 타당도라고 하는 것은 평가가 이론을 바탕으로 하고 있는지에 관한 것이다. 네 번째로 결과적 타당도(consequential validity)가 있는데, 이는 시험의 결과를 의미한다. 즉 시험이 주는 영향에 관한 것이다. 결과적 타당도는 시험이 학교나 사회에 주는 영향, 그리고 개인에게 주는 영향으로 나눠 생각할 수 있다. 마지막으로 안면 타당도(**face validity**)는 학생이 평가를 공정하고, 연관성이 있고, 학습을 향상시키는 유용한 도구라고 생각할 때 높아지는 타당성이다(Gronlund & Waugh, 2008). 즉 학생들이 시험을 치른 후 이 시험이 공정하다고 믿으면 안면 타당도가 높아진다.

네 번째 원칙은 진위도(**authenticity**)이다. 진위도란 평가가 얼마나 실생활에서 사용되는 목표 언어를 반영하는지에 관한 것이다. 진위적인 시험은 최대한 자연스러운 언어를 사용하며, 개별화된 문항이 아닌 내용 안에 포함된 문제를 이용하며, 유의미하고 흥미로운 주제를 포함하고 있으며 이야기와 같이 주제로 구성되어 있는 문항들을 사용하고, 실생활에서 사용하는 과업을 복제한 과업을 제공하는 시험이다(Brown & Abywickrama, 2010). 진위도는 의사소통 교수법이 활용되는 수업에서 그 중요성이 더 부각되었으며 이에 따라 문장이나 구 중심의 개별 문항보다는 문단 단위 이상에서 문항이 출제되고 말하기나 쓰기 영역이 시험에 포함되기 시작했다.

다섯 번째 원칙은 역류 효과(**washback**)인데 결과적 타당도(**consequential validity**)의 한 부분으로 볼 수도 있다. 결과적 타당도 중 시험이 학생의 언어 발달에 주는 영향을 특히 역류 효과라고 하는데, 역류 효과는 학습을 촉진시킬 수도 있고 억제할 수도 있다는 점에서 긍정적일 수도 있고 부정적일 수도 있다(Brown & Abywickrama, 2010). 긍정적인 측면을 중점으로 보자면 시험을 준비하면서 학생들은 언어 능력을 향상시킬 수 있고, 교사는 그 결과를 바탕으로 학생들에게 도움이 되는 정보를 제공할 수 있다. 역류 효과를 증진시키기 위해서 교사는 단순히 점수를 매긴 후 시험지를 돌려주는 것이 아니라 코멘트를 남기거나 피드백을 줄 수 있다.

9. Read the passage and follow the directions. 【4 points】

Mr. Lee wants to determine how well the scores from the College Entrance Exam (CEE) predict academic success in college. The scatter plot below includes high school seniors' CEE scores from 2014 and their college Grade Point Averages (GPAs) in the fall of 2016. Their CEE scores are placed on the horizontal axis and their college GPAs on the vertical axis.

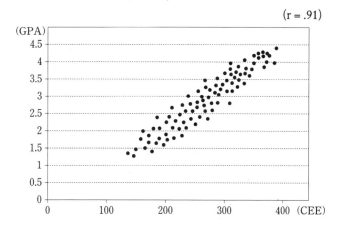

(r = .91)

Note: r = correlation coefficient

Students	CEE (Fall 2014)	GPA (Fall 2016)
A	389	4.43
B	246	2.58
C	304	3.15
D	322	3.27
E	211	2.10
F	328	3.62
G	314	3.18
H	288	2.83
I	372	4.00
J	368	3.85
⋮	⋮	⋮

Based on the information in the passage, identify the type of validity within the context of criterion-related validation and explain it with evidence.

1) 예측 타당도(predictive validity)에 관한 암시

● 문단의 처음에 수능 성적이 향후 대학 성적을 얼마나 잘 예견할 수 있는지 알고 싶다고 나와 있다.

● 도표와 표가 모두 수능 성적과 대학 성적이 긍정적인 관계가 있음을 나타내고 있다. 따라서 두 개의 시험이 긍정적인 상관관계에 놓여 있음을 알 수 있다.

● 마지막으로 문제에서 타당도의 한 종류이고 기준과 관련된 타당도를 밝히라고 되어 있다.

2) 예측 타당도(predictive validity)란?

● 타당도는 시험이 정말 테스트하고자 하는 것을 테스트 했나를 보는 척도이다. 타당도(validity)에는 구인 타당도(construct validity), 내용 타당도(content validity), 그리고 준거 타당도(criterion validity) 등이 있다. 구인 타당도(construct validity)란 시험에 적용되는 이론적 배경에 적절한가를 보는 것이고 내용 타당도(content validity)는 시험 내용이 테스트하고자 하는 전체 영역을 성공적으로 측정하는지를 보는 것이다. 준거 타당도(criterion validity)는 이미 타당하다고 여겨진 다른 평가 척도와의 상호관계에서 나타나는 타당성인데, 공인 타당도(concurrent validity)와 예측 타당도(predictive validity)가 이에 속한다. 공인 타당도가 하나의 평가 결과가 같은 능력을 측정하는 다른 평가 결과와 일치하는 지를 보는 것이라면 예측 타당도는 하나의 평가 결과가 미래에 행해지는 다른 평가의 결과와의 관련 정도를 나타낸다.

The type of validity is the predictive validity. The diagram and the table show the positive correlation between CEE scores and GPAs. The results indicate that CEE scores successfully predict college GPAs. Since the predictive validity refers to the degree to which a measurement can predict other measures of the same construct at some time in the future, the answer is the predictive validity.

13. Examine part of a test evaluation checklist by a head teacher and a student's reflective journal about the test, and follow the directions. 【4 points】

Mr. Kim, a head teacher of high school English, wanted to evaluate the achievement test of English reading in order to find to what extent the five major principles of language assessment (practicality, reliability, validity, authenticity, and washback) were applied to the test.

TEST EVALUATION CHECKLIST

Test-takers: 2nd year high school students.

Content	Scale		
	1	2	3
Subjectivity does not enter into the scoring process.	□	□	■
Classroom conditions for the test are equal for all students.	□	□	■
Test measures exactly what it is supposed to measure.	■	□	□
Items focus on previously practiced in-class reading skills.	■	□	□
Topics and situations are interesting.	□	□	■
Tasks replicate, or closely approximate, real-world tasks.	□	□	■

Note: 1=poor, 2=average, 3=good

Post-Exam Reflection

I studied really hard for the test because I wanted to move to a higher level class. But I got 76 and I was so disappointed. Since there were no errors in scoring, my score was dependable, I think. The topics were very relevant to my real life. But what was the problem? Did I use the wrong study skills? Actually I was very surprised when I first saw the test. Lots of tasks were very unfamiliar and I believe I've never done those kinds of tasks in class. Furthermore, after the test I actually expected the teacher to go over the test and give advice on what I should focus on in the future. It never happened. No feedback or comments from the teacher were given. I was not sure which items I got wrong. I will have the same type of test next semester and I'm not sure how I can improve my reading skills and get a better grade.

Identify TWO well-applied principles and TWO poorly-applied principles among the five principles of language assessment stated above based on all the data. Then support each of your choices with details from the post-exam reflection ONLY.

문제 분석 🔍

1) 답안 도출 단계

● 첫 문단에 언어 평가의 다섯 개의 원칙이 제시되어 있다(practicality, reliability, validity, authenticity and washback).

● "Test evaluation checklist"에 두 개의 잘 안된 점과 네 개의 잘 된 점이 제시 되어 있다. 문항의 내용을 분석해 보면 평가의 원칙 한 개당 두 개의 문항이 제시되어 있음을 알 수 있다.

● 따라서 "test evaluation checklist"의 어떤 문항이 언어 평가의 어떤 원칙에 해당되는지 파악한다. 처음의 두 개 문항은 각각 평가자 신뢰도(**rater reliability**)와 시험 시행 신뢰도(**test administration reliability**)이고, 그 다음 두 문항은 내용 타당도(**content validity**), 마지막 두 문항은 진위도(**authenticity**)임을 알 수 있다

● 학생이 시험 후 쓴 글은 성적은 믿을 수 있다는 점과 주제가 현실과 비슷했다는 점을 장점으로 들고 있으나 수업 시간에 하지 않은 내용이 출제된 점과 교사의 피드백이 없었다는 점을 단점으로 들고 있다.

- 따라서 "test evaluation checklist"와 학생의 "post-exam reflection"의 내용을 종합하면 신뢰도와 진위성은 높은 평가를 받았으나 타당도와 역류 효과는 낮은 점수를 받았음을 알 수 있다.

2) 평가의 다섯 가지 원칙

- **실용도(Practicality):** 평가가 실용적으로 구성되어 있는가를 보는 원칙이다. 시간, 재정, 관리, 채점, 해석이 편리하다면 실용성이라는 원칙이 잘 적용된 것으로 본다.

- **신뢰도(Reliability):** 평가 결과를 믿을 수 있는가를 보는 원칙이다. 시험의 구성, 시험 관리, 수험자, 그리고 채점자의 신뢰도가 전체 신뢰도를 구성하는 기본 구성이다.

- **타당도(Validity):** 시험이 측정하고자 의도했던 것을 측정하는지를 보는 원칙이다. 크게 내용 타당도(content validity), 구인 타당도(construct validity), 안면 타당도(face validity), 준거 타당도(criterion validity)로 나뉘며 준거 타당도는 다시 공인 타당도(concurrent validity)와 예측 타당도(predictive validity)로 나눠진다.

- **진위도(Authenticity):** 시험에 사용된 언어가 실제 생활에서 쓰이는 언어로 구성되어 있는 가를 보는 원칙이다.

- **역류 효과(Washback):** 역류 효과는 평가의 결과가 수험생의 강점과 약점을 진단해 다음 학습에 긍정적으로 영향을 미치는가를 보는 원칙이다. 역류 효과는 또한 시험을 준비함으로써 향후 수험생의 학습에 긍정적인 영향을 미치게 하는 도구로도 쓰인다.

예시 답안

According to the Test Evaluation Checklist and students' Post-Exam Reflection, reliability and authenticity are well applied, while validity and washback are poorly applied. The student's reflective journal about the test shows that there were no scoring errors. It indicates that the test had a high reliability. Also the student stated that the topics were relevant to real life, indicating well-applied authenticity. However, the student mentioned that the tasks on the test were new to the student, which meant that the test had low validity. In addition, there was no feedback from the teacher on the test, which meant no washback effect.

7. Read the passage and follow the directions. 【2 points】

At a high school English writing contest, contestants were given the instructions in the box and completed their compositions.

> Listen to a taped radio interview of Barbara Carrel, a famous writer, about her adventure to Africa. While listening, take notes. Then using the notes, write a story about her adventure. You will be given 30 minutes to complete the story.

Each contestant's composition was evaluated by two English teachers using the same rating scale. Below is part of the two teachers' scoring results.

Ratings of Contestants' Compositions

Students	Criteria	Teacher A	Teacher B
Giho Lim	Content	2	5
	Organization	1	4
	Vocabulary	3	4
	Grammar	2	5
Bomi Cho	Content	3	1
	Organization	5	1
	Vocabulary	4	2

* 1 = lowest ↔ 5 = highest

Complete the comments on the situation above by filling in each blank with ONE word. Write your answers in the correct order.

> The procedure used in the contest exemplifies ___①___ testing in terms of the number of skills assessed. One potential problem with the scoring process is low ___②___ reliability, which is most likely due to the subjectivity of the raters.

문제 분석

1) 답안 도출 과정

● 첫 번째 문단에 쓰기 경연 대회라고 주제가 주어졌으며 듣기를 바탕으로 쓰기가 행해졌음을 알 수 있다.

● 두 참가자의 점수를 보면, 두 명의 평가자가 세부 항목에 준 점수가 거의 일치하지 않고 큰 차이가 있음을 알 수 있다.

● ①번 답안이 들어가는 문장은 "경연 대회에서 사용된 과정은 평가된 스킬의 숫자라는 점에서 ①의 시험의 예를 보여준다"고 되어 있으며, ②번 답안이 들어가는 문장은 "채점 과정의 잠재적 문제점은 낮은 ② 신뢰도인데, 그것은 평가자의 주관성이 개입했기에 나타날 수 있다"라고 제시되어 있다.

2) 평가자 간 신뢰도(Interrater reliability)란?

● 평가의 주요 원칙 중 하나인 신뢰도(reliability)는 학생 관련 신뢰도(student-related reliability), 평가자 신뢰도(rater reliability), 시험 시행 신뢰도(test administration reliability), 시험 신뢰도(test reliability) 등으로 나눌 수 있는데, 그 중 평가자 신뢰도는 다시 평가자 간 신뢰도(interrater reliability)와 평가자 내 신뢰도(intra-rater reliability)로 나눌 수 있다. 채점 과정의 신뢰성을 높이기 위해서 채점자의 주관성을 최대한 배제하기 위한 여러 가지 방법을 쓰는데, 그 중의 하나가 두 명 이상의 채점자가 채점을 하여 일관적인 점수를 낼 수 있게 하는 것이다. 이를 평가자 간 신뢰도라고 한다.

예시 답안

① integrative
② interrater

3 평가의 설계(Assessment Design)

평가의 설계란 무엇보다도 우선 시험의 목적을 결정하는 것이다. 다음은 시험의 목적을 결정하기 위한 점검표이다.

1) 시험을 치를 필요가 있는가? 있다면 어떤 목적을 가지고 있는가?

2) 가르치고 있는 과목과 어떤 연관성을 가지고 있는가?

3) 다른 학생들의 실력과 비교할 필요가 있는가?

4) 시험 결과를 이용해 수업 목표를 성취했는가를 판단할 필요가 있는가?

5) 학생들이 역류 효과를 혜택을 보기를 원하는가?

6) 시험의 효과는 무엇일까?

(Brown & Abywickrama, 2010, p. 56에서 수정해서 사용됨)

위의 점검표는 평가의 종류와 원칙과 깊은 관계가 있음을 알 수 있다. 즉 시험의 목적을 잘 결정하면 어떤 종류의 시험을 만들어야 할지도 결정할 수 있고, 평가의 원칙도 충실히 지킬 수 있다.

다음 단계는 시험의 분명한 목표를 만드는 것이다. 단순히 시험을 보겠다고 했기 때문에 그 전까지 가르친 내용을 바탕으로 급하게 시험 문항을 만드는 것이 아니라 강의계획서에 명시된 학습 목표를 확인하고 그 목표를 학생들이 얼마나 성취했는가를 측정하기 위해 잘 설계된 문항을 만드는 것이다. 따라서 시험의 목표는 과목의 목표와 밀접한 관련이 있다. 이렇듯 시험의 목적과 목표를 바탕으로 평가의 기준이 만들어지게 된다.

세 번째 단계인 시험의 기준(test specifications)을 만드는 것은 시험의 형태를 결정한다. 다음은 시험의 기준에 공통적으로 들어가야 할 사항이다.

1) 시험 내용의 설명

2) 시험 문항의 종류(객관식, 주관식 등)

3) 과업(논술형 답안쓰기, 짧은 문단 읽기 등)

4) 기술(말하기, 쓰기, 읽기, 듣기)

5) 채점 기준

6) 점수 산정과 발표 방식

(Brown & Abywickrama, 2010, p. 56에서 수정해서 사용됨)

시험의 기준을 만드는 과정 중 하나인 채점 기준을 정하는데 있어서 특히 주관식 시험에 있어서는 평가 기준표(**rubrics**)를 만드는 것이 중요하다. 통상적으로 말하기와 쓰기 시험에서 채점 기준표가 많이 사용되는데, 분석적인 채점(**analytic scoring**)과 전체적인 채점(**holistic scoring**)의 두 가지 접근법이 있다. 분석적인 채점은 시험의 다양한 면을 구별해서 각각의 면을 독립적으로 채점하는 것이다. 예를 들어 내용, 정확성, 구성, 전달력 등으로 나눠서 말하기 능력을 평가한다면 각각의 영역에서 학생이 어떠한 장점과 단점을 가지고 있는지를 등급으로 평가한다. 분석적인 채점은 보다 객관적이고 일관적이라는 장점을 가지고 있어서 신뢰도가 비교적 높다. 반면 전체적인 채점은 전체적인 측면에서 학생의 등급을 고려하는 것으로써 각 등급 당 기준이 존재한다. 전체적인 채점은 덜 복잡하고 시간이 적게 걸린다는 장점을 가지고 있다. 과거에 토플 쓰기 시험이 전체적인 채점 방법을 택했고 현재 OPIc도 전체적인 채점 방식을 취하고 있다(Metruk, 2018).

그리고 마지막 단계가 시험 문항을 만드는 것인데 시험의 문항이 앞의 세 단계를 모두 반영하고 있어야 한다. 특히 객관식 문항을 만드는 것은 까다롭고 섬세한 작업을 요한다. 다음은 Brown과 Abywickrama(2010)이 제시한 객관식 문항을 만드는데 필요한 지침이다.

1) 각 문항이 하나의 목표를 측정해야 한다. 만일 어떤 문항이 문법 중 수동태에 관한 것이라면 답안이 수동태와 다른 형태와의 차이점을 알아낼 수 있는 능력에 집중해야지 다른 문법적 오류를 알아내는데 사용되면 안 된다. 즉, 수동태의 형태는 맞는데 전치사나 관사가 틀린 보기가 수동태 문항에 사용되면 안 되는 것이다.

2) 문제와 보기를 가능한 간단하게 만든다. 난이도를 높이기 위해서 혹은 다른 이유로 문제의 길이를 늘이거나 복잡한 문형을 사용하면 안 된다. 문제의 목표가 수동태의 형태를 알고 있는지를 측정하는 것인데, 단어의 난이도나 문장의 복잡성으로 인하여 제대로 측정할 수 없을 수 있기 때문이다.

3) 정답은 분명하게 하나여야 한다. 시험의 난이도를 높이기 위해서 오답을 만드는 것은 까다로운 일이다. 그러나 오답이 정답일 확률이 있어서는 안 된다.

4) 만일 객관식 문제라면 문항 지수(**item indices**)를 활용해 문항을 수정한다. 객관식 문항을 만드는데 없어서는 안 될 요소가 문항 지수이다. 보통 표준화된 공인 영어 시험을 만드는데 사용되지만 교실 수업에서도 활용될 수 있다. 다음은 문항 분석(**item analysis**)을 하기 위한 세 가지 문항 지수이다.

① **문항 난이도(item facility: IF):** 어떤 문항이 얼마나 쉽거나 어려운지 판단하는 기준이다. 만일 문항이 너무 어렵거나 너무 쉽다면 변별력이 없어진다. 적절한 문항 난이도는 0.15~0.85사이의 수치를 가진다.

$$IF = \frac{\#\ \text{문항을 맞춘 학생 수}}{\text{문항에 답을 한 전체 학생 수}}$$

② **문항 변별력(item discrimination: ID):** 문항이 잘하는 학생과 그렇지 않은 학생을 효과적으로 구별할 수 있는가를 판단하는 기준이다. 1점이 나온다면 가장 높은 변별력을 가지고 있는 것이고 0점이 나온다면 변별력이 없는 것이다. 0.5는 중간 정도의 변별력을 가지고 있다고 보면 된다.

$$ID = \frac{\text{잘하는 학생 그룹 중 문항을 맞춘 학생 수 -}\ \text{못하는 학생 그룹 중 문항을 맞춘 학생 수}}{1/2\ X\ \text{두 비교 그룹의 전체 학생 수}}$$

③ **오답 효율성(distractor efficiency):** 문항 변별력과 관련이 있는 또 하나의 수치는 오답 효율성이다. 즉, 실력이 부족한 학생들이 오답을 얼마나 많이 선택하는지 학생들이 모든 오답을 적절하게 선택하는지에 관한 것이다. 예를 들어 실력에 상관없이 아무도 선택하지 않은 오답이 있다면, 그 오답은 효율성이 없는 것이다. 또한 실력이 높은 학생이 낮은 학생보다 많이 선택한 오답이 있다면 그 오답 역시 효율성이 떨어진다고 할 수 있다. 그러나 특히 높은 실력을 가진 학생들이 정답을 더 많이 선택했다면 그 보기는 적절히 만들어진 것임을 알 수 있다.

이러한 단계를 통해 시험 문제를 다 만들었다면 수정하는 과정을 거쳐야 한다, 각 문항을 스스로 풀어보면서 지시 사항이 명료하게 기술이 되어 있는지, 문제를 풀기 위한 예시가 있는지, 정답이 명확하게 보이는지, 시간 안에 풀 수 있는지 등을 살펴본다. 시험 문제가 만들어 졌으면 시험 전에 학생들에게 시험에 관한 충분한 정보를 주고, 학생들이 시험 준비를 잘 할 수 있게 도와주며 질문에 대답할 수 있는 시간을 갖는다. 또한 시험 당일에도 미리 준비를 잘 해서 정시에 시작할 수 있도록 하고 시험이 끝나기 전에 남은 시간도 알려줘서 학생들이 문제를 제 시간에 풀 수 있도록 돕는다. 시험을 끝난 후에는 채점과 점수 부여 과정에서 실수가 없도록 유의하며 피드백을 주는 것을 잊지 않는다.

6. Read the passage and follow the directions. 【4 points】

A high school teacher wanted to develop a test in order to assess his students' English reading ability. He developed the test based on the following procedures:

• Step 1: Construct Definition

He started by clarifying what his test was intended to measure. He defined the construct of his English test as the ability to infer meanings from a given reading passage.

• Step 2: Designing Test Specifications

According to the construct definition in Step 1, he specified the test as consisting of a total of 20 multiple-choice items: 1) 10 items asking test-takers to infer meanings and fill in the blank with the most appropriate words or phrases (i.e., Fill-in-the-Blank), and 2) 10 items for finding the best order of scrambled sentences (i.e., Unscrambling).

• Step 3: Developing Test Items & Piloting

He finished item development. He piloted the test to examine whether the items had satisfactory test qualities.

• Step 4: Analyzing Item Facility & Item Discrimination

He analyzed item difficulty. To increase internal consistency, he removed the items with a high value of item discrimination.

• Step 5: Analyzing Reliability & Validity

Reliability was assessed by Cronbach's coefficient alpha. To investigate the concurrent validity of the test, he asked his colleagues to review the test items based on the test specifications.

• Step 6: Administering the Test

After making the necessary revisions, he administered the test to his students.

Based on the passage above, identify TWO steps out of the six that have a problem in the process of test development. Then, support your answers with evidence from the passage. Do NOT copy more than FOUR consecutive words from the passage.

문제 분석 〔lllQ〕

- 평가 설계에 관한 문제이다 평가의 원칙을 기반으로 해서 평가 설계 과정이 설명되어 있다. Step 1에서 구인(construct)을 읽기에서 의미를 유추하는 능력으로 정하고, Step 2에서 시험의 기준 및 사양은 빈 칸 채우기와 문장의 순서 정하기로 결정했다. 그 후 Step 3에서 문항을 만들고 질적으로 만족할 문항이 만들어졌는지 사전 점검을 한다. 여기까지는 큰 문제가 없다.

- Step 4에서 문항의 난이도(item facility)와 문항 변별력(item discrimination)을 분석할 때 내적 일관성(internal consistency)을 증가시키기 위해서 높은 변별력을 가진 문항을 제외했다고 되어 있다. 높은 변별력을 가진 문항은 시험의 신뢰도를 높이기 때문에 제거할 필요가 없다.

- Step 5에서 신뢰도는 "Cronbach's alpha"로 평가되었고, 공인 타당도(concurrent validity)를 알아보기 위해 동료에게 시험을 검토해달라고 부탁했다고 나와 있다. 그러나 공인 타당도는 시험의 결과가 타 시험의 결과와도 일치하는지를 알아보기 위한 것이기에 동료가 시험 문항을 검토하는 것과는 상관이 없다.

❏ 내적 일관성(internal consistency)

　　내적 일관성(**internal consistency**)은 통계 분석이나 연구를 위한 설문 조사 혹은 대단위의 시험 문제에서 문항들의 상관관계를 파악하기 위한 방법으로써 같은 목표를 가진 문항들이 비슷한 수치를 산출하면 내적 일관성이 높아진다. 이러한 내적 일관성은 주로 Cronbach's alpha로 측정되는데 Cronbach's alpha는 문항 간의 상관관계를 측정해서 보여주는 척도이다. 보통 Cronbach's alpha가 0.7이상이면 문항들의 내적 일관성이 좋다고 판단한다.

예시 답안

The two steps with a problem are Step 4 and Step 5. In Step 4, the teacher removed the items which would not increase internal consistencyy; If the value of item discrimination is high, the items should not be removed but be kept for better reliability. Also in step 5, reviewing the test items is nothing to do with the concurrent validity since the concurrent validity indicates if the test results are supported by other concurrent performance beyond the test itself.

10. Read the passage in <A> and the part of the individual conference in <B>, and follow the directions. 【4 points】

───────────── <A> ─────────────

The students in Mr. Lee's class did an oral presentation. Mr. Lee gave his students the following rubric in advance and let them know that their performance would be evaluated across four categories: (a) content & preparation, (b) organization, (c) language, and (d) delivery. After the students' presentations were over, Mr. Lee had a conference session with each student to discuss his or her strengths and weaknesses.

PRESENTATION ASSESSMENT FORM

Evaluation Categories	Scale				
	1 poor	2	3	4	5 excellent
I. Content & Preparation					
1. Interest & Value of topic	1	2	3	4	5
2. Informativeness of content	1	2	3	4	5
3. Preparedness	1	2	3	4	5
II. Organization					
1. Introduction (giving an overview)	1	2	3	4	5
2. Main body (supporting details & examples)	1	2	3	4	5
3. Conclusion (summarizing the presentation)	1	2	3	4	5
III. Language					
1. Accuracy (accurate use of grammar)	1	2	3	4	5
2. Appropriateness	1	2	3	4	5
3. Fluency	1	2	3	4	5
4. Pronunciation	1	2	3	4	5

IV. Delivery					
1. Confidence (not overly dependent on notes)	1	2	3	4	5
2. Gestures & Facial expressions	1	2	3	4	5

———————————— <B> ————————————

(The following is part of the individual conference that Mr. Lee had with one of his students, Yuna.)

Mr. Lee : Your presentation was pretty good.

Yuna : Thank you, Mr. Lee.

Mr. Lee : Yeah, you were really prepared. And so you got a perfect score on that area.

Yuna : I tried my best to make my PPT slides as informative as possible.

Mr. Lee : I know! They were really impressive. And your topic was really good.

Yuna : Thank you! How was my pronunciation?

Mr. Lee : Overall, I think your language was easy for the other students to follow. But you may want to try to use your language more appropriately. For example, some expressions you used like *you guys* and *you know,* may not be appropriate in this kind of presentation.

Yuna : I see. Thank you for your feedback.

Mr. Lee : I also noticed that you referred to your cue cards too frequently without looking at the audience.

Yuna : I did?

Mr. Lee : Yes, you did. Your presentation would have been much better if you had shown more confidence in your presentation task.

Yuna : I agree.

Mr. Lee : Other than that, everything looked fine.

Identify TWO of the four evaluation categories that Mr. Lee thinks reflect Yuna's weak points. Then, provide evidence for each identified category from <B>.

문제 분석

- 문단 <A>에서 말하기 발표의 평가 기준으로써 (a) content & preparation, (b) organization, (c) language, (d) delivery 네 가지가 제시되어 있다.

- 문단 <B>에서 교사와 학생의 대화를 분석해 보면 언어의 사용이 적절했다는 피드백을 받았으나 발표 중 다른 학생들을 보기 보다는 큐 카드에 의존했음을 알 수 있다.

- 이는 문단 <A>의 "Presentation Assessment Form"의 3번과 4번에 해당하는 언어와 전달력 부분에 해당한다.

예시 답안

The two evaluation categories that Yuna is weak in are "language" and "delivery". Mr. Lee mentions that Yuna needs to use her language more appropriately. Thus, "appropriateness" might be marked relatively low. Also he points that she referred cue cards too often during presentation. It means she was overly dependent on notes, which would lead to the lower scale on "confidence".

12. Read the English test task specifications in <A> and the teacher's reflective journal in <B>, and follow the directions. 【4 points】

——————— <A> ———————

Test Task Specifications	
Category	Description
Purpose	To determine students' current levels and place them into the most appropriate speaking courses
Time allocation	2 minutes (1 minute for preparation and 1 minute for speaking)
Task type	Picture-cued tasks
Scoring method	Analytic a. Criteria: Content, Fluency, Accuracy, Pronunciation b. Each criterion is worth 5 points and the score for this task is added up to 20.
Scoring procedure	a. Two examiners: a primary examiner who conducts the test and a secondary examiner who observes the test b. If there is a difference of more than 2 points in total, the examiners discuss rating disagreements based on the recorded test to arrive at a rating that they agree upon.

——————— <B> ———————

I understand that some students have potential strengths in learning languages, and in order to check my students' aptitude in English, I conducted a speaking test with picture-cued tasks. For each task, students looked at pictures and prepared for 1 minute and then described them for 1 minute. I found that 1 minute was not enough for my students to prepare their answers, so I felt that I needed to change the time allocation for the task. In addition, although my rating and the other examiner's rating seemed consistent, I realized that my approach, providing a global rating with overall impressions using a single general scale, was not very effective because the scores didn't give much helpful information to students. ⋯ There was one student's test yielding very different scores, so we (primary and secondary examiners) had a discussion about the recorded test and found that I gave the wrong score by mistake. It was good that we recorded the test even though both of us were present during the test.

Identify TWO categories that the teacher did NOT follow in the test task specifications from <A>. Then, support your answers with evidence from <B>.

문제 분석 Ⅲ○

● 문단 <A>에 "Test Task Specifications"와 각 기준의 세부 사항이 나와 있다. 그리고 문단 <B>에는 교사가 평가를 설계하고 실시한 내용이 나와 있다.

● 문단 <A>에서 나온 평가의 기준과 교사의 평가를 비교해 보면 "purpose"가 배치 시험 (placement test)으로 나온 반면, 교사는 적성 시험(aptitude test)을 설계했음을 알 수 있다. 또한 "time allocation"과 "task type"은 일치했으나 "scoring method"는 일치하지 않는다. 문단 <A>의 "Test Task Specifications"에는 분석적 채점 방식(analytic scoring)이 제시되어 있으나 교사는 "global rating"을 사용했다고 명시되어 있으므로 전체적인 채점 방식(holistic scoring)이 사용되었음을 알 수 있다. 다만 "scoring procedure"는 일치한다.

The two categories that the teacher did NOT follow are 1) Purpose and 2) Scoring method. In the teacher's reflective journal, the teacher indicates that s/he conducted a speaking test to find out students' aptitude in English. However, the Test Task Specifications in <A> shows that the purpose of the test is to place students into the appropriate course. Also, instead of an analytic scoring method suggested in the specification in <A>, the teacher used a global rating in <B>. Thus, the teacher did not follow the purpose and the scoring method in the Test Task Specifications.

3. Read the passage and follow the directions. 【2 points】

> Mr. Lee's English listening test consisted exclusively of four-option, multiple-choice items. After scoring the test, he calculated the response frequency for each item. Part of the results is presented below.

Item \ Option	Upper Group (N=100)				Lower Group (N=100)			
	A	B	C	D	A	B	C	D
1	50%*	27%	13%	10%	10%*	45%	25%	20%
2	13%	10%	70%*	7%	25%	27%	28%*	20%
3	20%	25%	18%	37%*	21%	26%	16%	37%*
...								
17	4%	0%	61%	35%*	66%	0%	29%	5%*
...								

Note: * indicates the correct response.

Complete the comments on item analysis by filling in each blank with ONE word. Write your answers in the correct order.

> Items 1 and 2 seem to be fulfilling their function. Item 3 has the problem of item ___①___ . Therefore, option D of item 3 needs to be revised or item 3 needs to be discarded. Item 17 has a problem with its ___②___ : No one from the upper group and lower group chose option B, and many upper group students incorrectly chose option C.

문제 분석 ⅢＱ

1) 답안 도출 과정

● 첫 번째 문단에서 듣기 시험 후에 "response frequency"를 계산했다고 나왔으므로 문항 분석

(item analysis)에 관한 문제임을 알 수 있다.

- 두 번째 문단에서 Item 3번이 문제가 있다고 나와 있다. 따라서 첫 번째 문단의 3번 문항을 분석해 보면 "upper group"과 "lower group"의 37%가 똑같이 정답 D를 선택했음을 알 수 있다. 즉, 이 문항은 "upper group"과 "lower group"을 구별하는 변별력이 부족하다.

- 두 번째 문단에서 Item 17번이 문제가 있다고 나와 있고 문제는 "upper group"과 "lower group" 중 아무도 B를 선택하지 않았으며 많은 "upper group"의 학생들이 오답인 C를 선택했다고 제시되어 있다. 즉, 오답인 B와 C에 문제가 있음을 알 수 있다.

2) 문항 분석(item analysis)이란?

문항 분석은 시험의 각 문항에 대한 학생들의 답변을 분석해서 각 문항의 질과 궁극적으로는 시험의 질을 높이는 방법이다. 문항 분석 결과는 다음 시험 구성을 향상시키고 교사의 시험개발 능력을 향상시키는 데 기여한다. 문항 분석에는 1) 문항 난이도(item facility), 2) 문항 변별도(item discrimination), 3) 오답 효율성(distractor efficiency) 혹은 문항 오답(item distractors) 등이 존재한다. 문항 난이도란 얼마나 많은 학생들이 정답을 맞혔는지에 관한 것이며 많이 맞출수록 쉬운 문제에 해당한다. 문항 변별도는 문항이 얼마나 효율적으로 상위 그룹과 하위 그룹을 구별해내는 변별하는지를 측정한다. 마지막으로 오답 효율성은 문항 오답 혹은 오답 효율성(item distractors/ distractor efficiency)으로 불리기도 하는데, 이는 오답의 효율성을 파악하는 수단으로써 너무 많은 상위 그룹 학생이 정답으로 선택하는 오답과 선택이 거의 되지 않는 오답은 효율성이 없는 오답으로 간주된다.

예시 답안

① discrimination
② distractors

기출 문제

영 어

수험번호 : (   )   성 명 : (   )

| 1차 시험 | 2교시 전공A | 21문항 50점 | 시험 시간 90분 |

○ 문제지 전체 면수가 맞는지 확인하시오.
○ 모든 문항에는 배점이 표시되어 있습니다.

※ **Write all answers in English.**

기입형 【1 ~ 15】

【1~3】 Listen to the dialogs and follow the directions.

1. Complete the statement about the woman by filling in the blank with ONE word. 【2 points】

> The only part of the gym that the woman is dissatisfied with is the _____.

2. Complete the statement about the professor's advice by filling in the blank with FOUR or fewer words. 【2 points】

> The professor says it is important to _____.

3. Complete the statement about the dialog by filling in the blank with TWO words. 【2 points】

> The woman and the man are discussing the _____ of children.

【4~5】 Listen to the talks and follow the directions.

4. Complete the statement based on the talk by filling in the blank with TWO words. 【2 points】

> The audience is composed mostly of people who _____.

5. Complete the main idea of the talk by filling in the blank with TWO words. 【2 points】

> _____ have played an important role in the history of rock.

6. Read the passage and follow the directions. 【2 points】

> We are born, each of us, with such self-centeredness that only the fact of being babies, and therefore cute, saves us. Growing up is largely a matter of growing out of that condition: we soak in impressions, and as we do so we dethrone ourselves—or at least most of us do—from our original position at the center of the universe. It is like taking off in an airplane: the establishment of identity requires recognizing how relatively small we are in the larger scheme of things. Remember how it felt to have your parents unexpectedly produce a younger sibling, or abandon you to the tender mercies of kindergarten? Or what it was like to enter your first public or private school? Or as a teacher, to confront your first classroom filled with sullen, squirmy, slumbering, solipsistic students? Just as you have cleared one hurdle, another is set before you. Each event diminishes your authority at just the moment at which you think you have become an authority.
>
> If that is what maturity means in human relationships—the arrival at identity by way of relative insignificance—then I would define historical consciousness as the projection of that maturity through time. We understand how much has preceded us, and how unimportant we are in relation to it. We learn our place, and we come to realize that it is not a large one. Even a superficial acquaintance with the existence, through millennia of time, of numberless human beings helps to correct the normal adolescent inclination to relate the world to oneself instead of relating oneself to the world. As historian Geoffrey Elton pointed out, "History teaches those adjustments and insights which help the adolescent to become adult, surely a worthy service in the education of youth."

Complete the main idea by filling in the blank with TWO consecutive words from the passage.

> History helps us mature by making us realize the _____ of ourselves in a wider context.

7. Read the passage and follow the directions. 【2 points】

At a high school English writing contest, contestants were given the instructions in the box and completed their compositions.

Listen to a taped radio interview of Barbara Carrel, a famous writer, about her adventure to Africa. While listening, take notes. Then using the notes, write a story about her adventure. You will be given 30 minutes to complete the story.

Each contestant's composition was evaluated by two English teachers using the same rating scale. Below is part of the two teachers' scoring results.

Ratings of Contestants' Compositions

Students	Criteria	Teacher A	Teacher B
Giho Lim	Content	2	5
	Organization	1	4
	Vocabulary	3	4
	Grammar	2	5
Bomi Cho	Content	3	1
	Organization	5	1
	Vocabulary	4	2

* 1 = lowest ↔ 5 = highest

Complete the comments on the situation above by filling in each blank with ONE word. Write your answers in the correct order.

The procedure used in the contest exemplifies ____①____ testing in terms of the number of skills assessed. One potential problem with the scoring process is low ____②____ reliability, which is most likely due to the subjectivity of the raters.

8. Read the interaction between a teacher and a student, and follow the directions. 【2 points】

(The teacher asks her student, Dongho, what he did over the weekend.)

T: Hi, Dongho, how was your weekend?
S: Hello, uh, have, had fun.
T: You had fun, oh, good. Did you go anywhere?
S: Yeah, uh, I go, go, went to uncle, uncle's home.
T: What did you do there? Did you do something interesting?
S: I play, played with childs. Uncle have childs, three childs.
T: Your uncle has three children?
S: Yeah, uh, one boy and two girls. So three childs.
T: Do you like them?
S: Yeah. They're fun. They're good to me.

* T = teacher, S = student

Complete the comments on the interaction by filling in the blank with ONE word.

Language errors may occur as a result of discrepancies between the learner's interlanguage and the target language. One main source of such errors is called _____, one example of which is seen in the student's use of *childs* in the given interaction.

9. Read the lesson procedure and complete the objectives by filling in each blank with TWO words. Write your answers in the correct order. 【2 points】

Students: 2nd year middle school students
Approximate time: 45 minutes
Lesson objectives:

Students will be able:
• to describe a daily routine using correct verb forms and ____①____ from a sample paragraph
• to revise writing through ____②____ on first drafts

Lesson Procedure

1. The teacher asks students what they do when they get home every day.
2. Students take turns asking and answering questions about their daily routine in pairs. Students take notes on each other's answers.
3. The teacher provides a sample paragraph, and students choose the correct expressions.

(As soon as/Since) Taebin finishes school, he goes to taekwondo. When he arrives, he puts on his workout clothes, and (first/then) he practices. (After/Before) he finishes, he rides his bike home. (As soon as/After that), he takes a shower. (After/Next), he eats his dinner. (Before/When) he finishes dinner, he does his homework. (Before/While) he goes to bed, he brushes his teeth.

4. Students use their notes to write a short paragraph about their partner's daily routine.
5. Students exchange writings and underline their partner's mistakes using the checklist.
   − Are the present forms of verbs used correctly?
   − Are the events described in time order?
   − Is time order indicated using the expressions focused upon in the sample paragraph?
   − Is punctuation used correctly?
6. Students rewrite their paragraph based on Step 5.

10. Below are an excerpt from a reading text and part of a student's think-aloud data generated while reading it. Based on the think-aloud data, identify the reading strategy that the student is using. Use ONE word. 【2 points】

> Computers have the potential to accomplish great things. With the right software, they could help make science tangible or teach neglected topics like art and music. They could help students form a concrete idea of society by displaying on screen a version of the city in which they live.
>
> In practice, computers make our worst educational nightmares come true. While we bemoan the decline of literacy, computers discount words in favor of pictures or video. While we fret about the decreasing cogency of public debate, computers dismiss linear argument and promote fast, shallow romps across the information landscape. While we worry about basic skills, we allow into the classroom software that will do a student's arithmetic or correct his spelling.

Well, nightmares? The author thinks computers do harm to education.

Hmm . . . the author is blaming computer software for a decline in basic skills.

11. Read the passage and fill in the blank with ONE word. 【2 points】

> In English, the lateral phoneme /l/ has two allophones: 'clear l', [l], and 'dark l', [ɫ], a velarized alveolar lateral. The articulatory difference between the two is that in the former the back of the tongue is lowered while in the latter it is raised toward the velum or retracted toward the uvula (without making contact in either case). Some examples with [l] and [ɫ] are:
>
> (1) limb [lɪm], climb [klaɪm], lock [lɑk]
> (2) miller [mɪlər], yellow [jɛlou], billow [bɪlou]
> (3) mill [mɪɫ], fill [fɪɫ], pile [paɪɫ], milk [mɪɫk]
> (4) middle [mɪdɫ], bubble [bʌbɫ], tunnel [tʌnɫ]
>
> We can see that [l] and [ɫ] are in complementary distribution. [l] appears in an onset position as in (1) and (2), while [ɫ] appears in a coda position as in (3). The rule involved seems to be that velarization takes place whenever /l/ is in a coda position. However, the cases in (4) cannot be explained by this rule because [ɫ] is syllabic and constitutes the nucleus, which is usually occupied by a vowel. By minimally modifying the above rule, we can obtain a more accurate rule: /l/ is velarized if and only if it is part of the _____.

12. Read the passage and follow the directions. 【2 points】

> In post-modification, to-infinitives can be interpreted as relative clauses or appositive clauses. When a to-infinitive is interpreted as a relative clause, the modified head noun corresponds to the relative pronoun, which is implicit in most cases, in the internal structure of the to-infinitive.
>
> (1) a. I will buy books to read.
>   b. I will buy books which I will read.
>
> The meaning of (1a) is equivalent to that of (1b). Since books is the antecedent of the object relative pronoun in (1b), it can be interpreted as the object of the verb in the internal structure of the to-infinitive in (1a). The modified head noun can also correspond to an implicit relative pronoun with other functions: the subject as in (2a), the object of the preposition as in (2b), and the object of the omitted preposition as in (2c).
>
> When a to-infinitive is interpreted as an appositive clause as in (2d), there is no implicit relative pronoun in the to-infinitive that corresponds to the head noun.
>
> (2) a. I need someone to help me with my homework.
>   b. Let's think about issues to deal with tomorrow.
>   c. We did not have money to buy food.
>   d. Do you have plans to travel abroad?

Analyze the sentences below and fill in the blanks with words from the passage. Write your answers in the correct order.

(i) The couples found places to stay before having dinner.
(ii) I am looking for doctors to consult regarding my mother's health.

> The underlined head nouns in (i) and (ii) correspond to ___①___ and ___②___ in the internal structures of the to-infinitives, respectively.

13. Read the passage and fill in each blank with ONE word from the passage. Write your answers in the correct order. 【2 points】

Every predicate is associated with an argument structure, which specifies the number of arguments it requires. The predicate assigns its arguments thematic roles including the following:

• Agent: the instigator of the action
• Theme: the entity affected by the action or state
• Experiencer: the entity experiencing the psychological state
• Instrument: the means by which the action or event is carried out

Thematic roles do not have a one-to-one relationship with grammatical functions such as the subject, the object, and so on. For example, the argument *the ball* is the object in (1a) and the subject in (1b), but it retains the same thematic role, Theme, in both sentences. Other examples can be seen in (2).

(1) a. David kicked the ball.
    b. The ball was kicked by David.
(2) a. A brick smashed the window.
    b. They expected the ship to sink.
    c. David opened the door slowly.
    d. Bob cut the tree with a saw.

The subject in (2a) and the object of the preposition in (2d) carry the role of _____①_____, whereas the subject of the subordinate clause in (2b) and the object in (2c) have the role of _____②_____.

14. Read the essay and follow the directions. 【2 points】

I learned this, at least, by my experiment; that if one advances confidently in the direction of his dreams, and endeavors to live the life which he has imagined, he will meet with a success unexpected in common hours. He will put some things behind, will pass an invisible boundary; new, universal, and more liberal laws will begin to establish themselves around and within him; or the old laws be expanded, and interpreted in his favor in a more liberal sense, and he will live with the license of a higher order of beings. In proportion as he simplifies his life, the laws of the universe will appear less complex, and solitude will not be solitude, nor poverty poverty, nor weakness weakness. If you have built castles in the air, your work need not be lost; that is where they should be. Now put the foundations under them.

Complete the idea that the essayist is conveying by filling in the blank with ONE word from the essay.

To reach 'castles in the air' we have to have, and believe in, _____.

15. Read the excerpt from a novel and follow the directions. 【2 points】

"For some days I haunted the spot where these scenes had taken place; sometimes wishing to see you, sometimes resolved to quit the world and its miseries for ever. At length I wandered towards these mountains, and have ranged through their immense recesses, consumed by a burning passion which you alone can gratify. We may not part until you have promised to comply with my requisition. I am alone, and miserable; man will not associate with me; but one as deformed and horrible as myself would not deny herself to me. My companion must be of the same species, and have the same defects. This being you must create."

The being finished speaking, and fixed his looks upon me in expectation of a reply. But I was bewildered, perplexed, and unable to arrange my ideas sufficiently to understand the full extent of his proposition. He continued —

"You, my creator, must create a female for me, with whom I can live in the interchange of those sympathies necessary for my being. This you alone can do; and I demand it of you as a right which you must not refuse to concede."

The latter part of his tale had kindled anew in me the anger that had died away while he narrated his peaceful life among the cottagers, and, as he said this, I could no longer suppress the rage that burned within me.

"I do refuse it," I replied; "and no torture shall ever extort a consent from me. You may render me the most miserable of men, but you shall never make me base in my own eyes. Shall I create another like yourself, whose joint wickedness might desolate the world? Begone! I have answered you; you may torture me, but I will never consent."

Below is an analysis of the excerpt above. Fill in the blank with ONE word from the excerpt.

Setting	a mountainous area
Characters	a creator and a being
Point of view	first-person narration
Conflict	a serious disagreement about the creation of a female creature which, the narrator imagines, would _____ the future of human beings

1. Read the passage and follow the directions. 【3 points】

If there is a single most important flaw in the current news style, it is the overwhelming tendency to downplay the big social, economic, or political picture in favor of the human trials, tragedies, and triumphs that sit at the surface of events. For example, instead of focusing on power and process, the media concentrate on the people engaged in political combat over the issues. The reasons for this are numerous, from the journalist's fear that probing analysis will turn off audiences to the relative ease of telling the human-interest side of a story as opposed to explaining deeper causes and effects.

When people are invited to take the news personally, they can find a wide range of private, emotional meanings in it. However, the meanings inspired by personalized news may not add up to the shared critical understandings on which healthy citizen involvement thrives. The focus on personalities encourages a passive spectator attitude among the public. Whether the focus is on sympathetic heroes and victims or hateful scoundrels and culprits, the media preference for personalized human-interest news creates a "can't-see-the-forest-for-the-trees" information bias that makes it difficult to see the big picture that lies beyond the many actors crowding center stage who are caught in the eye of the news camera.

The tendency to personalize the news would be less worrisome if human-interest angles were used to hook audiences into more serious analysis of issues and problems. Almost all great literature and theater, from the Greek dramas to the modern day, use strong characters to promote audience identifications and reactions in order to draw people into thinking about larger moral and social issues. News often stops at the character development stage, however, and leaves the larger lessons and social significance, if there is any, to the imagination of the audience. As a result, the main problem with personalized news is that the focus on personal concerns is seldom linked to more in-depth analysis. What often passes for analysis are opaque news formulas such as "He/She was a reflection of us," a line that was used in the media frenzies that followed the deaths of Britain's Princess Diana and America's John Kennedy, Jr. Even when large portions of the public reject personalized news formulas, the personalization never stops. This systematic tendency to personalize situations is one of the defining biases of news.

Describe the defining characteristic of the current news style, and explain how it differs from the common characteristic of great literature and theater. Do NOT copy more than FIVE consecutive words from the passage.

2. Read the passage in <A> and the conversation in <B>, and follow the directions. 【3 points】

---<A>---

A typical conversation organized around making requests has a common overarching sequence of interactional moves:

• A greeting exchange
• Preliminary moves toward a forthcoming request
• Making the request
• Short negotiation about the request
• Acceptance/Rejection of the request
• Closing/Thanking

---<B>---

(A low-proficiency English learner asks her roommate, a native speaker of English, to go buy some bread for her.)

Jisu: Hi, Kelly.
Kelly: Hi, Jisu.
Jisu: Buy me bread, OK?
Kelly: Do you want bread?
Jisu: Yeah.
Kelly: So, there's no bread in the fridge?
Jisu: Sorry?
Kelly: You don't have bread?
Jisu: No.
Kelly: So, do you want me to go to the supermarket and get some bread for you?
Jisu: What was that?
Kelly: Do you want me to get bread for you?
Jisu: Yeah.
Kelly: Do you want it right now?
Jisu: Tomorrow morning.
Kelly: OK. I'll get it for you later tonight.
Jisu: OK. Thank you.

* Jisu = low-proficiency learner, Kelly = native speaker of English

Explain how the conversation in <B> deviates from the sequence of interactional moves in <A>. Then identify the strategy that Jisu uses when she does not understand Kelly.

3. Read Mr. Park's comments in <A> and examine the results of a textbook evaluation by a review committee in <B>. Then follow the directions. 【3 points】

———————<A>———————

Mr. Park: The goal of my class is to help students use the language to communicate and perform authentic tasks. So I want to spend most of my class time letting students rehearse tasks they need to perform outside the classroom. I also want my students to have a lot of opportunities to work together so that they can use their linguistic knowledge to convey meaning rather than just practice form.

———————<B>———————

Evaluation Criteria	Textbook A			Textbook B			Textbook C		
	1	2	3	1	2	3	1	2	3
pattern drill activities		✓		✓					✓
role-play based on real-life situations		✓				✓		✓	
pronunciation tips			✓	✓					✓
regular grammar review			✓	✓			✓		
group projects	✓					✓		✓	

* 1 = poor, 2 = average, 3 = good

Considering the information in <A> and <B>, identify the textbook you would recommend for Mr. Park and provide TWO reasons for recommending it based on its characteristics.

4. Read the passage in <A> and the sentences in <B>, and follow the directions. 【4 points】

———————<A>———————

A constituent is a string of one or more words that syntactically and semantically behaves as a unit. The constituency of a string of words can be verified by a number of constituency tests, two of which are *movement* and *substitution*.

———————<B>———————

(1) Can you confirm your receipt of my application for membership?
(2) Call the reviewers of Bill's new book in a week.
(3) The music festival was crowded with young composers of jazz from Asia.
(4) Tina bears a striking resemblance to her mother.

Choose all the sentences where the underlined part qualifies as a constituent and identify the syntactic category of each constituent. Then explain how *movement* and/or *substitution* can be applied to verify the constituency of each string of words.

5. Read the passage and follow the directions. 【4 points】

There are two types of derivational suffix -al: the type that attaches to nouns and forms adjectives as in *central*, *coastal*, and *musical*, and the type that attaches to verbs and forms nouns as in *refusal*, *proposal*, and *recital*. The second type, called a deverbal suffix, can derive well-formed nouns only if three requirements are satisfied. One is that the final syllable of the verb it attaches to has stress, and based on this requirement, English lacks nouns like **fidgetal*, **promisal*, and **abandonal*. The data in (1) and (2) exemplify the other two requirements.

Requirement 2:
(1) betrothal, arrival, acquittal
    *rebukal, *impeachal, *detachal

Requirement 3:
(2) rental, dispersal, rehearsal
    *acceptal, *resistal, *engraftal

Some Distinctive Features for Consonants

Distinctive Features	Labials	Dentals/ Alveolars	Palato- alveolars	Velars
[anterior]	+	+	−	−
[coronal]	−	+	+	−

Distinctive Features	Nasal stops	Oral stops	Fricatives	Liquids/ Glides
[sonorant]	+	−	−	+
[continuant]	−	−	+	+

Describe Requirements 2 and 3 based on the data in (1) and (2), respectively. For each requirement, use ONE or TWO distinctive features from the list above.

6. Read the passage in <A> and examine the teaching procedure in <B>. Then follow the directions. 【3 points】

—————————<A>—————————

Processing instruction, a type of focus-on-form instruction, is based on the assumption that when processing input, L2 learners have difficulty in attending to form and meaning at the same time due to working memory limitations. Not surprisingly, they tend to give priority to meaning and tend not to notice details of form. Processing instruction uses several principles to explain what learners attend to in the input and why. Below are some of these principles.

The Lexical Preference Principle: In (1), both -*es* and *boy* convey the same information, 'the third person singular'. Yet, learners prefer to focus on the lexical item, *boy*, to arrive at meaning, and often ignore the grammatical item, -*es*, while processing the sentence.

  (1) The *boy* stud*ies* in the library, not at home.

The First Noun Principle: Learners tend to process the first noun or pronoun they encounter in a sentence as the agent of action. For example, they may misinterpret (2) as "Jack collected the data for the project."

  (2) *Jack* let *Joe* collect the data for the project.

The Event Possibilities Principle: Event possibilities refer to the likelihood of one noun being the agent of action as opposed to another. Since it is more likely in the real world that a dog would bite a man than the other way around, learners would likely misinterpret (3) as "The dog bit the farmer."

  (3) The dog was bitten by the farmer.

In processing instruction, teachers provide students with structured input activities, taking into consideration the principles above. In a structured input activity, students are forced to attend to form in order to comprehend a sentence.

—————————<B>—————————

Teaching Procedure

1. **Explicit Explanation**
   Explain how a past tense sentence is constructed in English. Then inform students of why they tend not to notice the past tense marker -*ed* and thus misinterpret past tense sentences.

2. **Structured Input Activity**
   Have students read six sentences and decide whether they describe an activity that was done in the past or usually happens in the present. Then, check the answers together.

Sentences	Present	Past
(1) They watched television at night.	☐	☐
(2) They watch television at night.	☐	☐
(3) I walk to school on Mondays.	☐	☐
(4) I walked to school on Mondays.	☐	☐
(5) We played soccer on weekends.	☐	☐
(6) We play soccer on weekends.	☐	☐

Identify the principle in <A> that the teaching procedure in <B> focuses on. Then explain how the structured input activity in <B> helps students correctly process the target form for meaning.

<수고하셨습니다.>

○ 문제지 전체 면수가 맞는지 확인하시오.
○ 모든 문항에는 배점이 표시되어 있습니다.

※ **Write all answers in English.**

서술형 【1 ~ 2】

1. Read the passage and follow the directions. 【5 points】

The population of a certain species tends to remain relatively stable over long periods of time. After domestic sheep became established on the island of Tasmania in the early nineteenth century, for instance, their population varied irregularly between 1,230,000 and 2,250,000—less than a factor of 2—over nearly a century. We know this because sheep were, and still are, very important to the economy of Tasmania, and their numbers were carefully recorded. In sharp contrast, populations of small, short-lived organisms may fluctuate wildly over many orders of magnitude within short periods. Populations of the green algae and diatoms that make up the phytoplankton may soar and crash over periods of a few days or weeks. These rapid fluctuations overlay changes with longer periods that occur, for example, on a seasonal basis.

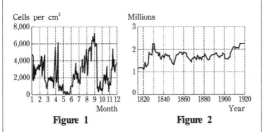

Figure 1   **Figure 2**

Why do sheep and algae show such disparate fluctuations in population? First of all, sheep and algae differ in their sensitivity to environmental change. Because sheep are larger, they have a greater capacity for homeostasis and better resist the physiological effects of environmental change. Furthermore, the populations of sheep and algae are differentially affected by birth rate fluctuations. Because sheep have a relatively long lifespan, short-term fluctuations in birth rate do not greatly affect the overall population at a given time. Thus, sheep populations possess a high intrinsic

---

stability. On the other hand, the lives of single-celled algal cells span only a few days, so these intrinsically unstable populations turn over rapidly.

* homeostasis: the maintenance of a stable equilibrium

Identify the figure that represents the fluctuations in sheep population and explain why the sheep population fluctuated the way the figure depicts. Do NOT copy more than FIVE consecutive words from the passage.

2. Read the poem and follow the directions. 【5 points】

Say not the struggle naught availeth,
　The labour and the wounds are vain,
The enemy faints not, nor faileth,
　And as things have been they remain.

If hopes were dupes, fears may be liars;
　It may be, in yon smoke conceal'd,
Your comrades chase e'en now the fliers,
　And, but for you, possess the field.

For while the tired waves, vainly breaking,
　Seem here no painful inch to gain,
Far back, through creeks and inlets making,
　Comes silent, flooding in, the main.

And not by eastern windows only,
　When daylight comes, comes in the light;
In front the sun climbs slow, how slowly!
　But westward, look, the land is bright!

* yon: over there
* fliers: runaway soldiers
* the main: the sea

Describe the theme of the poem and explain how the metaphor, "the main" (Line 12), is related to the theme.

논술형 【1 ~ 2】

1. Read the passage and follow the directions. 【10 points】

> Korea is quickly becoming an aging society. Consequently, we need to prepare so that we can effectively deal with the changes this situation will bring about. Clearly, these changes will have a wide-ranging impact on different facets of the nation. We should consider how we must prepare for the future from both individual and societal perspectives. Below are some of the points to consider within these two main areas.
>
> • **Possible preparation points at the individual level**
>   Develop life-long hobbies
>   Embrace healthier lifestyles
>   Seek financial self-sufficiency
>
> • **Possible preparation points at the societal level**
>   Re-examine mandatory retirement ages
>   Improve the healthcare system
>   Expand the existing pension system

How must we prepare for the future? Choose one preparation point that you think is most important at each level, and write a composition following the guidelines below.

> **<Guidelines>**
> • Write TWO paragraphs, one for each preparation point.
> • For each paragraph, include a topic sentence.
> • Support each preparation point with two specific reasons.
> • Use neat handwriting.

2. Examine the class observation checklist and notes completed by a middle school English teacher after observing a colleague's class, and follow the directions. 【10 points】

Observation Checklist

Instructor: *Sumi Kim*   Unit: *4. Personal Health*
Topic: *How to treat acne*   Function: *Giving advice*
Period: *2/8*   Date: *Nov. 11*

Areas	Criteria	Scale*
Lesson Preparation	• have a clearly developed lesson plan	1 -②- 3
	• prepare interesting multimedia materials	1 — 2 -③
Instructional Strategies	• give clear directions	1 -②- 3
	• use an appropriate grouping strategy for group activities	①- 2 — 3
	• provide level-appropriate activities	1 -②- 3
Affective Aspects	• create a warm and accepting atmosphere	1 — 2 -③

* 1 = poor, 2 = average, 3 = good

Notes

> - A fun video clip on acne. SS loved it.
> - T was kind and patient.
> - Group activity (same-ability grouping)
>   ▸ Higher-level students did well. Had no problems.
>   ▸ Lower-level students had a hard time completing the task. Seemed like they needed some help.

In one paragraph, identify one strong point and one weak point of the lesson based on the data above. Support each of your choices with details from both the checklist and the notes. In another paragraph, address the problems the lower-level students are experiencing by suggesting two possible solutions and supporting them with your rationales.

<수고하셨습니다.>

○ 문제지 전체 면수가 맞는지 확인하시오.
○ 모든 문항에는 배점이 표시되어 있습니다.

※ **Write all answers in English and use neat handwriting.**

기입형 【1 ~ 10】

1. Read the passage and fill in the blank with ONE word from the passage. 【2 points】

A psychology professor spent several decades studying the "fixed mindset entity theory." She refers to people who view talent as a quality they either possess or lack as having a "fixed mindset." People with a "growth mindset," in contrast, enjoy challenges, strive to learn, and consistently see potential to develop new skills.

Now Carol Dweck, the psychology professor, is extending her work on mindset beyond individuals. Can an organization, like an individual, have a fixed or a growth mindset? If so, how can managers help organizations embrace a growth mindset? To explore this issue, she conducted surveys and found that often top management must drive the change; for instance, a new CEO might focus on maximizing employees' potential. Dweck points to one emblematic growth mindset CEO who hired according to "runway," not pedigree, preferring big state university graduates and military veterans to Ivy Leaguers, and spent thousands of hours grooming and coaching employees on his executive team.

As this CEO's example shows, one area in which mindset is especially important is hiring. Fixed mindset organizations reflexively look outside their companies, while growth mindset organizations are likely to hire from within their ranks. "Focusing on _____ is not as effective as looking for people who love challenges, who want to grow, and who want to collaborate," Dweck says. Some companies appear to be making such a shift; these companies have recently begun hiring more people who have proven that they are capable independent learners.

Despite the survey results, not all employees will be happier in growth mindset organizations, Dweck acknowledges. In general, though, the early evidence suggests that organizations focused on employees' capacity for growth will experience significant advantages.

2. Read Mr. Han's materials for his level-differentiated classes, and follow the directions. 【2 points】

The original text is for 2nd year high school students.

Original

No sooner had my plane landed than I was charmed by Korea. I particularly like the outdoor street markets and the strength and openness of the people who work there.

(A)

When my plane landed I was charmed by Korea. I particularly like the outdoor street markets and the strength and openness of the people there.

(B)

No sooner had my plane landed than I was enthralled by Korea. I particularly like the outdoor street markets and the integrity and receptiveness of the people who work there.

Complete the comments by filling in each blank with ONE word. Write your answers in the correct order.

The original text has been adapted to suit the students' English proficiency levels. (A) shows how input is simplified through ____①____ modification to make the original text easier for the lower level students. (B) shows how input is adapted through ____②____ modification to make the original text more challenging for the upper level students.

3. Read the passage and follow the directions. 【2 points】

Mr. Lee's English listening test consisted exclusively of four-option, multiple-choice items. After scoring the test, he calculated the response frequency for each item. Part of the results is presented below.

Item\Option	Upper Group (N=100)				Lower Group (N=100)			
	A	B	C	D	A	B	C	D
1	50%*	27%	13%	10%	10%*	45%	25%	20%
2	13%	10%	70%*	7%	25%	27%	28%*	20%
3	20%	25%	18%	37%*	21%	26%	16%	37%*
...								
17	4%	0%	61%	35%*	66%	0%	29%	5%*
...								

Note: * indicates the correct response.

Complete the comments on item analysis by filling in each blank with ONE word. Write your answers in the correct order.

Items 1 and 2 seem to be fulfilling their function. Item 3 has the problem of item ___①___ . Therefore, option D of item 3 needs to be revised or item 3 needs to be discarded. Item 17 has a problem with its ___②___ : No one from the upper group and lower group chose option B, and many upper group students incorrectly chose option C.

4. Read the conversation and follow the directions. 【2 points】

T: The other day we were talking about the Battle of Waterloo. And we've already talked about the two main generals in that war. Does anybody remember who they are?

S1: Napoleon and Wellington.

T: Correct, but don't forget that Wellington is a title which he received for his military successes. Born Arthur Wesley, he became the Duke of Wellington in 1814. He received that title for ending the Peninsular War by storming what city?

S2: Toulouse.

T: That's right. Shortly after, Napoleon abdicated and was imprisoned on Elba. And when did the Battle of Waterloo take place?

S3: 1815.

T: Very good. Napoleon escaped Elba and was attempting to restore his rule. It wasn't until his defeat at Waterloo by Wellington that Napoleon's reign finally came to an end. Now we're going to see ...

Note: T = teacher, S = student

Complete the comments on the conversation above by filling in the blank with ONE word.

The conversation above is part of a teacher-student talk in the classroom in which a teacher and students mainly give and receive specific information. Among types of speaking functions, the type shown in the conversation refers to situations where the focus is on information rather than on the participants. The conversation above serves a(n) _____ function in that its priority is not the interpersonal function of speaking but information exchange.

5. Read the conversation between two high school English teachers, and identify the type of reading that Ms. Kim recommends to Mr. Hong. Use TWO words. 【2 points】

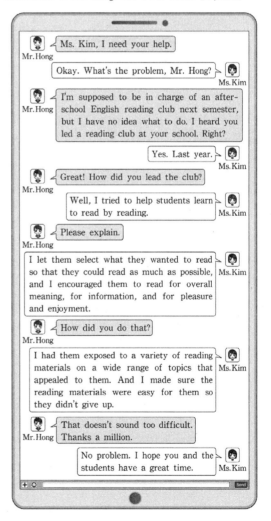

Mr. Hong: Ms. Kim, I need your help.

Ms. Kim: Okay. What's the problem, Mr. Hong?

Mr. Hong: I'm supposed to be in charge of an after-school English reading club next semester, but I have no idea what to do. I heard you led a reading club at your school. Right?

Ms. Kim: Yes. Last year.

Mr. Hong: Great! How did you lead the club?

Ms. Kim: Well, I tried to help students learn to read by reading.

Mr. Hong: Please explain.

Ms. Kim: I let them select what they wanted to read so that they could read as much as possible, and I encouraged them to read for overall meaning, for information, and for pleasure and enjoyment.

Mr. Hong: How did you do that?

Ms. Kim: I had them exposed to a variety of reading materials on a wide range of topics that appealed to them. And I made sure the reading materials were easy for them so they didn't give up.

Mr. Hong: That doesn't sound too difficult. Thanks a million.

Ms. Kim: No problem. I hope you and the students have a great time.

6. Read the poem and follow the directions. 【2 points】

> I look into my glass,
> And view my wasting skin,
> And say, "Would God it came to pass
> My heart had shrunk as thin!"
>
> For then, I, undistrest
> By hearts grown cold to me,
> Could lonely wait my endless rest
> With equanimity.
>
> But Time, to make me grieve,
> Part steals, lets part abide;
> And shakes this fragile frame at eve
> With throbbings of noontide.

Complete the statement by filling in the blank with ONE word from the poem.

> The speaker's distress will come to _____ when bodily and emotional deterioration go hand in hand.

7. Read the passage and fill in each blank with ONE word. Write your answers in the correct order. 【2 points】

> A glottal stop is the sound that occurs when the vocal cords are held tightly together. In many accents of English, a glottal stop is often realized as a(n) _____①_____ of /t/ in the words given in (1).
>
> (1) Batman   catnap
>   /t/   /t/
>   butler   atlas
>   /t/   /t/
>
> While the /t/ in the words in (1) can be produced as a glottal stop, the /t/ in the words in (2) cannot be realized as a glottal stop.
>
> (2) atrocious   attraction
>   /t/   /t/
>   atrophic   patrol
>   /t/   /t/
>
> The data given in (1) and (2) show that, unlike the /t/ in the words in (1), the /t/ in the words in (2) is in a(n) _____②_____ position of a syllable, and thus it cannot be produced as a glottal stop.
>
> *Note*: In the words in (1) and (2), the underlined spelling of *t* or *tt* represents /t/.

8. Read the passage and follow the directions. 【2 points】

> We know nothing of David Swan until we find him, at the age of twenty, on the road to the city of Boston, where he will work at his uncle's grocery store. After journeying on foot from sunrise till nearly noon on a summer's day, his tiredness and the increasing heat force him to rest in the first convenient shade, and wait for a stage-coach. As if planted on purpose, there soon appeared a small growth of maple trees, with a delightful clearing in the middle beside a fresh bubbling spring. He kissed it with his thirsty lips, and then flung himself beside it, pillowing his head upon some shirts. The spring murmured drowsily beside him and a deep sleep fell upon David Swan.
>
> While he lay sound asleep in the shade, other people were wide awake, and passed here and there along the sunny road by his bed. Some looked neither to the right nor to the left, and never knew he was there; some laughed to see how soundly he slept; and several, whose hearts were brimming with scorn, spoke aloud their criticism of David Swan. Soon, a wealthy merchant with no heir considered waking him to share his fortune, but walked away. A beautiful young woman, momentarily touched by his peacefulness, considered loving him, but continued on her way. Two dark and dangerous thieves considered taking his life for his wallet, but decided they did not have time. But disapproval, praise, amusement, scorn, and indifference, were all one, or rather all nothing, and had no influence on the sleeping David Swan.
>
> He slept, but no longer so quietly as at first. Now he stirred as a noise of wheels came rattling louder and louder along the road, until it rushed into the sleepy mist of David's rest—and there was the stage-coach. He rose, with all his ideas about him. He knew not that the possibility of Wealth or Love or Death had recently stood beside him—all, in the brief hour since he lay down to sleep.
>
> Sleeping or waking, we rarely hear the soft footsteps of the strange things that almost happen. Doesn't this argue that there is a superintending Providence that, while viewless and unexpected events throw themselves continually in our path, there should still exist enough regularity in mortal life for us to foresee at least some of the possibilities available to us?

Complete the commentary by filling in the blank with ONE word from the passage.

> **Commentary**
>
> The passage conveys that we are unaware of many events in our lives which could _____ our destiny. The occurrences are frequent but we do not notice them. Thus, we must wonder if it is better to know all of one's possibilities or if this knowledge is too much for an individual to comprehend.

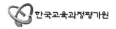

9. Read the excerpt from a play and follow the directions.
【2 points】

[PETER *reacts scoffingly.*]

Jerry: Yes, Peter; friend. That's the only word for it. I was heart-shatteringly et cetera to confront my doggy friend again. I came in the door and advanced, unafraid, to the center of the entrance hall. The beast was there . . . looking at me. And, you know, he looked better for his scrape with the nevermind. I stopped; I looked at him; he looked at me. I think . . . I think we stayed a long time that way . . . still, stone-statue . . . just looking at one another. I looked more into his face than he looked into mine. I mean, I can concentrate longer at looking into a dog's face than a dog can concentrate at looking into mine, or into anybody else's face, for that matter. But during that twenty seconds or two hours that we looked into each other's face, we made contact. Now, here is what I had wanted to happen: I loved the dog now, and I wanted him to love me. I had tried to love, and I had tried to kill, and both had been unsuccessful by themselves. I hoped . . . and I don't really know why I expected the dog to understand anything, much less my motivations . . . I hoped that the dog would understand. [PETER *seems to be hypnotized.*] It's just . . . it's just that . . . [JERRY *is abnormally tense, now.*] . . . it's just that if you can't deal with people, you have to make a start somewhere. WITH ANIMALS! [*Much faster now, and like a conspirator*] Don't you see? A person has to have some way of dealing with SOMETHING. If not with people . . . SOMETHING. . . . A dog. It seemed like a perfectly sensible idea. Man is a dog's best friend, remember. So: the dog and I looked at each other. I longer than the dog. And what I saw then has been the same ever since. Whenever the dog and I see each other we both stop where we are. The dog and I have attained a compromise; more of a bargain, really. We neither love nor hurt because we do not try to reach each other. And, *was* trying to feed the dog an act of love? And, perhaps, was the dog's attempt to bite me not an act of love? If we can so misunderstand, well then, why have we invented the word love in the first place?

[*There is silence. JERRY moves to Peter's bench and sits down beside him. This is the first time Jerry has sat down during the play.*]

The Story of Jerry and the Dog: the end.

[PETER *is silent.*]

Complete the commentary by filling in the blank with TWO consecutive words from the excerpt. Change the word form(s) if necessary.

Commentary

Jerry is desperate to have a meaningful conversation with Peter who lives in ignorance of the world outside his settled life. Jerry starts to _____ with an animal first in order to deal with Peter.

---

10. Read the passage and fill in the blank with ONE word.
【2 points】

The sentences in (1) show three types of NPs: the reflexive pronoun, the ordinary pronoun, and the proper noun.

(1) a. John likes himself.
    b. Mary met him.
    c. John came.

The reflexive pronoun should have the antecedent in the sentence from which it picks up its reference as shown in (2), with the coindexed NPs indicating the same referent. This sharply contrasts with the ordinary pronoun and the proper noun in (3).

(2) a. John$_i$ introduced himself$_i$ to Mary.
    b. *Himself came.

(3) a. John$_i$ introduced him$_j$ to Mary.
    b. John introduced Bill to Mary.

The existence of the antecedent in the sentence, however, is not a sufficient condition to license the reflexive pronoun, as shown in (4).

(4) a. *John$_i$ thinks that himself$_i$ is intelligent.
    b. John told Mary$_i$ about herself$_i$.

The examples in (2) and (4) show that the reflexive pronoun finds its antecedent in the smallest _____ that contains it. The sentences in (2b) and (4a) are thus ungrammatical in contrast to those in (2a) and (4b).

Note: * indicates that the sentence is ungrammatical.

---

1. Read the lesson procedure and write the TWO lesson objectives. Do NOT copy more than FIVE consecutive words from the passage. 【5 points】

The following is a sample lesson plan of culture-integrated language learning for 2nd year middle school students.

Lesson Procedure

(1) Students watch a video clip that shows an experiment, which is summarized below.

The experiment shows that American mothers used twice as many object labels as Japanese mothers ("piggie," "doggie") and Japanese mothers engaged in twice as many social routines of teaching politeness norms (empathy and greetings). An American mother's pattern might go like this: "That's a car. See the car? You like it? It's got nice wheels." A Japanese mother might say: "Here! It's a vroom vroom. I give it to you. Now give this to me. Yes! Thank you." American children are learning that the world is mostly a place with objects, Japanese children that the world is mostly about relationships. Relationships usually involve a verb. Verbs are more important in Asian languages than in English. Asians tend to use an expression like "Drink more?" rather than "More tea?" when they perceive there is a need. Americans are noun-oriented, pointing objects out to their children, naming them, and telling them about their attributes. Nouns denote categories.

(2) Students share their own experiences about noun-oriented expressions as opposed to verb-oriented ones, and discuss different ways of thinking for those expressions.

(3) Students do Activity 1 in order to learn a variety of noun-oriented English expressions.

<Activity 1> Fill in the blanks with appropriate words.

Verb-Oriented Expressions	Noun-Oriented Expressions
He works hard.	He is a hard worker.
My head aches.	I _____ .
He is very humorous.	He has a good _____ .
· · ·	· · ·

(4) Students discuss why noun-oriented expressions are more frequently used in English than verb-oriented ones.

(5) Students engage in the following activity to reinforce their awareness of the cultural difference between the West and the East.

Q: If you have a bad cold, which of the following wouldn't you say?
A: ① I've got a stuffy nose.
　 ② I have a runny nose.
　 ③ My nose is sick.

2. Read the passage in <A> and the conversation in <B>, and follow the directions. 【5 points】

―――――<A>―――――

In negotiation of meaning, "uptake" refers to an interlocutor's immediate response to his or her partner's signal of noncomprehension. In uptake, the interlocutor often uses a variety of communication strategies such as message abandonment, topic change, circumlocution, word coinage, foreignizing, and code switching.

―――――<B>―――――

The following is part of a teacher-student interaction that contains negotiation of meaning.

T: Hi, Sangjee. How was your weekend?
S: Hello. Well, I had a busy weekend.
T: Did you go anywhere?
S: No, I stayed home all weekend.
T: Why were you busy, then?
S: I had to fly ten chickens.
T: Uh, what? What did you do?
S: Uh, you know, put chickens in oil, very hot oil, kind of bake them.
T: Oh, you FRIED them!
S: Yeah, I fried them with my mother.
T: Why did you have to fry that many chickens?
S: We had a big party on Sunday. My grandfather's birthday. Many people came.
T: Oh, so that's why you fried so many. The party must have been a lot of fun.

Note: T = teacher, S = student

Identify where the uptake takes place by writing the specific utterance from <B>, and select the strategy used in the uptake from those in <A>. Then explain how the utterance in the uptake shows the selected strategy.

3. Read the excerpt and follow the directions. 【5 points】

(A) There is a time in the life of every boy when he for the first time takes a backward view of life. Perhaps that is the moment when he crosses the line into manhood. George is walking through the street of his town. He is thinking of the future and of the figure he will cut in the world. Ambitions and regrets awake within him. Suddenly something happens; he stops under a tree and waits as for a voice calling his name. Ghosts of old things creep into his consciousness; the voices outside of himself whisper a message concerning the limitations of life. From being quite sure of himself and his future he becomes not at all sure.

(B) If he be an imaginative boy a door is torn open and for the first time he looks out upon the world, seeing, as though they marched in procession before him, the countless figures of men who before his time have come out of nothingness into the world, lived their lives and again disappeared into nothingness. The sadness of sophistication has come to the boy. With a little gasp he sees himself as merely a leaf blown by the wind through the streets of his village. He knows that in spite of all the stout talk of his fellows he must live and die in uncertainty, a thing blown by the winds, a thing destined like corn to wilt in the sun. He shivers and looks eagerly about. The eighteen years he has lived seem but a moment, a breathing space in the long march of humanity. Already he hears death calling. With all his heart he wants to come close to some other human, touch someone with his hands, be touched by the hand of another. If he prefers that the other be a woman, that is because he believes that a woman will be gentle, that she will understand. He wants, most of all, understanding.

A rite of passage is a transition associated with a crisis or a change of status for an individual. With this in mind, explain the figurative meaning of the underlined words in section (B). Support your explanation with TWO examples from section (A). Do NOT copy more than FIVE consecutive words from the excerpt.

4. Read the passage in <A> and the sentence in <B>, and follow the directions. 【5 points】

―――――――<A>―――――――

Linguistic expressions are often ambiguous, and homonymy is one source of ambiguity. Homonyms are words that have different meanings but are pronounced the same, and may or may not be spelled the same. Another source of ambiguity is structure. Sometimes, homonymy creates even more ambiguity in combination with different structures.

(1) John admires intelligent professors and students.
(2) They are pitchers from America.
(3) Mary observed the man at the bank.

The ambiguity in (1) is created by different structures. The source of the ambiguity in (2) is homonymy, whereas (3) is ambiguous due to different structures and homonymy.

―――――――<B>―――――――

Mary saw John's nose ring.

Identify the source(s) of the ambiguity of the sentence in <B>. Then explain why the sentence is ambiguous and write the two readings of the sentence.

<수고하셨습니다.>

○ 문제지 전체 면수가 맞는지 확인하시오.
○ 모든 문항에는 배점이 표시되어 있습니다.

※ **Write all answers in English and use neat handwriting.**

서술형 【1 ~ 4】

1. Read the passage in <A> and the table in <B>, and follow the directions. 【5 points】

------------------------<A>------------------------

As part of an effort to maximize opportunities for her students to interact with others in English, Ms. Park, a high school English teacher, plans to design her lessons from a blended learning perspective. She is considering having the students interact with each other and her both online and offline. She designs lessons as follows: Online activities are based on a synchronous computer-mediated communication (CMC) interaction, and the transcripts of the online interaction are used a couple of days later for offline discussion.

Realizing that many of her students seem shy, frustrated, and uncomfortable with face-to-face discussion, she would like to use a CMC tool to help students get ready for an offline discussion. By examining their online production with peers and the teacher, she believes that CMC activities will guarantee more equalized opportunities for participation and make students' errors more salient and thus open to feedback and correction.

------------------------<B>------------------------

Evaluation of Three CMC Tools

Tools Criteria	Tool A	Tool B	Tool C
Easy to Use	Y	Y	Y
Saving and Archiving	Y	N	Y
Real-Time Interaction	N	Y	Y
Video Chatting	N	Y	N
Online Dictionary	Y	N	N

Note: Y = Yes, N = No

Based on the information in <A> and <B>, identify the tool you would recommend for Ms. Park, and provide TWO reasons for your recommendation.

2. Read the passage and follow the directions. 【5 points】

Scientists made a splash last week when they presented a radical new view of DNA, solving a puzzle that has long gnawed at investigators and shedding light on diseases such as cancer, heart disease, and Alzheimer's. Ever since decoding the human genome, scientists have been perplexed by the long strands of our DNA that appear to do nothing. They called the idle double helixes "junk DNA," thinking they were nothing but leftovers from ill-fitting assembly parts, useless bits of this and that, last season's models.

The days of junk status are now officially over. Working for almost 10 years on a collaborative project, 440 scientists from 32 labs across the globe announced that they have finally figured out just what the silent majority of our DNA does: It's middle management.

It seems these large branches of the DNA family tree—formerly called "junk" but now renamed as "dark matter"—run the factory but don't actually make anything. They're the deciders, the guys with administrative approval to greenlight a project or stop it cold—in this case to determine which genes step forward to produce a protein and which ones remain stalled, waiting for that second chance. And with a million supervisors for every 23,000 genes, a ratio of about 50 to 1, it appears middle management is well staffed.

Though perhaps a bit humbling to discover that our DNA is so bureaucratic, the insight is likely to result in substantial medical benefit. Up to now, therapies have focused on influencing the behavior of the gene itself—sometimes successfully but often not. The problem is that genetic mutations, though somewhat understood for many diseases, have proven difficult to fix. The realization that genes are surrounded by an entourage of promoters and suppressors expands the list of possible targets for intervention considerably. In cystic fibrosis, for example, we've discovered the genetic mutation that causes disease, but we've been unable to repair it. Using the new approach, researchers might defuse not the mutant gene itself but one of the bits of DNA responsible for greenlighting the bad gene's expression.

Describe what the underlined words mean in the above context, and explain why DNA's "middle management" could be the key to future cures.

3. Read the passage and follow the directions. 【5 points】

> Words such as *music* [mjuzɪk] and *cube* [kjub] are pronounced in the same way in both American English and British English. However, words such as *tuition, endure,* and *annuity* vary, as shown in (1a) and (1b).
>
> (1a) British English
>
> tuition [tjuɪʃən]   duration [djʊreɪʃən]
>
> endure [ɪndjʊə]   annuity [ənjuəti]
>
> perpetuity [pɜːpətjuəti]   voluminous [vəljumənəs]
>
> (1b) American English
>
> tuition [tuɪʃən]   duration [dʊreɪʃən]
>
> endure [ɪndʊr]   annuity [ənuəti]
>
> perpetuity [pɜpətuəti]   voluminous [vəlumənəs]
>
> While in British English we see a /j/ after the underlined consonants /t/, /d/, /n/, and /l/ in the words given in (1a), the expected American English pronunciations are without a /j/ after the same underlined consonants, as shown in (1b). The same difference is observed after the underlined consonants /s/ and /z/ for the words in (2a) and (2b).
>
> (2a) British English
>
> assume [əsjum]   superb [sjupɜːb]
>
> exude [ɪgzjud]   résumé [rɛzjʊmeɪ]
>
> (2b) American English
>
> assume [əsum]   superb [supɜb]
>
> exude [ɪgzud]   résumé [rɛzʊmeɪ]
>
> However, the words given in (3) show that the underlined alveolars /n/ and /l/ are followed by a /j/ in American English as well as in British English.
>
> (3) British English and American English
>
> continue [kəntɪnju]   biannual [baɪænjuəl]
>
> voluble [vɑljʊbəl]   valuation [væljueɪʃən]
>
> *Note*: Vowel differences in some words between British English and American English are not represented in the data above.

Based on the data given in (1b), (2b), and (3), state the condition(s) when /j/ cannot follow alveolar consonants and the condition(s) when /j/ can in American English.

4. Read the passage in <A> and the sentences in <B>, and follow the directions. 【5 points】

> ───────────<A>───────────
>
> Preverbal adverbs sometimes behave differently in terms of scope. The sentence in (1a) with the adverb *usually* can be paraphrased into (1b) and (1c). One can represent the two paraphrases using the schemata in (2a) and (2b), respectively.
>
> (1) a. John usually comes late for class.
>
> b. It is usual that John comes late for class.
>
> c. It is usually the case that John comes late for class.
>
> (2) a. It be ____X____ that ____Y____ .
>
> b. It be ____X____ the case that ____Y____ .
>
> In (2a), X stands for the adjective form of the adverb, and Y for the rest of the original sentence. In (2b), X stands for the adverb, and Y for the rest of the original sentence. In the meantime, sentences with a preverbal adverb such as *carefully* cannot be so paraphrased as illustrated in (3).
>
> (3) a. John carefully drives his car in winter.
>
> b. *It is careful that John drives his car in winter.
>
> c. *It is carefully the case that John drives his car in winter.
>
> *Note*: * indicates that the sentence is ungrammatical.
>
> ───────────<B>───────────
>
> (i) John rarely talks with philosophers.
>
> (ii) The fish slowly swims.

Based on the discussion of the two types of adverbs in <A>, a *usually* type and a *carefully* type, identify the type of the underlined adverbs in <B>. Then verify their type by writing the paraphrases of (i) and (ii), using the schemata in (2).

논술형 【1 ~ 2】

1. Read the passage and follow the directions. 【10 points】

All products may be considered as either disposable or durable. Disposable products are goods made for short-term usage, many even meant to be thrown away after one use. Manufacturing them requires constant development of new designs and the employment of large numbers of workers. This provides ongoing benefits for the growth of the economy. However, this type of production causes a great deal of waste. Some disposable products like plastic bags do not easily decompose and thus have anything but a positive impact on the environment.

Durable products are intended to last for a long time. As such, any given product would be sold less often. However, making products durable requires the support of secondary industries to supply parts and do repairs. This, in turn, establishes long-standing economic advantages. In addition, long-term use of products helps cut emissions of pollutants. As durable products also include less residual waste, landfill expansion is significantly reduced, which makes them a good environmental choice.

How do different types of products affect the economy and the environment? Write a composition following the guidelines below.

Guidelines
- Write TWO paragraphs based on the above passage: one a comparison paragraph regarding the effect on the economy and the other a contrast paragraph on the environment.
- Provide each paragraph with a topic sentence and two supporting pieces of evidence.
- Do NOT copy more than FIVE consecutive words from the passage.

2. Read two middle school students' opinions about an English lesson posted on the online bulletin board and their teacher's teaching log, and follow the directions. 【10 points】

Bulletin Board

Sumi

I loved today's lesson! When the teacher asked questions about the words and expressions related to cooking using the recipe from a cooking magazine, I was able to clearly figure out the meaning of what we were supposed to learn. It was really motivating to use the recipe for learning about the words and expressions used practically for cooking. But I made a few errors, such as telling the difference between "slice" and "chop," that I think I will repeat again despite the teacher's correction. When I make errors, I want him to give me some time to think about why I make them and how I can correct them myself.

Inho

When the teacher asked us to bring a recipe from a cooking magazine yesterday for today's lesson, I wondered why. But when he asked questions about some words and expressions related to cooking using the recipes we brought, I realized why. When asking and answering about them using the cooking material with the teacher and then with my partner, I came to clearly understand the meaning of the words and expressions. Plus, it was very fun and exciting. But I didn't like that he corrected my errors when I misused the word "pan" in "boiling water in the pan"; I prefer getting correction from my friends because it makes me feel more comfortable.

My Teaching Log

What I put emphasis on in today's class

I always want my students to have a clear understanding of what I teach, so today I tried to teach the points using materials used in real life rather than the ones in the textbook. To my surprise, they really loved the way I taught today. They participated in the lesson with a lot of enthusiasm.

The things I have to improve in the next class

While leading the activity, for convenience' sake, I corrected the errors that students made. Considering their opinions, however, I have to use alternate ways to give them a chance to correct their errors individually or in pairs.

In one paragraph, identify ONE feature of the teacher's lesson that the students liked, and explain TWO reasons why they liked it. In another paragraph, address ONE problem with the lesson, and suggest TWO solutions from the teacher's standpoint by supporting them with rationale. Both paragraphs must be based only on the bulletin board and the teaching log above.

《수고하셨습니다.》

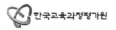

제1차 시험	2교시 전공A	14문항 40점	시험 시간 90분

○ 문제지 전체 면수가 맞는지 확인하시오.
○ 모든 문항에는 배점이 표시되어 있습니다.

※ **Write all answers in English and use neat handwriting.**

1. Read the lesson procedure and follow the directions.
【2 points】

Lesson Procedure

1. Ss listen to a recorded conversation about the topic of the lesson.
2. T asks Ss to make associations among key words and to guess the meaning of the words from context. Then T teaches new vocabulary.
3. Ss read passages and find semantic clues to get the main idea.
4. Ss reread the passages and scan for specific information.
5. Ss, in groups, do categorizing activities.
6. Ss discuss the topic and write a short comment on it.
7. T hands out the checklist and has Ss keep a daily log after school for one week.

A Daily Learning Log

Name: *Jihae Park*
※ Respond to each of the following statements with a checkmark (✔).

	Day 1			Day 2			Day 3			Day 4			Day 5		
	1	2	3	1	2	3	1	2	3	1	2	3	1	2	3
1. I make guesses to understand unfamiliar words.															
2. I first read over passages quickly, and then go back and reread them.															
3. I make summaries of the text that I read in English.															
19. I ask a friend questions about schoolwork.															
20. I write down my feelings in a language learning diary.															

Note: 1 = Never, 2 = Sometimes, 3 = Always

Note: T = teacher, S = student

Complete the comments by filling in the blanks with the SAME word.

The lesson procedure shows that the students are instructed to practice various kinds of _____ during the class. Also, they are encouraged to be aware of their use of _____ by keeping a daily learning log.

---

2. Read the poem and follow the directions. 【2 points】

Some time when the river is ice ask me
mistakes I have made. Ask me whether
what I have done is my life. Others
have come in their slow way into
my thought, and some have tried to help
or to hurt—ask me what difference
their strongest love or hate has made.

I will listen to what you say.
You and I can turn and look
at the silent river and wait. We know
the current is there, hidden; and there
are comings and goings from miles away
that hold the stillness exactly before us.
What the river says, that is what I say.

Complete the commentary by filling in the blank with ONE word from the poem.

Commentary

Out there will be the world confronting us both; we will both know we are surrounded by mystery, tremendous things that do not reveal themselves to us. That river, that world— and our lives—all share the depth and _____ of much more significance than our talk, or intentions. There is a steadiness and somehow a solace in knowing that what is around us so greatly surpasses our human concerns.

---

3. Read the activity procedure and identify the type of learning activity with ONE word. 【2 points】

	Activity Procedure
Step 1	• T places various information on a different job in each of the four corners in the classroom. (Each corner is labelled with a different letter, A, B, C, or D.) • T assigns individual Ss a letter (A, B, C, or D) in order to create four groups of four Ss, each of which is a base group composed of A to D.
Step 2	• T provides Ss in each base group with handouts. (Each handout has a set of questions about four different jobs.) • T helps Ss understand that they should be interdependent upon one another not only for their own learning but also for the learning of others throughout the activity. • T informs Ss which corner to go to based on their letter in order to form four different expert groups.
Step 3	• Ss move to their expert groups and find out information about different jobs through discussions and answer the questions on the handouts. • T circulates within the groups and makes sure each of the Ss has all the answers.
Step 4	• Ss return to their initial base groups and exchange the information through discussing what they learned in the expert groups. • All the base groups present their findings to the whole class and decide which job they would like most.

Note: T = teacher, S = student

4. Read the passage and write TWO consecutive words from the passage that show what Steve thinks psychoanalysis does. 【2 points】

HENRIETTA: It's like this, Mabel. You want something. You think you can't have it. You think it's wrong. So you try to think you don't want it. Your mind protects you—avoids pain—by refusing to think the forbidden thing. But it's there just the same. It stays there shut up in your unconscious mind, and it festers.

STEVE: Sort of an ingrowing mental toenail.

HENRIETTA: Precisely. The forbidden impulse is there full of energy which has simply got to do something. It breaks into your consciousness in disguise, masks itself in dreams, makes all sorts of trouble. In extreme cases it drives you insane.

MABEL [*with a gesture of horror*]: Oh!

HENRIETTA [*reassuring*]: But psychoanalysis has found out how to save us from that. It brings into consciousness the suppressed desire that was making all the trouble. Psychoanalysis is simply the latest scientific method of preventing and curing insanity.

STEVE [*from his table*]: It is also the latest scientific method of separating families.

HENRIETTA [*mildly*]: Families that ought to be separated.

STEVE: The Dwights, for instance. You must have met them, Mabel, when you were here before. Helen was living, apparently, in peace and happiness with good old Joe. Well—she went to this psychoanalyzer—she was "psyched," and biff!—bang!—home she comes with an unsuppressed desire to leave her husband. [*He starts work, drawing lines on a drawing board with a T-square.*]

MABEL: How terrible! Yes, I remember Helen Dwight. But—but did she have such a desire?

STEVE: First she'd known of it.

MABEL: And she *left* him?

HENRIETTA [*cooly*]: Yes, she did.

MABEL: Wasn't he good to her?

HENRIETTA: Why, yes, good enough.

MABEL: Wasn't he kind to her?

HENRIETTA: Oh, yes—kind to her.

MABEL: And she left her good, kind husband—!

HENRIETTA: Oh, Mabel! "Left her good, kind husband!" How naive—forgive me, dear, but how bourgeois you are! She came to know herself. And she had the courage!

MABEL: I may be very naive and—bourgeois—but I don't see the good of a new science that breaks up homes.

[STEVE *applauds*.]

5. Read the passage and fill in the blank with a distinctive feature. 【2 points】

In the syllable structure of English words, dependencies between peaks and codas provide evidence for the existence of rhyme as a constituent of syllable. For example, we can see the relationship between /aʊ/ peak and its coda as follows:

(1) town [taʊn]　　　　(2) *[taʊm]/*[taʊŋ]
　　 house [haʊs]　　　　　　 *[haʊf]
　　 rouse [raʊz]　　　　　　 *[raʊv]/*[raʊg]
　　 sprout [spraʊt]　　　　 *[spraʊp]/*[spraʊk]
　　 loud [laʊd]　　　　　　 *[laʊb]/*[laʊg]
　　 mouth [maʊθ]　　　　　 *[maʊf]
　　 couch [kaʊʧ]　　　　　 *[kaʊg]

The examples in (1) show that the coda following /aʊ/ has to be _____, while those in (2) show that it cannot be [labial] or [dorsal] to form a rhyme.

Note: * indicates a non-permissible form.

6. Read the passage and fill in the blanks. Write your answers in the correct order. 【2 points】

English suffixes can be grouped into three different types when they are added to a root: stress-bearing, stress-shifting, and stress-neutral. Stress-bearing suffixes attract the primary stress to themselves as in (1a). Stress-shifting suffixes move the stress to some other syllables as in (1b). Stress-neutral suffixes do not make any difference to the stress of the root as in (1c). Meanwhile, the suffix -*y* is classified into two classes. Noun-forming suffix -*y* in (2) belongs to ___①___ suffixes, while adjective-forming suffix -*y* in (2) belongs to ___②___ suffixes.

(1) a. engine-engineer, attest-attestation, statue-statuesque
　　 b. public-publicity, commerce-commercial, library-librarian
　　 c. clever-cleverness, consult-consultant, parent-parenthood

(2) summer-summery, telephone-telephony,
　　 synonym-synonymy, frump-frumpy, advisor-advisory,
　　 photograph-photography, velvet-velvety

7. Read the online discussion about Hyun's opinion and fill in the blank with TWO words from the passage. 【2 points】

 Hyun　As an international language, English has many varieties used and taught around the world. Have you ever thought about English varieties?

🖒 like it 28 | recommend it 15

 Sarah　Yes! There are many varieties of English. Americans, Australians, Brits and Canadians have many variations in how they use English. Naturally, this exists between non-native speakers, too. I think we should be aware of this reality. Many English teachers in the world today are non-native speakers of English. We need to consider this issue for teacher training and language instruction.

 Bill　I agree. Although I am a native English teacher, like many of you, we need to recognize the validity of a variety of Englishes, or better known as, _____. These include established outer-circle varieties such as Indian English, Singaporean English, and Nigerian English.

 Min　Perhaps, but what about standardization? Shouldn't we focus on one clearly understood form of the language for consistency and intelligibility?

 Jun　I don't think that is applicable in all cases, Min. The needs and attitudes of students, teachers, and administrators have an influence on the norm or standard adopted for instruction; it is thus best that local norms be respected whenever possible.

8. Read the conversation between a teacher and a student and follow the directions. 【2 points】

(Sujin, who is in an exchange programme in England, is having a conversation with her teacher, Ms. Connor.)

Sujin: Hi, how're you doing?

Ms. Connor: I'm doing well. Are you alright?

Sujin: Yes. Um . . . I have fun . . . but still intimidated by talking to people in English.

Ms. Connor: What's the problem?

Sujin: I have my British friend Kate in my class. Yesterday, she told me, "I like your jacket! Really unusual. Great on you." So I said, "Really? I don't think so." I felt she was rather embarrassed and something was wrong.

Ms. Connor: Oh, you should just say, "Thank you" in that situation. Remember, cultural norms involving language use differ from country to country. Don't worry, you're on the right track. It's a normal process of learning in a new culture.

Sujin: Oh, I see. I should have understood her and said, "Thanks." OK, thank you very much.

Complete the comments by filling in ① with TWO words and by filling in ② with ONE word. Write your answers in the correct order.

Sujin experienced misunderstanding as she performed a ____①____ of compliment response in an interaction with her British friend. Since cultures differ from one another and language is inextricably interwoven with culture, cultural knowledge of language use in context plays a crucial role in cross-cultural communication. This entails the concept of ____②____ competence, one of the core components of communicative competence, which enables learners to use the L2 in socioculturally appropriate ways.

---

9. Read the passage and follow the directions. 【4 points】

A little lamp with a white china shade stood upon the table and its light fell over a photograph which was enclosed in a frame of crumpled horn. It was Annie's photograph. Little Chandler looked at it, pausing at the thin tight lips. She wore the pale blue summer blouse which he had brought her home as a present one Saturday. It had cost him ten and elevenpence; but what an agony of nervousness it had cost him! How he had suffered that day, waiting at the shop door until the shop was empty, standing at the counter and trying to appear at his ease while the girl piled ladies' blouses before him, paying at the desk and forgetting to take up the odd penny of his change, being called back by the cashier, and finally, striving to hide his blushes as he left the shop by examining the parcel to see if it was securely tied. When he brought the blouse home Annie kissed him and said it was very pretty and stylish; but when she heard the price she threw the blouse on the table and said it was a regular swindle to charge ten and elevenpence for it. At first she wanted to take it back, but when she tried it on she was delighted with it, especially with the make of the sleeves, and kissed him and said he was very good to think of her.

Hm! . . .

He looked coldly into the eyes of the photograph and they answered coldly. Certainly they were pretty and the face itself was pretty. But he found something mean in it. Why was it so unconscious and ladylike? The composure of the eyes irritated him. They repelled him and defied him: there was no passion in them, no rapture. He thought of what Gallaher had said about rich Jewesses. Those dark Oriental eyes, he thought, how full they are of passion, of voluptuous longing! . . . Why had he married the eyes in the photograph?

He caught himself up at the question and glanced nervously round the room. He found something mean in the pretty furniture which he had bought for his house on the hire system. Annie had chosen it herself and it reminded him of her. It too was prim and pretty. A dull resentment against his life awoke within him. Could he not escape from his little house? Was it too late for him to try to live bravely like Gallaher? Could he go to London? There was the furniture still to be paid for. If he could only write a book and get it published, that might open the way for him.

Explain what the underlined words mean. Then write ONE word from the passage that best describes the emotional state of the main character in his home.

10. Read the passage in <A> and the sentences in <B>, and follow the directions. 【4 points】

<A>

There are two kinds of events or situations that predicates describe in sentences: One is telic and the other atelic. A telic event is the kind of event that has a natural finishing point and once it is completed, it cannot go on any further as shown in (1). In contrast, an atelic event does not have a natural finishing point and it can go on and on as shown in (2).

(1) a. They built the barn.
    b. They reached the summit.
(2) a. The room was sunny.
    b. The choir sang.

One of the tests for telicity is modification of the event duration by an adverbial led by *in* or *for*. Telic predicates take *in* adverbials; atelic predicates take *for* adverbials, as shown in (3-5) below. In the sentences describing a telic event in (3-4), *in* adverbials have either the event duration interpretation as in (3a) or the event delay interpretation as in (4a). In the latter interpretation, the time which elapses prior to the event is specified by *in* adverbials, and the event occurs at the end of the stated interval. Meanwhile, in the sentences describing an atelic event as in (5), *for* adverbials have the event duration interpretation only.

(3) a. They built the barn in two days.
    b. #They built the barn for two days.
(4) a. They reached the summit in half an hour.
    b. #They reached the summit for half an hour.
(5) a. #The room was sunny in an hour.
    b. The room was sunny for an hour.

It is essential to use simple past tense sentences when we do the above adverbial test; if *in* adverbials occur in future tense sentences, they can modify any type of predicate, including atelic predicates, and produce the event delay interpretation, as shown in (6a). This in turn leads to the following; certain unambiguous sentences with *in* adverbials may become ambiguous in the future tense as in (6b).

(6) a. The room will be sunny in an hour.
    b. They will build the barn in two days.

Note: # indicates that the sentence is anomalous.

<B>

(i) a. John walked to the park.
    b. John walked in the park.
(ii) a. John will arrive at the station in five minutes.
     b. John will eat the pizza in five minutes.
     c. John will play football in five minutes.

Based on the description in <A>, identify the type of event, telic or atelic, that each sentence of (i) in <B> describes. Then choose ONE ambiguous sentence in (ii) in <B> and explain why it is ambiguous.

11. Read the passage and follow the directions. 【4 points】

When it comes to climate, what counts is not only what humans do to reduce the buildup of greenhouse gases, but also how the earth responds. Currently half the carbon we release into the atmosphere gets absorbed by land and sea —much of it by plants, which take in carbon dioxide in the process of photosynthesis.

This cycle has the potential to change at any time. At issue is the balance between two natural phenomena. One is beneficial: as carbon-dioxide levels in the air rise, plants grow more quickly, absorbing more carbon in return. Scientists can measure this in the lab, but they don't know how much more fertile the new, carbon-enhanced environment will be for plants. The other is that as temperatures rise, permafrost, which holds an enormous amount of carbon from long-dead plants, tends to dry out, allowing decay and a release of carbon into the atmosphere. If this phenomenon, called "outgassing," were to kick in, it could inundate the atmosphere with carbon dioxide, perhaps doubling or tripling the effect of the past century of human industry.

Nobody knows for sure what might trigger outgassing, but preventing a global temperature increase of more than 2 degrees Celsius is considered essential. To stay below that limit, the consensus is that we should establish a maximum level of carbon in the atmosphere and do whatever is necessary to stay below it. A few years ago, scientists thought that a doubling of carbon concentrations over preindustrial times, to 550 parts per million, was a reasonable line in the sand; in recent years they've revised that figure downward, to 450 ppm. But reaching that would require a drastic 80 percent cut in emissions by midcentury.

Meanwhile, observations, though not conclusive, have been pointing in the wrong direction: temperatures are rising quickly at the poles, the north polar ice cap is in retreat, permafrost is showing troubling signs of change, and ocean currents may be weakening the uptake of carbon. As we feel good about driving hybrids and using fluorescent bulbs, our fate may be riding on an obscure contest between _____ and permafrost.

Fill in the blank with ONE word from the passage. Then explain what would happen to the permafrost if global temperature rises by more than 2 degrees Celsius.

12. Read the passage in <A> and the conversation in <B>, and follow the directions. 【4 points】

<A>

Mr. Jeon's Thoughts

There are various types of teacher corrective feedback on learners' grammatical errors, including clarification request, elicitation, metalinguistic feedback and recast. I believe that corrective feedback may not have an immediate impact but it should meet certain requirements in order to facilitate language learning. I think corrective feedback should not explicitly indicate that an error has occurred so that it does not embarrass the learner inadvertently and disrupt the flow of ongoing communication. I also find it important that corrective feedback should contain a targetlike alternative to the learner's ill-formed output. Such an alternative form enables the learner to make a comparison of his or her problematic form and its correct form, which constitutes a cognitive process facilitative of language learning.

<B>

S: I am very worried.
T: Really? What are you worried about, Minjae?
S: Math exam for tomorrow. I don't studied yesterday.
T: You didn't study yesterday?
S: No, I didn't studied.
T: Please tell me why. What happened?
S: I did volunteering all day long. So I don't had time to study.
T: Well, Minjae, "don't had" is not the right past tense form.
S: Uh, I didn't had time, time to study.

Note: T = teacher, S = student

Identify the teacher's TWO corrective feedback utterances in <B> and select their respective type from those mentioned in <A>. Then explain how only ONE of the utterances meets what Mr. Jeon believes is required for effective corrective feedback in <A>.

13. Examine part of a test evaluation checklist by a head teacher and a student's reflective journal about the test, and follow the directions. 【4 points】

> Mr. Kim, a head teacher of high school English, wanted to evaluate the achievement test of English reading in order to find to what extent the five major principles of language assessment (practicality, reliability, validity, authenticity, and washback) were applied to the test.

TEST EVALUATION CHECKLIST

Test-takers: 2nd year high school students

Content	Scale		
	1	2	3
Subjectivity does not enter into the scoring process.	□	□	■
Classroom conditions for the test are equal for all students.	□	□	■
Test measures exactly what it is supposed to measure.	■	□	□
Items focus on previously practiced in-class reading skills.	■	□	□
Topics and situations are interesting.	□	□	■
Tasks replicate, or closely approximate, real-world tasks.	□	□	■

Note: 1 = poor, 2 = average, 3 = good

> #### Post-Exam Reflection
>
> *I studied really hard for the test because I wanted to move to a higher level class. But I got 76 and I was so disappointed. Since there were no errors in scoring, my score was dependable, I think. The topics were very relevant to my real life. But what was the problem? Did I use the wrong study skills? Actually I was very surprised when I first saw the test. Lots of tasks were very unfamiliar and I believe I've never done those kinds of tasks in class. Furthermore, after the test I actually expected the teacher to go over the test and give advice on what I should focus on in the future. It never happened. No feedback or comments from the teacher were given. I was not sure which items I got wrong. I will have the same type of test next semester and I'm not sure how I can improve my reading skills and get a better grade.*

Identify TWO well-applied principles and TWO poorly-applied principles among the five principles of language assessment stated above based on all the data. Then support each of your choices with details from the post-exam reflection ONLY.

14. Read the passage and follow the directions. 【4 points】

> A paragraph in the papers of last week recorded the unusual action of a gentleman called Smith (or some such name) who had refused for reasons of conscience to be made a justice of the peace. Smith's case was that the commission was offered to him as a reward for political services, and that this was a method of selecting magistrates of which he did not approve. So he showed his contempt for the system by refusing an honour which most people covet, and earned by this such notoriety as the papers can give. "Portrait of a gentleman who has refused something!" He takes his place in (1) the gallery of the odd.
>
> The subject for essay has frequently been given, "If a million pounds were left to you, how could you do most good with it?" Some say they would endow hospitals, some that they would establish almshouses; there may even be some who would go as far as to build half a Dreadnought. But there would be a more decisive way of doing good than any of these. You might refuse the million pounds. That would be a shock to the systems of the comfortable— a blow struck at the great Money God which would make it totter; a thrust in defence of pride and freedom such as had not been seen before. That would be a moral tonic more needed than all the draughts of your newly endowed hospitals. (2) Will it ever be administered? Well, perhaps when the Declined-with-Thanks club has grown a little stronger.

Write TWO consecutive words from the passage that correspond to the meaning of the underlined words in (1). Then explain the implication of the underlined words in (2).

<5수고하셨습니다.>

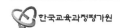

○ 문제지 전체 면수가 맞는지 확인하시오.
○ 모든 문항에는 배점이 표시되어 있습니다.

※ **Write all answers in English and use neat handwriting.**

1. Examine the survey results in <A> and part of the interview with the teacher who taught Practical English II in <B>, and follow the directions. 【4 points】

─────────── <A> ───────────

A school administrator conducted a survey with 60 students from two classes of Ms. Lee's Practical English II in order to improve the course in the future.

Evaluation of Practical English II				
Content	Number of respondents per category			
	1	2	3	4
(1) I feel I achieved my learning objectives as a result of taking this course.	4	9	25	22
(2) I feel more confident in my self-expression in English as a result of taking this course.	5	9	24	22
(3) I feel the supplementary material used in this course was helpful.	5	6	25	24
(4) I feel my speaking performance was assessed effectively based on the tests and assignments given.	29	22	8	1

Note: 1 = strongly disagree, 2 = disagree, 3 = agree, 4 = strongly agree

─────────── <B> ───────────

A: Your Practical English II was very satisfying for students. What do you think made it so successful?

T: Well, I thought it was necessary to make decisions about what would be taught and how it would be taught before designing a course, so I did a survey and interviews.

A: You mean you chose the teaching materials, contents, and activities based on what your students wanted to learn?

T: That's right. The results also provided me with a lot of information about what my students needed to learn or change, their learning styles, interests, proficiency levels, etc. Based on that information, I decided on the course objectives, contents, and activities.

A: You must have been very busy working on designing the course before it started. What about assessment?

T: Students just took one major test at the end of the semester. I regret that I evaluated only their learning product.

A: You mean just once over the semester?

T: Yes, I thought it was impossible to assess their speaking performance regularly by myself and I gave one major test to the students. So I was actually unable to gather information on the developmental process of their speaking abilities.

. . .

A: Okay. Thank you for your time.

Note: A = administrator, T = teacher

Describe ONE strong point with evidence of what the teacher did for the success of the Practical English II course. Then describe ONE weak point of what the teacher did in the course, and suggest ONE possible solution from the teacher's standpoint.

2. Read the passage and follow the directions. 【4 points】

─────────── <A> ───────────

In American English, alveolar stops can be pronounced as a flap, which is caused by a single contraction of the muscles so that one articulator is thrown against another. It is often just a very rapid stop gesture. This sound can be written with the symbol [ɾ] so that *fatty* can be transcribed as [fǽɾi]. Alveolar stops become a flap when they are located between a stressed vowel and an unstressed vowel as in *water* and *header*. In addition to this rule, there are two other rules that account for the contexts where flapping occurs.

─────────── <B> ───────────

autumn, riddle, monitor, saddle, humanity, daddy, battle, comedy, competing

Identify ALL the words from <B> that cannot be accounted for by the underlined rule in <A>. Then categorize them into TWO groups according to their occurrence contexts and state ONE rule for EACH group which accounts for each data set.

3. Read part of a lesson plan and follow the directions.

【4 points】

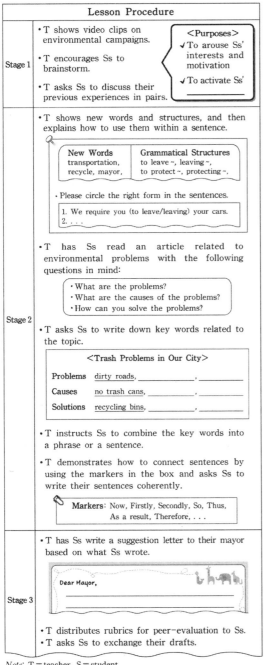

Lesson Procedure	
Stage 1	• T shows video clips on environmental campaigns. • T encourages Ss to brainstorm. • T asks Ss to discuss their previous experiences in pairs.	<Purposes> ✓ To arouse Ss' interests and motivation ✓ To activate Ss' _____

Stage 2
• T shows new words and structures, and then explains how to use them within a sentence.

New Words	Grammatical Structures
transportation, recycle, mayor,	to leave ~, leaving ~, to protect ~, protecting ~,

· Please circle the right form in the sentences.
1. We require you (to leave/leaving) your cars.
2. . . .

• T has Ss read an article related to environmental problems with the following questions in mind:

· What are the problems?
· What are the causes of the problems?
· How can you solve the problems?

• T asks Ss to write down key words related to the topic.

<Trash Problems in Our City>

Problems	dirty roads, _____, _____
Causes	no trash cans, _____, _____
Solutions	recycling bins, _____, _____

• T instructs Ss to combine the key words into a phrase or a sentence.

• T demonstrates how to connect sentences by using the markers in the box and asks Ss to write their sentences coherently.

Markers: Now, Firstly, Secondly, So, Thus, As a result, Therefore, . . .

Stage 3
• T has Ss write a suggestion letter to their mayor based on what Ss wrote.

Dear Mayor,
_____
_____

• T distributes rubrics for peer-evaluation to Ss.
• T asks Ss to exchange their drafts.

Note: T = teacher, S = student

Fill in the blank in the <Purposes> box in Stage 1 with ONE word. Then identify ONE way the teacher directly prepares students to write a well-organized suggestion letter in Stage 2, and explain it with evidence. Do NOT copy more than FIVE consecutive words from the passage.

4. Read the passage and follow the directions. 【4 points】

"The average Yaleman, Class of '24*, makes $25,111 a year." *Time* magazine reported.

Well, good for him!

But, come to think of it, what does this improbably precise and salubrious figure mean? Is it, as it appears to be, evidence that if you send your boy to Yale you won't have to work in your old age and neither will he? Is this average a mean or is it a median? What kind of sample is it based on? You could lump one Texas oilman with two hundred hungry free-lance writers and report *their* average income as $25,000-odd a year. The arithmetic is impeccable, the figure is convincingly precise.

In just such ways is the secret language of statistics, so appealing in a fact-minded culture, being used to sensationalize, inflate, confuse, and over-simplify. Statistical terms are necessary in reporting the mass data of social and economic trends, business conditions, "opinion" polls, this year's census. But without writers who use the words with honesty and understanding and readers who know what they mean, the result can only be semantic nonsense.

In popular writing on scientific research, the abused statistic is almost crowding out the picture of the white-jacketed hero laboring overtime without time-and-a-half in an ill-lit laboratory. Like the "little dash of powder, little pot of paint," statistics are making many an important fact "look like what she ain't."

_* graduates of 1924

Write TWO consecutive words corresponding to the underlined words from the passage. Then explain why the average Yaleman's annual income mentioned in the passage could be misleading.

5. Read the passage in <A> and examine the teaching procedures in <B>, and follow the directions. 【4 points】

-----------------------------<A>-----------------------------

Language learning can be classified into different types in various ways in terms of how learners process linguistic form to acquire rules that govern its use. One way is to distinguish inductive learning from deductive learning. This distinction is made by taking into account how a rule is learned in relation with its specific instances.

-----------------------------<B>-----------------------------

(Below are parts of two teachers' instruction procedures for teaching past tense verb forms in hypothetical conditionals.)

Teacher A's Class

- T explains to Ss that past tense verb forms should be used in sentences with *if* clauses to describe hypothetical situations.
- T asks Ss to complete sentences with appropriate verb forms to show hypothetical situations.

  1. I _____(can) fly to you, if I _____(be) a superhero.
  2. If he _____(have) a time machine, he _____(will) go back in time.

- T asks Ss to read a short text with sentences describing hypothetical situations.

  If I had a spaceship, I would fly to Mars. I would also build my own house there and live forever, if there were both oxygen and water. Unfortunately, I don't have lots of money to buy a spaceship. . . .

- T asks Ss to write a paragraph starting with the given expression.

  If I lived on Mars, . . .

Teacher B's Class

- T gives back the written texts about hypothetical situations Ss produced in the previous class and provides their reformulated texts T has produced at the same time. Only incorrect verb forms in Ss' writings are changed in T's reformulation as in the examples below.

  <A student's original writing>
  If I have last year to live over again, I will exercise more and eat less junk food because I can be healthier. I will spend more time with my friends and have better grades, if I am more active and watch less TV. . . .

  <The teacher's reformulated text>
  If I had last year to live over again, I would exercise more and eat less junk food because I could be healthier. I would spend more time with my friends and have better grades, if I were more active and watched less TV. . . .

- T asks Ss to compare T's reformulated sample with their writings and to underline all the words in the sample that are different from those in their writings.
- T asks Ss to find what the underlined words have in common and in what way they differ from the ones used in their original writings in terms of language form.
- T asks Ss to work out the rule that applies to all their underlined words based on their findings in the previous step.

Note: T = teacher, S = student

Identify the type of learning applied to each class in <B> based on <A>. Then explain how each class orients students toward its identified type of learning with supporting evidence.

6. Read the passage in <A> and the sentences in <B>, and follow the directions. 【5 points】

<A>

A PP modifier has distinct grammatical functions; it can be either a Complement exemplified by the underlined PP in (1a) or an Adjunct as in (1b).

(1) a. the specialist in phonology
    b. the specialist at the stage

Two types of syntactic arguments can be presented for the structural distinction between PP Complements and PP Adjuncts. First, they are strictly ordered when they both occur as postnominal modifiers, as the contrast in (2) shows.

(2) a. The specialist in phonology at the stage
    b. *The specialist at the stage in phonology

Another syntactic argument can be formulated in relation to Wh-movement, as shown in (3): NPs within PP Complements can be preposed, while NPs within PP Adjuncts cannot.

(3) a. What area of linguistics is he a specialist in?
    b. *Which place is he a specialist at?

Note: * indicates that the sentence is ungrammatical.

<B>
---

a. He is a contender with a knee injury.
b. He is a contender for the PGA title.

Based on the description in <A>, identify the grammatical function of the underlined PPs in <B>. Then provide two pairs of evidence for your identification, using BOTH sentences in <B>: a pair of NPs and a pair of *wh*-questions, with ungrammaticality marked with an asterisk (*) at the beginning of the evidence.

7. Read the passage and follow the directions. 【5 points】

Korea continues to expand its role in the global community culturally and economically. The effects are far reaching. Domestic businesses find themselves with new challenges and the public is exposed to a large number of new choices. At the same time, the outpouring of Korean made products, especially in the electronic and automotive industries, has been monumental. Along with these, as is the case with most successful adaptations to globalization, Korea has also found itself, at times inadvertently, shipping out culture, as well. From TV dramas, movies, K-pop, and food, Korean culture is simply what is hot right now, globally. The countries surrounding Korea have embraced everything from Korea. The reasons for all this are complex, to be sure, but it is clear it involved a bit of being in the right place at the right time and a lot of deliberate planning. It is not a coincidence that globalization is successful for Korea. Unlike many countries, it has dealt, and continues to deal, with the challenges and capitalizes on them. That being said, Korea's ongoing successful participation in the global sphere necessitates that it continue to carefully manage its role in globalization so that it can maintain the momentum it has created.

Write a summary following the guidelines below.

Guidelines
- Summarize the above passage in ONE paragraph.
- Provide a topic sentence, supporting evidence from the passage, and a conclusion.
- Do NOT copy more than FIVE consecutive words from the passage.

영 어 (6면 중 5 면)   한국교육과정평가원

8. Examine the consulting report about Ms. Song's English class and follow the directions. 【10 points】

Teacher: Ms. Song	Consultant: Mr. Cho	Date: Dec. 2nd

Before consul-tation	In my class, I taught grammatical structures as follows: . . . T: She will go swimming. (showing a picture of 'John riding a bike') "Ride a bike." S1: John will ride a bike. T: Good. (showing a picture of 'Mary playing the piano') "Play the piano." S2: Mary will play the piano. T: Very good. (showing a picture of 'Tom visiting a museum') "Visit a museum." S3: Tom visit a museum. T: No, you should say, "Tom will visit a museum." . . . T: (showing a picture of 'people going to a movie') What will they do? S4: They will go to a movie. T: Very good. (turning to S5, showing a picture of 'students singing a song') What will they do? . . . I expected my students to learn practiced structures, but they still had difficulty in using them in real context.
Mr. Cho's advice	The following are pieces of Mr. Cho's advice: • Utilize an e-portfolio. • Use other types of questions. • Employ various authentic materials. • Provide other types of feedback. • Assign specific roles to students in group work.
After consul-tation	After the consultation, I made changes in teaching grammar as follows: T: Good morning, class. Winter vacation is coming soon. I will go to Jeju Island and travel around. Minji, what will you do this vacation? S1: I go to Grandma's house in Busan. T: Minji, I go to Grandma's house? S1: Oh. . . eh. . . I will go to Grandma's house. T: Perfect! What about Bora? Do you have any plans? S2: Um. . . I. . . I take guitar lessons. T: I take guitar lessons? S2: Uh. . . I will take guitar lessons. T: Good! What a great plan! Why do you want to do that? . . .

Note: T = teacher, S = student

Write TWO paragraphs. In the first paragraph, identify the type of teaching technique which Ms. Song used before the consultation and explain the technique with evidence. In the second paragraph, identify TWO changes that Ms. Song made based on Mr. Cho's advice, and then explain those two changes by comparing the classes before and after consultation with evidence.

<수고하셨습니다.>

○ 문제지 전체 면수가 맞는지 확인하시오.
○ 모든 문항에는 배점이 표시되어 있습니다.

※ **Write all answers in English and use neat handwriting.**

1. Read the dialogue and follow the directions. 【2 points】

Student－teacher Meeting

T: Well, looking back over the last twelve weeks, I can see that you have written many drafts for the three essay writing assignments.

S: Yes, I have. I have a lot of things here.

T: Of all your essays, which one do you think is the best?

S: I think the persuasive essay I wrote is the best.

T: What makes you think so? Maybe you can tell me how you wrote it.

S: Well ... I think the topic I chose was quite engaging. I enjoyed the writing process throughout. And it feels good being able to see the progress I've made.

T: Yes, that's the benefit of this kind of project. I can see some improvement in your use of transitions. Your ideas are nicely connected and organized now.

S: Thanks. What else should I include?

T: Well, did you work on the self-assessment form and the editing checklist?

S: Yes, I did. I completed them and included them with all of my drafts right here.

T: Perfect! I'll be able to finish grading all of your work by the end of next week.

Note: T = teacher, S = student

Complete the following by filling in both blanks with ONE word. (Use the SAME word.)

_____ can include essays, reports, journals, video- or audio-recorded learner language data, students' self-assessment, teachers' written feedback, homework, conference forms, etc. As collections of these items, _____ can be useful for assessing student performance in that they can lead students to have ownership over their process of learning and allow teachers to pay attention to students' progress as well as achievement.

---

2. Read the passage and follow the directions. 【2 points】

M. Ringelmann, a French agricultural engineer, was one of the first researchers to study the relationship between process loss and group productivity. Ringelmann's questions were practical ones: How many oxen should be yoked in one team? Should you plow a field with two horses or three? Can five men turn a mill crank faster than four? Instead of speculating about the answers to these questions, Ringelmann set up teams of varying sizes and measured their collective power.

Ringelmann's most startling discovery was that workers— including horses, oxen, and men—all become less productive in groups. A group of five writers developing funny skits can easily outperform a single person, just as a team pulling a rope is stronger than a single opponent. But even though a group outperforms an individual, the group does not usually work at maximum efficiency. When Ringelmann had individuals and groups pull on a rope attached to a pressure gauge, groups performed below their theoretical capabilities. If person A and person B could each pull 100 units when they worked alone, could they pull 200 units when they pooled their efforts? No, their output reached only 186. A three-person group did not produce 300 units, but only 255. An eight-person group managed only 392, not 800. Groups certainly outperformed individuals—but as more and more people were added, the group became increasingly inefficient. To honor its discoverer, this tendency is now known as the Ringelmann effect.

Ringelmann identified two key sources of process losses when people worked together. First, Ringelmann believed some of the decline in productivity was caused by motivation losses: People may not work so hard when they are in groups. Second, coordination losses, caused by "the lack of simultaneity of their efforts," also interfere with performance. Even on a simple task, such as rope pulling, people tend to pull and pause at different times, resulting in a failure to reach their full productive potential.

Complete the main idea by filling in the blank with the ONE most appropriate word from the passage.

Groups were found to become more _____ as group size increased because the potential output that each member could contribute individually was not realized when they participated in groups.

---

3. Read the passage and fill in the blank with ONE word.
【2 points】

> While all vowels of English (except [ə]) can occur in stressed syllables, many of these vowels reveal alternations with an [ə] in reduced syllables in morphologically related words, as shown in (1).
>
> (1) **Stressed Syllable**   **Reduced Syllable**
> /i/ homogeneous [hoʊmədʒiniəs]   homogenize [həmɑdʒənɑɪz]
> /eɪ/ explain   [ɪkspleɪn]   explanation [ɛkspləneɪʃən]
> /ɛ/ perpetuate [pɔɹpɛtʃʊeɪt]   perpetuity [pɔɹpətʃuɑti]
> /ɑ/ demonstrable [dɪmɑnstɹəbəl] demonstration [dɛmənstɹeɪʃən]
> /ʌ/ confront   [kənfɹʌnt]   confrontation [kɑnfɹənteɪʃən]
> /ɑɪ/ recite   [ɹɪsɑɪt]   recitation [ɹɛsəteɪʃən]
>
> However, it is not uncommon to see an [ɪ] in reduced syllables of the words in (2).
>
> (2) a. selfish   [sɛlfɪʃ]   b. metric   [mɛtɹɪk]
>   sandwich [sændwɪtʃ]   running   [ɹʌnɪŋ]
>   marriage [mæɹɪdʒ]   allegation [ælɪgeɪʃən]
>
> In the examples in (2), [ɪ] occurs before palato-alveolars as in (2a) or before _____ as in (2b). (Your answer must account for all three examples in (2b).)

4. Read the passage and fill in the blank with ONE word.
【2 points】

> Trisyllabic laxing is a rule which changes a tense vowel into a lax vowel. This rule applies when the target vowel is pushed into the ante-penultimate syllable (i.e., the third syllable from the end) due to the attachment of a suffix, as exemplified below.
>
> supreme — supremacy
> apply   — application
> sane   — sanity
> divine — divinity
> opaque — opacity
>
> The tense vowels in words like 'nightingale' and 'ivory' do not undergo trisyllabic laxing although these words contain the minimum of three syllables required by the trisyllabic laxing rule. The explanation is that these forms are exempt from trisyllabic laxing since they do not have any _____.

5. Read the poem and follow the directions. 【2 points】

> The flower that smiles today
>   Tomorrow dies;
> All that we wish to stay,
>   Tempts and then flies.
> What is this world's delight?
> Lightning that mocks the night,
>   Brief even as bright.
>
> Virtue, how frail it is!
>   Friendship how rare!
> Love, how it sells poor bliss
>   For proud despair!
> But we, though soon they fall,
> Survive their joy and all
>   Which ours we call.
>
> Whilst skies are blue and bright,
>   Whilst flowers are gay,
> Whilst eyes that change ere night
>   Make glad the day,
> Whilst yet the calm hours creep,
> Dream thou—and from thy sleep
>   Then wake to weep.

Complete the statement by filling in the blank with the ONE most appropriate word from the poem.

> One theme in the poem is that all good things in life come to an end, and as a result, we are left with the feeling of _____.

6. Read the passage and follow the directions. 【2 points】

> The following is part of a lesson procedure that aims to facilitate students' comprehension of a text concerning global warming.
>
> **Steps:**
> 1. Before reading the text, T activates Ss' background knowledge concerning global warming and provides other relevant information to help Ss to have a better comprehension of the text.
> 2. T instructs Ss to read the text quickly in order to grasp the main ideas. In doing so, T tells them not to read every word.
> 3. T asks Ss to reread it quickly for specific information, such as the type of disasters caused by global warming.
> 4. T instructs Ss to read the text again at their own pace.
> 5. T checks Ss' overall comprehension by having them write a brief summary of the text.
> 6. T then checks Ss' understanding of the details by using a cloze activity.
>
> *Note*: T = teacher, S = student

Identify the two kinds of expeditious reading that the teacher instructs students to use in steps 2 and 3 with ONE word, respectively. Write them in the order that they appear.

7. Read the passage and fill in each blank with TWO words. (Use the SAME answer for both blanks.) 【2 points】

S: Could you give me some advice on how I can improve my pronunciation?

T: Yes, of course. Are you having trouble pronouncing a particular word?

S: I can't think of any right now, but there are a lot of sounds in English that I can't pronounce.

T: Can you give me an example?

S: The word *right*. *R* is very difficult for me.

T: Oh, that's because the consonant *r* doesn't exist in the Korean sound system. Then, you should practice pronunciation with a lot of ＿＿＿＿＿＿. For example, the words *river* and *liver* have only one sound difference in the same position, but it makes a big difference in meaning.

S: Oh, I see. So, I guess *fine* and *pine* would be another example of ＿＿＿＿＿＿, right?

T: Yes, you're right. If you want to be able to pronounce *right*, you first need to be able to hear the difference between *right* and *light*. There are so many other examples, like *rice* and *lice*, *rode* and *load*, etc.

S: I can't hear the difference between those words, either.

T: I know they are difficult, but with enough practice, you will be able to hear the difference and pronounce them correctly.

Note: T = teacher, S = student

8. Read the passages and follow the directions. 【2 points】

＜A＞

Non-verbal communication is an important aspect of intercultural communication. It includes the following categories, which also apply to cultural norms in public space. First, there is kinesics, which is the use of gestures or body language. A second category is oculesics, which refers to eye contact and eye movement. Eyes can provide signals as to one's mood, such as being interested, bored, empathetic, or annoyed. Third, there is proxemics, which relates to physical distance between interlocutors (and other people in public spaces). A fourth category is kinesthetics (also called haptics), meaning touching or making physical contact with someone. Across cultures, norms relating to these categories can vary significantly, which can lead to misunderstandings or inappropriate behavior in cross-cultural situations.

＜B＞

A group of students in Ms. Lee's school won a regional English contest and they received an all-expense-paid trip to Seattle as a reward. In preparation, Ms. Lee tutored them on how to be polite, which included lessons comparing cultural norms and non-verbal communication in Korea and America. However, the following event occurred.

After arriving in Seattle, they were hungry, so they asked their shuttle bus driver to stop at the nearest fast food restaurant, but it was busy and the line was long. A student, Gyumin, led the group through the line. As the line moved, so did Gyumin, inching ever so closer to the front. He was excited — this was his first time in a restaurant abroad — and he was eager to order his meal. However, Ms. Lee noticed something recurring. Gyumin was closely following a middle-aged American man in line, and as the line moved forward, Ms. Lee saw that the man frequently turned his head to the side and, with a scrunched forehead, gazed down at Gyumin for a moment as if to tell him something. Ms. Lee quietly pulled Gyumin aside and the following exchange occurred:

T: Gyumin, do you remember what I taught you about lining up?

S: You mean not to bump into anyone? I didn't!

T: No, no, not that. Rather, do you remember the arm's length rule?

S: Oh, that!

T: It's okay. Just remember it for next time. We want to be polite while we are here.

S: Okay. I got it.

Note: T = teacher, S = student

Given the information in ＜A＞, write the ONE most appropriate category that Gyumin violated in ＜B＞ in regards to cultural norms in America.

9. Read the passage and follow the directions. 【4 points】

Mr. Lee wants to determine how well the scores from the College Entrance Exam (CEE) predict academic success in college. The scatter plot below includes high school seniors' CEE scores from 2014 and their college Grade Point Averages (GPAs) in the fall of 2016. Their CEE scores are placed on the horizontal axis and their college GPAs on the vertical axis.

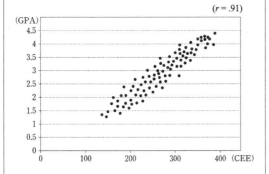

($r = .91$)

Note: r = correlation coefficient

Students	CEE (Fall 2014)	GPA (Fall 2016)
A	389	4.43
B	246	2.58
C	304	3.15
D	322	3.27
E	211	2.10
F	328	3.62
G	314	3.18
H	288	2.83
I	372	4.00
J	368	3.85
⋮	⋮	⋮

Based on the information in the passage, identify the type of validity within the context of criterion-related validation and explain it with evidence.

10. Read the passage and follow the directions. 【4 points】

As time went by, Freddie Drummond found himself more frequently crossing the Slot and losing himself in South of Market . . . .

Somewhere in his make-up there was a strange twist or quirk. Perhaps it was a recoil from his environment and training, or from the tempered seed of his ancestors, who had been bookmen generation preceding generation; but at any rate, he found enjoyment in being down in the working-class world. In his own world he was "Cold-Storage," but down below he was "Big" Bill Totts, who could drink and smoke, and slang and fight, and be an all-around favorite. Everybody liked Bill, and more than one working girl made love to him. At first he had been merely a good actor, but as time went on, <u>simulation became second nature</u>. He no longer played a part, and he loved sausages, sausages and bacon, than which, in his own proper sphere, there was nothing more loathsome in the way of food.

From doing the thing for the need's sake, he came to doing the thing for the thing's sake. He found himself regretting as the time drew near for him to go back to his lecture-room and his inhibition . . . .

Explain what the underlined part means by including one example of "simulation" from the passage. Do NOT copy more than FOUR consecutive words from the passage.

Then, complete the commentary below with TWO consecutive words from the passage.

Freddie, whose job is a college professor, experiences something unusual as he starts to mingle with people outside "his own proper sphere." Until then, Freddie used to do things for the _____, such as giving a lecture.

11. Read the passage and follow the directions. 【4 points】

> *(Sitting weakly in the wheelchair, Vivian recites a poem and continues with a monologue.)*
>
> Vivian:
>
> > This is my playes last scene, here heavens appoint
> > My pilgrimages last mile; and my race
> > Idly, yet quickly runne, hath this last pace,
> > My spans last inch, my minutes last point,
> > And gluttonous death will instantly unjoynt
> > My body, 'and soule
> >
> > John Donne. 1609.
>
> I have always particularly liked that poem. In the abstract. Now I find the image of "my minute's last point" a little too, shall we say, *pointed*.
>
> I don't mean to complain, but I am becoming very sick. Very, very sick. Ultimately sick, as it were.
>
> In everything I have done, I have been steadfast, resolute — some would say in the extreme. Now, as you can see, I am distinguishing myself in illness.
>
> I have survived eight treatments of Hexamethophosphacil and Vinplatin at the *full* dose, ladies and gentlemen. I have broken the record. I have become something of a celebrity. Jason Posner is simply delighted. I think he foresees celebrity status for himself upon the appearance of the medical journal article he will no doubt write about me.
>
> But I flatter myself. The article will not be about *me*. It will be about my ovaries, which, despite his best intentions, are now crawling with cancer.
>
> What we have come to think of as *me* is, in fact, just the specimen jar, just the dust jacket, just the white piece of paper that bears the little black marks.

Based on the passage, explain what makes Vivian feel personal about John Donne's poem cited in her monologue. Then, based on the passage, identify Jason Posner's occupation.

12. Read the passage in <A> and the sentences in <B>, and follow the directions. 【4 points】

> —————————<A>—————————
>
> Not all intransitive verbs are of the same kind. Compare the two sentences in (1) and (2).
>
> (1) An angel jumped on the hill.
> (2) An angel appeared on the hill.
>
> Although both of the above sentences are intransitive, they are not of the same kind. They have different syntactic and semantic properties. In (1), the subject originates in the specifier position external to the V-bar constituent, receiving an Agent role. Verbs like *jump* are known as unergative verbs. However, in (2), the superficial subject originates in the complement position within the immediate V-bar projection of the verb, receiving a Theme role. Then it moves to subject position. Verbs like *appear* are known as unaccusative verbs.
>
> The two types of intransitive verbs can be distinguished by means of tests such as the following. Unaccusative verbs like *appear* allow a word order called *there* inversion, where the underlying complement remains in its original position after the verb. On the other hand, since the subject of unergative verbs like *jump* does not originate in the complement position of the verbs, it isn't allowed to appear in that position after the verbs with *there* inversion, as shown below.
>
> (3) *There jumped an angel on the hill.
> (4) There appeared an angel on the hill.
>
> *Note*: * indicates that the sentence is ungrammatical.

> —————————<B>—————————
>
> (i) Several people ate in the Korean restaurant.
> (ii) Several customers shopped in the new shopping center.
> (iii) Several students remained in the school library.
> (iv) Several soldiers saluted in the military ceremony.
> (v) Several complications arose in the medical experiment.

Identify the TWO sentences containing an unaccusative verb in <B>, and explain the reason by using the test described in <A>.

13. Read the passage and follow the directions. 【4 points】

> It was once assumed that reading comprehension could be understood as a kind of serial processing—that is, reading comprehension entails processing discrete units of words and sentences sequentially. This was one of the main assumptions behind the phonics approach.
>
> However, F. Smith explained that the serial processing operations underlying the phonics approach are contradicted by the fact that it is often impossible to make decisions about the sound of upcoming letters and words until the context (e.g., such as a word context or a sentence context) surrounding the item has been understood. When decoding an isolated word starting with 'ho-', for example, it would be impossible to assign a(n) _____ value to 'o' until one knew whether the whole word was 'house', 'horse', 'hot', or 'hoot'. In the same way, when decoding the word 'read' at the sentence level, it is impossible to assign a(n) _____ value to the vowel sequence 'ea' until it is known whether the sentence containing the word 'read' refers to the past or the present.

Fill in both blanks with the ONE most appropriate word from the passage. (Use the SAME word.) Then write the main idea of the passage. Do NOT copy more than FOUR consecutive words from the passage.

14. Read the passage and follow the directions. 【4 points】

> The early 20th century was not a great time for grocery shoppers. Sure, industrialization meant that more food products were available than ever before, and at lower prices, too. But in the days before the FDA, who knew what those products were really made of? A bottle of ketchup might contain dyed pumpkin, ground ginger might be mixed with bits of tarred rope, and cans labeled "potted chicken" might include no chicken at all.
>
> All those things happened, and worse. Once the public became aware of the extent of the problem, the Pure Food and Drug Act of 1906 was passed. The legislation laid out standards for food safety: You could no longer mix poisonous, dirty, or rotten ingredients into a product. It also stopped outright mislabelling: You could not call something a particular food if it was not that food.
>
> This was going to hurt the bottom line for manufacturers of cheap imitation food, so they came up with a way around the new rules. What if you technically did not say a product was something it was not? What if you are calling a product that is mostly cornstarch *Puddine*, expecting that people will think it is real pudding?
>
> That strategy worked for a while. A "distinctive name" proviso was inserted into the law that allowed clever names. In addition to Puddine (mostly cornstarch), consumers could buy Grape Smack (imitation grape juice) and Bred Spred (a nearly fruit-free sugar-pectin mixture in a jam jar). If buyers thought they were getting pudding, grape juice, and strawberry jam—well, it was not the companies' fault. They did not *say* their products were those other things.
>
> The courts agreed. In the marvelously titled cases *United States v. 150 Cases of Fruit Puddine, United States v. 24 ⁷/₈ Gallons of Smack,* and *United States v. 15 Cases of Bred Spred,* the distinctive name proviso let the imitators off the hook. But the rules got stricter with the 1938 Food, Drug, and Cosmetic Act, which mandated that products could still bear fanciful names, but if they looked a lot like something they were not, they had to be explicitly labeled a(n) _____.

Fill in the blank with the ONE most appropriate word from the passage. Then explain why manufacturers started to use so-called 'distinctive names'.

<수고하셨습니다.>

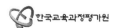

○ 문제지 전체 면수가 맞는지 확인하시오.
○ 모든 문항에는 배점이 표시되어 있습니다.

1. Read the passages and the teaching journals, and follow the directions. 【4 points】

---<A>---

Form-focused instruction (FFI) can be split into two types: focus on form*S* and focus on form. According to R. Ellis (2001), FFI "includes both traditional approaches to teaching forms based on structural syllabi and more communicative approaches, where attention to form arises out of activities that are primarily meaning-focused" (p. 2).

---<B>---

[**Mr. Song**]

My students often tell me that they feel overwhelmed by the number of grammatical structures they have to learn. While thinking about ways to help students develop grammatical competence, I decided to teach grammar explicitly in class. Today I spent most of the class time on explaining grammatical rules using meta-linguistic terms. Although some of the students initially showed some interest in learning about the rules, many of them got bored, with some dozing off after ten minutes or so.

[**Miss Oh**]

Most of my students find grammatical rules difficult and boring. So I decided to implement a new approach. For this approach, I typed up the reading passage in the textbook and deliberately italicized the target structures, hoping that this would help my students notice how the target structures function. After I passed out the reconstructed reading passage, I had my students read it by themselves and then work together in groups, cross-checking their understanding.

Referring to the terms in <A>, identify the type of form-focused instruction exemplified in each of the teachers' teaching journals, and explain with supporting evidence from <B>. Do NOT copy more than FOUR consecutive words from the passage.

2. Read the passages and follow the directions. 【4 points】

―――――――――<A>―――――――――

Materials can be adapted for many reasons, for example, to localize, to modernize, or to personalize. We can localize materials to make them more applicable to our local context. We can modernize materials when they are outdated in terms of English usage or content. We can also personalize materials by making them more relevant to learner needs and interests. Materials adaptation can be carried out by using a number of different techniques, as shown in the figure.

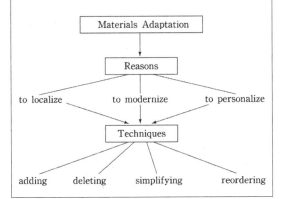

―――――――――<B>―――――――――

Mr. Lee is teaching first-year middle school students whose proficiency levels are very low. After conducting a needs analysis, he has learned that the students find the writing sections of the textbook difficult and that they are interested in sports. While he is planning a writing lesson for next week, he realizes that there is only one pre-writing activity in Unit 1 of the textbook. He thinks that one activity is not enough for his students to develop ideas for writing. Thus, he is going to increase the number of the pre-writing activities from one to three. In addition, thinking that the reading passage on sports in Unit 3 will better suit learner interests than the reading text in Unit 1, he decides to switch the two reading texts. He believes that this change will help his students become better prepared for writing and more engaged in English language learning.

Referring to the terms in <A>, explain the reason why Mr. Lee wants to adapt the materials, and identify which techniques he is going to use for materials adaptation. Do NOT copy more than FOUR consecutive words from the passage.

3. Read the passage and follow the directions. 【4 points】

The schwa vowel /ə/, which is a reduced or weak vowel in English, can be deleted in fast speech, as exemplified in (1).

(1) Schwa Deletion

	Careful Speech	Fast Speech
camera	[ˈkæməɹə]	[ˈkæmɹə]
veteran	[ˈvɛtəɹən]	[ˈvɛtɹən]

However, schwa deletion is not observed in fast speech for the following words.

(2) No Schwa Deletion

	Careful Speech	Fast Speech	
facilitate	[fəˈsɪləteɪt]	[fəˈsɪləteɪt]	*[fəˈsɪlteɪt]
famous	[ˈfeɪməs]	[ˈfeɪməs]	*[ˈfeɪms]

In the following examples of morphologically related words, schwa deletion may or may not be observed.

(3)

	Careful Speech	Fast Speech	
a. principal	[ˈpɹɪnsəpəl]	[ˈpɹɪnspəl]	
principality	[pɹɪnsəˈpæləti]	[pɹɪnsəˈpæləti]	*[pɹɪnˈspæləti]
b. imaginative	[ɪˈmædʒənətɪv]	[ɪˈmædʒnətɪv]	
imagination	[ɪmædʒəˈneɪʃən]	[ɪmædʒəˈneɪʃən]	*[ɪmædʒˈneɪʃən]

Note: * indicates a non-permissible form.

In the data given in (1) and (3), schwa deletion occurs in fast speech under two conditions related to a preceding and a following phonetic environment. State the two phonetic conditions for schwa deletion.

4. Read the passages and follow the directions. 【4 points】

<A>

Meaning-negotiation strategies such as comprehension checks, clarification requests, and confirmation checks may aid comprehension during conversational interaction. First, comprehension checks are defined as the moves by which one interlocutor seeks to make sure that the other has understood correctly. Second, clarification requests are the moves by which one interlocutor requests assistance in understanding the other's preceding utterance. Finally, confirmation checks refer to the moves used by one interlocutor to confirm whether he or she correctly has understood what the other has said.

<B>

Miss Jeong has been instructing her students to actively utilize meaning-negotiation strategies stated in <A> during speaking activities. One day, she interviewed two of her students, Mijin and Haerim, about the strategies that they had used during previous speaking activities. The following are excerpts from the interview:

Mijin : When I didn't understand what my friends said during speaking activities, I usually said, "Could you repeat what you said?" or "I am sorry?" Sometimes I tried to check whether my friends clearly understood what I said by saying, "You know what I mean?"

Haerim : Well, during speaking activities, when I had difficulties comprehending what my friends said, I didn't say anything and pretended to understand what they said. I felt it embarrassing to show my lack of understanding to my friends. However, when I talked about something during speaking activities, I often said, "Do you understand?" in order to see if my utterances were understood well by my friends.

Based on the passage in <A>, write down all the meaning-negotiation strategies that Mijin and Haerim used respectively, along with their corresponding utterances from each student in <B>.

5. Read the passages and follow the directions. 【4 points】

<A>

The English article system seems deceptively simple because there are only two articles: the indefinite article *a(n)* and the definite article *the*. There are, however, many situations in which a noun phrase is considered definite and thus requires the definite article. Described below are five common uses for the definite article:

(1) second mention―when the speaker wants to refer to something that has already been mentioned, e.g., *She has a brother and a sister. The brother is a university student. The sister is still in high school.*
(2) situational use―when the speaker wants to refer to something specific that is present in the environment and visible to the listener, e.g., *Can you pass me the salt?*
(3) associative use―when the speaker can assume that the listener knows about the relationships that exist between certain objects and things usually associated with them, e.g., *I bought a book yesterday, and I spoke to the author today.*
(4) post-modification―when relative clauses are used to define or specify something, making it specifically identifiable and hence definite, e.g., *She's never met the girl I dated in college.*
(5) generic reference―when a noun refers generally to members of a species or class, e.g., *The penguin is a flightless bird.*

<B>

A taxi was involved in a terrible accident last night. Luckily, neither the driver nor the passengers were injured.

Identify which of the five uses of the definite article described in <A> best accounts for the use of the two definite articles in <B>. Then explain the reason.

6. Read the passage in <A> and the sentences in <B>, and follow the directions. 【5 points】

---<A>---

Anaphors such as *each other* have to be bound by their antecedent. An anaphor must satisfy two conditions to be bound. An anaphor can be bound if it is coindexed (i.e., coreferential) with its antecedent and is also c-commanded by that antecedent within the smallest clause or noun phrase containing the anaphor. A node c-commands its sister and all the descendents of its sister. For example, in (1), B c-commands C, D, E, F, G, H, I, J, and K; however, I c-commands only H, which is its sister. It does not c-command any other nodes.

(1)
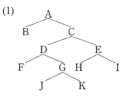

Consider the two structures for the verb phrase in the double object construction (2). (3) is a ternary (three) branching structure, which is a kind of multiple branching structure, and (4) a binary branching structure.

(2) Tom will give Mary a book.

(3)   (4)
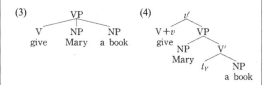

In (3) and (4), the direct and indirect objects have different structural relations.

---<B>---

(i) Mary showed the boys$_i$ each other$_i$.

(ii) *Mary showed each other$_i$ the boys$_i$.

(In the examples *the boys* and *each other* refer to the same people.)

Note: * indicates that the sentence is ungrammatical.

Identify which VP structure, (3) or (4), can account for the ungrammaticality of sentence (ii) in <B>. Then, explain why one, but not the other structure, can account for the ungrammaticality by using the c-command relation described in <A>.

7. Read the passage and follow the directions. 【5 points】

Have you ever felt overwhelmed trying to do too many things at once? In modern times, hurry, bustle, and agitation have become a regular way of life for many people—so much so that we have embraced a word to describe our efforts to respond to the many pressing demands of our time: multitasking. Used for decades to describe the parallel processing abilities of computers, in the 1990s the term multitasking became shorthand for the human attempt to simultaneously do as many things as possible, as quickly as possible, and with the help of new technologies.

It was originally assumed that multitasking was a useful strategy for increasing productivity. More recently, however, challenges to the presumed advantages of multitasking began to emerge. For example, numerous studies have addressed the sometimes fatal danger of driving and using cell phones or other electronic devices at the same time. As a result, several countries have now made that particular form of multitasking illegal. Researchers have also found that multitasking in the workplace can actually decrease productivity because the constant attention paid to emails, messaging apps, and phone calls temporarily impairs our ability to solve complex problems. Moreover, multitasking may negatively influence how we learn. Even if we learn while multitasking, that learning is likely to be less flexible and more fragmented, so we cannot recall the information as easily. As the research on multitasking implies, perhaps it is time to challenge the assumption that doing more is better.

Write a summary following the guidelines below.

Guidelines

- Summarize the above passage in ONE paragraph.
- Provide a topic sentence, supporting ideas from the passage, and a concluding sentence.
- Do NOT copy more than FIVE consecutive words from the passage.

8. Read the two lesson procedures for teaching comparatives in <A> and <B>, and follow the directions. 【10 points】

<A>

Class A

Lesson objectives: Ss will be able to discuss and present their travel experiences using comparatives.

1. T tells a story about travel experiences.

> *Let me tell you about two trips I took, one to Singapore and the other to Bangkok. I really enjoyed my trip to Bangkok. It was more interesting than my trip to Singapore. Singapore was a little more boring than Bangkok. Although Singapore was cleaner and nicer, I thought Bangkok was a more fun city to travel in.*

2. T articulates the lesson objectives and asks Ss to form groups of six.

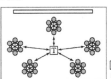

T : Teacher
◎ : Student

3. Ss begin a consensus building activity. During this activity, Ss compare locations according to a list of given adjectives (e.g., *safe, beautiful, historic*) on a worksheet. (T helps Ss as needed.)

	Your chosen place	Your group's agreed-upon place
safe	*Busan*	*Daegu*
beautiful	*Jeju*	*Jeju*
historic		
...		
_____ (your idea)		

Ss compare and discuss their ideas using comparatives. (T gives feedback. Ss correct ill-formed utterances.)

> S : Busan is beautifuler.
> T : Beautifuler?
> S : Beautiful, more beautiful.
> T : More beautiful?
> S : Busan is more beautiful.
> T : More beautiful. OK.

4. In groups, Ss discuss where the better and worse places to visit are.

(T walks around the classroom to see if all the Ss are participating in the discussion. If Ss are reluctant to join in group work, T encourages them to participate.)

5. Ss work on a summary together within their group. T allows Ss to choose a role within their group (e.g., leader, timekeeper, note-taker, reporter). (T monitors their work and helps out as needed.)

6. Each group presents their summary to the class.

....

Note: T = teacher, S = student

<B>

Class B

Lesson objectives:
(1) Ss will learn comparative forms;
(2) Ss will be able to make sentences using comparatives.

1. T explains the grammatical form of comparatives and writes the following chart on the board:

safe	safer
beautiful	more beautiful
cheap	cheaper
expensive	more expensive
....	....

(T stays at the front of the class the entire time, and Ss sit in orderly rows in silence.)

2. T instructs Ss to pay attention to the lesson.

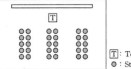

T : Teacher
◎ : Student

3. T plays a recording line-by-line, and Ss listen and repeat. (T instructs them to repeat in unison.)

Recording	Students
A: What is cheaper, taking trains or taking buses?	What is cheaper, taking trains or taking buses?
B: Taking buses is cheaper than taking trains.	Taking buses is cheaper than taking trains.
A: Which one is safer?	Which one is safer?
B: Taking trains is safer than taking buses.	Taking trains is safer than taking buses.
....	....

4. T checks if Ss understand the comparative forms. (T asks questions, Ss answer individually, and T gives feedback.)

> T : What is the comparative form of 'safe'?
> S : Safer.
> T : Good. What about 'beautiful'?
> S : More beautiful.
> T : Very good. Then what about 'cheap'?
> S : More cheaper.
> T : No, not 'more cheaper'. It's 'cheaper'.

5. Ss do more choral repetition. (T plays the recording again, pausing it after key phrases, and Ss repeat them immediately.)

6. T asks Ss to repeat key phrases individually. (T corrects Ss' errors explicitly.)

....

Note: T = teacher, S = student

Write TWO paragraphs. In the first paragraph, identify and compare the roles of the teacher in each class, and explain them with evidence from the text. In the second paragraph, explain and compare how the teacher in each class manages the classroom with evidence from the text.

<수고하셨습니다.>

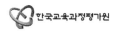

제1차 시험	2교시 전공A	14문항 40점	시험 시간 90분

○ 문제지 전체 면수가 맞는지 확인하시오.
○ 모든 문항에는 배점이 표시되어 있습니다.

※ **Write all answers in English and use neat handwriting.**

1. Read the passage and follow the directions. 【2 points】

> Learning a second language (L2) may be viewed as the gradual transformation of performance from controlled to less controlled. This transformation has been called proceduralization or automatization and entails the conversion of declarative knowledge into procedural knowledge. According to this argument, the learning of skills is assumed to start with the explicit provision of relevant declarative knowledge and, through practice, this knowledge can hopefully convert into ability for use. At the same time, it is important to understand that learning an L2 may proceed in a different way. For example, some have wondered if incidental L2 learning is possible as a consequence of doing something else in the L2. Simply put, the question is about the possibility of learning without intention. The answer is still open, but, at present, it appears that people learn faster, more and better when they deliberately apply themselves to learning.

Read Mr. Lee's teaching log below and fill in the blank with the ONE most appropriate word from the passage above.

> Through my teaching experience, I've learned that different students learn in different ways. Considering the current trend in teaching and learning, I believe that students should be provided with more opportunities to be exposed to the _____ learning condition. Minsu's case may illustrate that point. At the beginning of the semester, Minsu introduced himself as a book lover. He wanted to read novels in English but was not sure if he could. I suggested that he didn't have to try to comprehend all the details. Indeed, Minsu has benefitted a lot from reading novels. He said he learned many words and expressions even though he did not make attempts to memorize them. I will continue observing his progress as his way of learning is of great interest.

2. Read the passage and follow the directions. 【2 points】

> From the very beginning of school we make books and reading a constant source of possible failure and public humiliation. When children are little we make them read aloud, before the teacher and other children, so that we can be sure they "know" all the words they are reading. This means that when they don't know a word, they are going to make a mistake, right in front of the whole class. Instantly they are made to realize that they have done something wrong. Perhaps some of the other children will begin to wave their hands and say, "Ooooh! O-o-o-oh!" Perhaps they will just giggle, or nudge each other, or make a face. Perhaps the teacher will say, "Are you sure?" or ask someone else what he thinks. Or perhaps, if the teacher is kind, she will just smile a sweet, sad smile－often one of the most painful punishments a child can suffer in school. In any case, the child who has made the mistake knows he has made it, and feels foolish, stupid, and ashamed, just as any of us would in his shoes.
>
> Before long many children associate books and reading with mistakes, real or feared, and penalties and humiliation. This may not seem sensible, but it is natural. Mark Twain once said that a cat that sat on a hot stove lid would never sit on one again－but it would never sit on a cold one either. As true of _____ as of cats. If they, so to speak, sit on a hot book a few times, if books cause them humiliation and pain, they are likely to decide that the safest thing to do is to leave all books alone.

Fill in the blank with the ONE most appropriate word from the passage.

3. Read the dialogue and follow the directions. 【2 points】

> T1: There's no doubt that young children beginning school need the basics of reading, writing, and math.
>
> T2: I agree, but the big problem is determining the best way for them to get it. I think the classic mode of a teacher at the chalkboard, and books and homework is outdated.
>
> T1: True. That's why I have been looking at some teaching literature based on the ideas Jonathan Bergman and Aaron Sams came up with.
>
> T2: What do they suggest?
>
> T1: Well, they have reconsidered the role of the traditional classroom and home. So home becomes a classroom, and vice versa in this way of learning. Students view lecture materials, usually in the form of videos, as homework before class.
>
> T2: That's interesting. What's the focus in class?
>
> T1: That's the best part. Class time is reserved for activities such as interactive discussions or collaborative work supervised by the teacher.
>
> T2: I like it. But how does it benefit the students?
>
> T1: They can study the lectures at home at their own pace, or re-watch the videos, if needed, or even skip parts they already understand.
>
> T2: Right. And then, in class the teacher is present when they apply new knowledge. What about traditional homework?
>
> T1: That can be done in class, too. So, the teacher can gain insights into whatever concepts, if any, their students are struggling with and adjust the class accordingly.
>
> T2: What does the literature say about its effectiveness?
>
> T1: Amazingly, according to one study, 71% of teachers who have tried this approach in their classes noticed improved grades, and 80% reported improved student attitudes, as well.
>
> T2: That's fantastic. Let me read that when you're done. I want to look further into this.
>
> *Note*: T = teacher

Fill in the blank with the ONE most appropriate word.

> The teaching approach discussed by the two teachers is known technically as _____ learning in educational settings.

4. Read the passage and follow the directions. 【2 points】

> It is well known in English that we get antepenultimate stress in nouns of at least three syllables when the penultimate syllable is light:
>
> (1) antepenultimate syllable stressed
>   *cinema, asterisk, America, Canada, animal*
>
> When the penultimate syllable ends with a coda, or has a long vowel or a diphthong, stress, however, falls on that heavy penultimate syllable:
>
> (2) penultimate syllable stressed
>   a. *utensil, agenda, synopsis*
>   b. *aroma, horizon, arena*
>
> In the above examples in (2a), it is clear that a syllable boundary seats itself between word-internal consonantal sequences such as -ns- (in *utensil*), -nd- (in *agenda*), and -ps- (in *synopsis*), since English phonotactic constraint does not permit such consonantal sequences to occur as an onset cluster. However, the word-internal consonantal sequence -st- poses an interesting challenge for syllabification. Unlike the -ns-, -nd-, or -ps-, the -st- sequence could be an onset cluster (as in *student, stupid*) or a coda cluster (as in *list, mist*).

Fill in the blank with the ONE most appropriate word from the passage above.

> Considering the stress placement in the words given in (3) where -st- occurs, we can claim that the underlined s is in _____ position.
>
> (3) antepenultimate syllable stressed
>   *amnesty, minister, pedestal*

5. Read the passage and fill in each blank with the ONE most appropriate word, respectively. 【2 points】

The examples in (1) show that word final consonant clusters formed by the addition of an inflectional suffix undergo voicing assimilation.

(1) cats   [kæts]   dogs   [dɔgz]
    cans   [kænz]   bells   [bɛlz]
    baked   [beɪkt]   popped   [pɑpt]
    farmed   [fɑɪmd]   sealed   [sild]

The examples in (2) illustrate the voicing agreement patterns in word final consonant clusters of the underived lexical items.

(2) a. apse   [æps]   *[æpz]   adze   [ædz]   *[æds]
      apt   [æpt]   *[æpd]   lift   [lɪft]   *[lɪfd]
      act   [ækt]   *[ækd]   cast   [kæst]   *[kæsd]

    b. mince   [mɪns]   *[mɪnz]   belch [bɛltʃ]   *[bɛldʒ]
      purse   [pəɹs]   *[pəɹz]   pump [pʌmp]   *[pʌmb]
      mint   [mɪnt]   *[mɪnd]   elk   [ɛlk]   *[ɛlg]

Unlike the lexical items with inflectional suffixes in (1), voicing agreement selectively occurs for the underived lexical items in (2). As can be seen in (2b), there are cases where clusters composed of _____ and _____ do not agree in voicing.

Note: * indicates a non-permissible form.

6. Read the passage and follow the directions. 【2 points】

A king. He waits. A musician enters.

King   : Ah. Didn't see you come in. You're a ... .
Composer : Bachweist, your Majesty.
King   : And what can you do for me?
Composer : I can make you immortal.
King   : Already been taken care of.
Composer : I can delight you.
King   : Kings don't delight, Bachweist, children delight.
Composer : I can carry you away on gossamer wings of melody.
King   : Bachweist, you better kneel down. [*Bachweist does.*] I'm not interested in your talent, man, it's peripheral to the real business of governing, or even living for that matter. Oh, it's useful with women, but my position is a stronger attraction than that. Only other musicians could possibly be interested in music in any meaningful way. And critics, of course, as a way of making a reputation. No, Bachweist, what I want from you is the following: a few ceremonial pieces on demand, hummable, naturally. A printable paragraph on my respect for and understanding of art. Some good groveling to make clear my position, and a resolute and articulated belief that you haven't been censored in anyway. Satire might sometime be a problem, Bachweist, but that's beyond the province of serious music, in any case.

Complete the commentary below by filling in the blank with the TWO most appropriate consecutive words from the passage.

The king is not satisfied with the composer's replies as to the possible services that he can offer. What is interesting, though, is the way the king clarifies his dissatisfaction. He has the composer "groveling" not just figuratively but also literally by commanding the composer to _____, a command that makes clear his "position."

7. Read the dialogue and follow the directions. 【2 points】

(A teacher and a student are talking after seeing a video-clip of a baseball game.)

T: What was happening in the video?

S: A ball, uh, a ball.

T: A ball was thrown.

S: Thrown?

T: Yes, thrown. A ball was thrown.

S: A ball thrown.

T: And who threw the ball?

S: Pitcher. Thrown pitcher.

T: Thrown by the pitcher.

S: By pitcher.

T: Yes, by the pitcher. A ball was thrown by the pitcher.

S: Ball thrown by pitcher.

Note: T = teacher, S = student

Fill in the blank with the FOUR most appropriate words.

From a socio-cultural perspective, effective learning takes place when what a student attempts to learn is within his or her _____. This is the distance between what a student can do alone and what he or she can do with scaffolded help from more knowledgeable others like teachers or more capable peers. For learning to be effective, such help should be provided to a student through interaction like the teacher's utterances offered to aid the student in the above dialogue.

---

8. Read the dialogue and fill in both blanks with the ONE most appropriate word. (Use the SAME word in both blanks.) 【2 points】

S: Ms. Lee, can I ask you a question?

T: Sure, go ahead.

S: I went over your feedback on my essay, and I really appreciate it. You pointed out the expression "die" could be revised to "pass away."

T: Yes, I did.

S: I don't understand the difference between the two expressions. As far as I understand, they have the same meaning.

T: Oh, I see. That's actually an example of a(n) _____.

S: Hmm … .

T: Let me make it clearer with another example. How do you think someone would feel if they were called "poor"?

S: Well, they may feel bad.

T: Okay, what about "less privileged"?

S: Oh, I understand your point. Two words or expressions may mean the same thing, but we may have different feelings and attitudes about them.

T: That's the point. A(n) _____ is a polite word or expression that you use instead of a more direct one, to avoid shocking or upsetting someone.

S: Interesting!

T: Good.

S: Thank you, Ms. Lee. Your feedback is always helpful.

Note: T = teacher, S = student

---

9. Read the passage and follow the directions. 【4 points】

There are expressions that are ambiguous because of scope interaction between a quantifier and another quantifier or between a quantifier and a negative expression. Consider the following sentences.

(1) a. Every boy likes a girl.
  b. Every student respects a professor.

Sentence (1a) and sentence (1b) are ambiguous because *every boy* and *every student* can have a wide scope over *a girl* and *a professor*, and *a girl* and *a professor* can have a wide scope over *every boy* and *every student*, respectively.

(2) a. Every student has not done their assignment.
  b. I have not eaten all the cookies.

In (2a) and (2b), *every student* and *all the cookies* can have a wide scope over *not*, and *not* can have a wide scope over *every student* and *all the cookies*.

Sentence (3) below is ambiguous. Write TWO possible meanings of the sentence and state how its ambiguity can be explained in terms of scope interaction.

(3) Mary refused to visit every city that Tom visited.

10. Read the passages and follow the directions. 【4 points】

─< A >─

Task-based language teaching (TBLT) holds a central place in current second language acquisition research and also in language pedagogy. Some suggest there are six main steps in designing, implementing, and evaluating a TBLT program.

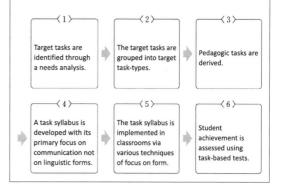

─< B >─

Mr. Kim designed and implemented a TBLT program based on the six steps described in <A>.

- Step 1. He did some questionnaire surveys with his students and interviewed fellow teachers to identify what his students would really want to do in everyday life.

- Step 2. He grouped the identified real-world tasks (e.g., purchasing a train ticket, booking a room, renting a car) into more general categories (e.g., planning a trip).

- Step 3. He developed tasks that his students would perform in the classroom. Those tasks were expected to elicit communicative language use in the classroom.

- Step 4. He designed a syllabus with a central aim of presenting different grammatical items one at a time and teaching them separately.

- Step 5. He drew student attention to linguistic forms when needed, while the primary focus of the lessons was still on communication during task performance.

- Step 6. He assessed the student outcomes, focusing on whether and how much they accomplished each given task.

Identify the step in <B> that does not match with its corresponding suggestion in <A>. Then, explain how that identified step deviates from its suggestion in <A>. Do NOT copy more than FOUR consecutive words from the passage.

11. Read the poem and follow the directions. 【4 points】

Rite of Passage

As the guests arrive at my son's party
they gather in the living room —
short men, men in first grade
with smooth jaws and chins.
Hands in pockets, they stand around
jostling, jockeying for place, small fights
breaking out and calming. One says to another
How old are you? Six. I'm seven. So?
They eye each other, seeing themselves
tiny in the other's pupils. They clear their
throats a lot, a room of small bankers,
they fold their arms and frown. *I could beat you
up*, a seven says to a six,
the dark cake, round and heavy as a
turret, behind them on the table. My son,
freckles like specks of nutmeg* on his cheeks,
chest narrow as the balsa* keel of a
model boat, long hands
cool and thin as the day they guided him
out of me, speaks up as a host
for the sake of the group.
We could easily kill a two-year-old,
he says in his clear voice. The other
men agree, they clear their throats
like Generals, they relax and get down to
playing war, celebrating my son's life.

*nutmeg: a powdered brown spice
*balsa: a tropical American tree or the wood from this tree

Considering the title of the poem, explain why the speaker describes the guests as "short men" (line 3), not little boys. Then, complete the commentary below with the TWO most appropriate consecutive words from the poem.

The birthday cake shaped like "a turret" juxtaposes playfulness and violence because a birthday cake evokes enjoyment, whereas the word "turret" reminds us of a military weapon. In a related way, the activity of _____ can be interpreted to symbolize the same contradictory elements.

12. Read the passage and follow the directions. 【4 points】

It is well known that coordinate conjunctions can conjoin constituents of the same grammatical category but cannot conjoin constituents of different grammatical categories, as exemplified in (1) and (2).

(1) a. fond of a dog and afraid of a tiger
    b. very slowly and very steadily
    c. a princess of Denmark and a prince of the United Kingdom
    d. I think that Mary likes poems and Susan novels.
    e. I think that Mary likes poems and that Susan likes novels.

(2) a. *like a dog and afraid of a tiger
    b. *slowly and the car
    c. *a princess of Denmark and with long hair
    d. *I believe Mary to be honest and that Susan is kind.
    e. *I believe that Mary is honest and Susan to be kind.

AP can conjoin with another AP, AdvP with another AdvP, NP or DP with another NP or DP, TP with another TP, and CP with another CP.

TP, meaning Tense Phrase, is a clause that does not include a complementizer like *Mary likes poems* in (3a). CP, meaning Complementizer Phrase, is a clause that includes a complementizer. The embedded clause of sentence (3a) has the structure in (3b).

(3) a. I think that Mary likes poems.
    b.

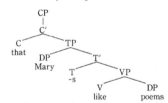

Note: * indicates the ungrammaticality of the sentence.

State whether sentence (4) and sentence (5) can be conjoined with the coordinate conjunction *but* as in sentence (6). Then, explain why, identifying the grammatical category of sentence (4) and that of sentence (5).

(4) I am feeling thirsty.
(5) Should I save my last cola till later?
(6) I am feeling thirsty but should I save my last cola till later?

13. Read the dialogue and follow the directions. 【4 points】

> T: Come here, Sumin. How was your vacation?
>
> S: Pretty good. Thank you, Ms. Kim. Actually, I'm so happy to be taking English classes from you this year.
>
> T: Good! You're really welcome in my class. Okay, then, let's talk about the test you had.
>
> S: You mean the reading test you gave us in the first class? Actually, I was wondering why you gave us a test instead of going directly into the textbook.
>
> T: Right, your class hasn't had a lesson yet. It was mainly to see how much you are ready for this semester and give you individual attention for any strong and weak points you have.
>
> S: I see. So, how were the results?
>
> T: Hmm … . Overall, you did quite well. Especially, you did well on the grammar questions. But it appears you had a bit of trouble with some words in the reading texts.
>
> S: You're right. Some words are really hard to memorize although I keep trying.
>
> T: I understand. Well, why don't you try to learn them through a context particularly relevant to you? That will be helpful, I believe.
>
> S: Thank you for your advice, Ms. Kim.
>
> *Note*: T = teacher, S = student

Fill in the blank with the ONE most appropriate word. Then, support your answer with evidence from the dialogue.

> Tests can be categorized according to the purposes for which they are carried out. In this respect, the test that Ms. Kim and Sumin are talking about is an example of a(n) _____ test.

14. Read the passage and follow the directions. 【4 points】

> For at least 10,000 years, humans have been manipulating their own brains by drinking alcohol. And for at least the last few decades, researchers have wondered whether alcohol had a positive effect on physical health. Study after study seemed to suggest that people who imbibed one alcoholic beverage per day — a 12-ounce beer, a 6-ounce glass of wine, or a 1.5-ounce shot of spirits — had healthier hearts than did people who abstained from drinking altogether. A drink a day, it seemed, kept the cardiologist away.
>
> Yet the methods in these studies may be flawed. When Kaye Fillmore, a researcher at the University of California, San Francisco, and her team analyzed 54 published studies on how moderate drinking affects the heart, they found that most of the drink-a-day studies had not used random assignment. In studies with random assignment, researchers used coin tosses or the like to decide into which condition — the control group or various experimental groups — each study participant should go. By letting chance dictate who goes into which group, researchers are more likely to end up with truly comparable groups.
>
> Instead of randomly assigning participants to drinking and non-drinking groups, though, 47 of the 54 studies compared people who were already having one drink daily to people who were already teetotaling. Why is this design method a problem? In the United States, where most of these studies took place, many people have a drink once in a while. Usually, people who never drink abstain for a reason, such as religious prohibitions or medical concerns.
>
> In fact, Fillmore and her team found that many of the nondrinkers in these studies were abstaining from alcohol for medical reasons, including advanced age or a history of alcoholism. In other words, the nondrinking groups in most of the studies included more unhealthy people *to begin with*, compared to the drinking groups. As a result, these studies didn't show that drinking alcohol led to better health. Instead, they showed that better health often leads to a level of alcohol consumption that is moderate.

First, describe the characteristics of the participants in the two groups in 47 of the 54 studies. Second, explain why those 47 studies were flawed in design.

<수고하셨습니다.>

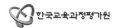

영 어

수험 번호 : (   )   성 명 : (   )

제1차 시험	3교시 전공B	8문항 40점	시험 시간 90분

◦ 문제지 전체 면수가 맞는지 확인하시오.
◦ 모든 문항에는 배점이 표시되어 있습니다.

※ **Write all answers in English and use neat handwriting.**

1. Read the passage and follow the directions. 【4 points】

In a number of dialects of British English, a glide is inserted in certain environments, as shown in (1) and (2).

(1) /j/ insertion

being	/biɪŋ/	[bijɪŋ]
my other (car)	/maɪʌðə/	[maɪjʌðə]
free a (prisoner)	/friə/	[frijə]
enjoy ice cream	/ɛndʒɔɪaɪskɹim/	[ɛndʒɔɪjaɪskɹim]

(2) /w/ insertion

sewer	/suə/	[suwə]
few arrests	/fjuaɹɛsts/	[fjuwaɹɛsts]
now or never	/naʊɔnɛvə/	[naʊwɔnɛvə]
go away	/gouəweɪ/	[gouwəweɪ]

However, in such dialects, glide insertion is not attested in the examples in (3). Instead, /ɹ/ is inserted.

(3) No glide insertion

drawing	[dɹɔɹɪŋ]	*[dɹɔjɪŋ]	*[dɹɔwɪŋ]
ma and pa	[maɹənpa]	*[majənpa]	*[mawənpa]
law and order	[lɔɹənɔdə]	*[lɔjənɔdə]	*[lɔwənɔdə]
media event	[midiɹaɪvɛnt]	*[midiəjɪvɛnt]	*[midiəwɪvɛnt]

Note: * indicates a non-permissible form.

Based on the data given in (1)-(3), provide one single generalization for glide insertion. Then, state the condition(s) for /j/ insertion and the one(s) for /w/ insertion, respectively.

2. Read the passage and follow the directions. 【4 points】

While Ashbury was still in New York, he had written a letter to his mother which filled two notebooks. He knew, of course, that his mother would not understand the letter at once. Her literal mind would require some time to discover the significance of it, but he thought she would be able to see that he forgave her for all she had done to him. For that matter, he supposed that she would realize what she had done to him only through the letter.

If reading it would be painful to her, writing it had sometimes been unbearable to him – for in order to face her, he had had to face himself. "I came here to escape the slave's atmosphere of home," he had written, "to find freedom, to liberate my imagination, to take it like a hawk and set it 'whirling off into the widening gyre' (Yeats) and what did I find? It was not capable of flight. It was some bird you had domesticated, refusing to come out!" The next words were underscored twice. "I have no imagination. I have no talent. I can't create. I have nothing but the desire for these things. Why didn't you kill that too? Woman, why did you pinion me?"

Explain why Ashbury thinks that his mother might not immediately grasp the message he wants to get across through his letter. (Do NOT copy more than THREE consecutive words from the passage.) Then, complete the commentary below by filling in the blank with the ONE most appropriate word from the passage.

Ashbury employs figurative language to represent his imagination as a(n) _____ animal in contrast to Yeats' wild hawk.

---

3. Read the passage and follow the directions. 【4 points】

The act of searching for and finding underground supplies of water using nothing more than a rod is commonly known as "dowsing." Many dowsers in Germany claim that they respond to "earthrays" that emanate from water. These earthrays, say the dowsers, are a subtle form of radiation potentially hazardous to human health. As a result of these claims, the German government in the mid-1980s conducted a 2-year experiment to investigate the possibility that dowsing is a genuine skill.

A group of university physicists in Munich, Germany, were provided a grant of 400,000 marks to conduct the study. Approximately 500 candidate dowsers were recruited to participate in preliminary tests of their skill. To avoid fraudulent claims, the 43 individuals who seemed to be the most successful in the preliminary tests were selected for the final, carefully controlled, experiment.

The researchers set up a 10-meter-long line on the ground floor of a vacant barn, along which a small wagon could be moved. Attached to the wagon was a short length of pipe, perpendicular to the test line, that was connected by hoses to a pump with water. The _____ along the line for each trial of the experiment was assigned using a computer-generated random number. On the upper floor of the barn, directly above the experimental line, a 10-meter test line was painted. In each trial, a dowser was admitted to this upper level and required, with his or her rod, stick, or other tool of choice, to ascertain where the pipe with water on the ground floor was located.

Over the 2-year experimental period, the 43 dowsers participated in a total of 843 tests. The experiment was "double blind" in that neither the researcher on the top floor nor the dowser knew the _____, even after a guess was made.

For each trial, an examination of the actual pipe's location (in decimeters from the beginning of the line) and the dowser's guess were recorded. The German physicists from these data concluded in their final report that although most dowsers did not do particularly well in the experiments, "some few dowsers, in particular tests, showed an extraordinarily high rate of correct guesses, which can scarcely if at all be explained as due to chance ... a real core of dowser-phenomena can be regarded as empirically proven ... ."

Fill in the blank with the TWO most appropriate consecutive words from the passage. (Use the SAME consecutive words for both blanks.) Then, write the two factors used to determine the underlined words, "correct guesses."

4. Read the passage in <A> and the dialogue in <B>, and follow the directions. 【4 points】

<A>

The modal auxiliary *will* can be used to express a neutral prediction of what will happen in the future or have a volitional meaning for describing what one will do, as exemplified in (1).

(1) a. It will snow tomorrow.
    b. I will go to the U.S. next year for further studies.

However, the simple present tense is used instead of the auxiliary *will* to express future time in adverbial time clauses, as in (2a).

(2) a. He will help the scientists when he gets to the research center.
    b.*He will help the scientists when he will get to the research center.

Note: * indicates the ungrammaticality of the sentence.

<B>

W: You're going to attend the international conference, aren't you?
M: Yes, I am.
W: How do you feel about the conference?
M: I am glad I can go to the conference with you. I'll be excited when the conference will begin.
W: Do you think Helen will come, too?
M: I don't know if she will come. Have you finished your preparation for the presentation?
W: Not yet. I need to work on it several more hours. It will be nice if it's finished by tomorrow, but I am not sure if it will be possible.
M: I hope you'll have it finished by tomorrow.
W: But it seems very difficult. Could you help me?
M: Sure. I'll be happy to.
W: Thank you very much. With your help I'll be able to complete it by tomorrow.
M: Don't worry. I'll help you until you will finish it.

Note: M= man, W= woman

Identify TWO ungrammatical sentences that contain incorrect usages of the auxiliary *will* in <B>. Then, explain why they are incorrect, based on the description given in <A>.

5. Read Ms. Lee's opinions about the grammar lesson in <A> and the sample lesson plan in <B>, and follow the directions. 【4 points】

―――――<A>―――――

I think teachers should keep in mind that the ultimate goal of any grammar lesson is to build up communicative ability. In order to achieve this goal, I believe that classroom activities should not focus on practicing structures and patterns in a meaningless way. Instead, they should be designed to involve students in real communication. By doing so, grammar lessons will be able to encourage the students' interest in learning and elicit more active and meaningful interaction with others in the classroom.

―――――<B>―――――

Subject	High School English	Students	1st-year students
Title	Lesson 9 My Dream	Date	Nov. 24th
Objec-tives	• Students will familiarize themselves with the expression "If I were … ." • Students will be able to communicate using the expression "If I were … ."		

Teaching-Learning Activities		
Introduc-tion	Greeting & Roll-call	• T and Ss exchange greetings. • T checks if all the Ss are present.
	Review	• T reviews materials from the previous lesson.
	Stating the Objectives	• T introduces the objective of the lesson.
Develop-ment	Activity 1	• T hands out a text that contains several instances of "If I were … ." • Ss scan the text and highlight all the sentences including "If I were … ." • Ss check the ones they highlighted with T. • T tells Ss to pay attention to the verb form "were."
	Activity 2	• T tells Ss that she is going to read a passage on "My Dream." • T explains difficult words in the passage. • T reads the passage at a normal pace. • Ss jot down the key words in the passage as T reads.
		• Ss reconstruct the passage individually. • T hands out the original text to Ss.
	Activity 3	• T has Ss form groups of three. • T asks Ss to think of a job that they would like to have in the future. • Ss use "If I were … " to share their opinions about their future dream jobs. • Assuming that their dreams come true, two Ss take a reporter's role and interview the other S asking how he or she feels about his or her job. • Ss take turns and continue the activity.
	Activity 4	• T hands out a worksheet. • Ss put together sentence fragments to form complete sentences. • T reads out complete sentences and each S checks their own answers. • T writes three more sentences using "If I were … " on the board. • T asks Ss to read the sentences.
Consoli-dation	Review	• T reviews what Ss learned.
	Closure	• T hands out homework and announces the next lesson. • T says goodbye to Ss.

Note: T = teacher, S = student

Based on <A>, choose the ONE most appropriate activity in the development stage that reflects Ms. Lee's opinions. Then, support your choice with evidence from <B>. Do NOT copy more than FOUR consecutive words from the passage.

6. Read the passages and follow the directions. 【5 points】

<A>

Sentences must satisfy various principles to be grammatically correct. Consider the following sentences.

(1) a. It seems that Tom admires Mary.
  b. *Tom seems that he admires Mary.

Sentence (1a) is grammatical but sentence (1b) is ungrammatical since the matrix subject *Tom* has no theta role.

Next, consider sentences containing an anaphor.

(2) a. Tom thinks that Mary$_i$ admires herself$_i$.
  b. *Tom$_i$ thinks that Mary admires himself$_i$.

(3) a. Tom expects Mary$_i$ to admire herself$_i$.
  b. *Tom$_i$ expects Mary to admire himself$_i$.

Sentences (2a) and (3a) are grammatical since the reflexive pronoun *herself* is in the same clause as, and bound by, the antecedent *Mary*. However, sentences (2b) and (3b) are ungrammatical since the reflexive pronoun *himself* does not occur in the same clause as the antecedent *Tom*, violating the binding condition, which requires a reflexive pronoun to be bound by its antecedent in its binding domain, which is the smallest clause containing the anaphor.

Finally, consider the following sentences.

(4) a. It seems that Tom is believed to admire Mary.
  b. *Tom seems that it is believed to admire Mary.

Sentence (4a) is grammatically correct since no violation of grammatical principles has occurred. However, sentence (4b) is ungrammatical since the movement of the matrix subject has violated a constraint which bans a subject from crossing another subject.

Note: * indicates the ungrammaticality of the sentence.

<B>

Consider the following sentence.

(5) Tom$_i$ appears to Mary to be believed by his friends to brag about himself$_i$.

In the above sentence, the reflexive pronoun *himself* is in the lowest embedded clause, whereas its antecedent *Tom* is in the subject position of the matrix clause.

State whether sentence (5) in <B> is syntactically well-formed or ill-formed. Then, explain why, discussing whether the matrix subject can be assigned a theta role, whether it violates any movement constraint, and whether the anaphor can be bound.

7. Read the passage and follow the directions. 【5 points】

As children, many of us were taken to museums. In most cases this was probably with a group of fellow students from our school on a field trip. We were there to learn. The displays were static and the importance of the so-called great works escaped many in attendance. As a result, many adults rarely revisited museums. Museums were only seen as cultural repositories. In the last few decades, however, they have changed their purpose and role in society.

Throughout human history, museums collected the extraordinary as evidence of the past. More recently, they have reevaluated the purpose of their collections and put much more effort into collecting the ordinary and everyday, in recognition of the fact that it is this material which best represents the lives of most people. Such a change in their collections enables museums to show their relevance to people who previously were underrepresented, and thus uninterested in museums.

Museums have started to play a new role in society through their partnerships, as well. It is no longer an option for a museum to remain isolated and aloof. Museums are social constructs and have assumed their place in mainstream contemporary life. They are now networking their value to all sectors of society, not just with traditional allies like the education sector. Political associations and business and community sectors are now included.

In these ways, the institutions that once were just hallowed halls of important objects are now quickly adapting with new attitudes towards what they collect. They also have evolved to interact and work with a variety of members within their communities. Modern museums are reinventing themselves as the center of contemporary culture.

Write a summary following the guidelines below.

<Guidelines>
- Summarize the above passage in one paragraph.
- Provide a topic sentence, two supporting ideas, and a concluding sentence based on the passage.
- Do NOT copy more than FIVE consecutive words from the passage.

8. Read the passage in <A> and the teacher talk in <B>, and follow the directions. 【10 points】

―――――――――<A>―――――――――

(Below are notes that Ms. Shin, a new teacher, took of her senior teacher's advice on how to make her class communicatively oriented.)

Senior teacher's suggestions

- Objective: Get class centered on language functions rather than grammatical structures.

- Error targeted: Focus only on global errors impeding communication of meaning.

- Strategy: Encourage the use of communication strategies.

- Feedback: Provide correction implicitly.

―――――――――<B>―――――――――

(Below is Ms. Shin's talk at the beginning and closure of her single-activity class.)

Today, you are going to practice how to make requests using the question forms you learned from the last class. To do this, you will be doing an activity in pairs where you need to fill in a book order form by asking your partner for the necessary information. While doing this, you will get a chance to use the question forms to make requests. If you can't come up with the exact words to express the meaning you intend during the activity, you can try using similar words you know or even gestures, instead. Now, I will hand out the copies of the order form. Then, you can begin the activity with the student next to you. You'll work in pairs. OK, here are your copies.

⋮

All right, now it's time to wrap up. I think you all did a great job on the form-filling activity exactly as I told you when the class started. But there is one and only one language element I want to briefly point out today. I noticed some of you missed 's' in some verbs like "He come" while talking. It should be "comes" not "come" though meaning is still clear without 's.' Apart from this, you seem to be fairly familiar with making requests now. Next time, we will focus on how to ask for permission.

Write TWO paragraphs based on <A> and <B>. In the first paragraph, identify TWO suggestions from <A> that Ms. Shin's class conforms to and provide evidence for each identified suggestion from <B>. In the second paragraph, identify TWO suggestions from <A> that Ms. Shin's class does <u>not</u> conform to and explain how with evidence from <B>.

<수고하셨습니다.>

○ 문제지 전체 면수가 맞는지 확인하시오.
○ 모든 문항에는 배점이 표시되어 있습니다.

※ **Write all answers in English and use neat handwriting.**

1. Read the questionnaire in <A> and the teacher's note in <B>, and follow the directions. 【2 points】

<A>

This questionnaire is designed to identify students' learning styles. Each category (A, B, C, D) has 10 items. Students are asked to read each item and check their preferences.

	Learning Style Questionnaire	4	3	2	1
A	1. I understand better when I hear instructions.				
	2. I remember information better when I listen to lectures than when I read books.				
	3. I like to listen to radio shows and discussions more than reading the newspaper.				
	⋮				
B	1. I like to look at graphs, images, and pictures when I study.				
	2. I follow directions better when the teacher writes them on the board.				
	3. I can easily understand information on a map.				
	⋮				
C	1. I enjoy working with my hands or making things.				
	2. I remember things better when I build models or do projects.				
	3. I like to 'finger spell' when I learn words.				
	⋮				
D	1. I like activities that involve moving around.				
	2. I prefer to learn by doing something active.				
	3. I learn the best when I go on field trips.				
	⋮				

Note: 4=strongly agree, 3=agree, 2=disagree, 1=strongly disagree

<B>

Based on the findings of the questionnaire conducted in my class, I have noticed that four students each have a major learning style.

Scores of the four students			
Youngmi	Minsu	Taeho	Suji
A=38	A=18	A=15	A=13
B=11	B=36	B=12	B=14
C=10	C=10	C=40	C=12
D=12	D=12	D=11	D=36

This week, I am going to teach names of wild animals, like 'ostrich' and 'rhinoceros,' by trying different activities to address these students' different learning styles. Youngmi scored the highest in category A, showing that she is an auditory learner. So I will let her listen to a recording and say the names of animals out loud. Minsu's high score in category B shows that he is a visual learner. I will let him look at images of animals and read the corresponding names. The person who had the highest score in C was Taeho, who is a tactile learner. I am going to use origami so he can use his hands to fold papers into animal shapes. This will help him learn their names better. Lastly, Suji's score in category D shows that she is a(n) _____ learner. For her, I am planning to do an animal charade activity where she acts like different animals and others guess the names of them. I think she will enjoy moving around the classroom. In these ways, I want to maximize students' learning outcomes in my class.

Based on the information in <A> and <B>, fill in the blank in <B> with the ONE most appropriate word.

2. Read the conversation between two teachers and follow the directions. 【2 points】

> T1: My students are having trouble with plural nouns. I'm thinking of trying a new task.
> T2: What's your idea?
> T1: I'm planning to give a short text where every seventh word is blanked out. Students have to guess the correct word for each blank to make a complete sentence.
> T2: Well, that might be a bit difficult for beginning level students. I did a similar activity last semester. I gave a text where I blanked out only plural nouns so that students could focus on them.
> T1: Oh, I see.
> T2: You can also give students only parts of words in the blanks and ask them to restore each word in the text.
> T1: Hmm, that seems interesting. Well, then, for my students, I'll try to use only plural nouns in the written text and ask my students to fill in the blanks. Thanks for the suggestion.
>
> *Note*: T1=teacher 1, T2=teacher 2

Complete the comments by filling in the blank with the ONE most appropriate word.

> In the above dialogue, the two teachers are talking about teaching plural nouns through three types of gap-filling tasks which require students to read the texts and fill in the blanks. The gap-filling described by the teachers here is _____, which can be readily adapted for pedagogical tasks in classrooms.

3. Read the dialogue and follow the directions. 【2 points】

> T: What are you going to do this weekend?
> S: I will go to a market with my mom.
> T: Is there anything you want to buy?
> S: Eggs. Many eggs.
> T: Is that all you want?
> S: No. I will buy many bread and cheese, too.
> T: (1) Well, you said you will buy... buy...
> S: Buy bread and cheese. Ah, buy a lot of bread. I will buy a lot of bread and cheese.
> T: Why will you buy them?
> S: I like to make sandwiches. I will make many sandwiches.
> T: Do you have any other plans?
> S: I have many homework so I will study for many hours.
> T: (2) Well, what word do we use with homework?
> S: Many homeworks? No, a lot of? Yes, a lot of homework.
>
> *Note*: T=teacher, S=student

Fill in the blank with the ONE most appropriate word.

> _____ refers to a type of the teacher's corrective feedback that directly induces the correct form of an error from the learner. One technique of this is to induce the correct form of an error by prompting the learner to reformulate the error and complete his or her own utterances, which is seen in the teacher's first corrective feedback, (1), in the dialogue. Another technique is to use questions to lead the learner to produce correct forms as shown in the teacher's second corrective feedback, (2), in the dialogue.

4. Read the passage and fill in each blank with the ONE most appropriate word. Write your answers in the correct order. 【2 points】

> Across morpheme boundaries, obligatory nasal assimilation to bilabials or alveolars applies without restriction, as shown in (1).
>
> (1) compose   composition
> symbol   symbolic
> sympathy   sympathetic
> condemn   condemnation
> intone   intonation
> indent   indentation
>
> On the other hand, obligatory nasal assimilation to velars applies selectively, as shown in (2). (Note that optional nasal assimilation may apply postlexically to derive 'co[ŋ]cordance,' 'co[ŋ]gressional,' etc.)
>
> (2) Nasal assimilation   No nasal assimilation
> co[ŋ]cord   co[n]cordance
> co[ŋ]gress   co[n]gressional
> co[ŋ]quer   co[n]cur
> co[ŋ]gruous   co[n]gruity
> sy[ŋ]chrony   sy[n]chronic
> i[ŋ]cubate   i[n]clude
>
> The examples in (2) illustrate that obligatory nasal assimilation applies only when preceded by a(n) ___①___ vowel and followed by a(n) ___②___ vowel with a velar involved.

5. Read the passage and fill in the blank with the most appropriate IPA symbol. 【2 points】

> Two different definitions are employed for the tense-lax distinction. One is the phonetic definition given in (1).
>
> (1) Phonetic definition
>   a. A tense vowel has a higher tongue position than its lax counterpart.
>   b. A tense vowel has greater duration than its lax counterpart.
>   c. A tense vowel requires a greater muscular effort in production than a lax vowel.
>
> The other is a phonologically defined tense-lax separation in terms of the different kinds of syllables in which the vowels can occur.
>
> (2) Phonological definition
>   Tense vowels can appear in open syllables with stress while lax vowels cannot.
>
> The distributionally based phonological classification of tense-lax comes into conflict with the phonetically based classification in several respects. First of all, both /oʊ/ and /ɔ/ are tense in the phonological classification while they are separated as tense and lax, respectively, in the phonetic classification. Second, there is a problem with regard to duration, which the phonetically based criterion focuses on. While it is true that several of the lax vowels are short, _____ is not. Indeed, this vowel has equal duration with, or even greater duration than typically long and tense vowels.

6. Read the excerpt from a play and follow the directions. 【2 points】

> PARRITT: What do they do for a living?
> LARRY: As little as possible. Once in a while one of them makes a successful touch somewhere, and some of them get a few dollars a month from connections at home who pay it on condition they never come back. For the rest, they live on free lunch and their old friend, Harry Hope, who doesn't give a damn what anyone does or doesn't do, as long as he likes you.
> PARRITT: It must be a tough life.
> LARRY: It's not. Don't waste your pity. They wouldn't thank you for it. They manage to get drunk, by hook or crook, and keep their pipe dreams, and that's all they ask of life. I've never known more contented men. It isn't often that men attain the true goal of their heart's desire. The same applies to Harry himself and his two cronies at the far table. He's so satisfied with life he's never set foot out of this place since his wife died twenty years ago. He has no need of the outside world at all. This place has a fine trade from the Market people across the street and the waterfront workers, so in spite of Harry's thirst and his generous heart, he comes out even. He never worries in hard times because there's always old friends from the days when he was a jitney Tammany politician, and a friendly brewery to tide him over. Don't ask me what his two pals work at because they don't. Except at being his lifetime guests.

Complete the commentary below by filling in the blank with the TWO most appropriate consecutive words from the passage.

> <Commentary>
> The different types of characters mentioned in Larry and Parritt's conversation in Harry Hope's bar dwell on _____. They sentimentally reminisce about their glory days while loafing around doing nothing. It is self-delusion rather than self-knowledge that sustains them.

7. Read the passage and follow the directions. 【2 points】

When I came to my castle, for so I think I call'd it even after this, I fled into it like one pursued; whether I went over by the ladder as first contriv'd, or went in at the hole in the rock, which I call'd a door I cannot remember; nor, nor could I remember the next morning, for never frighted hare fled to cover, or fox to earth, with more terror of mind than I to this retreat.

I slept none that night; the farther I was from the occasion of my fright, the greater my apprehensions were, which is something contrary to the nature of such things and especially to the usual practice of all creatures in fear: But I was so embarrass'd with my own frightful ideas of the thing, that I form'd nothing but dismal imaginations to my self, even tho' I was now a great way off of it. Sometimes I fancy'd it must be the devil; and reason joyn'd in with me upon this supposition: For how should any other thing in human shape come into the place? Where was the vessel that brought them? What marks was there of any other footsteps! And how was it possible a man should come there? But then to think that Satan should take human shape upon him in such a place where there could be no manner of occasion for it, but to leave the print of his foot behind him, and that even for no purpose too, for he could not be sure I should see it; this was an amusement the other way; I consider'd that the devil might have found out abundance of other ways to have terrify'd me than this of the single print of a foot. That as I liv'd quite on the other side of the island, he would never have been so simple to leave a mark in a place where 'twas ten thousand to one whether I should ever see it or not, and in the sand too, which the first surge of the sea upon a high wind would have defac'd entirely: All this seem'd inconsistent with the thing it self, and with all the notions we usually entertain of the subtilty of the devil.

Complete the commentary below by filling in the blank with the ONE most appropriate word from the passage.

<Commentary>

In this scene, instead of rejoicing at the possibility of rescue or of a companion, the narrator reacts with fear. His apprehension is intensified because where he expected to find a trail of _____, he only found one.

8. Read the passage and follow the directions. 【2 points】

Ancient Easterners saw the world as consisting of continuous substances while ancient Westerners tended to see the world as being composed of discrete objects or separate atoms. Remarkably, it is still the same in the modern era.

In a survey of the values of middle managers, Hampden-Turner and Trompenaars examined whether respondents from both Eastern and Western cultures thought of a company as a system to organize tasks or as an organism coordinating people working together. They asked respondents to choose between the following definitions:

(a) A company is a system designed to perform functions and tasks in an efficient way. People are hired to fulfill these functions with the help of machines and other equipment. They are paid for the tasks they perform.

(b) A company is a group of people working together. The people have social relations with other people and with the organization. The functioning is dependent on these relations.

About 75 percent of Americans chose the first definition, and more than 50 percent of Canadians, Australians, British, Dutch, and Swedes chose that definition. About a third of a group of Japanese and Singaporeans chose it. Thus for the Westerners, especially the Americans and the other people of primarily northern European culture, a company is an atomistic, modular place where people perform their distinctive functions. For the Easterners, a company is an organism where the social relations are an integral part of what holds things together.

Fill in the blank with the ONE most appropriate word from the passage.

Research shows that people from Western cultures tend to see the world in a more atomistic way. This view leads them to see a social institution like a workplace as a system to perform distinctive functions. On the other hand, according to the Easterners' perspective, a company is seen as an interdependent organism. Its function is made possible by _____ among its members as well as between the members and the organization. Knowledge of such differences can be helpful for intercultural understanding.

9. Read the passages and follow the directions. 【4 points】

<A>

Clausal modifiers of NPs which function as the Subject or the Object can move to the end of the sentence, which is called 'extraposition,' as shown in (1) and (2), respectively. The extraposed CP can be adjoined to VP or TP.

(1) a. A man [who has red hair] just came in.
    b. A man just came in [who has red hair].

(2) a. John won't turn a friend [who needs help] away.
    b. John won't turn a friend away [who needs help].

Let's take a closer examination of the extraposition of the CP from the Object position in (2b). As confirmed in (3), VP preposing can be further applied to (2b) and the resulting sentence is grammatical. This suggests that the extraposed CP from the Object position is adjoined to VP, since only phrasal constituents can move.

(3) John said that he wouldn't turn a friend away who needs help, and [turn a friend away who needs help] he won't.

The whole process can be represented as in (4): from the structure in (4a) the clausal modifier CP adjoined to VP in (4b) and the resulting VP constituent moved to the front of the sentence in (4c).

(4) a. [TP John won't [VP turn [NP a friend [CP who needs help]] away]]
    b. [TP John won't [VP [VP turn a friend t$_i$ away] [CP who needs help]$_i$]]
    c. [[VP [VP turn a friend away] [CP who needs help]]$_j$ [TP John won't t$_j$]]

From the brief observation, it can be proposed that an extraposed CP is adjoined to the first phrasal constituent containing the NP out of which it is extraposed.

<B>

(i) Few people who knew him$_i$ would work with John$_i$.
(ii) Few people would work with John$_i$ who knew him$_i$.
(iii) Work with John$_i$ who knew him$_i$ few people would.

Based on the proposal in <A>, first identify in <B> what syntactic category the extraposed CP in (ii), derived from (i), is adjoined to. Second, state whether the preposing in (iii), derived from (ii), is grammatical or not, and then explain why.

10. Read the poem and follow the directions. 【4 points】

Promise me no promises,
So will I not promise you;
Keep we both our liberties,
Never false and never true:
Let us hold the die uncast,
Free to come as free to go;
For I cannot know your past,
And of mine what can you know?

You, so warm, may once have been
Warmer towards another one;
I, so cold, may once have seen
Sunlight, once have felt the sun:
Who shall show us if it was
Thus indeed in time of old?
Fades the image from the glass
And the fortune is not told.

If you promised, you might grieve
For lost liberty again;
If I promised, I believe
I should fret to break the chain:
Let us be the friends we were,
Nothing more but nothing less;
Many thrive on frugal fare
Who would perish of excess.

Complete the commentary below by filling in the blank with the ONE most appropriate word from the poem. Then, explain what the underlined part means. Do NOT copy more than TWO consecutive words from the poem.

<Commentary>

In the poem the speaker tells the man, "Promise me no promises." She is unwilling to be committed to the man, suggesting that they should remain as _____.

11. Read the passage in <A> and the teacher's log in <B>, and follow the directions. 【4 points】

―<A>―

Language transfer refers to the effects of the learner's previous language knowledge or performance on subsequent language learning. Transfer can be categorized into positive and negative transfer. Negative transfer can be further divided into two types―overgeneralization and interference.

―<B>―

(Following is a teacher's reflection on a task for her Korean students.)

Teacher's log

I conducted a task that required students in pairs to ask and answer questions in class yesterday. At the beginning of the task, I heard a student asking, "Don't you like bananas?" His partner answered, "No, I eat them everyday. They are good for my health." And another student said, "Yes, I never eat them. But I like mangos," when responding to "Don't you like oranges?" I noticed many other students make such errors later in the course of the task. So I decided to tap into the errors and explained them to students after the task. I gave them further question-and-answer exercises to provide opportunities to practice what I explained before the class was over.

Identify the type of negative transfer in <B> based on <A>. Then, provide TWO examples of the identified type from <B> and explain why they exemplify the identified type in terms of whether transfer occurs intralingually or interlingually.

12. Read the English test task specifications in <A> and the teacher's reflective journal in <B>, and follow the directions. 【4 points】

―<A>―

Test Task Specifications

Category	Description
Purpose	To determine students' current levels and place them into the most appropriate speaking courses
Time allocation	2 minutes (1 minute for preparation and 1 minute for speaking)
Task type	Picture-cued tasks
Scoring method	Analytic a. Criteria: Content, Fluency, Accuracy, Pronunciation b. Each criterion is worth 5 points and the score for this task is added up to 20.
Scoring procedure	a. Two examiners: a primary examiner who conducts the test and a secondary examiner who observes the test b. If there is a difference of more than 2 points in total, the examiners discuss rating disagreements based on the recorded test to arrive at a rating that they agree upon.

―<B>―

I understand that some students have potential strengths in learning languages, and in order to check my students' aptitude in English, I conducted a speaking test with picture-cued tasks. For each task, students looked at pictures and prepared for 1 minute and then described them for 1 minute. I found that 1 minute was not enough for my students to prepare their answers, so I felt that I needed to change the time allocation for the task. In addition, although my rating and the other examiner's rating seemed consistent, I realized that my approach, providing a global rating with overall impressions using a single general scale, was not very effective because the scores didn't give much helpful information to students. … There was one student's test yielding very different scores, so we (primary and secondary examiners) had a discussion about the recorded test and found that I gave the wrong score by mistake. It was good that we recorded the test even though both of us were present during the test.

Identify TWO categories that the teacher did NOT follow in the test task specifications from <A>. Then, support your answers with evidence from <B>.

13. Read the passage and follow the directions. 【4 points】

There's no shortage of therapies for autism, some of which work well, some not so well. But there is one simple treatment that hasn't been getting the attention it may deserve: time. According to a new study in the *Journal of Child Psychology and Psychiatry*, some children who receive behavioral interventions to treat autism might be able to age out of their symptoms, outgrowing them like last year's shoes.

The idea of maturing out of psychological ills is not new. All 10 personality disorders, for example—including schizoid, which shares features with schizophrenia—can lessen as people age. Some of this may be attributable to patients' learning to manage their symptoms, but it's also possible that the brain, which is still developing into our late 20s, is improving too. "The fact that these things aren't engraved in granite is terribly exciting," says psychologist Mark Lenzenweger of the State University of New York at Binghamton.

There have been hints that this kind of remission might be possible in autism, but previous studies were plagued with questions about whether the children who had apparently shed their autism were properly diagnosed with the disorder in the first place. In the current analysis, a team led by psychologist Deborah Fein of the University of Connecticut looked at 34 people ages 8 to 21 who had been diagnosed with autism but no longer met the criteria for the disorder. It compared them with 44 patients in the same age group who still had symptoms. Both groups had received similar treatments. After the researchers corrected for other variables, the subjects with the better outcomes seemed simply to have matured out of the condition.

"I view it as a landmark kind of study," says Geraldine Dawson, chief science officer for Autism Speaks. Others disagree. It's possible, they say, that some kids just mask their symptoms, imitating healthy behaviors that they come to appreciate as desirable. Still, it's hard to dismiss Fein's work entirely. The 34 subjects whose symptoms had vanished were able to attend school without one-on-one assistance and needed no further social-skills training. Something had to account for that, and maturation, in this research at least, is the best answer.

Describe what the underlined part refers to. Provide TWO pieces of evidence showing that the group of 34 subjects in Fein's work had recovered from autism. Do NOT copy more than THREE consecutive words from the passage.

14. Read the passage in <A> and part of a lesson procedure in <B>, and follow the directions. 【4 points】

―――――――――<A>―――――――――

(Below are suggestions from a conference for teaching L2 writing.)

To help students to write effectively...

(a) Start with pre-writing activities with little emphasis on ungrammaticalities and incorrect spelling.

(b) Have drafting and revising stages in a recursive way.

(c) Provide meaning-focused feedback.

(d) Offer students opportunities to think about their own writing.

―――――――――<B>―――――――――

(The following is part of Ms. Song's lesson procedure for teaching how to write an argumentative essay.)

Steps:

1. T provides background information about artificial intelligence and Ss watch videos related to the topic.
2. Ss discuss the topic in groups and brainstorm.
3. Ss sketch their ideas and write the first drafts, focusing on content.
4. T reviews Ss' drafts and provides corrective feedback that reformulates ill-formed expressions.
5. Ss revise their drafts once, based on the feedback, and then hand in their final drafts to T.
6. T asks Ss to write reflective journals about their writing.

Note: T=teacher, Ss=students

Identify TWO suggestions from <A> that Ms. Song does NOT implement in <B>. Then, support your answers with evidence from <B>.

<수고하셨습니다.>

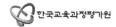

○ 문제지 전체 면수가 맞는지 확인하시오.
○ 모든 문항에는 배점이 표시되어 있습니다.

※ **Write all answers in English and use neat handwriting.**

1. Read the passages and follow the directions. 【4 points】

< A >

The vast majority of adjectives in English can appear in both attributive and predicative positions. Attributive adjectives modify the head noun in an NP and occur before that head noun (e.g., That elephant has a really *big* trunk). In contrast, predicative adjectives appear after a verb, not in an NP, and function as a predicate (e.g., That elephant's trunk is really *big*). However, a number of adjectives function only as attributive. Listed below are four types of attributive-only adjectives.

(1) Adjectives of Degree－describe the degree of the property expressed by the head noun, e.g., a *complete* ballplayer
(2) Quantifying Adjectives－indicate the amount, quantity, or frequency of the head noun, e.g., an *occasional* cloud
(3) Adjectives of Time and Location－place a head noun within a particular time frame or location, e.g., a *previous* version
(4) Associative Adjectives－do not express literal properties of a head noun but instead describe it in terms of some entity that is associated with it, e.g., a *nuclear* physicist

< B >

It was a hot and humid day when a cool, crisp breeze came over the mountain. The wind brought sweet relief; it was an absolute welcome, piercing the scorching humidity and cooling the sweat dripping down my brow. Nature－in its stunning beauty, with the ebb and flow of its continuous cycles－once again provided in a time of need. I'm so thankful to our urban planners for keeping this park.

Based on the description in <A>, identify TWO attributive-only adjectives in <B>. Then, state what type of adjectives each belongs to.

2. Read the passage and follow the directions. 【4 points】

The alveolar lateral approximant /l/ presents appreciable differences among different varieties. In British English, we find the clear 'l,' which is articulated with the tongue tip in contact with the alveolar ridge, in words such as *like, law, leaf, light*, etc. On the other hand, /l/ is realized as the velarized dark 'l,' which has a quality similar to /u/ with raising of the back of the tongue toward the velum, in words such as *fall, file, belt, milk*, etc. In Welsh English, /l/ is always pronounced as the clear 'l.'

In some varieties of American English (AE), however, the clear 'l' may hardly be found; most commonly, the realizations differ in terms of shades of the dark 'l.' Thus, a dark 'l' is found in words given in (1a), a more velarized darker 'l' variety in words in (1b), and the darkest 'l' in words in (1c).

(1) Realizations of /l/ in some AE varieties
  a. dark 'l'
     lip, left, lash, leaf
  b. darker 'l'
     loose, low, lawn, lock
  c. darkest 'l'
     full, bolt, help, hill

In African American Vernacular English (AAVE), /l/ may vocalize to [ʊ] as in (2a) and may be deleted as in (2b).

(2) Realizations of /l/ in AAVE
  a. vocalization of /l/

bell	[bɛl]	or	[bɛʊ]
milk	[mɪlk]	or	[mɪʊk]
football	[fʊtbɔl]	or	[fʊtbɔʊ]
children	[tʃɪldɹən]	or	[tʃɪʊdɹən]

  b. deletion of /l/

help	[hɛlp]	or	[hɛp]
elm	[ɛlm]	or	[ɛm]
wolf	[wʊlf]	or	[wʊf]
twelve	[twɛlv]	or	[twɛv]

Based on the data given in (1a)－(1b), state the environment(s) for dark 'l' and darker 'l,' respectively, in some AE varieties. Then, based on the data given in (2a)－(2b), state the environment(s) for the vocalization of /l/ and the deletion of /l/, respectively, in AAVE.

3. Read the passage and follow the directions. 【4 points】

(A) When about midway of a certain block the policeman suddenly slowed his walk. In the doorway of a darkened hardware store a man leaned, with an unlighted cigar in his mouth. As the policeman walked up to him the man spoke up quickly. "It's all right, officer," he said, reassuringly. "I'm just waiting for a friend. It's an appointment made twenty years ago. Sounds a little funny to you, doesn't it? Well, I'll explain if you'd like to make certain it's all straight. About that long ago there used to be a restaurant where this store stands—'Big Joe' Brady's restaurant." "Until five years ago," said the policeman. "It was torn down then." The man in the doorway struck a match and lit his cigar. The light showed a pale, square-jawed face with keen eyes, and a little white scar near his right eyebrow. His scarfpin was a large diamond, oddly set.

(B) The policeman twirled his club and took a step or two. "I'll be on my way. Hope your friend comes around all right. Going to call time on him sharp?" "I should say not!" said the other. "I'll give him half an hour at least. If Jimmy is alive on earth he'll be here by that time. So long, officer." "Good night, sir," said the policeman, passing on along his beat, trying doors as he went.

(C) About twenty minutes he waited, and then a tall man in a long overcoat, with collar turned up to his ears, hurried across from the opposite side of the street. He went directly to the waiting man. "Is that you, Bob?" he asked, doubtfully. "Is that you, Jimmy Wells?" cried the man in the door. "Bless my heart!" exclaimed the new arrival, grasping both the other's hands with his own. "It's Bob, sure as fate. I was certain I'd find you here if you were still in existence. Well, well, well!—twenty years is a long time. The old restaurant's gone, Bob; I wish it had lasted, so we could have had another dinner there. How has the West treated you, old man?" "Bully; it has given me everything I asked it for. You've changed lots, Jimmy. I never thought you were so tall by two or three inches." "Oh, I grew a bit after I was twenty."

(D) At the corner stood a drug store, brilliant with electric lights. When they came into this glare each of them turned simultaneously to gaze upon the other's face. The man from the West stopped suddenly and released his arm. "You're not Jimmy Wells," he snapped. "Twenty years is a long time, but not long enough to change a man's nose from a Roman to a pug." "It sometimes changes a good man into a bad one," said the tall man. "You've been under arrest for ten minutes, 'Silky' Bob. Chicago thinks you may have dropped over our way and wires us she wants to have a chat with you. Going quietly, are you? That's sensible. Now, before

we go to the station here's a note I was asked to hand you. You may read it here at the window. It's from Patrolman Wells." The man from the West unfolded the little piece of paper handed him. His hand was steady when he began to read, but it trembled a little by the time he had finished. The note was rather short. "Bob: I was at the appointed place on time. When you struck the match to light your cigar I saw it was the face of the man wanted in Chicago. Somehow I couldn't do it myself, so I went around and got a plain clothes man to do the job. JIMMY."

Situational irony occurs when expected outcomes do not happen, or when they are the opposite of what is expected. First, identify the section (A, B, C, D) where the irony is revealed. Then, regarding the underlined part, explain what he couldn't do and why he couldn't do it.

4. Read the passages and follow the directions. 【4 points】

<A>

(Below is a student's writing and a conversation with his teacher about the writing.)

Student writing

> Someone first showed the bicycle to the public in the late 18th century. People first thought it was not safe or comfortable. But many creative people improved it. So, many people use the bicycle widely as a form of transportation or for exercise today. Bicycle makers manufacture lighter, faster and stronger bicycles now than before. Because of that, more people ride the bicycle around the world these days than any time in the past. But they used some unique types of cycles in the old days like the four-cycle.

Teacher-student one-on-one conference

T: What is this writing about?

S: It's about the bicycle. Do you ride a bicycle?

T: Yes, I sometimes do. So your writing is not about people who produce or use the bicycle.

S: That's right.

T: OK, the main theme is the bicycle. But none of the sentences has the bicycle as its subject.

S: I know. But if the bicycle becomes the subject, then I have to use many passives. They are complicated and difficult. So I tried not to use them.

T: But it would be better to use the bicycle as the subject in most sentences. That way, it will become clear that the main focus of your writing is the bicycle.

S: Well, okay. I'll try.

T: You used the word "manufacture." Did you know this word?

S: No, I didn't. At first, I wanted to use "make" but then the sentence looked a bit awkward because the subject is "makers." It would go like "Bicycle makers make."

T: I see.

S: So I looked up a different word in a dictionary that has the same meaning as "make."

T: That works. What about this word "four-cycle?" What do you mean? Are you trying to describe a bicycle but with four wheels?

S: Yes, I am. I added "four" to "cycle" just like "bi" is put before "cycle" in bicycle.

T: Oh, it is called "quadricycle." "Quadri" means four just as "bi" means two.

Note: T=teacher, S=student

<B>

When writing as well as speaking in a second language, learners who have limited command of the second language may have to use a variety of strategies that can compensate for their lack of knowledge of the target language grammar and vocabulary in order to effectively get their intended meaning or message across to a reader or listener. Strategies employed for this purpose include avoidance, code switching, word coinage, appeal to authority, and using prefabricated patterns. As these strategies constitute a significant part of strategic competence, advances in the learners' ability to effectively use them play a considerable role in promoting their communicative competence.

Based upon the student's writing and his dialogue with the teacher in <A>, identify THREE strategies the student used from those mentioned in <B>. Then, provide corresponding evidence for each identified strategy from <A>.

5. Read the passage and follow the directions. 【4 points】

Inanimate objects are classified scientifically into three major categories. The goal of all inanimate objects is to resist man and ultimately to defeat him, and the three major classifications are based on the method each object uses to achieve its purpose.

As a general rule, any object capable of breaking down at the moment when it is almost needed will do so. The automobile is typical of the category. With the cunning typical of its breed, the automobile never breaks down while entering a filling station. It waits until it reaches a downtown intersection in the middle of the rush hour. Thus it creates maximum inconvenience, frustration and irritability among its human cargo, thereby reducing its owner's life span.

Many inanimate objects, of course, find it extremely difficult to break down. Keys, for example, are almost totally incapable of breaking down. Therefore, they have had to evolve a different technique for resisting man. They get lost. Science has still not solved the mystery of how they do it, and no man has ever caught one of them in the act of getting lost. The most plausible theory is that they have developed a secret method of locomotion which they are able to conceal the instant a human eye falls upon them.

Scientists have been struck by the fact that things that break down virtually never get lost, while things that get lost hardly ever break down. A furnace, for example, will invariably break down at the depth of the first winter cold wave, but it will never get lost. A woman's purse, which after all does have some inherent capacity for breaking down, hardly ever does. Some persons believe this constitutes evidence that inanimate objects are not entirely hostile to man, and that a negotiated peace is possible.

The third class of objects is the most curious of all. These include such objects as cigarette lighters and flashlights. It is inaccurate, of course, to say that they never work. They work once, usually for the first few hours after being brought home, and then quit. Thereafter, they never work again. In fact, it is widely assumed that they are built for the purpose of not working.

They have truly defeated man by training him never to expect anything of them, and in return they have given man the only peace he receives from inanimate society. He does not expect his cigarette lighter to light or his flashlight to illuminate, and when they don't it does not raise his blood pressure. He cannot attain that _____ with furnaces and keys, and cars and women's purses as long as he demands that they work for their keep.

Fill in the blank with the ONE most appropriate word from the passage. Then, state THREE methods that inanimate objects use to resist man.

6. Read the passages and follow the directions. 【5 points】

<A>

Despite their similarity on the surface, sentences in (1) are of different types, as suggested in their paraphrasing in (2). Sentences like (1a) are called 'Control' construction; the ones like (1b) 'Raising/ECM' construction. Unlike the latter, an empty pronominal NP PRO is postulated in control constructions.

(1) a. John persuaded Sue to obey her parents.
    b. John believed Sue to be obedient to her parents.
(2) a. John persuaded Sue that she should obey her parents.
    b. John believed that Sue was obedient to her parents.

In fact, there are two kinds of PRO. One is called 'arbitrary PRO,' whose meaning is basically "someone" as shown in (3a). Arbitrary PRO is like a referring expression or a pronoun in that it can get its meaning from outside the sentence. The other is 'non-arbitrary PRO,' which can be further distinguished into two varieties: 'obligatory control' and 'optional control.' The optional control is exemplified in (3b). PRO here can either refer back to *John* or it can have an arbitrary PRO$_{arb}$ reading. The obligatory control is exemplified in (3c) and (3d): PRO in (3c) obligatorily refers back to the main clause Subject, hence called 'subject control,' while PRO in (3d) obligatorily refers back to the main clause Object, hence called 'object control.'

(3) a. [PRO$_{arb}$ to go to college] is not essential for success in life.
    b. John$_i$ knows that it is essential [PRO$_{i/j}$ to be well-behaved].
    c. John$_i$ tried [PRO$_{i/*j}$ to behave].
    d. John persuaded Sue$_i$ [PRO$_i$ to obey her parents].

Note: * indicates the ungrammaticality of the sentence.

<B>

(i) a. [PRO to improve himself], John should consider therapy.
   b. John is easy [PRO to talk to].
(ii) a. John motivated Sue to study harder.
    b. John reported Sue to be obnoxious.
    c. John threatened Sue$_i$ to leave her$_i$.

Based on the description in <A>, first, identify whether PRO in (ia) and (ib) is arbitrary or non-arbitrary, and for non-arbitrary PRO, whether it is obligatory control or optional control. Second, in (ii), identify control constructions only, and then state whether they are subject control or object control.

7. Read the passage and follow the directions. 【5 points】

Melatonin—a hormone naturally produced by the pineal gland—is released when darkness falls, signaling to the body that it is time to rest. While it is well known for its sleep-inducing properties, now, as a result of growing research, scientists know that the substance not only induces sleep but also keeps the brain in order.

One way it does so is as an antidepressant. Seasonal affective disorder is a form of depression common during winter months, thought to be the effect of a mismatch between one's normal sleep cycle and the shifting light-dark cycle. For some people this rhythm mismatch depresses mood. However, this disorder can be readily treated with melatonin. Research has shown that low doses of melatonin along with bright light therapy can realign the sleep-wake cycle and alleviate symptoms of seasonal affective disorder.

Another way it keeps the brain in order is by slowing the cognitive impairment associated with age-related diseases such as Alzheimer's. Amyloid beta and tau proteins are toxic and they build up in patients with this disease, leading to cognitive decline. Melatonin helps to offset the toxic effects of these proteins, but people with Alzheimer's disease produce one fifth the amount of melatonin as healthy young adults. Therefore, melatonin supplements can improve cognitive function in these patients by countering the toxic influence of these two harmful proteins.

These promising newly found effects of this hormone have attracted much attention and have stimulated further research to make humans healthier and happier. What is clear is that melatonin is no longer just an alternative to counting sheep.

Write a summary following the guidelines below.

<Guidelines>
· Summarize the above passage in one paragraph.
· Provide a topic sentence, two supporting ideas, and a concluding sentence based on the passage.
· Do NOT copy more than FIVE consecutive words from the passage.

8. Read the passage in <A> and the two teachers' reflections in <B>, and follow the directions. 【10 points】

<A>

Mr. Kim and Ms. Jo, English teachers, attended a workshop for language teachers where they both gained a lot of useful information to promote student learning. Below is part of the information from the workshop.

Teachers need to...
(1) keep in mind that their course goals and/or procedures can be modified.
(2) offer students a variety of learning strategies to develop learner autonomy.
(3) involve students in self-/peer-evaluation instead of evaluating them alone.
(4) assess students frequently throughout the semester.

<B>

(Below are the two teachers' reflections after the workshop.)

Mr. Kim's reflection

To develop English writing abilities, my students engaged in writing activities. I simply assumed that paragraph writing would be enough for my students. However, I realized that I should change the initial course goal after assessing my students' first classroom writings. Their writing abilities were well above my expectations so I changed the goal set earlier and included essays. Since I believe that one-shot assessment at the end of the course is not effective for enhancing student learning, I carried out assessment periodically over the whole course period. I also believe assessment should be objective and that students' self-assessments are rather subjective in some ways. So, I did all the periodic assessments by myself, not asking students to evaluate their own work.

Ms. Jo's reflection

In my class, students were expected to develop debating skills in English. I organized my lesson in this way: brief mini-lectures, short video presentations to provide content for debating practice, followed by small group debating practice. I taught a range of learning strategies so that my students could become independent language learners utilizing those strategies whenever needed. For improving students' oral skills, I thought that arranging assessments multiple times, not just once, would be better. So I carried out assessments every two weeks during my instructional period. Based on the results of the assessments, I noticed that strictly following the lesson procedure was rather challenging to my students. However, I kept the same procedure over the course period since I believe maintaining consistency is crucial in order not to confuse students.

Write TWO paragraphs based on <A> and <B>. In the first paragraph, identify TWO elements from <A> that Mr. Kim employed in his course and ONE element that he did not employ, and provide evidence from <B> for each identified one. In the second paragraph, identify TWO elements from <A> that Ms. Jo employed in her course and ONE element that she did not employ, and provide evidence from <B> for each identified one.

<수고하셨습니다.>

o 문제지 전체 면수가 맞는지 확인하시오.
o 모든 문항에는 배점이 표시되어 있습니다.

※ **Write all answers in English and use neat handwriting.**

1. Read the passage in <A> and the teacher's journal in <B>, and follow the directions. 【2 points】

─────── < A > ───────

Vocabulary is a core component of language knowledge and provides much of the basis for how well learners listen, speak, read, and write. Without extensive knowledge of vocabulary or diverse strategies for acquiring new words, learners are often unable to produce as much language as they would like.

Knowing a word does not simply mean knowing its surface meaning. Rather, it involves knowing diverse aspects of lexical knowledge in depth including phonological and morphological forms and syntactic and semantic structures. Therefore, activities that integrate lexical knowledge of form, meaning, and use should be included in class.

─────── < B > ───────

Teacher's Journal

Ms. Kang and I read an article on teaching vocabulary and discussed how we can improve the way we teach vocabulary. We realized that we have been heavily focused on expanding the size of our students' vocabulary. As a result, they seem to know a lot of words but do not understand or use them properly in context. So, we came up with the following activities that we believe help our students develop _____ of vocabulary knowledge across form, meaning, and use.

Vocabulary activities to be implemented:
• Trying to pronounce the target words by listening to a recorded text
• Analyzing parts of the target words (e.g., prefixes and suffixes)
• Guessing the meanings of the target words using contextual cues
• Studying concordance examples to see various contexts and collocation patterns
• Writing a short story using the target words

Fill in the blank in <B> with the ONE most appropriate word from <A>.

2. Read the passage in <A> and a teacher's note in <B>, and follow the directions. 【2 points】

─────── < A > ───────

Curriculum design is a series of systematic efforts to develop a curriculum that satisfies the target learners as well as teachers. Researchers suggest that there are five main stages in the process of designing a curriculum.

```
┌─────────────────────────┐
│                         │
└─────────────────────────┘
           ⇓
┌─────────────────────────┐
│   Goal Specifications    │
└─────────────────────────┘
           ⇓
┌─────────────────────────┐
│  Materials Development   │
└─────────────────────────┘
           ⇓
┌─────────────────────────┐
│ Language Teaching & Learning │
└─────────────────────────┘
           ⇓
┌─────────────────────────┐
│   Curriculum Evaluation  │
└─────────────────────────┘
```

─────── < B > ───────

Teacher's Note

I am planning to develop a new English course for winter session, so I wanted to establish the basis for developing the curriculum. The first step of this process requires me to systematically collect and analyze areas of necessity for my students in order to satisfy their language learning requirements. So, I created a survey which asked students questions about their English deficiencies and the difficulties they face in performing certain language tasks in their current classes. It also asked them about the methods they enjoy learning through as well as the types of English skills that they want to improve. For the second step of this process, I wanted to get more information about the students' preferred learning styles and interests, so I referred to my classroom observation notes to learn about them. I then asked my school's principal to show me the results of their placement tests to gain an understanding of their levels of linguistic proficiency and background experience. Furthermore, I interviewed students both in groups and individually to get more detailed information. In short, I conducted _____ by collecting all these data.

Based on the information in <A> and <B>, fill in the blanks in <A> and <B> with the TWO most appropriate words. Use the SAME words in both blanks.

---

3. Read the passage in <A> and the conversation between two teachers in <B>, and follow the directions. 【2 points】

<A>

The way you speak is affected in many ways. For example, how much attention you are paying to your speech may be one factor. When you are not paying much attention to the way you are speaking, your speech may be more casual. By contrast, if you are conscious about the way you are speaking, your output will be less casual. The social position of the person with whom you are engaging in conversation may also affect your language output. It is natural to use more formal language when you speak to someone whose social position is above yours. The sociolinguistic concept of solidarity should also be considered. If your interlocutor comes from the same speech community or shares a similar social or cultural identity with you, you will feel connected to him or her, and this will affect the way you deliver your message. In addition, where you are affects the formality of your output. When you are in a formal situation, such as a business meeting, you naturally use more formal language, and the opposite is true as well. Lastly, the channel or medium of language, that is, whether you deliver your message through speech or writing, can be another critical factor that affects your speech. All of these things need to be considered carefully, because they constitute what is called pragmatic competence which relies very heavily on conventional, culturally appropriate, and socially acceptable ways of interacting.

<B>

T1: What are you writing?

T2: Oh, this is a recommendation letter for Miri.

T1: I see. She is very active in school activities, so you must have a lot to write about her.

T2: Yes, she is a good student, but she doesn't know how to adapt her conversational style when making a request.

T1: Hmm... what do you mean by that?

T2: When Miri approached me, she said, "Hi, teacher, can you write me a recommendation letter?"

T1: Haha... I understand what you mean. Some of my students also seem to have trouble making their speech style appropriate to the situation. Miri is just one example.

T2: Exactly! Still, I feel it's my responsibility to show them how speech styles differ across various situations. Hey, why don't we offer a special lecture on this topic?

T1: Definitely! We can invite a guest speaker who can show the importance of selecting the appropriate conversational style to match the _____ of the situation.

Note: T = teacher

Fill in the blank in <B> with the ONE most appropriate word from <A>.

4. Read the passage and fill in the blank with the ONE most appropriate word. 【2 points】

Diphthongs such as [aɪ] and [aʊ] are vowels that exhibit a change in quality within a single syllable. This is due to tongue movement from the initial vowel articulation toward another. In English, this combinatory sound is considered one vowel, as it behaves as a single unit. That is, the words *hide* [aɪ] and *loud* [aʊ] are monosyllabic, as are *heed* [i] and *hid* [ɪ]. Diphthong vowels are different from two consecutive monophthongs as in *seeing* [siɪŋ] and *ruin* [ɹuɪn], which are counted as two syllables.

A similar phenomenon is also observed among consonant sequences. Consider the following examples where two different consonants occur together at the end of a word:

(1) a. ni<u>nth</u> [nθ], war<u>mth</u> [mθ]   b. lau<u>ghs</u> [fs], twel<u>fth</u> [fθ]
    c. ma<u>ps</u> [ps], wi<u>dth</u> [dθ]   d. ma<u>tch</u> [tʃ], ba<u>dge</u> [dʒ]

When the words in (1) are followed by a word beginning with a vowel, such as *is/are* as in (2), the second member of the consonant sequences in (2a)–(2c) can move to the next syllable:

(2) a. Leaving on the ni<u>nth is</u> fine with me. ([nθ] or [n.θ])
    b. His lau<u>ghs are</u> heard from down the hall. ([fs] or [f.s])
    c. Ma<u>ps are</u> useful when you travel abroad. ([ps] or [p.s])
    d. A ma<u>tch is</u> found in the box. ([tʃ] but not [t.ʃ])

In (2a), for example, the second consonant of the underlined part [nθ] forms a new syllable in fast speech. That is, [θ] in *ninth* is a coda of the syllable, but it can move to the next syllable and in turn, it becomes the onset of [θɪz]. However, this resyllabification does not happen in (2d). That is, (2d) is pronounced [mæ.tʃɪz] and not [mæt.ʃɪz]. This is because English treats them differently: the consonant sequences in (2a)–(2c) are two consonant clusters while the one in (2d) is a single sound. This class of sounds is indeed inseparable just like diphthongs, and a member of this class is called a(n) _____ .

Note: '.' represents a syllable boundary.

5. Read the passage in <A> and the interaction in <B>, and follow the directions. 【4 points】

<A>

Different words and phrases can be used to organize the structure and manage the flow of ongoing conversations. Language elements of this function include different types such as conjunctions, cataphoric words, hedges, and back channel cues. Conjunctions join words, phrases, or clauses together. Cataphoric words refer forward to other words which will be used later in the conversation. Hedges are words or phrases employed not to express the truth of a statement categorically, and back channel cues indicate that one is paying attention to his or her interlocutor's speech. As using these types of language is associated with discourse and strategic competence, the ability to use them in an effective way constitutes part of communicative competence.

<B>

(Two students are doing a task on finding differences between each other's pictures without showing them to each other.)

S1: Do you see any people in your picture?
S2: I have a man. He is tall.
S1: Is he the only person?
S2: I also have a woman in my picture.
S1: There are two in mine, too. What are they doing?
S2: They are sitting together.
S1: That's one difference. They are standing in mine.
S2: What is the woman wearing?
S1: She is wearing a jacket.
S2: What color is it?
S1: It's black.
S2: That is the same in my picture.
S1: Oh, wait, on her jacket, I found this. There is a letter P on it.
S2: I also see a P on her jacket in my picture.
S1: What about the man? What is he wearing?
S2: He is in a blue coat. It is sort of neat.
S1: The man's coat is brown in mine. That's another difference.

Note: S = student

Identify TWO types among those mentioned in <A> that are used in <B>. Then, provide evidence for each identified type from <B>.

6. Read the passage and follow the directions. 【4 points】

<A>

There is a class of words, such as *yet* and *any*, called 'Negative Polarity Items (NPIs).' They are allowed in sentences containing a negative word such as *not*, as illustrated below.

(1) a. The defense strategy had not been determined yet.
    b. *The defense strategy had been determined yet.

However, there is an additional structural condition for an NPI to be licensed by the negation *not*. As shown in (2), the negation has to c-command the NPI.

(2) *Any defense strategy had not been determined.

(3) A node c-commands its sister nodes and all the daughter nodes of its sister nodes.

In (2), given the definition of c-command in (3), *not* does not c-command *any*. Hence, the sentence is ungrammatical.

Temporal and locational adverbials can be structurally ambiguous in that they can modify either a matrix element or an embedded element. In (4a) below, *yesterday* can modify the embedded *knew the answer*, as illustrated in (4b). Let us refer to this reading as 'embedded reading.' In the embedded reading, it is asked whether Mark knew the answer yesterday. By contrast, *yesterday* can also modify the matrix predicate *wondered*, as shown in (4c). Let us refer to this reading as 'matrix reading.' In the matrix reading, yesterday is when Celin wondered about Mark.

(4) a. Celin wondered if Mark knew the answer yesterday.
    b. [Celin wondered [if Mark knew the answer yesterday]]: embedded reading
    c. [Celin wondered [if Mark knew the answer] yesterday]: matrix reading

Note: '*' indicates the ungrammaticality of the sentence.

<B>

(i) Mary said that Justin did not sing in any room.
(ii) Mary did not say that Justin sang in any room.

For the sentences in <B>, identify whether each sentence has a matrix reading, embedded reading, or both. Then, explain your answer on the basis of the description in <A>.

7. Read the passage in <A> and the dialogue in <B>, and follow the directions. 【4 points】

─────────<A>─────────

One of the most effective ways of testing a learner's pronunciation is to observe and record repeated errors in a variety of situations. Speech contexts often change the way a given word is pronounced. Careful or emphasized speech is usually employed to show how to pronounce words clearly. In a connected or conversational speech, words are often contracted and the pronunciation of a word can change through the phenomena in (1) and sound rules in (2):

(1) a. That is nice > That's   (Contraction)
    b. missed *[d], Ms. *[s]   (Spelling pronunciation)

(2)

	Careful speech	Connected speech	Sound rules
a. can't you	[t j]	[tʃ]	Palatalization
b. because	[ə]	-	Vowel deletion
c. greater	[t]	[ɾ]	Tapping
d. advantage	[nt]	[n]	Consonant deletion

It is worth mentioning that spelling often influences learners' pronunciation of words. When spelling pronunciation errors are found in learners' pronunciation, they can sometimes be critical. For instance, if the plural form of *sea*, *seas*, is pronounced [sis] rather than [siz], it can be misunderstood as the word *cease* [sis] by listeners.

Note: '*' indicates incorrect pronunciation.

─────────<B>─────────

(Two students are talking about what they wrote during a dictation task without looking at each other's notes.)

S1: Can you tell me what you got for the second sentence? I wrote down, 'Last [wɪnɚ] (winner) was colder,' and it does not make sense to me.

S2: Why? It means what it says. 'Last [wɪntɚ] (winter) was colder.' How (i) did you understand it?

S1: Oh, it is [wɪntɚ] (winter), the season! I thought it was winner. That is why the sentence did not make sense to me.

S2: [wɪntɚ] (winter), [wɪnɚ] (winter), ... yes, when you say it quickly, it does sound the same.

S1: Thanks! Wait, did you hear the last word in the fourth sentence? Can you tell me what it was?

S2: 'My dog's skin is irritated by [fliz] (fleas).'

S1: What is [fliz] (fleas)? Can you spell it for me?

S2: F-L-E-A-S! Don't you know what fleas are?

S1: Yeah, but isn't that pronounced as (ii) [flis] (fleas)? It is confusing.

S2: Let's ask the teacher later why 's' sounds like 'z' here.

Note: S = student

Identify ONE phenomenon or sound rule from <A> that changes the pronunciation of (i) in <B> and explain how your answer applies to the given words. Then, identify ONE phenomenon or sound rule that causes S1's confusion in (ii) and explain how your answer applies to the given word based on the description in <A>.

8. Read the passage and follow the directions. 【4 points】

According to W. Ury and R. Fisher's best-selling book, you can walk away from any negotiation. The authors purport that by having a good walk-away option (BATNA: Best Alternative to a Negotiated Agreement), you protect yourself from difficult opponents. They advocate walking away from more powerful opponents so you don't give away the store, or at the very least, make a sale that doesn't "make sense."

In theory, this might make sense, but in the world of selling when you haggle with your customers, it is folly.

Telling a salesperson to walk away from the table and kissing off a sale is a bit cavalier for an expert who's never had to make a living by making a quota. For those of us who have spent a significant portion of our careers in sales, we know we would never just up and walk away from a potential sale, no matter how slim the chances are of actually getting the business. That is one of the characteristics that makes salespeople successful: <u>irrational optimism in the face of certain defeat</u>.

Technically, you might have the ability to abort settling on a big sale, but you still have a quota to make and a job to keep.

With that said, however, salespeople are always better dealers when they've already reached their quota. Why? Because they don't need the business. Still, they may indeed walk away from a potential sale, but they always come back as the situation changes.

As a sales manager, I urged my team to have as many potential prospects as possible. I encouraged them to be working on many potential deals, not just because it would help them make quota, but also because it made them tougher negotiators. They were all much better at holding their ground when they didn't feel desperate to have a customer's business.

Here's an important side note:

At times, I get the opportunity to ask about the skills taught in the *Getting to Yes* seminar with people who attended the workshop in the past. I always ask them, "What is the thing you most remember about the Ury and Fisher tenet?" to which I receive the almost universal response: "The thing I remember most is to make sure you know your BATNA."

Even though most cannot recall what the initials stand for, they believe that knowing which options they have if a settlement can't be reached empowers them a bit. I find it curious that the term most remembered from a course designed specifically to improve negotiation skills is one that describes how to walk away from the table—in other words, by refusing to _____.

Fill in the blank with the ONE most appropriate word from the passage. Then, explain what the underlined part means. Do NOT copy more than FOUR consecutive words from the passage.

9. Read the passage and follow the directions. 【4 points】

Included in the possible outcomes of culture learning are several not always desirable results, such as alienation from the native culture and marginality. Marginality refers to a situation in which a person, for a variety of reasons (such as race or religion) remains on the outskirts of a social or cultural group. Marginal individuals or groups are isolated, and, in the words of John Lum, their actions "do not reflect well any one culture." Marginality is not necessarily always a(n) _____ factor. It plays a part in all cultural change; it is part of the lives of children whose parents remain monocultural while they become bicultural. Richard Rodriguez' poignant book *Hunger of Memory* recounts the pains of cultural transition and the agonies of the loss of cultural identity. In anthropology, the marginal person has often been seen as the one most likely to accept change and to be willing to deal with the foreigner (e.g., the anthropologist) who comes along and asks such seemingly stupid questions.

That marginality and mediation are lonely states is also beautifully expressed in an often-quoted passage from the autobiography of Nehru:

I have become a queer mixture of the East and the West, out of place everywhere, at home nowhere. Perhaps my thoughts and approach to life are more akin to what is called Western than Eastern, but India clings to me, as she does to all her children, in innumerable ways; and behind me lie, somewhere in the subconscious, racial memories of a hundred, or whatever the number may be, generations of Brahmans. I cannot get rid of either that past inheritance or my recent acquisitions. They are both part of me, and, though they help me in both the East and the West, they also create in me a negative feeling of spiritual loneliness not only in public activities but in life itself. I am a stranger and alien in the West. I cannot be of it. But in my own country also, sometimes, I have an exile's feeling.

Lum concludes that "marginal people who fall may be rootless or alienated; those who rise may be <u>synthesizers</u>." They may become marginal in all cultures, belonging wholly to none and without cultural identity. On the other hand, they may cross cultural boundaries and leap cultural chasms.

Fill in the blank with the ONE most appropriate word from the passage. Then, explain what the underlined part means. Do NOT copy more than FOUR consecutive words from the passage.

10. Read the passage in <A> and the lesson plan in <B>, and follow the directions. 【4 points】

<A>

Teachers can employ a variety of techniques when teaching reading that will help enhance students' reading comprehension. For instance, at the preparation stage, the prediction technique can be used: Pictures or photos and titles can be viewed quickly to give the students an idea of the overall content of the text. While reading, if students find some words difficult, the teacher may help them to guess their meanings by looking at the surrounding words. Also, as for the reading content, the teacher can employ the outlining technique, which can help the students see the overall organization of the text by reconstructing the ideas or events. After reading, diverse techniques can be used in order to check the students' level of comprehension: scrambled stories, finding the author's purpose, and examining grammatical structures.

<B>

(Below is part of Mr. Kim's lesson plan. He is preparing a handout for his students.)

Objectives	• Students will read the text about modern tourists and find the main idea. • Students will identify the topic and the details of the text based on the handout. • Students will write a summary about the text based on information given in the handout.
Teaching-Learning Activities	

Introduction	Greeting & Roll-call	• T and Ss exchange greetings. • T checks if all the Ss are present.
Development	Activity 1	• T hands out a reading text, "Tourists Today." • T asks Ss to skim through the text. • T asks if Ss understand the gist of the text. • T asks Ss to read the text again. • T distributes the handout about the reading text.

Note: T = teacher, S = student

Tourists Today

Many contemporary tourists avoid encountering reality directly but thrive on psuedo-events in their tourism experiences thus affecting tourism entrepreneurs and indigenous populations. For one, many tourists prefer to stay in comfortable accomodations, thereby separating themselves from the local people and environment. For instance, sleeping in a hotel filled with the comforts of home may insulate them from the fact that they are in a foreign land. In addition, much of the tourism industry is bolstered by the use of tourist-focused institutions such as museums and shopping centers. The needs of the contemporary tourists have induced entrepreneurs to build tourist attractions for the sole purpose of entertaining visitors. This detracts from the colorful local culture and presents a false view of the indigenous cultures. The other group affected by modern tourism is the local population. These people find themselves learning languages in a contrived way based on the changing tides of tourist groups solely for marketing purposes. Furthermore, when curious visitors do venture outside their cultural bubbles, they enjoy, albeit intrusively, watching locals doing their daily tasks, thereby making them the subject of the tourist gaze. In sum, while tourism is on the rise, the trend is to maintain a distance from the real environment rather than to see the locations for their own values, and this negatively affects tourism entrepreneurs and local people.

Handout

Topic sentence: Modern tourists' demands _____

_____

A. Effects on tourism entrepreneurs
  • Provide comfortable accommodations
  • Create tourist-focused entertainment attractions

B. Effects on local populations
  • Learn tourists' languages
  • Become the objects of the tourist gaze

Based on <A>, identify the technique that the teacher employed in the handout in <B>. Then, complete the topic sentence in the handout. Do NOT copy more than FOUR consecutive words from <B>.

11. Read the passage and follow the directions. 【4 points】

You can learn a lot about a society by examining who or what it reveres. You can learn even more by studying what it is afraid of, as a new exhibit at the Morgan Library and Museum in New York proves. "Medieval Monsters" takes the visitor on a jaunt through Europe's Middle Ages via its beasties. Artefacts such as illuminated manuscripts and tapestries are adorned with unicorns, dragons, antelopes with forked tails, blemmyes—humanoids with no heads, their faces instead on their chests—and more.

Monsters were often dispatched in the service of a specific ideology. Medieval power brokers used incredible creatures as a medium to display their magnificence: saints, clergymen and kings were depicted as slayers to show that they were extraordinary. King Henry VI's rule over his land was symbolized through heraldry, which featured an antelope with horns thought to be sharp enough to cut down trees. Maps provided another opportunity to wield _____. A 16th-century plot of Iceland shows the island ringed by various mythological beasts. Their purpose was to scare off competing traders and keep the waterways clear for colonial powers.

Most of the early manuscripts were produced by monks by virtue of their education, and monsters were a medium through which the divine and the unknowable could be visualized. As ships went farther afield in the 15th and 16th centuries, the recurrence of "sea swine" and (1) Leviathan-esque water creatures may reflect an increasing fear of an endless and deadly sea. Demons and the gaping "maw of hell" could illustrate a fear of death, or dying without absolution. Drawings of unicorns, mermaids and sphinxes reveal a sense of wonder about the supernatural.

How do the insights of the exhibition apply to modern monsters, and contemporary Western anxieties? (2) Killer robots point to a fear of indestructible, clever, artificial intelligence-powered computers. Angela Becerra Vidergar, a scholar at Stanford, suggests that the fascination with zombies and the undead in media is one of the creative legacies of the Second World War, when the Holocaust and the use of the atomic bomb changed perceptions about humanity's propensity for mass destruction. Modern art and society are not yet rid of the instincts found in the Morgan's medieval collection.

Fill in the blank with the ONE most appropriate word from the passage. Then, identify ONE common human emotion that (1) and (2) represent, and explain the reason why the identified emotion is represented by (2). Do NOT copy more than FOUR consecutive words from the passage.

12. Read the passage and follow the directions. 【4 points】

We've come to assume that just about any bug we're saddled with—from strep to staph—can be wiped out with a quick round of antibiotics. But in the U.S. alone, roughly 2 million people every year get infections that can't be treated with antibiotics, and 23,000 of them die as a result. The bacteria to blame are now present in every corner of the planet, according to a landmark report from the World Health Organization (WHO). In some countries, about 50% of people infected with *K. pneumoniae* or *E. coli* bacteria won't respond to our most powerful antibiotics, say global health experts. That suggests doctors are increasingly running out of (1) the ammunition they rely on to fight these harmful microbes.

Bacteria have been evolving to resist the drugs designed to kill them since the first antibiotic was discovered in 1928. But our overuse of antibiotics in farming, prescription drugs and antibacterial soaps has supercharged (2) the process. The WHO report was a sober warning of a dire future, but globally, progress is slowly being made.

France used to have the highest rate of antibiotic prescription in Europe, but a government mandate helped lower the number of doctor-issued Rxs by 26% in six years.

In Sweden, regulations to phase out preventive use of antibiotics in agriculture—in which low doses are given to keep animals healthy and plump—cut sales of the drugs for farming by 67% since 1986. The Netherlands and Denmark have also restricted antibiotic use on livestock.

Progress in the U.S. has been slower. The Food and Drug Administration recently tried to encourage farmers to voluntarily reduce antibiotics in farming. The agency is also taking steps to curb use of antibacterials in some consumer goods, requiring manufacturers to prove that antibacterials are better than simple soap and water in keeping germs at bay.

Before antibiotics, something as minor as a cut or a sore throat could be a death sentence. While some _____ has recently been made in the right direction, some might say that much more needs to be done.

Fill in the blank with the ONE most appropriate word from the passage. Then, specify what the underlined parts (1) and (2) refer to, respectively. Do NOT copy more than THREE consecutive words from the passage.

<수고하셨습니다.>

○ 문제지 전체 면수가 맞는지 확인하시오.
○ 모든 문항에는 배점이 표시되어 있습니다.

※ **Write all answers in English and use neat handwriting.**

1. Read the passage and follow the directions. 【2 points】

There is an intriguing phenomenon in English in which two semantically related constituents are separated, as shown below.

(1) a. All the students will work hard.
　　b. The students will all work hard.

In both (1a) and (1b), the quantifier *all* modifies the subject *the students*. What is interesting is that in sentence (1b), the quantifier positioned after the subject forms a discontinuous constituent with no major change in meaning.

This fact can be straightforwardly accounted for if it is assumed that the entire constituent *all the students* is base-generated in the _____ position of VP. As illustrated in (2a), *all the students* undergoes movement to the surface subject position. By contrast, in (2b), just part of the constituent, *the students*, moves to the subject position, leaving *all* behind in its base position, marked as [*all* t$_i$].

(2) a. [$_{TP}$ [all the students]$_i$ will [$_{VP}$ t$_i$ work hard]]
　　b.

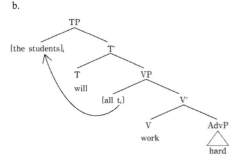

This account is based upon 'VP-internal subject hypothesis,' which states that a subject is base-generated in the _____ position of VP and in turn moves to the _____ position of Tense Phrase (TP).

Fill in the three blanks with the ONE most appropriate word. Use the SAME word for all the blanks.

2. Read the conversation between two teachers and follow the directions. 【2 points】

(Two teachers are evaluating two textbooks, Textbook A and Textbook B, in order to select the one that their students are going to use next year. This is part of their conversation.)

T1: So, why don't we start with the first criterion? I went with Textbook A.
T2: May I ask you why?
T1: I think that the illustrations and graphics in Textbook A portray people in the target culture more realistically.
T2: Yeah! Textbook A contains very realistic visuals that can provide our students with cultural information more accurately.
T1: Good! Then, what about the second criterion?
T2: Well, I think Textbook B is the better of the two. I couldn't give Textbook A a good score, because it appears to aim at explicit learning with many contrived examples of the language.
T1: Hmm... could you clarify your point a bit more?
T2: Well, I mean the texts and dialogues in Textbook A are oversimplified.
T1: I had the same impression, but don't you think that they may help our students by focusing their attention on the target features?
T2: You may be right, but I think that such texts might deprive them of the opportunities for acquisition provided by rich texts.
T1: Oh, I see. That's a pretty good point.
T2: So, in my opinion, Textbook B can provide more exposure to language as it is actually used in the real world outside the classroom.
T1: Yeah! From that point of view, Textbook B will be intrinsically more interesting and motivating to our students.
T2: I agree. Okay, then, I think we are ready to move on to the next evaluation criterion.

Note: T = teacher

Fill in the blank with the ONE most appropriate word.

There are many criteria that can be used in textbook evaluation. The teachers, T1 and T2, are mainly focusing on, first, the criterion of reality of visuals and then, the other criterion of _____. In the dialogue, the latter is specifically related to language use shown in the textbooks.

3. Read the passage and follow the directions. 【4 points】

> Some morphemes in English are pronounced differently depending on their phonetic environments. These variants of the same morpheme are called *allomorphs*. An important question is how we know which allomorph appears for a given word.
>
> Consider the following examples in (1), where the negative morphemes *il-* and *ir-* are added to a base:
>
> (1) a. *il-*: illegal, illogical, illiterate, illegible
>   b. *ir-*: irregular, irrational, irreducible, irrecoverable
>
> Comparing the examples in (1a) with the ones in (1b), a simple distribution is observed for the two allomorphs [ɪl] and [ɪɹ]. That is, [ɪl] and [ɪɹ] are selectively combined with their bases conditioned by the initial sound of the base: when the base begins with /l/, the prefix *il-* is chosen, and when the base begins with /ɹ/, the prefix *ir-* is chosen.
>
> There is another case where [l] and [ɹ] alternate between allomorphs. The adjectival suffix has two allomorphs: *-ar* [əɹ] and *-al* [əl], as shown in (2):
>
> (2) a. *-ar*: singular, popular, solar, velar
>   b. *-al*: rural, plural, viral, moral
>
> These suffixes *-ar* [əɹ] and *-al* [əl] are attached to the base depending on the final consonant of the base. (1) and (2) are different in where the morpheme is attached: (1) precedes the base, which is a prefix, and (2) follows the base, which is a suffix. On the other hand, these two morphemes are similar in that the allomorphs for different morphemes show the same alternation between [l] and [ɹ]. It is interesting to find the two apparently different phonemes /l/ and /ɹ/ are involved in the alternation of the allomorphs *il-/ir-* and *-al/-ar*.
>
> The two sounds /l/ and /ɹ/ share many phonetic properties such as voicing, the place of articulation, and the manner of articulation. They only differ in terms of the way air passes through the mouth. This characteristic difference can be made using the distinctive properties known as the distinctive feature [lateral].

Identify TWO phonological processes involved in (1) and (2) in the correct order. Then, using the distinctive feature [lateral] (i.e., [+lateral] or [−lateral]), generalize the distribution of the allomorphs *-al* and *-ar*.

4. Read the passage in <A> and the interaction in <B>, and follow the directions. 【4 points】

> —<A>—
>
> When problems in conveying meaning occur in conversational interactions, interlocutors need to interrupt the flow and negotiate meaning in order to overcome communication breakdowns and to understand what the conversation is about. A negotiation routine may have a sequence of four components:
>
> • A *trigger* is an utterance that causes communication difficulty.
> • An *indicator* alerts the speaker of the trigger that a problem exists.
> • A *response* is the component through which the speaker of the trigger attempts to resolve the communication difficulty.
> • A *reaction to response* can tell the speaker of the trigger whether or not the problem has been resolved.

> —<B>—
>
> *(The following is a student-student talk occurring in the morning.)*
>
> S1: You didn't come to the baseball practice yesterday. What happened?
> S2: Nothing serious. I had to study for an exam.
> S1: I am sorry you missed the practice. Have you taken the exam yet?
> S2: Yes. I took it a little while ago.
> S1: How did you do?
> S2: Hopefully I did OK. I didn't get any sleep last night.
> S1: I guess you must be drained.
> S2: Drained? What do you mean?
> S1: It's similar to 'tired.'
> S2: Oh, I see. Yeah, I am very tired.
> S1: You need to take a break.
> S2: I sure do, but I think I am going to eat something first.
>
> *Note*: S = student

Identify an utterance from <B> that is a *response* mentioned in <A>, and explain how the speaker attempts to resolve the communication difficulty with the identified utterance. Then, identify an utterance from <B> that is a *reaction to response* mentioned in <A>, and explain whether the communication difficulty is resolved with the identified utterance.

5. Read the excerpt from a novel and follow the directions. 【4 points】

> My father is a failed documentary filmmaker. I say failed because he made only one film in his life. But for a short time in the late seventies, when I was growing up, he achieved what he would later refer to as moderate fame. The source of his moderate fame was a short documentary film about a group of Shoshone Indians living in southern Nevada. I doubt that anybody remembers the film now, but in the weeks and months that followed its release, my father received critical acclaim at several small film festivals, earned some grant money, and garnered enough [. . .] courage to continue making films for another ten years. To my knowledge, he never completed another film after that, but instead spent the next ten years of his life jumping around from one project to the next, shooting for several weeks or months, then eventually abandoning the current film for another that he believed had more _____ .
>
> My mother and I were living in southern California, where she worked as a lawyer, and every few months my father would call from a different part of the country with news of his latest concept—it was always his best yet—and ask my mother to sell something of his, or cash a bond, or take out another mortgage on the house. And finally, when there was nothing left to sell, he began to simply ask her for loans. Technically my parents were separated by then, but my mother was still very much in love with him, never stopped loving him, and worse, she believed with an almost stubborn myopia in his talent. She wanted my father to succeed, perhaps even more than he did, and to this day I still think this was her greatest flaw.
>
> I can say now, twenty years later, that my father was never destined for the type of fame he once hoped to achieve. He was never meant to be a great filmmaker (few documentarians are), and he was never meant to receive even the lesser distinctions that so many of his contemporaries enjoyed. The small amount of talent he did possess only seemed to serve as a source of frustration for him, a constant reminder of some vague, unrealized potential. But at the time—this was in my early childhood—I believed fully in his potential, and though I missed him dearly, I never once faulted him for being away so often.

Fill in the blank with the ONE most appropriate word from the excerpt. Then, explain the underlined part in terms of the life-goal of the narrator's father.

6. Read the passage and follow the directions. 【4 points】

> A high school teacher wanted to develop a test in order to assess his students' English reading ability. He developed the test based on the following procedures:
>
> • Step 1: Construct Definition
> He started by clarifying what his test was intended to measure. He defined the construct of his English test as the ability to infer meanings from a given reading passage.
>
> • Step 2: Designing Test Specifications
> According to the construct definition in Step 1, he specified the test as consisting of a total of 20 multiple-choice items: 1) 10 items asking test-takers to infer meanings and fill in the blank with the most appropriate words or phrases (i.e., Fill-in-the-Blank), and 2) 10 items for finding the best order of scrambled sentences (i.e., Unscrambling).
>
> • Step 3: Developing Test Items & Piloting
> He finished item development. He piloted the test to examine whether the items had satisfactory test qualities.
>
> • Step 4: Analyzing Item Facility & Item Discrimination
> He analyzed item difficulty. To increase internal consistency, he removed the items with a high value of item discrimination.
>
> • Step 5: Analyzing Reliability & Validity
> Reliability was assessed by Cronbach's coefficient alpha. To investigate the concurrent validity of the test, he asked his colleagues to review the test items based on the test specifications.
>
> • Step 6: Administering the Test
> After making the necessary revisions, he administered the test to his students.

Based on the passage above, identify TWO steps out of the six that have a problem in the process of test development. Then, support your answers with evidence from the passage. Do NOT copy more than FOUR consecutive words from the passage.

7. Read the poem and follow the directions. 【4 points】

> In summer's mellow midnight,
> A cloudless moon shone through
> Our open parlor window
> And rosetrees wet with dew.
>
> I sat in silent musing,
> The soft wind waved my hair:
> It told me Heaven was glorious,
> And sleeping Earth was fair.
>
> I needed not its breathing
> To bring such thoughts to me,
> But still it whispered lowly,
> "How dark the woods will be!
>
> "The thick leaves in my murmur
> Are rustling like a dream,
> And all their myriad voices
> Instinct* with spirit seem."
>
> I said, "Go, gentle singer,
> Thy wooing voice is kind,
> But do not think its music
> Has power to reach my mind.
>
> "Play with the scented flower,
> The young tree's supple bough,
> And leave my human feelings
> In their own course to flow."
>
> The wanderer would not leave me;
> Its kiss grew warmer still —
> "O come," it sighed so sweetly,
> "I'll win thee 'gainst thy will.
>
> "Have we not been from childhood friends?
> Have I not loved thee long?
> As long as thou hast loved the night
> Whose silence wakes my song.
>
> "And when thy heart is laid at rest
> Beneath the church-yard stone
> I shall have time enough to mourn
> And thou to be alone."

* Infused

Complete the commentary below by filling in each blank with the ONE most appropriate word from the poem, respectively. Then, explain what the underlined part in the poem means.

<Commentary>

Personification gives the attributes of a human being to an animal, an object, or a concept. In the poem, the "wind" is personified as a(n) "_____" and a(n) "_____." This use of personification offers clues to understanding the speaker's relationship with nature.

8. Read the passage and follow the directions. 【4 points】

―――――〈A〉―――――

Sentences containing [be + past participle] can fall into two subtypes, based on whether the past participle form is a verb or an adjective, as shown in (1).

(1) a. The cat was bitten by the mouse.
    b. He had always been interested in Korean history.

In (1a), *bitten* is a verb, and in (1b), *interested* is an adjective.
    There are two syntactic properties that distinguish adjectives from verbs. First, adjectives can be modified by degree modifiers, whereas verbs cannot, as shown in (2).

(2) a. I couldn't stand his overly offensive behavior.
    b. She was so embarrassed by his demeaning attitude toward her.
    c. *He very solved the difficult problem.
    d. *The ball was very bounced against the wall several times.

The fact that *offensive* and *embarrassed* in (2a) and (2b) can be modified by degree modifiers whereas *solved* and *bounced* in (2c) and (2d) cannot suggests that the former are adjectives and the latter are verbs. For an adjective to be modified by a degree modifier, it should be gradable. Such modification is not possible with non-gradable adjectives. This is illustrated in (3).

(3) a. The meeting was rather serious.
    b. *The situations were too impossible.

Second, other than *be*, verbs such as *remain* can be followed by adjectives, but not by verbs, as given in (4).

(4) a. The visitors remained assembled outside the museum for over an hour.
    b. *The safe remained broken by the burglars.

Note: '*' indicates the ungrammaticality of the sentence.

―――――〈B〉―――――

(i) They were married at the church.
(ii) They were married until last Christmas.

Identify whether *married* in (i) and (ii) is an adjective or a verb, respectively. Then, for the sentence containing the adjective *married*, provide TWO sentences, each of which has a property described in <A>. Each sentence should have a different property. Put an '*' before the ungrammatical sentence.

9. Read the passage and follow the directions. 【4 points】

What could be better than studying physics under Albert Einstein? A lot, it turns out. While geniuses have done much to help society progress and flourish, perhaps they don't belong in front of the classroom. While logic dictates that the best teachers would be the most capable and accomplished people, there are two other qualities that are more vital than intelligence.

The first quality of effective teachers is that they had to put forth a lot of effort into their studies. While this may seem counterintuitive, it is probably more helpful to be guided by a person who had to work daily to master difficult concepts than by someone for whom learning was a breeze. Students often gravitate toward prodigies like Einstein because their expertise seems so effortless, but that's a mistake. It makes more sense to study under people who had to struggle to become experts because they've gone through the process of building their knowledge one concept at a time.

The next quality is a little more obvious but is often overlooked: being able to explain content clearly. A teacher who has a long list of publications probably isn't going to remember how to methodically explain the basics. In the first university course he taught, Einstein wasn't able to attract much interest in the esoteric subject of thermodynamics: Just three students signed up, and they were all friends of his. The next semester he had to cancel the class after only one student enrolled. This example shows how someone who has inborn genius may not be able to relate to students' ignorance to help them understand abstract concepts.

It's often said that those who can't do teach, yet the reality is that the best doers are often the worst teachers. So, teachers' most important qualities are having had the experience of building their knowledge and having the ability to make content easy to grasp. Being a great physicist doesn't make one a great physics teacher. Rather than taking an introduction to physics class with Einstein, it would be more valuable to learn from his protégé who spent years figuring out how to explain what it would be like to chase a beam of light.

Write a summary following the guidelines below.

―――――〈Guidelines〉―――――

• Summarize the above passage in one paragraph.
• Provide a topic sentence, two supporting ideas, and a concluding sentence based on the passage.
• Do NOT copy more than FIVE consecutive words from the passage.

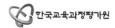

10. Read the passage in <A> and the part of the individual conference in <B>, and follow the directions. 【4 points】

---<A>---

The students in Mr. Lee's class did an oral presentation. Mr. Lee gave his students the following rubric in advance and let them know that their performance would be evaluated across four categories: (a) content & preparation, (b) organization, (c) language, and (d) delivery. After the students' presentations were over, Mr. Lee had a conference session with each student to discuss his or her strengths and weaknesses.

PRESENTATION ASSESSMENT FORM

Evaluation Categories	Scale				
	1 poor	2	3	4	5 excellent
I. Content & Preparation					
1. Interest & Value of topic	1	2	3	4	5
2. Informativeness of content	1	2	3	4	5
3. Preparedness	1	2	3	4	5
II. Organization					
1. Introduction (giving an overview)	1	2	3	4	5
2. Main body (supporting details & examples)	1	2	3	4	5
3. Conclusion (summarizing the presentation)	1	2	3	4	5
III. Language					
1. Accuracy (accurate use of grammar)	1	2	3	4	5
2. Appropriateness	1	2	3	4	5
3. Fluency	1	2	3	4	5
4. Pronunciation	1	2	3	4	5
IV. Delivery					
1. Confidence (not overly dependent on notes)	1	2	3	4	5
2. Gestures & Facial expressions	1	2	3	4	5

---<B>---

(The following is part of the individual conference that Mr. Lee had with one of his students, Yuna.)

Mr. Lee : Your presentation was pretty good.

Yuna : Thank you, Mr. Lee.

Mr. Lee : Yeah, you were really prepared. And so you got a perfect score on that area.

Yuna : I tried my best to make my PPT slides as informative as possible.

Mr. Lee : I know! They were really impressive. And your topic was really good.

Yuna : Thank you! How was my pronunciation?

Mr. Lee : Overall, I think your language was easy for the other students to follow. But you may want to try to use your language more appropriately. For example, some expressions you used like *you guys* and *you know*, may not be appropriate in this kind of presentation.

Yuna : I see. Thank you for your feedback.

Mr. Lee : I also noticed that you referred to your cue cards too frequently without looking at the audience.

Yuna : I did?

Mr. Lee : Yes, you did. Your presentation would have been much better if you had shown more confidence in your presentation task.

Yuna : I agree.

Mr. Lee : Other than that, everything looked fine.

Identify TWO of the four evaluation categories that Mr. Lee thinks reflect Yuna's weak points. Then, provide evidence for each identified category from <B>.

11. Read the excerpt from a play and follow the directions.

【4 points】

The sappers* have already mapped most of the area. YOLLAND's official task, which OWEN is now doing, is to take [. . .] — every hill, stream, rock, even every patch of ground which possessed its own distinctive Irish name — and Anglicize it, either by changing it into its approximate English sound or by translating it into English words. [. . .] OWEN's official function as translator is to pronounce each name in Irish and then provide the English translation.

OWEN: Now. Where have we got to? Yes — the point where that stream enters the sea — that tiny little beach there. George!

YOLLAND: Yes. I'm listening. What do you call it? Say the Irish name again?

OWEN: Bun na hAbhann.

YOLLAND: Again.

OWEN: Bun na hAbhann.

YOLLAND: Bun na hAbhann.

OWEN: That's terrible, George.

YOLLAND: I know. I'm sorry. Say it again.

OWEN: Bun na hAbhann.

YOLLAND: Bun na hAbhann.

OWEN: That's better. Bun is the Irish word for bottom. And Abha means river. So it's literally the mouth of the river.

YOLLAND: Let's leave it alone. There's no English equivalent for a sound like that.

OWEN: What is it called in the church registry?

[*Only now does YOLLAND open his eyes.*]

YOLLAND: Let's see . . . Banowen.

OWEN: That's wrong. [*Consults text.*] The list of freeholders calls it Owenmore — that's completely wrong: [. . .] And in the grand jury lists it's called — God! — Binhone! — wherever they got that. I suppose we could Anglicize it to Bunowen; but somehow that's neither fish nor flesh.

[*YOLLAND closes his eyes again.*]

YOLLAND: I give up.

OWEN: [*At map.*] Back to first principles. What are we trying to do?

YOLLAND: Good question.

OWEN: We are trying to denominate and at the same time describe that tiny area of soggy, rocky, sandy ground where that little stream enters the sea, an area known locally as Bun na hAbhann . . . Burnfoot! What about Burnfoot!

YOLLAND: [*Indifferently.*] Good, Roland. Burnfoot's good.

OWEN: George, my name isn't . . .

YOLLAND: B-u-r-n-f-o-o-t?

OWEN: I suppose so. What do you think?

YOLLAND: Yes.

OWEN: Are you happy with that?

YOLLAND: Yes.

OWEN: Burnfoot it is then. [*He makes the entry into the Name-Book.*] [. . .]

YOLLAND: You're becoming very skilled at this.

OWEN: We're not moving fast enough.

YOLLAND: [*Opens eyes again.*] Lancey lectured me again last night.

OWEN: When does he finish here?

YOLLAND: The sappers are pulling out at the end of the week. The trouble is, the maps they've completed can't be printed without these names. So London screams at Lancey and Lancey screams at me. But I wasn't intimidated. [. . .] 'I'm sorry, sir,' I said, 'But certain tasks demand their own tempo. You cannot rename a whole country overnight.' Your Irish air has made me bold.

* Soldiers whose job involves digging, building, and map-making

Complete the commentary below by filling in the blank with the ONE most appropriate word from the excerpt. Then, regarding the underlined part, explain what Owen thinks of the word "Bunowen."

<Commentary>

Yolland has been commissioned to remap Ireland with Anglicized place-names. For some reason, however, he shows little concern about finishing the mission on time. He even ignores his superior officer Lancey's order to increase his _____.

<수고하셨습니다.>

참고문헌

오경애. (2019). 『중등교사 임용시험을 위한 언어 습득론』. 도서출판 한필

Amerian, M.& Khaivar, A. (2014). Textbook selection, evaluation, and adaptation procedures. *International Journal of Language Learning and Applied Linguistics World. 6*(1). 523-533.

Bachman, L. F. (1990). *Fundamental considerations in language testing.* Oxford: Oxford University Press.

Bergmann, J., & Sams, A. (2014). *Flipped learning: Gateway to student engagement.* Eugene, OR: International Society for Technology in Education.

Brewer, B. A. (2008). *Effects of lexical simplification and elaboration on ESL readers' local-level perceived comprehension.* (Master thesis). Brigham Young University, Utah, The United States.

Brown, H. D. & Abywickrama, P. (2010). *Language assesment: Principles and classroom practices.* New York: Pearson Education.

Brown, H. D. (2014). *Principles of Language Learning and Teaching: A Course in Second Language Acquisition.* (4th ed.) New York: Pearson

Brown, H. D. (2015). *Teaching by principle: An interactive approach to language pedagogy.* New York: Pearson Education.

Cain, K., & Oakhill, J. (1999). Inference making ability and it's relation to comprehension failure in young children, *Reading and Writing: An Interdisciplinary Journal, 11*(5), 489-503.

Canale, M., & Swain, M. (1980). Theoretical bases of communicative approaches to second language teaching and testing. *Applied Linguistics, 1,* 1-47.

Caro, K., & Mendinueta, N. R. (2017). Lexis, lexical competence and lexical knowledge: A review. *Journal of Language Teaching and Research, 8*(2). 205-213.

Celce-Murcia, M., Brinton, D. M, & Ann Snow, M. (2014). *Teaching English as a second or foreign Language.* Boston: National Geographic Learning.

Celce-Murcia., & McIntosh, L. (1979). *Teaching English as a second or foreign language.* Cambridge: Newbury House Publishers.

Cetinasci, B. M. (2014). Contextual factors in guessing word meaning from context in a foreign language. *Procedia-Social and Behavioral Sciences, 116.* 2670-2674.

Cohen, A. D., & Weaver, S. J. (2005). *Styles and strategies-based instruction: A teachers' guide.* Minneapolis, MN: Center for Advanced Research on Language Acquisition, University of Minnesota.

Cohen, A. D., Weaver, S. J., & Li, T-Y. (1998). The impact of strategies-based instruction on speaking a foreign language. In A. D. Cohen, *Strategies in learning and using a second language* (pp. 107-156). Harlow, England: Longman.

Dekeyser, R. (2007b). Skill acquisition theory. In B. VanPatten & J. Williams (Eds.), *Theories in second language acquisition: An introduction* (pp. 97-113). New Jersey: Lawrence Erlbaum Associates, Inc.

Ellis, N. (2012). Frequency-based accounts of second language acquisition: The role of frequency, form, and function. *The Modern Language Journal, 93,* 329-335.

Eslami, Z., Moody, S., & Pashmforoosh, R. (2019). Educating pre-Service Teachers about World Englishes: Instructional activities and Teachers' Perceptions, *TESL-EL,. 22*(4). 1-17.

Garinger, D. (2002). Textbook selection for the ESL classroom. *Center for Applied Linguistics Digest.* Retrieved from http://www.cal.org/resources/Digest/0210garinger.html

Gronlund, N. E. & Waugh, C. K. (2008). *Assessment of student achievement* (9th ed.). Boston: Allyn & Bacon.

Halim, S. & Halim T. (2016). Adapting materials: Revisiting the needs for learners. *International Journal of Humanities and Cultural Studies, 2*(4). 633-641.

Harmer, J. (2004). *How to teach writing.* Essex, UK: Pearson Education. Limited.

Hosseinpour, N., Biria, R., & Revani, E. (2019). Promoting academic writing proficiency of Iranian EFL learners through blended learning. *Turkish Online Journal of Distance Education, 20*(4).99-116.

Hulstijn, J. H. (2013). Incidental learning in second language acquisition. In C. A. Chapelle (Ed.), *The encyclopedia of applied linguistics* (Vol. 5, pp. 2632-2640). Chichester: Wiley-Blackwell.

Ishikawa, S. (2015). Noun/verb ratio in L1 Japanese, L1 English, and L2 English: A corpus-based study. *Proceedings of The Second International Conference on Language, Education, Humanities & Innovation.* 134-145.

Joos, Martin. (1967). *The style of five clocks. In current topics in language: Introducing reading,* Nancy Ainworth Jhonson (ed), Massachusetts: Winthrop Publisher, Inc

Kaweera, C. (2013). Writing error: A review of interlingual and intralingual interference in EFL context. *English Language Teaching, 6*(7). 9-18.

Kelly, J. (2000). *How to teach pronunciation.* Essex, UK: Pearson Education.

Lan, Y. (2019). Interlingual interfaces in Chinese language learning and its use: Exploring language transfer errors in Chinese writing. *Journal of Language Teaching and Research, 10*(3). 437-445.

Long, M. (1985). A role for instruction in second language acquisition: task-based language teaching. In K. Hyltenstam and M. Pienemann (eds.), *Modelling and assessing second language acquisition.* (pp. 77-79). Clevedon: Multilingual Matters.

Long, M. (2015). *Second Language Acquisition and Task-based Language Teaching.* West Sussex, UK: John Wiley and Sons, Inc.

Lyster, R., & Ranta, L. (1997). Corrective feedback and learner uptake: Negotiation of form in communicative classrooms. *Studies in Second Language Acquisition, 20,* 37-66.

Matsuda, A. (2017). *Preparing teachers to teach English as an international language.* Bristol: Multilingual Matters.

Masrizal, M. (2014). The role of negotiation of meaning in L2 interaction: An analysis from the perspective of Long's interaction hypothesis. *Studies in English Language and Education, 1*(2). 96-105.

Metruk, R. (2018). Comparing holistic and analytic ways of scoring in the assessment of speaking skills. *The Journal of Teaching English for Specific and Academic Purposes, 6*(1). 179-189.

Mishra, S. (2018). Nonverbal communication: An influential tool for effective management. *International journal of Business and General Management, 7*(3). 19-24.

Nam, Jung-Mi. (2019). Attitudes and perceptions of Korean college students toward world Englishes and current English teaching in Korea. *English Language Teaching, 31*(3), 111-126.

Nunan, D. (1988) *The learner-centered curriculum: A study in second language teaching.* Cambridge: Cambridge University Press.

Nunan, D. (2004). *Task-based language teaching.* Cambridge: Cambridge University Press.

O'Malley, J. M. & Valdez, P. L. (1996). *Authentic assessment for English language learners: Practical approaches for teachers.* White Plains, NY: Addison-Wesley.

Reid, J. (1995). *Learning Styles in the ESL/EFL Classroom.* New York: Heinle and Heinle.

Rhouma, W. B. (2016). Perceptual Learning Styles Preferences and Academic Achievement. *International Journal of Arts & Sciences, 9*(2). 479-492.

Richards, J., Platt, J. & Webber, H. (1986). *A dictionary of applied linguistics.* London: Longman.

Sari, E. M. P. (2016). Interlingual errors and intralingual errors found in narrative text written by EFL students in Lampung. *Jurnal Penelitian Humaniora, 17*(2). 87-95.

Selinker, L. (1972). Interlanguage. *International Review of Applied Linguistics, 10.* 201-231.

Siegel, A. (2014). What should we talk about? The authenticity of textbook topics. *ESL Journal, 68*(4). 363-375.

Sierocka, H. (2012). Developing LSP / ESP materials for legal professionals. *The University of Bialystok: Poland* retrieved from http://fl.uni-mb.si/wpcontent/uploads/2012/10/SIEROCKA.

Skehan, P. (1998). Task-based instruction. *Annual Review of Applied Linguistics, 18,* 268-286.

Taie, M. (2014). Skill acquisition theory and its important concepts in SLA. *Theory and Practice in Language Studies, 9*(4). 1971-1976.

Tan, J. G. (2015). Using Outline to Enhance Reading Comprehension in a High School English Language Classroom. *American Journal of Educational Research, 3*(7), 893-896.

Thornbury, S. (1999). *How to teach grammar.* Essex, UK: Pearson Education Limited.

Uhm, C. J. (2000)). Investigating the empirical aspects of communication strategies. *Linguistics, 8*(1). 353-377.

VanPattern, B. (2004). *Processing instruction: Theory, research, and Commentary.* Mahwah, US: Lawrence Erlbaum Associates.

Wardhaugh, R. & Fuller, J. M. (2015). *An Introduction to Sociolinguistics.* West Sussex: Blackwell Publishers Ltd.

Wei, X. (2012). An introduction to conversational interaction and second language acquisition. *English Linguistics Research, 1*(1). 111-117

Wu, Y. (2016). *Effects of form-focused instruction, corrective feedback, and individual differences on the acquisition of Chinese wh-questions and classifiers.* (Doctoral dissertation). Boston University, Massachusettes, The United States.

Yeh, H., & Lai, W. (2019). Speaking progress and meaning negotiation processes in synchronous online tutoring. *System, 81.* 179-191.

Yusuf, Q., Yusuf, Y. Q., Yusuf, B., & Nadya, A. (2017). Skimming and scanning techniques to assist EFL students in understanding English reading texts. *Indonesian Research Journal in Education, 1*(1). 43-57.

Zhao, B. (2009). Corrective feedback and learner uptake in primary school EFL classrooms in China. *The Journal of Asia TEFL, 6*(3). 45-72.

영문 색인

(M)

manager 159

meaning negotiation 30

meaningful minimal pairts 123

meaningful technique 158

measurement 187

mechanical drill 158

mechanical technique 158

message abandonment 33

message avoidance 33

metacognitive strategies 74

metalinguistic feedback 61

mime 33

minimal pairs 123

mistakes 55

modernizing 134

modified input 30

modified interaction 30

modifying 134

(N)

Natural Approach 100

needs analysis 71, 144

negative transfer 55

negotiated syllabus 146

nonverbal communication 44

norm-referenced tests 189

notional-functional syllabus 145

(O)

objective needs 144

objectives 145

observations 191

oculesics 46

olfactics 46

open-ended technique 157

opinion exchange 161

organizational competence 43

outer circle 27

outlining 86

output 16

overgeneralization 55, 104

(P)

pair work 159

paraphrase 33

pedagogical tasks 70

peer assessment 191

peer-editing 161

perceptual preference 22

performance-based assessment 189

perlocutionary force 43

personality preference 22, 23

personalizing 134

phonological avoidance 33

placement tests 189

practicality 196

pragmatic competence 43

prediction techniques 85

prediction, predicting 85

predictive validity 197, 203

prefabricated patterns 33

problem solving 160

procedural knowledge 14

procedure 157

Processing Instruction: PI 102, 116

processing preference 22

productive skill 16

proficiency tests 189

project-based language learning 146

proxemics 46

국문 색인